T0385462

SPECIAL DUTY

SPECIAL DUTY

A HISTORY OF THE JAPANESE
INTELLIGENCE COMMUNITY

RICHARD J. SAMUELS

CORNELL UNIVERSITY PRESS
Ithaca and London

First published 2019 by Cornell University Press

Library of Congress Cataloging-in-Publication Data

Names: Samuels, Richard J., author.
Title: Special duty : a history of the Japanese intelligence community / Richard J. Samuels.
Description: Ithaca [New York] : Cornell University Press, 2019. | Includes bibliographical references and index.
Identifiers: LCCN 2019010374 (print) | LCCN 2019012009 (ebook) | ISBN 9781501741593 (e-book pdf) | ISBN 9781501741609 (e-book epub/mobi) | ISBN 9781501741586 | ISBN 9781501741586 (hardcover ; alk. paper)
Subjects: LCSH: Intelligence service—Japan—History.
Classification: LCC JQ1629.I6 (ebook) | LCC JQ1629.I6 S26 2019 (print) | DDC 327.1252—dc23
LC record available at https://lccn.loc.gov/2019010374

In memory of Chalmers Johnson, the bold and brilliant Asia scholar, and of Wakamiya Yoshibumi, the generous and open-minded journalist for whom the adjective "intrepid" is entirely inadequate.

Speaking of the recently deceased U.S. covert operative Alden Pyle, a colleague noted "in a low voice tense with ambiguity: 'He had special duties' . . . He was a very quiet American."

—Graham Greene, *The Quiet American*

CONTENTS

PREFACE

One often hears Japanese refer to their country as a unique small island trading nation, precariously dependent on imported raw materials and adrift in a hostile world. Apart from the fact that all nations claim to be unique, that Japan is not small economically or demographically, and that its dependence on imports is no greater than that of many other countries, there is some truth in this mantra. Japan's neighborhood, and the world in which its businesses and citizens operate, have always been filled with threats. This has never been truer than it is today, when shifts in Tokyo's relations with its colossal Chinese and nuclear-armed North Korean neighbors portend modification of relations with its powerful U.S. ally. Japan's intelligence officers have to judge the speed, trajectory, and certainty of transformations in the balance of power, and policy makers need to decide what measures to take to protect those businesses and citizens. In the decades of study of Japan's evolving security community, virtually no sustained attention has been paid to its once expansive—and then atrophied—intelligence community. This community is atrophied no longer; a close look at its past, present, and future is overdue.

Japan was in ruins and its intelligence community was at its feeblest at the end of the Asia-Pacific War, a time of momentous institutional enhancement of the U.S. intelligence community. In January 1946, when the triumphant President Harry S. Truman created a National Intelligence Authority and the post of director of central intelligence to coordinate government-wide intelligence activities, he seized the chance to have some fun. The president gave his senior deputies black cloaks, mustaches, and wooden daggers. The fortified U.S. intelligence apparatus—and those of its allies—were not always playgrounds for practitioners, but thanks more to novelists, screenwriters, cartoonists, and comedians than to scholars, "licensed skullduggery"—and the secret agents who practice it—became Cold War stereotypes and satirical fodder. Who did not appreciate James Bond, George Smiley, or Jason Bourne? And who was not amused by Boris Badenov, Natasha Fatale, Maxwell Smart, or Austin Powers?[1]

Of course, real spies have always been among us, many associated with the wisdom of our greatest leaders. According to Numbers 13, Moses sent spies into Canaan under God's direct order to report on the land conditions. In Kings 2, the Assyrians drew on an extensive intelligence network during their invasion of the kingdom of Judah in 701 BC. Julius Caesar noted that the Gauls regularly interrogated travelers and merchants for information about distant lands to gain strategic advantage, which they thereupon squandered for lack of analytic skills.[2] George Washington relied on spies during the Revolutionary War, and upon becoming president in 1790, he persuaded Congress to establish a "Contingent Fund of Foreign Intercourse," a secret intelligence kitty that grew to 12 percent of the entire federal budget within three years.[3] In 1861, President Abraham Lincoln personally recruited a southern businessman to provide intelligence to Washington.[4] And as recently as the eve of America's entry into World War II, President Franklin D. Roosevelt was dispatching personal friends to gather information on war-torn Europe.

By then—actually by the end of World War I—intelligence had already become as much a matter for professional bureaucrats as for spies and their derring-do. Indeed, our embrace of the exploits of secret agents belies both how difficult the intelligence business is and the deadly serious role it plays in national security affairs. Members of an intelligence community—shorthand for the network of collectors of adversaries' secrets and analysts of threat—are in the business of helping decision makers manage uncertainty. They must separate potential and distant challenges from real and near ones in an environment in which their enemies' intentions are often the most closely guarded of all secrets. They must separate what matters from what only seems to matter, to distinguish what is known from what is unknown, and to know what they do not know.[5] Then, as if this were not difficult enough, they have to transmit their evaluations to decision makers who have multiple reasons to discount or misuse them. As one unnamed senior State Department intelligence official described his unit's role, "A good day is when we prevent a bad policy decision from being made."[6] Walter Laqueur offers a fitting metaphor: intelligence is "the Cinderella of contemporary politics: long hours, unpleasant work, humiliation, lack of recognition, and no Prince Charming in sight."[7] Once we acknowledge that all this takes place in the context of existential threat, intelligence ceases to appear all fun and games, and getting its organization right becomes imperative.

Our perceptions of the intelligence community have been shaped predominantly by American, British, Soviet, and Israeli espionage—by Ludlum's CIA, le Carré's MI6, *The Americans'* KGB, or Reicher Atir's Mossad—and we may have been led to believe that spies are less suave and resourceful elsewhere. This may be why few Japanese spies have been popularly associated with either wisdom or heroism in Western accounts, though some were both wise and heroic. Nor have many been the benign objects of satire. More often, their malign caricature abroad was formed out of a supposed orientalist capacity for treachery, such as this from the British historian Peter Elphick, who insisted that "the Japanese national psyche" explains why expatriate Japanese who were "required to serve as part of a subversive network [were] deeply honored they were serving their emperor" as spies. Then there is the purported native incapacity of Japanese to act independently, as in this from the U.S. Strategic Services Unit immediately after the Asia-Pacific War: "Jap mentality is completely unsuited to listening post work. They are slow, cautious thinkers, and can never make a quick decision or take prompt action before thinking up a suitable reason or excuse [that is] sufficiently watertight to [protect] against loss of face."[8] Even the Chinese have waved the essentialist culture card at the Japanese. Chiang Kai-shek, the Chinese Nationalist leader who once served in the Imperial Japanese Army, reportedly declared that "everyone Japanese, both male and female, is a born spy."[9] The popular allure of ninjas notwithstanding, clearly there is some confusion abroad regarding whether the Japanese are or are not inherently adept at espionage. As we shall see, there was no inherent intelligence deficit preventing the Japanese intelligence community from expanding or from having its share of success during the first half of the twentieth century.

Meanwhile, the joke at home in Japan has been about the bureaucracies, not the secret agents. In the standard Japanese narrative, during the Cold War Japan had no CIA but did have a "KGB": Keisatsu (National Police Agency), Gaimushō (Foreign Ministry), and Bōeichō (Defense Agency). This speaks to a fundamental truth that will inform much of the analysis in this book: these separate government agencies—like those elsewhere within Japan and in intelligence communities abroad—seem to have forever been engaged in intense (sometimes petty) jurisdictional competition, captive in silos inhibiting coordination. The Japanese intelligence community, like the U.S. and British ones, took a sharp bureaucratic turn—perhaps even earlier and more sharply than in Washington or London. In the Japanese narrative, more of the country's heroes—many of whose photos are in this volume— were celebrated as military and government officials than as gallant national champions. They were patriots, of course, but in the first instance they were cashiered soldiers in the former Imperial Japanese Army who were joined by diplomats in the Ministry of Foreign Affairs (MOFA), crime fighters in the National Police Agency (NPA), economists in the Ministry of International

Trade and Industry (MITI) and the Ministry of Finance (MOF), and lawyers in the Justice Ministry's Public Security Intelligence Agency (PSIA). They belonged as much to their competing units as to the Japanese state. And many, of course, were politicians vying for power. Japan's intelligence units were small, non-comprehensive, uncoordinated, underfunded, and, as a result of lingering political sensitivities (especially regarding the use of spies), unnecessarily baroque. They all operated in an environment of mutual distrust with limited central authority and even more limited public support. Kotani Ken, a leading historian of Japanese intelligence, tells us that the government "never succeeded in managing the central intelligence system effectively," and even today, many observers simply throw up their hands and declare, "Japan has no intelligence *community*."[10]

So this term will be used with caution in these pages. And indeed, we can recognize that not all the problems encountered (or created) by the Japanese intelligence bureaucracies should be connected to the domestic structure of strategic policy making. Subordination to Washington also muted interest in developing Japan's postwar intelligence community. During the Occupation—and even well after Japan regained sovereignty—its intelligence function was derivative, underdeveloped, and narrowly aimed at domestic enemies and foreign firms. The larger strategic horizon was monitored by its ally the United States. Resentment of Japan's subservience to its U.S. partner—what one intelligence journalist has called a persistent "master-servant relationship" (*shujū kankei*)—never independently forced the shape and pace of Japanese intelligence reform, but it did become a more persistent problem than is normally acknowledged.[11] Most Cold War Japanese intelligence and security professionals accepted that they had little choice but to accommodate to U.S. power. As a result—and notwithstanding that there remain gaps in sharing and trust—there has been increasing integration of the two intelligence communities.

While accommodation to the preferences and practices of the U.S. intelligence community was a defining feature of the first decades after the war, the Japanese intelligence community—like the military overall—was also stifled by clear and insistent public opposition to any practice redolent of wartime governance. Above all this meant that engaging in (or even debating the merits of) intelligence—especially counterintelligence, but also counterterrorism—was problematic. Every plan, each discussion of the topic, raised hackles among those who feared (not without cause) that the Japanese could slide down a slippery slope back to unrestrained practices like domestic surveillance and foreign aggression that destroyed millions of lives and their nation.

After the Cold War, thoughtful Japanese national security strategists—in both the bureaucracy and the political class—took up intelligence reform with new energy. They began to tinker, reconceive, and, finally, to restructure Japan's national security apparatus—and with it Japan's intelligence community. These, then, are the transitions that are identified and followed in this volume: the expanding, accommodating, tinkering, reimagining, and reengineering of the intelligence community of one of the world's great powers. It will be a story that shifts from a focus on individuals and their exploits to organizations and their competitions. We will discover how Japan was propelled on this century-long course, why reform was so constant and difficult, and what consequences this had for Japan's national security.

Like most policy change, in Japan or anywhere else, intelligence reform cannot be reduced to a single cause—at least not without sacrificing accuracy. Chapter 1 identifies three generic drivers that affect the shape, pace, and direction of intelligence reform. None is surprising. The first consists of shifts in the strategic environment. After all, threats and balances of power change. Consider, for example, how and why the OSS became the CIA as the Cold War set in after World War II and the United States found itself having to adjust to being one of two superpowers in a suddenly bipolar world. For their part, Japanese strategic thinkers have always been sensitive to Japan's geostrategic circumstances, and often have responded with intelligence reform at moments of strategic uncertainty. The Foreign Ministry built intelligence capabilities to undermine tsarist Russia at the turn of the twentieth century, the imperial military began to rely heavily on private intelligence sources in China in the 1920s, the police strengthened counterintelligence and counterterrorism capabilities in the 1920s at the moment when mass parties were mobilizing (in some cases with foreign support), and every agency beefed up its collection and analysis capabilities in the 1930s when war with the United States seemed imminent.

After losing that war, the Japanese intelligence community endured an extended period of subordination to the United States from which it only recently has begun the delicate process of freeing itself by enhancing indigenous capabilities without denying itself the benefits of U.S. intelligence support. As I have already briefly noted—and as I examine in detail in chapters 3 and 4 of this book—Washington's domination of Japan's intelligence community throughout the Cold War generated considerable resentment in the Japanese security community. The U.S. Department of Defense reportedly blocked Japanese acquisition of surveillance satellites for a long time, and Japanese Ground Self-Defense Force intelligence units were run under code names that were kept secret from their U.S. partners. Remnants of this resentment persisted after the Cold War, affecting some more than others, but the depth of this resentment varied and never rivaled geostrategy as an independent driver of intelligence reform. U.S. frustration with Japanese intelligence leaks generated pressure from Washington that was as problematic for the Japanese intelligence community as the leaks themselves.

Strategists are fully aware that the global balance of power has shifted several times since the end of the Cold War, and many are quite naturally concerned that continued dependence for security and intelligence on a United States in relative decline renders Japan vulnerable in new ways. As we shall see, this was evident to many well before Donald Trump's campaign and election in 2016 elevated their concerns. Nearly a decade earlier—even before China's military threat became palpable and North Korea's acquisition of nuclear weapons openly challenged the U.S. position—a former chief of MOFA's Intelligence and Analysis Service argued that Japan could not effectively reform its intelligence community until it realized that Washington would not necessarily provide for Japan's security and came to grips with the need to formulate a truly independent diplomatic strategy.[12] Just as Prime Minister Abe Shinzō was preparing to reengineer Japan's foreign policy and intelligence system in 2013 by creating a National Security Council (NSC), three Diet representatives from different parties—one of whom would become Abe's foreign minister in 2017—issued a vigorous call for an independent Japanese intelligence service, justifying it with this assessment, rhetorical question, and prescription:

> Japan's diplomacy and national security have never been in such a tight fix. America's relative power is declining and China's military rise, as well as its expanding claims in the ocean, are striking. . . . Is Japan responding effectively to the historic shift in world order? . . . Even if an NSC is established, there is still a missing piece—a foreign intelligence [unit].[13]

The second driver of intelligence reform has been technological change. The most prominent intelligence-related technologies have had to do with the way intelligence is collected: human intelligence (HUMINT), radio and other signals intelligence (SIGINT), and image intelligence (IMINT) are the most widely known and are all widely practiced. Cyber-based intelligence harvesting is just the latest tool to which intelligence communities have to adjust. The Japanese intelligence community has been an active, indeed voracious, technology follower for well more than a century. The imperial military first experimented with aerial reconnaissance balloons in 1877, during the Satsuma Rebellion, and their first operational use came in 1904, during the Russo-Japanese War. It was during that conflict when the Imperial Japanese Navy stood up its first SIGINT unit and broke Russian codes. By that time, and for decades after, Japanese agents—some official, many not—were engaged in extensive espionage activities across Eurasia using advanced tools, including encrypted communication devices. Even so, Japanese messaging proved vulnerable to interception. Washington was privy to Japan's negotiating positions during the Washington Naval Conference in 1921–22 and used its SIGINT advantages to intercept much of Japan's military and diplomatic communications during World War II.

Even if its counterintelligence capabilities sometimes trailed its collection technologies, Japan was never too slow off the technological mark. Despite self-imposed constraints on the military use of space, Japan deployed transponders on the satellites of civilian agencies that transmitted images for the use of military intelligence starting at least as far back as the 1980s. Today, Japanese analysts use many of the most advanced space-based image-processing technologies—reportedly being able to differentiate among five pilots and a lone protocol officer standing in line on the deck of China's aircraft carrier.[14] And, like those of most other advanced nations, Japan's intelligence community is struggling to militarize cyber capabilities to deter, if not to protect against, unwelcome intrusion.[15]

Failure is the third, and often the most proximate, driver of intelligence reform. Clausewitz famously acknowledged intelligence failure in *On War*: "Many intelligence reports in war are contradictory; even more are false, and most are uncertain."[16] Indeed, although their successes are often well hidden, intelligence communities have failed famously; Hitler's surprise of Stalin with the treacherous Operation Barbarossa and U.S. complacency before Japan's attack at Pearl Harbor are just two prominent examples from World War II. Another involved Major General Charles Willoughby, who played a singularly prominent role in the postwar history of the Japanese intelligence community and who engineered "one of the most glaring failures in U.S. military intelligence history" in Korea—both on behalf of General Douglas MacArthur.[17] The failure to coordinate intelligence on the 9/11 terrorist attacks, Washington's willful ignorance of Saddam Hussein's abandonment of weapons of mass destruction, and the counterintelligence failures that abetted Russian interference in the 2016 presidential election are more recent American examples.

But intelligence failure has nowhere been more plentiful or storied than in Japan. The nineteenth-century shogunate was shaken to its knees once the capabilities of Commodore Perry's "black ships" became known; imperial militarists and pan-Asianists were unprepared for U.S. resolve in the

Asia-Pacific War; and the most famous tactical intelligence failure of the Asia-Pacific War occurred after a U.S. signals unit located Admiral Yamamoto Isoroku near the Solomon Islands in April 1943, allowing Admiral Chester Nimitz's pilots to ambush his plane. In the 1970s, Richard Nixon pulled the rug out from under Japan not once but *twice* in "shocks" that upended the global financial community and brought China in from the cold. Subsequent unannounced and unanticipated visits by a Soviet MiG-25 in 1976 and by a North Korean missile in 1998 justified immediate changes in the way Japan practiced intelligence.

These three drivers—strategic change, technological development, and failure—forced the pace of intelligence reform in Japan in much the same way that they compelled reform elsewhere. But this is not merely a story of Japan as a normal nation. We can more easily detect what is distinctive about the history and practice of intelligence in Japan when we observe how the drivers converge with the specific activities in which national intelligence communities are engaged—the "elements" of intelligence. This volume identifies and examines six such elements over time: collection, analysis, communication, protection, covert action, and oversight.

Japan's dominant mode of intelligence collection has varied over time. While Japan's intelligence community was rapidly expanding—from roughly 1895 until 1945—it depended on human intelligence, often in the form of secret collaboration for covert action among ultranationalist freelancers, military spy masters, diplomats, and corporate sponsors. Over time, and after many failures, tradecraft and foreign language training advanced in places like the Imperial Army's Nakano School in Tokyo and the privately run East Asia Common Cultural College (Tōa Dōbun Shōin) in Nanjing. By the end of the Asia-Pacific War, Japan had also acquired a competent SIGINT capability.

Afterwards, with spying and covert action (indeed with the entire security community) held in disrepute, and with Japanese intelligence (indeed with the entire security community) subordinated to Washington, most overt HUMINT was eschewed. SIGINT and, later, IMINT and open source intelligence (OSINT) became the collection technologies of choice. As we shall see, Japan proved adept at each. It was Tokyo's interception of Soviet military orders to shoot down a Korean Airlines commercial jetliner in 1983 that confirmed Moscow's complicity before the United Nations. Meanwhile, in 1997, Japan stood up its SIGINT- and IMINT-centered Defense Intelligence Headquarters (DIH). The DIH is by far the largest unit in the Japanese intelligence community, even if it is but a fraction of the size of the U.S. National Security Agency (NSA), with which it is often compared, and for which it has performed important functions. During the period of U.S.-Japan "trade frictions" in the 1980s, much ado was made of the legal (and sometimes illegal) use of trading companies and other firms to collect (sometimes proprietary) economic data in order to enhance the competitive position of Japanese firms in the global market. The connection between the Japan External Trade and Research Organization (JETRO) and its parent Ministry of International Trade and Industry (MITI, now Ministry of Economy, Trade, and Industry, or METI) with the Japanese intelligence community and with the Ministry of Foreign Affairs raised considerable speculation that HUMINT had never really been abandoned. These efforts notwithstanding, the consensus among Japan's conservative political leadership had long been just as Abe Shinzō, the future prime minister, framed it when he was deputy chief cabinet secretary in 2003: "Most postwar Japanese have overlooked the importance of intelligence collection capabilities."[18]

Analysis is the effort to make sense of data that cannot speak for themselves. Analysts rely on the logics of precedent and analogy and on their knowledge of the doctrines, cultures, and practices of their subject. They must also know the difference between possibilities and probabilities.[19] Above all—and unlike their tenured cousins in academia who enjoy job security even when sloppy or slow—analysts have to trade rigor for speed.[20] This has been a problem for the Japanese intelligence community of every era. Before World War II, most analysis took place in MOFA and in the military, where there were too few specialists, too much ideology, and too many preconceptions. For decades after the war, Japan had no centralized intelligence capacity, and the mutual insularity of Japan's competing intelligence units was allowed to calcify. It was not until Prime Minister Abe's ambitious reengineering project—including creation of a centralized NSC in 2013 and its intelligence coordinating unit, the National Security Secretariat—that the government acted on its oft-stated determination to upgrade Japan's intelligence analysis capacity.

Communication operates on three axes—vertically, between analysts and policy makers; horizontally, among (often competing) intelligence units; and cross-nationally, between allies. Until the Abe reforms examined in chapter 6, surprisingly little had changed since the Asia-Pacific War in the way Japanese analysts and policy makers communicated. The Japanese government had not established an effective system for formulating and issuing intelligence priorities, and political leaders rarely tasked the intelligence community with requests for national intelligence estimates. So, strategic decision making often operated in the dark.[21] Horizontal communications have always been even more problematic for Japan. As indicated by the persistent joke introduced earlier about Japan's "KGB," the Japanese intelligence community has always suffered from extreme stovepiping, a problem endemic to intelligence communities everywhere, but one that has famously plagued the Japanese bureaucracy overall. Even if "the evils of bureaucratic sectionalism" (*tatewari gyōsei no heigai*) are particularly pronounced and widely acknowledged in Japan, intelligence silos are a universal affliction, a result in no small measure of the requirement that intelligence be collected, analyzed, and communicated in secret. Still, Japanese practice has been extreme, never more harmfully so than during the Asia-Pacific War, when, unbeknownst to each other, the Imperial Army and Imperial Navy built identical signals intercept facilities, and the Foreign Ministry routinely withheld intelligence from the military and vice versa.

The Asia-Pacific War not only destroyed much of Japan physically but also cast a shroud on the legitimacy of its national security enterprise. This, combined with the heightened dependence of Japan on U.S. intelligence in a strategic environment that had radically changed, had a profoundly deleterious effect on the Japanese intelligence community. Together they created conditions rife with moral hazard and, thereby, ripe for the extreme underdevelopment of intelligence and, especially, counterintelligence. Much as with the larger national security infrastructure and the military itself, intelligence was rejected by many as prima facie invalid. Throughout the Cold War, intelligence cooperation with the United States remained fraught. Repeated Japanese leaks to Soviet, Chinese, and North Korean agents went largely unpunished and led the United States to withhold information from its Japanese ally. Many Japanese intelligence officers came to resent U.S. domination, and some who were reportedly "anti-American" (*kenbei*) took pains to conceal their activities from Washington.[22] After the Cold War, Washington's pressure on Tokyo on trade and technology poisoned bilateral intelligence cooperation for a time. This seemed to change after 9/11, but even after a bilateral intelligence-sharing pact, the General Security of Military Information Agreement (GSOMIA), was signed in 2007 and the Japanese intelligence community was being openly reimagined, Washington felt it had to hold information back. Its reserve seemed to evaporate, however, in 2013, after a determined reengineering of Japanese intelligence that included promulgation of a state secrets law and creation of the NSC.

We shall also see how covert action had been an active element of Japanese practice for more than half a century. Some of the few storied intelligence agents were those like Akashi Motojirō, who, at the turn of the twentieth century, devoted himself (and considerable Foreign Ministry resources) to undermining the Romanov dynasty in Russia. Groups of "unaffiliated" nationalist agitators and war profiteers were active across Eurasia well into the 1930s, when the imperial military began formally standing up the "special duty units" (*tokumu kikan*) that inspired the title of this volume to support and mobilize anticolonial fighters from Malaya, through India, and into China. Others worked undercover for the imperial military and the Foreign Ministry in the United States in the 1930s and 1940s. We learn, too, that postwar patriots, such as Ao Hiromasa, were active covertly in Taiwan and Southeast Asia well into the 1970s. And even officers from domestically oriented counterintelligence and counterterrorism units, such as the Justice Ministry's Public Security Intelligence Agency, occasionally operated abroad. It bears mentioning, however, that none of Japan's known covert actions had the impact of America's, which, after all, took down regimes from Iran to Chile and sustained anticommunist governments in Japan, Italy, and elsewhere, in part by enriching conservative politicians to sustain the Cold War Pax Americana.[23]

Finally, there is the matter of oversight. Oversight is rarely included in lists of intelligence functions. But it is critically important to the effective functioning of an intelligence community in any democratic state. It is typical of bureaucrats and politicians to resist the creation or strengthening of oversight units that in their view would compromise the secrecy and effectiveness of the intelligence apparatus, especially in democracies. It is also typical that the opposing view—that secrecy must be balanced by transparency and accountability—forces compromises by which intelligence oversight is nested in national legislatures, in the judiciary, or even in the offices of inspectors general in the executive branch itself. As we shall see, Japan has been no stranger to debates about secrecy and oversight—not least because of its wartime experience with authoritarianism. But after Japanese hostage incidents in the Middle East and the suicide of a compromised Japanese consular official in Shanghai laid bare weaknesses in Japan's intelligence community, a committee of the ruling Liberal Democratic Party (LDP) got out ahead of the issue. Its June 2006 report calling for intelligence reform also recommended creation of a Diet Intelligence Committee to conduct oversight.

As often happens, the more ambitious hopes for oversight were quashed, and the oversight structure that finally congealed does not allow elected representatives to peer inside the intelligence black box. Thus, intelligence oversight in Japan has fallen to citizens' movements, the media, and the judiciary by default, leaving its many critics dissatisfied. Nonetheless, since acknowledgment of the importance of oversight has emerged from the most conservative wing of Japan's conservative ruling party, there is reason to expect further reforms that will bring Japanese practice into line with that of other democratic states.

By now my purpose here should be clear. This book, much like others I have produced, is designed to render Japan—in this case, the history of Japan's strategic intelligence—comparable to other states. It uses public records and open source material to assess the politics and organization of these under-studied but critical elements of Japan's security apparatus and to map within a generic framework how they have changed over time. Without such a history and comparative mapping, it is impossible to establish a clear and comprehensive portrait of the Japanese intelligence community or to anticipate how it will change going forward. And without such a portrait or an ability to anticipate change, public understanding of the institutions of Japanese national security decision making will remain inadequate. This, of course, would impair oversight. We turn now, then, to developing the more nuanced understanding of the generic historical drivers and comparative elements that will frame this volume and, I hope, make this portrait come to life.

ACKNOWLEDGMENTS

I am grateful to Cullen Nutt and Mayumi Fukushima for their excellent research assistance on this project. Cullen played a critical role in educating me as I was just learning how to think seriously about intelligence. In addition to helping me identify and plow through Japanese language materials, often correcting my awkward translations and transliterations, Mayumi carefully proofread draft chapters. She also conducted several interviews on my behalf, a task I had never before assigned to an RA and which I am happy to acknowledge. A great many other colleagues have been subjected to my interrogations and/or have read portions of early drafts. In particular, I want to thank Eichiro Azuma, Thomas Berger, Dennis Blair, Joel Brenner, Edward Drea, Chas Freeman, Lance Gatling, Sheldon Garon, Michael Green, Hayashi Yasuo, Paul Heer, Bill Heinrich, Lowell Jacoby, Robert Jervis, Kanehara Nobukatsu, Kaneko Masafumi, Kotani Ken, Kunimi Masahiro, Kinomura Kenichi, David Leheny, John McManus, Stephen Mercado, Michishita Narushige, Morimoto Satoshi, Nishi Masanori, Danny Orbach, Otsuka Umio, Shinoda Tomohito, Shiraishi Takashi, Henry Sokolski, Suzuki Michihiko, Tanaka Hitoshi, Gregory Treverton, Eric Van Slander, Corey Wallace, Yamato Taro, Yoshida Yoshihide, Urs Matthias Zachmann, James Zobel, and an even larger number of interlocutors inside the Japanese and U.S. intelligence and policy communities who prefer to remain anonymous.

I owe a special debt to my old friend Tanaka Akihiko, president of the National Graduate Institute for Policy Studies in Tokyo, where I was based for my fieldwork with support from the Smith Richardson Foundation, and to Verena Blechinger, director of the Center of East Asian Studies at the Freie Universität Berlin, where much of the writing was undertaken with the support of the Albert Einstein Foundation of Berlin. I am grateful, too, for the support of the MIT Security Studies Program and the MIT Japan Program. Back at MIT, Laurie Scheffler once again maintained order in my absence, and colleague Eric Heginbotham generously and incisively read the entire manuscript, saving me from numerous unforced errors. Those that remain are mine alone.

It has been a special privilege to work with Roger Haydon again. This was not our first rodeo together, and I am immensely grateful that even after thirty-five years of collaboration, he can still slice and dice a manuscript without making this author abandon hope. And far above all, I must acknowledge the unwavering support of my wife, Debbie. We've been at this for nearly half a century now, and unlike each of us corporally, life together never gets old.

Abbreviations

AESA – Active Electronically Scanned Array
AEWG – Airborne Early Warning Group
ASDF – Air Self-Defense Force
BADGE – Base Air Defense Ground Environment
CGP – Clean Government Party
CIA – Central Intelligence Agency
CIC – Central Intelligence Corps
CIRO – Cabinet Intelligence and Research Office
COMINT – communications intelligence
CPI – Counter Psychological Intelligence Program
CRC – Cabinet Research Chamber
CSIC – Cabinet Satellite Intelligence Center
CTUJ – Counterterrorism Unit of Japan
DIH – Defense Intelligence Headquarters
DPJ – Democratic Party of Japan
DPRK –Democratic People's Republic of (North) Korea
DSSL – Designated State Secrets Law
EADB – East Asia Development Board
ELINT – electronic intelligence
FSA – Financial Services Agency
GHQ – General Headquarters of the Supreme Commander of the Allied
    Powers
GIA – Geospatial Information Authority
GSDF – Ground Self-Defense Force
GSOMIA – General Security of Military Information Agreement
G-2 – Military Intelligence Section
HUMINT – human intelligence
IDE – Institute of Developing Economies
IJA – Imperial Japanese Army
IJN – Imperial Japanese Navy

IMINT – image intelligence
INA – Indian National Army
ISR – intelligence, surveillance, and reconnaissance
JADGE – Japan Aerospace Defense Ground Environment
JAXA – Japan Aerospace Exploration Agency
JCG – Japan Coast Guard
JCP – Japan Communist Party
JDA – Japan Defense Agency
JETRO – Japan External Trade and Research Organization
JSP – Japan Socialist Party
KCIA – South Korean Central Intelligence Agency
KGB – Committee for State Security of the Soviet Union
LDP – Liberal Democratic Party
MASINT – measurement and signal intelligence
METI – Ministry of Economy, Trade, and Industry
MEXT – Ministry of Education, Science, and Technology
MITI – Ministry of International Trade and Industry
MOC – Ministry of Communications
MOD – Ministry of Defense
MOF – Ministry of Finance
MOFA – Ministry of Foreign Affairs
MSDF – Maritime Self-Defense Force
NDC – National Defense Council
NDSL – National Defense Security Law
NGO – nongovernmental organization
NIDS – National Institute for Defense Studies
NIE – national intelligence estimate
NISC – National Information Security Center
NPA – National Police Agency
NPR – National Police Reserve
NSA – National Security Agency
NSC – National Security Council
NSS – National Security Secretariat
OSINT – open source intelligence
OSS – Office of Strategic Services
PLA – People's Liberation Army
PLAN – People's Liberation Army Navy
PRC – People's Republic of China
PSEC – Public Security Examination Commission
PSIA – Public Security Intelligence Agency

ROK – Republic of (South) Korea
SAPA – Subversive Activities Prevention Act
SCAP – Supreme Command of the Allied Powers
SCJ – Security Council of Japan
SDF – Self-Defense Forces
SIGINT – signals intelligence
USFJ – United States Forces Japan
USFK – United States Forces Korea

CHAPTER 1

Driving Intelligence

There are many ways to tell the history of intelligence reform, but it cannot be told accurately without exploring the transformation of what had long been a "hobby of princes" to its more organized role in national security policy making.[1] Intelligence was driven into the arms of professional bureaucrats during World War I, and by 1918, most European states had established centralized intelligence capabilities as a matter of national survival.[2] The United States was late to that war, and was even later in realizing the enduring need for a permanent intelligence establishment. Only America's shocking vulnerability at Pearl Harbor two decades later and a second "total war" would shake Washington out of its lethargy. I shall attempt to explain why it has taken Japan even longer to make the administrative changes that undergird effective intelligence. Much longer.

Paradoxically, as the intelligence business became more professional, its institutions became less fixed. The organizational forms, analytical missions, and operational roles of intelligence communities have always and everywhere been the repeated objects of change, even when they were not the problem—and, it must be acknowledged, even when reform was not the solution. Demands for intelligence reform (typically politicized demands) periodically have nudged the fundamental elements of every intelligence community—collection, analysis, communication, protection, covert action, and oversight—in new directions. Three permanent facts of life have stimulated these demands and have deprived most intelligence communities of stable institutional form, if not permanent identities: shifting balances of regional and global power; rapid technological change; and repeated, costly, and visible intelligence failures. Reforms introduced in this punctuated evolution somehow never forestall the next crisis or inhibit consequent demands for further change.[3]

Wars, of course, can activate all three of these mechanisms simultaneously—and conflict certainly has framed most prominent intelligence failures. But balances of power and technology also shift in peacetime, ahead of the next war and in the wake of the last one. And as they do, intelligence establishments are among the first expected to make sense of what these changes might mean for national security. Sometimes they accomplish their task with aplomb and sometimes they fail—famously. But they are seldom at rest for long. This chapter explores the three drivers of intelligence reform and the six mechanisms that are targeted for change, each in turn. Together they provide the historical and comparative framework for a subsequent analysis of the Japanese intelligence community.

The Drivers

Systemic

Senior intelligence officials—usually those unencumbered by demands for tactical evaluations—are often tasked with assessing the distribution of international power. They have to stare coldly at facts regarding their own vulnerabilities and search for those of adversaries. They have to judge the ambitions of foreign leaders who may theretofore have been comfortably disregarded. What motivates these leaders? Are they rational? How do they process information? Will they understand the signals sent to them? Do they suffer from the same cognitive and organizational impediments to effective policy that affect us? For how long will rising powers accept the status quo? Must the emergence of potential foreign adversaries be accompanied by the inflation of the threat they pose?[4]

Working with this broad palette, analysts have to anticipate how shifts in the balance of power and the thinking of foreign actors will affect policy makers' ability to tip the forces of history to their own advantage and in the direction of their own choosing. Consider three possibilities. First, there are moments when major threats simply disappear. In the United States, the end of the Cold War marked the beginning of a decade-long search by the CIA for a new raison d'être. Some officials tried to redefine their role by augmenting capacities in economic intelligence. Others refocused on demographic or environmental dangers. Then, when immediate threats again became kinetic, many shifted back to more familiar terrain.

Second, there is the shift away from relatively stable unipolar or bipolar global balances of power to the relatively more unstable multipolarity. Here the intelligence community must redirect itself toward understanding myriad threats and challenges, including the prospects for the formation and dissolution of alliances—both adversarial and friendly—as well as for concomitantly, and possibly unacceptably, higher risks of strategic surprise.[5] One prominent example is how the early twenty-first-century rise of China stimulated new forms of intelligence cooperation across East, South, and Southeast Asia: the Philippines agreed to enhance intelligence cooperation with Australia in 2008; Indonesia signed an intelligence cooperation agreement with Australia in August 2014; and India began training Vietnamese intelligence officers in 2015.[6] Japan, for its part, responded to the rise of China and the relative decline of the United States by pivoting in Asia and actively diversifying its strategic relationships. It now has enhanced ties with India and Australia, including intelligence cooperation.[7]

International political change influences the shape and functioning of intelligence communities in other ways as well. For example, altogether new constellations of actors and threats—and the blurring of the distinctions among foreign, transnational, and domestic ones—can make concerns about the balance of power seem quaint. Indeed, the ever more porous boundary between domestic and international threats has forced considerable change upon intelligence communities worldwide. In the post-9/11 United States, once separate domestic and foreign intelligence domains began to share policy makers' attention and budgets, and entirely new intelligence units based on function, such as terrorism/counterterrorism or proliferation/counter-proliferation, were established.[8] Likewise in France, where "the global war on terror" had long had a powerful domestic presence, stovepiped intelligence units were rearranged to incentivize collaboration across functional boundaries.[9] This may have been easier in states such as the UK, Canada, and Australia, where domestic intelligence services were already regarded as legitimate, relatively transparent, and reasonably well supervised by elected legislators.[10] As we shall see, because they started from lower levels of legitimacy, transparency, and oversight, Japanese policy makers had their own problems. Playing catch-up in the face of a shifting regional balance of power, they created a stiff new state secrets law and reorganized the intelligence function within the cabinet in 2013, and then passed a controversial anti-conspiracy law in 2017. The world was rapidly changing, and intelligence communities everywhere were struggling to follow suit.

Technological

Technological shifts have also forced many changes in the structure and function of intelligence agencies. By the late nineteenth century, industrial development made it risky, if not always foolish, to undertake military operations while relying entirely on human intelligence—individual spies or the interrogation of prisoners (HUMINT).[11] States needed more timely and more complete information about an adversary's capabilities and intentions. Initially this took two forms: signals intelligence (SIGINT)—the interception (and possible decrypting) of an opponent's telegraph, telephone, and radio messages—and, later, remote sensing. SIGINT got a boost during the U.S. Civil War, when War Department code-breakers serving President Lincoln and his commanders had notable successes. By 1863, the Union established the Bureau of Military Intelligence under the leadership of General Joseph Hooker, commander of the Army of the Potomac, to consolidate HUMINT and SIGINT data. It was considered "the best run intelligence operation of the Civil War," and was in any event America's first professional, "all source" intelligence agency.[12] After the war, though, the unit was shuttered, reflecting a U.S. preference for maintaining intelligence capabilities only in wartime. In 1917 the army reestablished a robust signals intelligence unit and tasked this "MI-8" with deciphering military communications. The "MI-8" survived for a few years after World War I and, by decoding Japanese communications, enabled Washington to reach a favorable capital ship ratio in its negotiations with Tokyo.[13] But it was disbanded by President Herbert Hoover in 1921 at the conclusion of the Washington Naval Conference. This is a reminder that, like military power, technology-based intelligence capabilities may degrade sharply after a war.[14]

Remote sensing using aerial photography (photographic intelligence, or PHOTINT) was first developed for use by Union forces in the U.S. Civil War in 1860. Japan was not far behind. Imperial forces experimented with reconnaissance balloons during the Satsuma Rebellion in 1877, and deployed them during the Russo-Japanese War in 1904. PHOTINT came into widespread use by all militaries during World War I. Aerial night photography—relying largely on flares and flash bombs to light the skies—was first used in the 1930s by the British and the Russians, but the United States was not far behind, with superior strobe technology developed by Harold "Doc" Edgerton at the Massachusetts Institute of Technology.[15] In the 1950s, the U.S. Air

Force was flying routine missions over Soviet territory at altitudes that made the collecting U-2 aircraft undetectable and invincible—until one crashed in May 1960. A few months later, in August, the United States launched its first spy satellite, the KH-1, which used photographic film released in canisters that parachuted back to earth.[16] By the end of the Cold War, a panoply of air-, space-, and sea-based platforms operated by every great (and some middle) powers could support remote sensing using an array of geospatial imaging (IMINT), including thermal, microwave, and light detection and ranging (LIDAR) technologies.[17] On some accounts, as information became available "in torrents," response times grew dangerously short and analysis was often bypassed as raw intelligence was reported directly to policy makers and, in some cases, even to pilots and other weapons operators. This—along with the development of missile delivery—increased the possibility and danger of false positive detections. Yet there was an upside. John Lewis Gaddis calls the development of the reconnaissance satellite "the greatest success of the Cold War for both sides," pointing out how "transparency became a mutual benefit" by diminishing mutual fear of surprise attack.[18] Later, measurement and signal intelligence (MASINT) was added to the remote sensing toolkit. MASINT includes a wide range of technologies that can detect, track, identify, and describe the distinctive characteristics ("signatures") of targets by analyzing their sounds, chemical properties, and gaseous emissions.

SIGINT was critical during World War II; IMINT came to dominate Cold War intelligence; and MASINT became diffused widely (especially for submarine and missile tracking) after 1986. Funds for each mushroomed over time. Verifiable, and generally more comprehensive than even the most reliable human informants, remote sensing also came to consume expanding swaths of bureaucratic space, often crowding out HUMINT where the technology could be developed, applied, and afforded.[19] These and other remote sensing technologies, including telemetry, acoustics, and air sampling, which formed the backbone of "national technical means," have been used to verify international arms treaties and to monitor the proliferation of weapons of mass destruction globally, and their use expanded the size and number of organizations within which complex collection and analysis had to be coordinated.

By the early twenty-first century, a powerful new high-tech Swiss army knife was added to the arsenals of state (and non-state) actors: the uninvited, secret, and unfriendly penetration of adversaries' computer networks. Since such cyber operations could be used defensively to surveil and exploit (collect) as well as offensively degrade or destroy an adversary's military and economic capabilities, an entirely new domain was added to national security affairs. Indeed, "domain" is not a metaphor; in 2010 the United States Cyber Command, a sub-unified command subordinate to the United States Strategic Command, was created to nurture collection and offensive and defensive cyber capabilities. Israel followed suit in May 2011, and the next month the British Ministry of Defense announced it had stood up its own cyber warfare joint force command.[20] In 2014 the Chinese People's Liberation Army (PLA) shifted its "strategic guideline"—for only the ninth time ever—to elevate cybersecurity to the "commanding heights" of national defense.[21] Japan's Ministry of Defense (MOD) established a Cybersecurity Strategic Headquarters and released a new cybersecurity strategy in 2015.[22] In 2018, MOD announced it would increase personnel in this domain by 40 percent, from 110 to 150 staff, and launch a new command to deal with space and cyber, the "fourth and fifth battlefields" after land, sea, and air.[23]

Many of the world's most sophisticated defense contractors mirrored (and likely lobbied for) these organizational changes. Cyber divisions at U.S. firms like Northrop Grumman, Raytheon, and General Dynamics began working with ministries of defense to develop cyber espionage as well as offensive capabilities.[24] The number of cyber consultancies—both corporate and boutique—mushroomed. So have their revenues. Civilians and businesses reportedly spent under $70 billion annually on cybersecurity in 2014, an estimated $5 billion more the next year, and $93 billion in 2018.[25] Nor will this "cyber military-industrial complex" deflate anytime soon. On one account, global cyber spending is projected to exceed $170 billion annually by 2020, while another predicted in 2018 that global spending on cybersecurity would exceed $1 trillion cumulatively from 2017 to 2021.[26] There is no reliable public estimate of private sector Japanese cybersecurity spending, but Fujitsu, NEC, Toshiba, Mitsubishi Electric, NTT, and other military contractors compete for a share of Japanese public spending on cybersecurity, which rose a striking 37 percent in 2019 to a record 85 billion yen.[27]

Apart from their awesome capability to disable or degrade the command and control of adversaries' weapons systems and to sabotage their industrial infrastructures, cyber tools also move well beyond HUMINT and SIGINT to provide new avenues of access to the intellectual property, codes, weapons designs, and other classified information of potential adversaries. Data storage has evolved from human memory to paper documents in desk drawers, to computer files, and now to clouds; data mining now enables sifting through haystacks of information to find the menacing needle; botnets can reside secretly in targets' computers while providing a window on their data. Russia's intervention in the 2016 U.S. presidential election was only the first prominent indication of the colossal potential for cyber offense and the colossal challenge for cyber defense. Although we are wise not to imagine that emerging technologies always live up to their hype, they are shaking up intelligence communities worldwide.[28]

The latter has attracted more attention: ministries of defense and related government agencies everywhere have been the object of cyber probes. A classified system of the British MOD was hacked in May 2012, files were stolen from the Indian Defense Ministry's Defense Research and Development Organization in March 2013, and data were stolen from the Dutch Defense Ministry in October 2014.[29] More than a year before it was confirmed by U.S. intelligence agencies that Russian hackers had penetrated the Democratic Party's presidential campaign offices, the head of U.S. Cyber Command, Admiral Michael Rogers, told the U.S. Senate that hackers probe U.S. military networks for vulnerabilities "thousands of times per day."[30] It is not known how many of these incursions are undertaken by—or at the behest of—foreign governments, but the Chinese People's Liberation Army, the Russian government, and the North Korean regime have all been associated with some of them by the U.S. Department of Defense and the FBI.[31] While it is not clear how much U.S. cyber activity is offensive, how much is defensive, and how much is for intelligence gathering, the United States and its intelligence partners have been aggressive in this domain as well.[32] It is estimated that by 2018, cyber accounted for at least 8 percent of the U.S. intelligence budget.[33] It is more difficult to break out an equivalent number in the overall Japanese intelligence budget. But it has been reported that annual government spending on cyber security in Japan averaged $529.5 million from 2013 to 2017, the half decade after cyberattacks hit nearly all government departments, including the Diet, the Nuclear Energy Safety Organization, the Atomic Energy Agency, and the Japan Aerospace Exploration Agency. The record-high 85 billion yen budgeted for 2019 was still comparatively low.[34] It is difficult to determine just how much public cyber spending is used for intelligence. In 2017, the portion of cybersecurity-related spending allocated to ministries and agencies that were formally part of the Japanese intelligence community was less than 1 percent of the total Japanese intelligence budget.[35]

Failure

No matter how sophisticated technologically, no intelligence system has ever been (or ever can be) immune to failure—the "mismatch between the estimates and what later information reveals."[36] Because failures are closely observed while even spectacular successes may pass unnoticed—and because they are often so costly in blood and lucre—failures have served politicians and policy makers repeatedly as primary justifications for reorganization. The rate of intelligence failure may be no higher than in economic forecasting, but the stakes and visibility of intelligence failure are much greater.[37] Whereas academics may declare success if their analyses are correct four out of five times, intelligence analysts cannot get it wrong that one important time.[38] One senior diplomat, recognizing that political leaders looking for fault will rarely look in the mirror, has observed ironically that "there are no policy failures. There are only policy successes and intelligence failures."[39] So it is the latter that immediately become the objects of reform.

There are, of course, both intelligence failures and intelligence-related policy failures. In either event, the great irony is that failure-inspired reorganizations—usually the result of exhaustive studies by blue ribbon panels and/or legislative oversight in democratic systems—have led to the enlargement of intelligence communities more often than they have led to their contraction. Intelligence failures may stall out the careers of individual analysts and operatives, but they invariably also lead to increased missions and budgets.[40] Indeed, the expansion of the intelligence communities—without regard to their marginal utility or high costs—may be the most impressive example of rewarded failure in the history of public policy.[41]

The recognition that, as Richard Posner points out, "there are no organizational panaceas" in the intelligence world has never prevented politicians from hoping that their next reform would solve the problem and that failure could somehow be "baked out" of the intelligence process.[42] New units are created to do what old units did, but with more resources. Experts tinker with tradecraft; "red teams" and "blue teams" are formed to examine underlying preconceptions; devil's advocacy is introduced—or abandoned; scenario development is reconfigured; key assumptions are reexamined; counterfactuals are privileged or banished. That nothing stands still under these episodic reforms is not to say progress is inexorable. Even intelligence communities that learn and reform may not improve as quickly as their adversaries' ability to conceal and deceive.[43] In fact, the government often finds itself "fixing the organizational chart rather than the quality of the intelligence."[44] To its credit, the CIA undertook the first review of its performance in January 1948, less than a year after the agency was established. And it never ceased probing its own failures through the 1950s and 1960s. By the early 1970s, a Product Review Division was established in the CIA to study seven highly visible intelligence failures. Failure proved uncomfortably resilient to review and reform, and the exercise was repeated a decade later—and continued through 9/11 to the present. No U.S. administration, and few Congresses, have failed to initiate their own studies of failure, but there has never been a lasting fix.[45] Consequently, post-failure studies and reorganizations continue intermittently, rarely without prompting organizational and operational tinkering, the suboptimal practice that, as we shall see, characterized Japan's approach to intelligence reform for the first decade after the Cold War.

This appears to be a universal phenomenon. After Israel's intelligence failure in the 1973 Yom Kippur War, a Commission on the Preparedness of Israel for the October War was empowered to determine what went wrong. Its final report included a long list of recommendations for institutional change, many of which were quickly implemented.[46] In the aftermath of the Falklands War of 1982, a parliamentary committee inquired into the performance of the British government before the Argentine invasion of the islands. Though it did not directly blame British intelligence or mandate organizational changes, the committee faulted British spies for their inattention to Argentine press reports and recommended staffing reforms in the cabinet-based Joint Intelligence Organisation.[47] Pakistan's surprise military incursion that precipitated the Kargil War of 1999 spurred a similar inquest in India. Delhi's Research and Analysis Wing came in for stinging criticism from a parliamentary committee. Among other reforms, the Indian government established a Defense Intelligence Agency in response.[48]

History is filled with strategic surprise. In the U.S. case, during the War of 1812, military intelligence failed to discover British troops advancing on Washington, D.C., until they were just sixteen miles from the capital.[49] A national intelligence estimate (NIE) predicting that armed hostilities were unlikely was issued in June 1950, just days before the North Korean military crossed the 38th parallel into South Korea.[50] In the 1960s—at least until the Pentagon Papers were written—most U.S. analysts discounted the possibility that North Vietnam could long sustain its war footing. Analysts also failed to anticipate the overthrow of the Shah of Iran in 1979, the collapse of the Soviet Union in 1991, and the 9/11 attacks in 2001.[51]

Although intelligence success may be less visible than intelligence failure, it is neither a stranger to, nor in any way the enemy of, intelligence reform.[52] Although less widely known until well after the fact, many successes have transformed the way intelligence is conducted. U.S. and British decrypting of imperial Japan's "Purple" cipher system and the compromising of the German "Enigma" machine by the Poles, the French, and the British each contributed dramatically to a shortened war, to an Allied victory, and to permanent changes in cryptology.[53] Thus, as Robert Jervis reminds the methodologically self-conscious among us, looking only at failure is akin to "selecting on the dependent variable," one of the cardinal sins in the social sciences.[54] After all, when an informed warning is heeded, failures are for-gone. And if the intelligence community learned only from failure, it would miss the chance to capitalize on lessons from its successes.[55] That is not how the intelligence community works, according to one recent director of the U.S. National Intelligence Council. Successes are viewed as processes that are studied and codified for the benefit of future analyses.[56] Persistent study of success—and of failures within the successes—have reportedly led to organizational change, though with less fanfare than failure generates.[57]

In a perfect world, intelligence professionals would know everything, deliver their analyses in a timely way, and be believed.[58] Collection would be comprehensive and communication seamless. And, of course, intelligence successes have saved however many thousands of lives and shortened wars—such as when Allies' moles inside the German Foreign Office and Gestapo provided critical early intelligence on the V1 and V2 rocket programs; when British intelligence turned German soldiers into double agents in the famed Double-Cross System, allowing London to flood Berlin with wartime misinformation; or when the Magic decrypt of Japanese government messaging enabled Allied decision makers to know Hitler's dispositions before his Japanese partners did. But no such perfect world has ever existed, and no reasonable analyst or policy maker can expect intelligence success each time.[59] Although an elegant piece of collection will occasionally fill in a piece of a puzzle or fix an outstanding problem, analysts cannot know everything, much less stimulate uniformly appropriate action on that which they cannot know with certainty. The intelligence business produces critical successes and spectacular failures and learns from both.

Although the National Security Agency, America's premier signals intelligence organization, has crowed publicly about its successes and referred in its strategic planning documents to creating a "Golden Age of SIGINT" in which it could acquire information from "anyone, anytime, anywhere," the contemporary U.S. intelligence system was actually born of failure—the near-mythic failure of Pearl Harbor.[60] Foreigners had long underestimated the capabilities—and misread the intentions—of the Japanese. In March 1929, the Plans Division of the British Admiralty observed that Japan's educational and banking systems and its innovative spirit were all so underdeveloped that the Japanese military and industry were certain to continue to lag behind those of the other great powers.[61] A bit more than a decade later, on the basis of U.S. naval intelligence reports that "no move against Pearl Harbor appears imminent or planned for the foreseeable future," U.S. Secretary of the Navy Frank Knox vowed just three days before the 7 December 1941 attack that "the U.S. Navy is not going to be caught napping" in Hawaii.[62] All this is especially poignant when viewed from Japan's perspective: Its stunning intelligence success at Pearl Harbor was tactical. It is still living with the consequences of its larger strategic intelligence failure.

For the most part, failures are due less to incompetence or malfeasance than to a lack of resources, common mistakes, and, most simply, the impossibility of omniscience. Thomas Schelling uses the example of Pearl Harbor to make just this point: "There is a tendency in our planning to confuse the unfamiliar with the improbable. The contingency we have not considered seriously looks strange; what looks strange is thought improbable; what is improbable need not be considered seriously."[63] And so intelligence communities fail and reform. In doing so—and in responding to shifts in the strategic environment and technological shifts—they encounter what Richard Betts refers to as the "familiar pathologies" that impede effective national intelligence.[64] Some are cognitive, others bureaucratic, but they are ubiquitous and reside in each of the six functions performed within every intelligence community: collection, analysis, communication, protection, covert action, and oversight—the elements on which this volume focuses most closely.

The Elements

The first four of these functional elements are often connected in one or another version of an idealized "intelligence cycle" said to be the brainchild of Sherman Kent.[65] In this "old-fashioned" closed-loop model, policy requirements derive from planning collection efforts, the results of which are processed for analyses that are eventually reported to decision makers who will thereupon act and generate new requirements.[66] But it is rarely so simple in the real world, where each node may be connected to every other node in a cybernetic network that is more complex than Kent's original call and response model. After all, policy consumers may not know what they need, collectors may not know how to find what they are looking for, and communication may be hindered by bureaucratic or political constraints that engender workarounds. Moreover, although collection and analysis are jobs assigned to intelligence units, communication is a divided responsibility between intelligence professionals who disseminate and policy makers who are expected to listen, but are free to interrogate the transmitter and/or ignore what they are told. Political leaders may fail despite receiving properly collected, analyzed, and transmitted information from the intelligence community. Despite the predictable "blame game" and finger pointing, the distinction between policy failure and intelligence failure is not clear-cut. Successful or not, policy makers are a node in a chain of communication in which each side transmits and receives. How the policy community listens, absorbs, understands, and acts on intelligence will shape future collection, analysis, and dissemination by the intelligence community.

Although the Japanese government formally embraced the "intelligence cycle" model in its 2013 intelligence overhaul, its practices conform no more closely to Kent's textbook than do others'. As we shall see in chapters 4 through 6, during the Cold War—and even for years afterwards—Japan's most senior leaders had little appetite for intelligence estimates. Few were ordered up, produced, served, or consumed. And even after the ambitious reform of 2013, the topics of intelligence estimates have been selected as often by analysts as by decision makers. I therefore examine Japan's intelligence process as I would those of other states—as discrete, multiply connected elements rather than as a cycle.[67] In addition, I treat covert action as a fifth element because it is an activity in which every intelligence community is deeply engaged—and because the history of the Japanese intelligence community is richly embroidered with clandestine activities. And finally, since the classical model neglected to incorporate domestic politics, I examine a sixth element that has been remarkably (and, to some, unexpectedly) important in the postwar Japanese discourse on intelligence reform: oversight.

Collection

Collection is sometimes associated with espionage, tradecraft, and intrigue. Often it is conflated with the broader term "operations," and includes not only the clandestine acquisition of information that the target would wish not to have shared but also the "secret manipulation of events that affect adversaries," including propaganda, disinformation, political destabilization, and even the secret transfer of weapons to insurgents—components of "covert action" that will be discussed separately later on.[68]

Information comes to collectors through two channels—from sources (when people share it with them) and from methods (when they find ways to produce it)—both often undertaken under hostile conditions.[69] Secretly obtaining secrets is not easy; alert adversaries try to deceive and deny. But, as noted earlier—and as the 2016 Russian hacks into the Democratic National Committee's computer system illustrated—this has not prevented the persistent addition of innovative new means of collection, particularly those that are cyber-based.[70]

Collection may always have to confront and overcome the deliberate planting of false information, but it is undertaken by a range of additional means beyond HUMINT. In the United States, budgets for SIGINT and

IMINT have been seven times larger than for HUMINT since the 1960s, and each has its own deeply resourced institutional home, the National Security Agency (NSA) and the National Geospatial-Intelligence Agency, respectively. Soon after IMINT came online, the NSA budget doubled that of the CIA, itself twice the size of the budget of the State Department.[71] In 2016, the seventeen federal agencies constituting the U.S. intelligence community—including the Office of the Director of National Intelligence—spent a total of about $72 billion.[72] The exact proportion dedicated to collection—including HUMINT, IMINT, and MASINT—is classified and does not include the enormous cost of satellite development.[73] Owing to the high cost of the technical platforms they employ, the lion's share of U.S. intelligence spending likely supports collection as opposed to analysis. The first director of the Defense Intelligence Headquarters, Japan's largest image and signals collection unit, explained that the sprawling U.S. operation cannot be Japan's model and suggested instead that "the British model is closer in size, scope, and historical relevance."[74]

Collection need not be covert, of course. As Loch Johnson, a former staff director of the House Committee on Intelligence Oversight, has noted, "A good librarian can be as valuable as a good spy."[75] Open source intelligence (OSINT)—newspapers, speeches, conference papers, industrial displays, operational manuals, and gray materials of all sorts—has advantages of speed, availability, cost, quality, clarity, and ease of use.[76] In one striking case, analysts in the Office of Strategic Services (OSS) combed through local newspaper obituaries of Wehrmacht officers during World War II to assess how Germany was doing on the Eastern Front. The information they collected was public, but the intelligence they generated from it had to be kept secret so that a valuable window on the enemy's military situation would not be shuttered.[77] Johnson estimates that OSINT may account for as much as 80 to 95 percent of the data in final intelligence reports.[78] Knowing this, policy makers often bypass the intelligence community entirely. In a 2013 survey of 234 former senior U.S. policy makers, two thirds ranked the newspaper as a very important source of information for policy making. This put newsprint in a dead heat with classified U.S. government reports. The authors of the survey, Paul Avey and Michael Desch, call this a "striking" result that "lend[s] more credence to the widely recognized—if seldom acknowledged—fact that most policy is made based upon open sources."[79]

Finally, there is the issue of boundary transgression by collectors. There is no international law against espionage, and it has been practiced by all states. But what is acceptable foreign policy is often unacceptable at home. This is an irony in the United States, where bulk data collection is a business model and an election campaign tool. For a time after 9/11, the American public accepted a more intrusive state. But until the 2013 revelations of NSA contractor Edward Snowden, it was not known that the U.S. Department of Justice and the Foreign Intelligence Surveillance Court had interpreted Section 215 of the USA Patriot Act as permitting the bulk collection of U.S. citizens' telephone metadata. Intelligence officials insisted that U.S. citizens are protected against all but incidental collection by the Fourth Amendment of the Constitution and that they had to demonstrate "reasonable suspicion" to gain access to specific personal data, but the notion that the intelligence community targets "all Americans" became widely embraced.[80] As a result, the intelligence community once again came under pressure for reform, and Section 215 of the nearly fourteen-year-old Patriot Act was eliminated in its successor, the so-called Freedom Act of 2015.

Meanwhile, Britain, France, and other democratic states with longer histories of domestic terrorism continue to enjoy broad power to conduct the equivalent of Section 215 bulk collection and to spy on their citizens. Unit 8200, Israel's equivalent of the NSA, is the largest single unit in the Israeli Defense Forces. It routinely surveils Israeli citizens, as well as Palestinians in the Occupied Territories.[81] Until 2013, the German government was reportedly one of the NSA's key partners in collecting data on its own citizens, and *Le Monde* has reported that the French Direction Générale de la Sécurité Extérieure collects telephone, text, and social media data.[82] As we shall see, the Japanese government assumed broader surveillance powers in 2017. And these are just some of the democracies. Collection continues apace both at home and abroad, in new forms and old.

Analysis

Analysis—the assessment and interpretation of collected data that cannot speak for themselves—generates its own problems. According to Betts, analysts and collectors have entirely different personalities: "A careful analyst will be more like Hamlet; an effective operator, more like Patton."[83] Indeed, there are likely no pearl-handled revolvers or swagger sticks on the desktops of intelligence analysts. To the contrary, these scholarly professionals are routinely described as the "stepchildren" of the intelligence community, second fiddles to the more storied collectors and policy makers.[84] But neither the heroics of field operations nor the grandeur of remote-sensing data—nor even the allure of decision making—is more critical than the requirement that raw information be transformed into accurate, timely, and relevant intelligence. This means that analysts working from some of the least glamorous desktops in national capitals must interpret photos, signals, documents, and field reports that are at best incomplete and ambiguous. Their estimates have to provide insight not merely into adversaries' capabilities, a hard enough task in itself, but also into their intentions, a more difficult job.[85] As Sherman Kent once acknowledged, "Estimating is what you do when you do not know."[86]

Analytic success is often impaired by both cognitive and structural factors.[87] One of the most critical problems is the tendency for intelligence analysts to seek consensus. Some individuals self-censor, hoping to reinforce workplace solidarity and keep their analytic team together. As more analysts work together in groups, the more costly it becomes for any individual to confront an emerging consensus, and the more likely it is that group leaders will seek unanimity through compromise. In this way, minority views may be relegated to footnotes or squeezed out altogether. But this may also be the result of simple bureaucratic procedure: as information travels from collectors to analysts—and is then sent on for evaluation and corroboration—final judgments can become less definitive, more hedged, and less suited to decisive action.[88] This is most likely when policy makers who do not have the time or interest to read multiple evaluations expect a single definitive document. While coordination and editing are vital for quality control and rigor—and while dissenting opinions are routinely sought—"over-coordinated" and "excessively edited" NIEs in the United States are often criticized for expressing just this sort of "group think."[89] Despite ubiquitous (and tiresome) claims to the contrary, Japan has no monopoly on "consensus decision making."

There is also the problem of how analysts use—and misuse—data. Reliance on history and analogue, a cognitive filtering process that includes some data and excludes others, is well recognized. So is the likelihood that the problem being addressed may, for one or more reasons, not be fully comparable to its antecedents because, much as with Heraclitus's river, conditions have changed. Data are also misused by analysts who selectively use (cherry-pick) facts from the deluge of collected information in order to rationalize extant policy or justify their own recommendations.[90] This is made easy because, as Anthony Cordesman points out, "intelligence collection is filled with vast amounts of contradictory information."[91] The selective, possibly malfeasant use of data may be especially pronounced in the intelligence world, where secrecy is the rule, data are fragmentary and ambiguous, and political pressure for an answer is enormous. This all reinforces tendencies toward "confirmation bias," misjudgment that is all the more difficult to overcome when an analyst is confronted by facts that contradict years of experience—the very basis of one's expertise.[92] Ariel Levite wisely notes that beliefs, expertise, preconceptions, and wishful thinking converge to form a "crucial barrier" because they "raise the standard of evidence required of discrepant information before it gains acceptance."[93] It has long been acknowledged that for these reasons and others—and despite efforts to ameliorate the problem—fact-based falsification may be harder to come by inside an intelligence community than outside one.[94]

If expertise can inhibit or even disable analysis, so can nescience. It is not uncommon for even the most highly skilled and experienced generalists to embrace an inaccurate picture of an adversary because they do not understand its values, motivations, or goals. Analysts who are unfamiliar with particular adversaries have more difficulty reading their signals and resort to imagining that their adversary will make the same calculations they themselves would make in the same situation. Imposing one's own rationality on an adversary—what is known as "mirror-imaging"—is surprisingly common and unsurprisingly costly. Perhaps the most widely recognized case was in 1962, when the chief of the Office of National Estimates, Sherman Kent, thought that Nikita Khrushchev would not introduce nuclear weapons into Cuba because doing so would be irrational.[95] A decade later, in 1973, the CIA again imposed its version of rationality on Anwar Sadat, who, its analysts believed, would never jeopardize his plans for economic growth by launching a surprise attack on Israel. The U.S. intelligence community discounted a possible Soviet invasion of Afghanistan in 1979 for the same reason. In each case, the intelligence community projected its idea of rationality on an irrational—or at least differently rational—leader. The dark joke circulating in the intelligence community regarding these last two cases was that *they* got it right but that the Arabs and Soviets got it wrong.[96]

Communication

Even if there were no mirror-imaging, even if intelligence analysis were impeccable, and even if independent opinions were actively encouraged and accurately represented, collection and analysis would be useless unless communication across intelligence agencies and between analysts and policy makers was timely and effective.[97] Communication operates on a third axis as well—cross-nationally, between allies.

We begin with the problem of horizontal communication—the ubiquitous, deeply entrenched structural impediment of "silos" or "stovepipes," the institutional separation of agencies that impedes communication across units within the intelligence community. President George W. Bush's July 2008 executive order amending existing regulations on intelligence activity specified roles and responsibilities of nearly *twenty* different U.S. government units. One leading analyst refers to the term "intelligence community" as "quaint," adding that "the word community describes precisely what it is not; it is somewhere between a fiction and an aspiration."[98] It seems better understood as a scrum, filled with more and less powerful competitors pursuing their own interests and budgetary advantage in a bruising contest between mutually exclusive organizations. In the process they may exaggerate their capabilities and inflate the threats before them—and they almost certainly resist sharing data acquired at steep cost.

This is a general problem, well known to organization theorists, who understand that individual units in business or government develop "proprietary instincts" about what is their information and what is others', what their territory is and what is others'.[99] But the intelligence community is different in one critical respect. Normal selfish bureaucratic instincts are magnified by legitimate requirements for concealment justified by the need to protect sources.[100] While silos and secrecy might generate competing estimates that sharpen choices for policy makers and analysts, competing intelligence is not necessarily better than unshared intelligence.[101]

Stovepiping, information hoarding, and turf battling among mutually insular intelligence units have long been universal facts of life. Testifying before the Armed Services Committee of the U.S. Senate in April 1947, General Hoyt S. Vandenberg, the director of central intelligence, described the "internal bickering" and "continual sniping" that characterized Germany's spy organizations: "They all developed a policy of secrecy, [and] coordination went out the window."[102] Postwar efforts to eliminate turf battles and smooth coordination across the various stakeholders in the British intelligence community date from the so-called Mountbatten reforms of 1957, but never fully succeeded.[103] In France, where the intelligence community "has long looked like a divided house or a field full of battling tribes," a 2013 reorganization was conducted to consolidate the combatants and create a central authority to authorize all foreign interventions with the oversight of the National Assembly.[104] Australia stood up a Joint Counter Terrorism Intelligence Coordination Unit in 2002 "to better coordinate counter-terrorism intelligence" both domestically and globally.[105] German homeland security officials came under considerable pressure in late 2011 after a neo-Nazi terror cell was discovered to be operating with the uncoordinated knowledge of the federal government's segregated intelligence units. A new joint center for preventing domestic terrorism was quickly established to overcome "siloism."[106] And, as we shall see, this phenomenon—known as "vertical administration" (*tatewari gyōsei*) in Japanese—long ago became a fixture within the

Japanese bureaucracy in general, and has been endemic to its intelligence community in particular.

The U.S. case may simply be the best documented.[107] A formal investigation of Pearl Harbor found that the military failed to disseminate intercepted tactical intelligence on the Japanese attack—"not only between the Washington headquarters of the Army and Navy and their field commands, but also between the services themselves in Hawaii."[108] During the early years of the CIA, the U.S. military refused to provide it with operational documents for inclusion in the daily briefing of the president, including General Douglas MacArthur's reports from Tokyo and General Lucius Clay's reports from Berlin.[109] Indeed, the agency's first NIE was delayed for a year as a result of mistrust between it and the military.[110] Just over a decade later, the 1961 failure of the Bay of Pigs operation was attributed in part to the refusal of the CIA's operations directorate to consult the CIA's intelligence directorate during its operational planning.[111] In his memoirs, a former director of central intelligence, Admiral Stansfield Turner, bluntly declared that "the NSA . . . collaborates with the military services to keep the CIA out of the analysis of major military issues."[112] So far, the most famous twenty-first-century horizontal "communications lapse" was the failure by the CIA to provide the FBI with timely information about Khalid al-Midhar and Nawaq Alhazmi, two of the nineteen 9/11 hijackers, which might have prevented the attacks.[113]

This was supposed to have been corrected in the predictable reforms that followed. But a blue ribbon panel reported to the president after the next major intelligence failure—in Iraq in 2003—that U.S. intelligence remained insufficiently networked and that "individual departments and agencies continue to act as though they own the information they collect, forcing other agencies to pry it from them."[114] Many of the provisions for the 2004 Intelligence Reform and Terrorism Prevention Act, including the establishment of the Office of the Director of National Intelligence, were designed primarily to improve coordination across the U.S. intelligence community.[115] But one year after the 2013 Boston Marathon bombing, the U.S. House of Representatives Committee on Homeland Security reported that the Russian security services had notified both the FBI and the CIA of links between bomber Tamerlan Tsarnaev and radical groups in the Caucasus, and that neither followed up with the other or with local law enforcement officials.[116] A government report prepared for the inspectors general of the CIA, the Department of Justice, and the Department of Homeland Security was issued a month later. In a departure from past practice, it found "no basis to make broad recommendations for changes in information handling or sharing." But truer to form, it did recommend that the FBI "consider sharing threat information with state and local partners more proactively."[117] An earlier report of the National Defense Intelligence College on this topic plaintively asked, "Can't We All Just Get Along?"[118]

The problems inherent in vertical communication—reports upward to the policy community from intelligence analysts and requests for analysis from the policy maker to the analyst—seem just as intractable. The path from the analyst's desk to the policy maker's brain—and back again—is also strewn with a great many obstacles and broken links along the way, what Joshua Rovner calls the "pathologies of intelligence-policy relations." He examines three closely: when policy makers ignore or cherry-pick analysts' warnings, he speaks of "neglect"; "excessive harmony" occurs when analysts massage their estimates to conform to what they believe are the policy makers' views; and "politicization" is the effort by the policy maker to manipulate intelligence in order to come to a preset conclusion or to signal to the intelligence community the desired analytic conclusion.[119]

There are several explanations for these pathologies. Perhaps the most obvious (and most generous) is the demand on policy makers' time. The analyst must not assume that an equivocal warning buried in a sheaf of last week's documents will have surfaced and caught the attention of someone who can do something about it. Political leaders and senior government officials may focus intensely on a terrorist event after it occurs, but as successive administrations' treatment of al-Qaeda cells in the United States before 9/11 amply illustrate, warnings of its imminence may easily get lost amidst the daily flood of information and the crisis *du jour*. So persistence is a virtue in the analytic community.

Like most folks, policy makers do not often appreciate hearing news or receiving estimates that undermine their preconceptions or extant policy positions. As Robert Jervis has pointed out, even when intelligence services submit accurate estimates, "they are likely to bring disturbing news, and this incurs a cost."[120] Joseph Stalin's disregard of warnings from Soviet military intelligence of Hitler's impending double-cross—Operation Barbarossa— in 1941 provides arguably the highest-cost example.[121] His ally Winston Churchill famously (and inadvertently) helps illustrate this point in a more relevant democratic setting. A few years earlier, in 1938, Churchill learned of ominous developments in the imperial Japanese military, but as Chancellor of the Exchequer, he had to limit military spending and block expansion of British naval capacity in the Far East. "A war with Japan!" he declared. "I do not believe there is the slightest chance of it in our lifetime."[122]

Getting the relationship right between analyst and policy maker is one of the most enduring and difficult problems in intelligence. It is an asymmetrical relationship, "a meeting between an expert without authority, and an authority without expertise," who must wrestle to find the "delicate balance between intimacy and detachment."[123] It is a conversation between specialists who must be objective but who know too much to be certain, and generalists, whose views about how the world works are a matter of public record (and hence are more difficult to abandon) and who may not understand or appreciate subtleties.[124] Gregory Treverton insists that "intelligence and policy making are such different cultures that it is a surprise that they even connect at all. . . . Analysts think analytically of what can go wrong, while policy officials tend to think wishfully of what might go right."[125] Jervis adds, "It is . . . not surprising that intelligence officials, especially at the working level, tend to see political leaders as unscrupulous and careless, if not intellectually deficient, and that leaders see their intelligence services as timid, unreliable, and often out to get them."[126] This emerged in full public view during Special Counsel Robert Mueller's investigation of President Donald Trump's 2016 campaign ties to Russia. In what was viewed by many as an effort to intimidate and delegitimate the intelligence community, Trump revoked the security clearance of former CIA chief John Brennan, a leading critic, and announced that others—including a serving Justice Department official involved in the probe—could also have their clearances stripped.[127]

Finding a way to optimize vertical communication has long occupied intelligence experts.[128] The standard view has been that analysts must keep their distance and wait to be tasked before undertaking their work without reference to their clients' politics. William Donovan made this argument himself when he pressed successfully for the creation of the CIA in 1946.[129] His view was reprised in 1951 by CIA director Allen Dulles, who reminded his staff that it was their job to make sense of facts, not to make policy. Once an analyst "exceeds that role," Dulles insisted, "he becomes useless."[130] The central concern for a firewall between the intelligence community and the policy world, later championed by Sherman Kent, holds that if analysts and decision maker are too close, intelligence will be distorted by the analyst's natural instinct to tailor intelligence to the preferences of the client—what has been called "intelligence to please."[131]

Recognizing the problem of politicized intelligence and fixing it are two different things, of course. After the "red line" between analysis and policy was violated in 2002 when the George W. Bush administration cooked the intelligence books to gain support for the Iraq War, the Senate Select Committee on Intelligence concluded misleadingly in 2004 that this was not politicization but merely a failure to communicate.[132] Throwing the intelligence community under the bus and lamely trying to exculpate themselves, the senators determined that "the intelligence community did not accurately explain to policy makers the uncertainties behind the judgments in the October 2002 NIE" that justified the April 2003 invasion of Iraq.[133] Policy makers, wearing "ideological blinders," and using intelligence "the way a drunk uses a lamppost—for support rather than for illumination," apparently still expect the intelligence community to find evidence that supports their prior decisions, and oversight bodies apparently are still willing to shift blame away from the policy makers.[134] Some things never change.

And some things should not change. There is legitimate reason to be concerned that intelligence can be irrelevant if it does not address directly the specific concerns of the policy community. Close relations with policy makers may be the best way for analysts to know where to direct their limited resources.[135] On this view, "intelligence is irrelevant without policy while policy is blind without intelligence. . . . [A]n analyst who is not on the verge of being politicized is not doing his job."[136] If intelligence is so far removed from policy that it cannot be infected by politics, it runs the parallel risk of becoming inconsequential. Even Sherman Kent came around to the view that "intelligence must be close enough to policy, plans, and operations to have the greatest amount of guidance, and must not be so close that it loses its objectivity and integrity of judgment."[137]

Politicization, segmentation, and each of the other issues that have been identified contribute to a related pair of communication problems that deserve attention: threat inflation (the overestimation of an adversary's strength) and "crying wolf" (false positives about the imminence of attack). Both are natural and ubiquitous outcomes of intelligence systems designed to warn but riven by competition for budgets and missions. Some place the blame for threat inflation at the feet of the military. Loch Johnson, for example, argues that "military analysts are notorious for portraying their adversaries as ten feet tall, armed to the hilt, and ready to storm the home front at any moment."[138] And even the former military officer Admiral Stansfield Turner accused the Defense Intelligence Agency of consistently overestimating Soviet capabilities when he was director of central intelligence.[139] But there has been plenty of finger pointing back at civilian analysts for crying wolf. Secretary of state Dean Rusk was famously credited with the quip that the CIA "predicted twelve of the last four crises."[140] Since both the military and the intelligence community have allies in the media, academia, and the think tank world upon whom they can count to ring alarm bells—and since they have organizational incentives to encourage them to do so—we hear alarm bells constantly.

Finally, there are the problems of cross-border intelligence sharing—communication between allied intelligence communities—problems that ironically may be less pronounced in wartime. In November 1940, after President Franklin Roosevelt had appealed to Prime Minister Winston Churchill for access to intercepted and decrypted Axis communications, the United States and Great Britain secretly agreed to a full exchange of intelligence regarding German, Japanese, and Italian cryptographic systems.[141] In the spring of 1941, U.S. agents delivered a model of the Japanese "Purple" code machine to British analysts at Bletchley Park and in return received an assortment of advanced cryptographic equipment. This cooperation was deepened by detailed protocols for handling encrypted data and by the exchange of personnel and agreements on the division of labor in the collection and analysis of Axis communications in the so-called Ultra project.[142] Once the United States entered the war, British-American intelligence sharing was expanded to include the other Anglo-Saxon states whose intelligence services had originally been branches of the British one. Canada provided the Allies full access to its decoded intercepts of both Japanese and German communications, while Australia and New Zealand collected and shared Japanese signals communication.

Agreement on peacetime Anglo-American signals intelligence sharing was reached even before the war ended, in April 1945, as part of Atlantic Charter planning for the postwar order.[143] The first task for Allied intelligence cooperation after World War II was a "cryptanalytic attack on Soviet codes and ciphers," approved in September 1945 by President Truman. This effectively created the global SIGINT network comprising Canada, the UK, Australia, the United States, and New Zealand, known officially as the anodyne United Kingdom–United States of America Agreement and informally as "Five Eyes." The arrangement was later formalized in a secret intergovernmental agreement that established shared code words and classification schemes. As a preview of how dominant Washington would become in the postwar effort to contain Moscow and its allies, the Five Eyes agreement lists the United States as the "first party" and each of the other four partners as "second parties." This meant that the United States would be responsible for issuing clearances and other procedural requirements, ensuring that there would be no intelligence sharing without Washington's approval. Soon thereafter, Five Eyes' remit was expanded to include ocean surveillance of Soviet vessels. Over time, the Five Eyes partners instituted mechanisms to share with so-called "third parties": Norway in 1952, Denmark in 1954, and West Germany in 1955. The five principals, however, share intelligence with these parties on a far more limited scale than they do with one another. Documents leaked by Edward Snowden refer to a second-tier circle known as "Nine Eyes" which includes Denmark, Norway, the Netherlands, and France.

They also reference a group of "Fourteen Eyes" which adds Germany, Sweden, Spain, Belgium, and Italy. We will explore in chapter 5 how Japan has supported Five Eyes by virtue of its extensive collaboration with the NSA and other U.S. intelligence agencies while formally remaining on the sidelines.

Finally, as if a reminder were even needed, cross-border intelligence sharing reminds us that there are limits to trust in even the closest alliance relationships and that alliances shift in international politics. Perhaps the most prominent example of the latter was the agreement reached after Richard Nixon's 1972 visit to the People's Republic of China to set up two SIGINT stations in western China built by the CIA near the Soviet border and staffed by Chinese to intercept and share information about Soviet missile tests and military communications.[144]

But even model relationships are "laced with ambivalence and caution."[145] Although cooperation may reduce costs and compensate for gaps in collection and analysis by any single partner, there is always the chance of discord, withholding, and deceit. There are many specific examples of British or Australian or American intelligence officers compromising or disrupting the activities of Five Eyes partners.[146] This had become such a problem even before the Snowden revelations that a federally established commission advised President Bush in 2005 "to significantly reduce damaging losses in collection capability that result from unauthorized disclosures of classified information" stemming from intelligence sharing with foreign governments.[147] But as Snowden's documents revealed in 2013, the NSA regularly tapped into the private communications of the leaders of an exhaustive list of allied nations, most notably France and Germany, but also Japan.

Protection

I have discussed, but still not exhausted, the range of trade-offs that plague the intelligence community. Problems associated with the trade-off between sharing and surveilling, between warning too little and warning too much, and those associated with finding the right balance between intimacy with and distance from the political class are met by similarly intractable problems associated with the trade-offs between secrecy and efficiency on the one hand and between security and privacy on the other. Each of these latter trade-offs is connected to the fourth element of intelligence, the imperative to protect national secrets in order to ensure national security counterintelligence, often in the service of counterterrorism.

As virtually everyone acknowledges, much of the intelligence community's work must proceed in secret to be effective. But we have learned to our consternation that secrecy can be used to conceal corruption or abuse and can be used to justify surveillance that trespasses on individuals' rights to privacy. In the view of Tessa Morris-Suzuki, "the state, as law maker and law giver, creates agencies which it authorizes to break its own laws in the interest of preserving the state itself."[148] Remedies for excessive secrecy are difficult to impose, even in democratic states where leaking to the media is accepted as a norm, where whistle-blowing is protected by law, and where oversight of classified activities resides in national legislatures and/or the courts. In 1974, after reports surfaced regarding the Nixon White House's order for the illegal collection of information on political dissidents by U.S. intelligence agencies, Senator Frank Church initiated what came to be the most extensive review of intelligence activities ever undertaken in public view. One result was declassification of more than fifty thousand documents, a figure dwarfed a generation later, in 2013, when Edward Snowden passed on some 1.7 million classified documents to journalists, stimulating more hearings and endless rounds of formal review.[149] Standard operating procedure was challenged yet again when the Obama administration moved to reform the NSA by amending Section 215 of the Patriot Act that allowed the NSA to collect data on personal phone communications, and by reforming the Foreign Intelligence Surveillance Court by appointing a special privacy advocate.[150]

Defenders of classification may acknowledge that privacy must be protected and that there must be limits to surveillance at home but insist that openness can degrade security. Partly for this reason, the intelligence community and its policy customers err on the side of caution and mark virtually all communications and reports secret. They manage programs under the shroud of secrecy in order to prevent "damage," "serious damage," or "exceptionally grave damage" to national security.[151] Many intelligence professionals believe that even if secrecy reduces efficiency, openness—particularly unauthorized disclosures—can compromise security in even more costly ways, including lives lost, sources compromised, reputational damage, economic loss, stunted morale, opportunity costs associated with the use of personnel redirected to assess damage and plug leaks, loss of control of the geostrategic narrative, and loss of future intelligence.[152]

This debate—never more heated or more public than after the Snowden revelations—has been joined in creative ways. One observer tried to reframe the extant positions, arguing that the treatment of the exposure of secrets as an unmitigated good and the view that any unauthorized disclosure of classified information is an assault on national security are both "untenably extreme."[153] Neither of these views gets to the most important trade-off, that between preservation of privacy and protection of the community. Before citizens of democratic states and their representatives can distinguish between legitimate whistle-blowing and illegitimate leaks, they must first distinguish between legitimate and illegitimate classification. This task was taken up with some success by a group of nearly two dozen NGOs and academic centers coordinated by the Open Society Justice Initiative. Their fifteen "Principles on National Security and the Right to Information" were issued in June 2013 in Tshwane, South Africa, "to address questions of how to ensure public access to government information without jeopardizing legitimate efforts to protect people from national security threats."[154] These "Tshwane Principles" include the public right to access government information, the right to know about surveillance, protection of whistle-blowers, freedom of the press, carve-outs for human rights violations, rules for classification that measure value against harm to the public, clarity on the process for declassification, and independent oversight, inter alia. These principles became a central part of national debates over secrecy and classification in a number of democratic systems where civil society groups took the lead in challenging government plans to introduce new classification schemes, including South Africa, Poland, and, as we shall see in chapter 6, Japan, whose multiple well-developed counterintelligence and counterterrorism units are connected to trans-war histories of repression and postwar incompetence, and that recently have been given enhanced legal standing with broadened remits.

Covert Action

Covert action is an instrument of foreign policy designed to achieve national goals abroad secretly. It is intended to create public effects without any attribution to (or at least with plausible deniability for) public officials.[155] Covert action differs from "clandestine activity," which refers to the tactical secrecy of an operation rather than to the secrecy of its sponsor.[156] Since it does not involve the mobilization of military force, cannot be undertaken officially by diplomats, requires secrecy, and involves more than collection and analysis, it usually falls to the "special projects" and "operations" units within intelligence communities.[157] As we shall see, the Japanese called these "special duty units" (*tokumu kikan*) during the Asia-Pacific War and beyond. Although these units often reside under the same organizational umbrellas as those that collect, analyze, and communicate intelligence, their mission is less about generating actionable knowledge than about political action itself. Their work is undertaken to shape favorable outcomes, not to judge their

possibility or understand their implications. Covert action is usually understood to include four broad classes of activity: propaganda, such as planting
stories (true or false) in foreign media using paid (or compromised) agents;
political interventions, such as supporting parties and politicians; economic
interventions, such as manipulating markets and/or currencies; and paramilitary operations, such as assisting guerrilla insurrections.[158] It can be as in-
expensive as the cost of a dinner for a graffiti artist, a few hundred dollars to
keep a foreign editor on retainer, or thousands to a union leader to organize
strikes.[159] But this, of course, is the lower end. Engineered market or supply
chain disruptions, and especially paramilitary operations (such as secret ren-
ditions), are orders of magnitude more expensive. We may never know how
much the Kremlin spent to insert itself in the 2016 U.S. presidential election,
nor do we know the size of its "active measures" budget. But we do know
that covert action remains all too effective a tool in international affairs.[160]

This is nothing new. Covert action has a long history. Roman emperors secretly advanced the careers of friendly foreign leaders and supported factions
abroad that could shift the balance of political power in their favor.[161] Later,
co-opting a king's councilor or mistress was a standard tool in the covert action kit bag.[162] The German government supplied German American political organizations with propaganda to try to tamp down enthusiasm for U.S.
entry into World War I, and Churchill used "agents of influence" to try to tip
U.S. policy toward intervention in Europe before Pearl Harbor.[163] During the
Cold War, the British term for covert action shifted from "special operations"
to "special political action," and then to "disruptive action," none of which
was ever clearly defined. The Soviets, for their part, stuck to the term "active
measures," which, as chapter 3 documents, they practiced very successfully
in Tokyo. The term returned to common parlance after Russian meddling
in the 2016 U.S. presidential campaign, when it became the object of House,
Senate, and Justice Department investigations.[164]

In the United States, where the term "dirty tricks" once dominated the
discourse, covert action dates back to the Revolutionary War, when the
French used sham businesses to import supplies for Washington's army.[165]
Teddy Roosevelt used it to foment a revolution to force a split of Panama
from Colombia that could provide the United States with territory to build
its canal.[166] Covert action was the raison d'être for General Donovan's wartime OSS, and he and George Kennan argued vigorously for "organized political warfare" to promote the liberation of eastern Europe early in the Cold
War.[167] The Office of Special Projects (later renamed the Office of Policy
Coordination), the U.S. government's first peacetime covert action unit, was
created in June 1948 and grew from 300 to 2,800 staff by 1952.[168] Successive

administrations deployed agents to support anticommunist parties in Italy and Japan, and to destabilize left-leaning regimes in Iran, Indonesia, Guatemala, Cuba, and elsewhere during the Cold War.[169] In some cases (e.g., Radio Free Europe and the National Endowment for Democracy), covert political activities were offloaded from the CIA and transplanted into the public sphere. War hero General Jimmy Doolittle offered a candid, if unsavory, evaluation of these "repugnant" activities in 1954 when he argued that "there are no rules in this competition. . . . If the United States is to survive, longstanding American concepts of fair play must be reconsidered. We must . . . learn to subvert, sabotage, and destroy our enemies."[170]

Enthusiasm for covert action has waxed and waned in the United States.[171] It may have reached its nadir in 1975, when U.S. intervention in Chile and elsewhere from 1964 to 1974 led Senator Frank Church to refer to the CIA as a "rogue elephant." He and other members of Congress demanded fuller oversight of the U.S. intelligence community, and President Gerald Ford issued an executive order prohibiting any U.S. involvement in, or sanction of, assassinations of foreign leaders. Congress's investigation also led to the creation of permanent intelligence oversight committees with broad powers in both the House of Representatives and the U.S. Senate.[172] So what once was celebrated by many as an essential instrument of foreign policy, and dismissed by others as a "necessary evil," had come to be seen by many as "an imminent threat to the liberal body politics."[173] As James Baker notes, "Cold War covert action was largely conducted in a statutory vacuum" in which congressional oversight was "informal" at best.[174] As we shall see in chapter 2, covert action—supervised by diplomats, undertaken by special duty military units, or freelanced by less decorous "patriotic" cousins outside the government—was thought to be central to establishing, sustaining, and expanding Japanese empire. In chapter 3 we will see how Japanese covert action survived and was nurtured under the guidance of the U.S. Occupation, and in chapters 4 through 6 we will examine what little of this is left in public view.

Oversight

And so we arrive at our final, but hardly least important, element—oversight. As we have seen, the same secrecy that binds covert action to collection, analysis, communication, and protection collides with demands for transparency from interested and affected, but often underinformed, publics in democratic states. Covertness is, after all, "the very antithesis of open debate and public decision."[175] Public opinion focuses episodically on how best to balance the need for secrecy with transparency and accountability in the intelligence community. The central problem is that those who want to watch the watchdogs—that is, those who demand safeguards against unauthorized action and the politicization of intelligence—are not likely to be the same as those whose first priority is to improve the ability of intelligence services to collect, analyze, communicate, and protect secrets efficiently.[176] This was exemplified in a 1991 report by the Twentieth Century Fund that recommended new restrictions on covert action. While it concluded that "covert action inherently conflicts with democratic aspirations," it also noted that there are circumstances in which—under proper controls—such actions can advance national objectives beyond the capacity of overt actions.[177] Rahul Sagar frames this problem well: "The question at the heart of the contemporary debate on state secrecy is not about whether or not there should be state secrecy; rather it is about what sort of regulatory framework will ensure that state secrecy will be used to protect national security and not to conceal the abuse of power."[178]

This framework—the institutions of oversight designed to ensure that intelligence services properly implement laws and policies—takes many forms in the industrial democracies.[179] Indeed, there are often multiple institutions of oversight in the same state. Independent commissions, special courts, executive branch ombudspersons (inspectors general), declassification units, and national audit offices are ubiquitous, but delegation of oversight to legislatures is probably the most common. The first legislature-based oversight system was established in the Netherlands in 1952, with Dutch consociationalism requiring that each of five major political parties share responsibility for supervising the intelligence units.[180] Three decades later, after German unification, the Bundestag was assigned oversight responsibility—a provision it had trouble digesting for some time.[181] The problem, of course, is that national parliaments that oversee most government activity at the line item level cannot always do so in matters of intelligence, where operations and capabilities must be kept secret. A parallel problem arises when intelligence oversight is allocated to judges, whose judicial proceedings must be undertaken in secret. This is why so much oversight is delegated to the executive branch. Oversight of the Dutch, Norwegian, and Canadian intelligence communities is delegated to professional managers to a greater extent than elsewhere, and, for all the congressional machinations, the U.S. system of intelligence oversight also relies on inspectors general resident in the intelligence community itself. And this system became even more difficult to manage in 2017, after President Trump began in earnest to delegitimate the U.S. intelligence community after it reported in 2017 that his election campaign had been abetted by Russian agents.

In states where domestic terrorism has been prominent in national political life and where publics may be more inured to their activities—such as in Israel and France—intelligence services are relatively more transparent and their legitimacy is questioned less often. In the United States, by contrast, the problem began with the moral outcry in the 1970s, when it was discovered that U.S. intelligence services had been surveilling civil rights groups and plotting the assassination of foreign leaders. Indeed, until the 1974 Hughes-Ryan Amendment to the Foreign Assistance Act of 1961, covert action was not subject to congressional oversight at all.[182] Demands for enhanced oversight of intelligence only became more urgent in the intervening decades, as the imperative of "guarding the guardians" and making sure they adhere to professional and constitutional standards was expanded beyond the once exclusive province of civil-military relations.[183] The Iran-contra affair—a complex covert action during Ronald Reagan's second term involving arms sales to an embargoed Iran in exchange for the release of hostages held in Lebanon to generate funds diverted to Nicaraguan rebels—led to the even more formal congressional oversight.[184] And Edward Snowden's revelations of domestic surveillance by the NSA stimulated probably the most extensive mobilization ever of citizens and media demanding intelligence oversight.[185]

In the end, though, the institutions of intelligence oversight are imperfect and are therefore objects of constant public scrutiny. As Wolfgang Krieger points out, it takes "a leap of faith" to assume that oversight might "make intelligence services less dangerous to their own citizens."[186] Debate over how to improve oversight has thus become—along with debate over the role of the media—a permanent fixture in debates about the connection of oversight to democratic practice. The persistent institutional tinkering with oversight through constant monitoring of intelligence activities undertaken in the name of national security may be the last best option for mobilized citizens hoping to limit the moral hazard that secrecy generates, and thereby hoping to minimize the space available for violation of civil rights and the abuse of power.[187] As Kobayashi Yoshiki, a Japanese National Police Agency official who has studied oversight, has argued, "In the long run, oversight is the best way to convince the public that a strong intelligence community is desirable."[188] In chapters 4 through 6, we will see its contentious and imperfect adoption in post–Cold War Japan.

In this chapter I have sought to develop a common language for historical comparison of Japan's intelligence community to those of other nations. The discussion has directed us toward several issues that will become particularly salient as the Japanese case is brought into focus. The first has to do with the imperatives of the international system. We have seen how the United States government dismantled successful wartime intelligence units after World War I and World War II, and how it established its first centralized agency only when it was on the cusp of becoming a global power, believing it could no longer depend on British intelligence. We will explore whether a parallel dynamic is at work in Japan today. Is Tokyo investing in intelligence reform to enhance the alliance? Or is its effort animated by a declining faith in the quality of U.S.-supplied intelligence and a hedge against American abandonment? First spoiler alert: both motives are in play. A related issue raised by bilateral intelligence cooperation concerns the extent to which Washington has been able to use Tokyo's dependence on U.S.-provided intelligence to force changes in Japan's famously leaky classification system.

We have seen how, in the United States and other countries, one of the greatest challenges to intelligence reform has been "not how to make the intelligence bureaucracy work better, but rather how to make the intelligence community operate less like a bureaucracy."[189] Most states have attacked this problem by attempting to break down stovepipes and flatten hierarchies—precisely what Japanese leaders have always stated as their aims but have found most difficult to accomplish. Complicating this are the difficulties Japan has had with political control of its bureaucracy, a stubbornly persistent parallel to imperial era difficulties with civilian control of the military. This directs us to pay special attention to the civil-military-intelligence triad within Japan's intelligence community today. Japan's ubiquitous stovepipe problem is amplified by the need for someone to be in charge. Since centrifugal forces can easily dominate in a highly competitive and distributed system such as an intelligence community, leaders must be especially vigilant and capable. As we shall see, Abe Shinzō took office in 2013 and attacked this problem head-on—albeit not to everyone's satisfaction. But what has been called Japan's "leadership deficit" could reappear and cripple the reformed Japanese intelligence community going forward.

Followership is no less a potential problem for Japan. We have learned that dissent is critically important for any effective intelligence community and that the intelligence analyst must be prepared to call attention to what Sherman Kent dubbed "the stubborn fact."[190] Reliable intelligence estimates cannot be the product of self-censorship or submission to a consensus view.[191] But Japanese scholars and pundits are the first to acknowledge that dissent does not emerge easily in their organizational settings and rarely is rewarded. We thus are drawn to examine how much room there is for the proverbial nails to stick up without being hammered down in the evolving Japanese intelligence community.

Still another personnel issue is salient here. Analysts tell us that in the U.S. and other militaries, the status of those on the intelligence track has been lower than for those on the war-fighting track. Intelligence, lore has it, is usually left for officers deemed unfit for more important tasks—whether because they lack command potential or because they see too many shades of gray.[192] This may no longer be the case in the United States, but since it was true of the imperial Japanese military—and since more intelligence is done today in the MOD than elsewhere—the question is whether and to what extent the Japanese government will overcome biases against intelligence as a profession.

This speaks to issues associated with flexibility and "lock-in" in easily politicized environments like the intelligence world. We have learned from a range of cases that once an intelligence agency issues an analytic conclusion, it is very difficult to change it, even in the face of new and contradictory data.[193] Analysts who do not wish to be judged as having been incompetent often stubbornly ignore the possibility that they were wrong the first time. Again, we have comparative context for an issue that many Japanese organizations under the public microscope find particularly problematic.[194] This is associated with the political use of intelligence—the selective cherry-picking of warnings that elevates the interests of the political class over those of the state and its citizens. Michael Handel suggests that "the temptation to exploit intelligence for political purposes is greatest in democratic societies. Both a government and its opposition will scramble to take advantage of intelligence information when appealing to public opinion, to the legislature, and to the mass media."[195] We will see how intelligence is used and abused in a robustly democratic—some would say "rough and tumble"—Japan, and by whom.

First, though, we will review the prewar and wartime institutions of the Japanese intelligence community to explore how they comport with the drivers of reform and the elements of intelligence outlined in this chapter. Second spoiler alert: the drivers of Japan's intelligence reform are not exceptional. As elsewhere, Tokyo has shifted its intelligence structure in response to dramatic analytical and organizational failures—in conjunction with changes in the regional and global balance and sudden technological developments—across the Pacific and Cold Wars. That said, particular elements of the intelligence enterprise seem distinctive to Japanese practice. We will discover which ones and learn why in the chapters that follow.

CHAPTER 2

Expanding Special Duties (1895–1945)

> The key to military success is to know your enemy
> and yourself. . . . I cannot neglect intelligence for even
> a single day at the General Staff.
>
> —Field Marshal Yamagata Aritomo, 1880

The beginning of modern Japanese intelligence gathering is often attributed to the spies dispatched by the Tokugawa shogunate (1603–1868) to report on the activities of "recalcitrant daimyo and samurai." Their "connected eyes" (*metsuke*) monitored both corruption and sedition. And even though this was a time of enforced isolation, the shogunate gathered intelligence on foreign as well as domestic developments, receiving reports from the Dutch at Dejima, the island off the coast of Nagasaki used by the government as its only official window on the outside world. They also monitored developments through visiting Korean embassies. Separately, the Satsuma domain gained intelligence on Chinese developments via its Ryukyu connection.[1] The Tokugawa era *oniwaban* (garden guards), a cadre of elite undercover agents who worked for the shogun, were the "ninjas" who have been celebrated in endless period dramas in theaters and on television and in the movies—in Japan and worldwide.[2]

The now fetishized throwing stars (*shuriken*) and swords (*katana*) of Japan's "samurai culture" began receding into pop culture soon after Japan first established a professional intelligence bureaucracy at the beginning of the Meiji era in the late nineteenth century. Japan's modern intelligence community started taking shape in much the same way that other Japanese institutions did after 1868: leaders of the new government identified the need for timely and accurate information about foreign adversaries, closely studied foreign practices and technologies, and selectively applied what they believed would best serve the national interest. In 1869, the Meiji state dispatched its first students—including Yamagata Aritomo, who would become Japan's most influential grand strategist—to study Germany's military. This visit convinced Yamagata that Japanese security required a powerful state at home protected by a powerful and well-informed military abroad. He soon became war minister and, wasting little time, sent Japan's first military attachés and diplomats to practice tradecraft in China in 1875 and set up a "system of espionage in North China" that revealed Chinese weaknesses.[3]

But Yamagata neglected to establish a professional track for career intelligence officials, and at least until the 1930s, Japanese intelligence relied as much on expatriate freelancers as on military intelligence officers. Danny Orbach aptly refers to the network of (often criminal, sometimes pan-Asianist and nationalist) freelance spies and their secret government and business sponsors as a "military-adventurous complex [in] a multi-layered system of deniability."[4] These now storied "continental adventurers" (tairiku rōnin) enjoyed extraterritorial privileges and consular protection in China—a textbook breeding ground for moral hazard. As a result, a significant part of Japan's intelligence effort was launched on the backs of "agents of chaos," as HUMINT resources were devoted more to covert action than to intelligence collection.[5] But the early Japanese intelligence community was more than HUMINT on steroids. In its formative years, it was plagued by many of the enduring pathologies common to intelligence communities everywhere identified in chapter 1: deep internal rivalries, costly failures to cooperate, the subordination of political to military intelligence, a scarcity of reliable analyses, and the refusal of top officials to listen.

As is so often the case with new institutions, professionalizing the Japanese intelligence community involved structural experimentation and the efforts of influential figures. In 1890 the military created the Japan-China Trade Research Institute (Nisshin Bōeki Kenkyūjo), a notionally market-oriented information-gathering and economic analysis unit that became the base of Japanese intelligence activities in China and the prototype for future intelligence units. General (later Viscount) Fukushima Yasumasa showed how a talented intelligence analyst could succeed in the Imperial Japanese Army (IJA), despite institutional barriers. Before becoming Japan's senior intelligence officer in Manchuria during the Russo-Japanese War, Fukushima had gone off to India in 1892–93 on a legendary "intelligence ride," and had served as military attaché in Berlin. He then crossed Siberia from the west on horseback, ending in Vladivostok. His analytic dispatches were read by Yamagata, who wrote in October 1893 that Fukushima's reports were instrumental in the development of his strategic thinking, particularly his determination to stiffen the Japanese military in continental Asia. Fukushima ended his career as chief of staff of the First Army and led Japan's expeditionary forces into China during the Boxer Rebellion.[6]

As this chapter will show, the early evolution of the Japanese intelligence community did not always go smoothly. The half century from Japan's first modern foreign war against China to the larger Asia-Pacific War that ended in 1945 may have been "in part consecrated to the establishment of a modern intelligence system,"[7] but the extent of this challenge across each of our three drivers, and the relative inexperience of Japanese strategists, produced uneven performance by an unsteady intelligence community across each of the six elements under study here.

At first, Japan's grand strategy seemed straightforward enough. For the army, Russia was the only hypothetical threat, so control of China and Korea—Japan's near abroad—would be an effective prophylactic. If Japan could acquire high-quality intelligence on Russian (and, later, Soviet) capabilities and intentions in Russia's Far East, and if it could develop adequate military strength, Japan could be safe in an unstable region. The expanding Imperial Japanese Navy (IJN), of course, soon came to be concerned about the British and U.S. fleets, matters of scant interest to the army until the 1920s. Indeed, the Imperial Army was more concerned about growth of the Imperial Navy, and we know now that the latter spied on the former as early as 1912.[8]

By World War I, even with the considerable help Japan was getting from allies such as Great Britain, from firms operating abroad, and from its paid agents on the continent, the task at hand soon was too complex for Japan's still pre-professional intelligence community. The strategic environment was in constant motion, and before long Tokyo found itself chasing too many hares at once—in the USSR, Korea, China, and, later, Southeast Asia and across the Pacific—to be able to develop a well-coordinated and centralized intelligence operation in the first decades of the twentieth century. These challenges were compounded by the tumult of political divisions over the premiership, the cabinet, and military funding priorities. Moreover, as Japan became more muscular, it appeared to threaten the major powers, a development that, in turn, demanded more and better intelligence from Tokyo. We begin a decade earlier, though, to explore the basis of the intelligence community's unruly expansion and the origins of some of its lasting pathologies.

In the Beginning

To be sure, Japan enjoyed some early intelligence successes. In the decade between the Sino-Japanese War and the Russo-Japanese War, the Telegraph

Section of Japan's Ministry of Foreign Affairs (MOFA) succeeded in intercepting Chinese diplomatic cable traffic but was unable to accomplish the same breakthrough with the more sophisticated Russians. Indeed, the Japanese government was concerned that imperial Russia had cracked Japanese codes as early as 1901.[9] It was ironic, then, that Japan's first military intelligence successes were technological triumphs in its victory over tsarist Russia in 1905. After Russian cruisers sank several Japanese troop transports in successive raids in the Sea of Japan in early 1904, the Imperial Navy broke Russian codes and stood up its first SIGINT unit, which used wireless intercepts to monitor the Russian transmissions and cut off successive raids throughout the war.[10]

Early SIGINT successes presaged what would become a permanent divide within Japan's military and between the military and diplomatic intelligence services. The Imperial Navy was first out of the blocks. It stood up its first service-wide intelligence unit in 1896 to collect and analyze reports on the disposition of foreign ships, and in 1903 it created its Third Bureau for Foreign Intelligence.[11] As the Russo-Japanese War neared, the army remained more cautious, forming only a Committee on Foreign Intelligence Compilation (Kaigai Jōhō Hensan Iinkai) to collect reports from military attachés for the General Staff.[12] Virtually all of its efforts during this period were directed at collection and analysis of intelligence regarding Russia. Meanwhile, the navy continued to expand the reach of its intelligence services. The Imperial Army did not create its first intelligence unit until the General Staff was reorganized in 1908.

These early military intelligence units attracted the cooperation of a range of interesting characters. One was Ishimitsu Makiyo. Soon after graduating from the Imperial Army College in 1889, the young second lieutenant left the military to study Russian. He claimed to have done so at his own expense, but since Ishimitsu changed his Japanese name and assumed a Russian alias, we can presume that he was still acting in an official capacity.[13] In August 1900, Ishimitsu opened a laundry in Harbin, where he gathered intelligence from his customers—mostly Russian soldiers—regarding Russian operations in Manchuria. A year later he opened a photo studio, which enabled him to travel and take snapshots without suspicion. By October 1903 his studio had branches in Manzhouli, Lüshun, Dalian, Liaoyang, and Blagoveshchensk. Russian soldiers and Eastern Chinese Railway officers snapped pictures of railway infrastructure, bridges, and other important buildings to be sent to their office headquarters, which Ishimitsu developed and delivered to the Japanese General Staff as well.[14]

The early Japanese intelligence community was bolstered institutionally by idealistic pan-Asianists like the aristocrat Konoe Atsumaro, who sought to construct a "same race alliance" between Japan and China. He was not a spy, but he did anticipate the need for effective intelligence in China, and the East Asia Common Culture Society (Tōa Dōbunkai), which he created after the Sino-Japanese War to improve Sino-Japanese relations, supplied a great many operatives and analysts to support Japanese expansion there.[15] In 1900 the society—what Douglas Reynolds identifies compellingly as a pioneer in "area studies" forty years before the term was "invented" in the West—opened the East Asia Common Cultural College (Tōa Dōbun Shoin) in Nanjing, which recruited Japanese students seeking to learn Chinese language and culture.[16] Although its graduates were not trained in tradecraft, they were highly sought after for their language skills and deep knowledge of China by the Japanese military intelligence services and the related Research (Intelligence) Department of the South Manchuria Railway Company.[17]

The Tōa Dōbunkai was the more respectable cousin of ultranationalist groups that served the military on the Asian continent without official cover or acknowledged support. The most famous among these was the nationalist Genyōsha (Dark Ocean Society), founded by Tōyama Mitsuru, which ran a

FIGURE 2.1 "Area studies" may have been invented at the East Asia Common Cultural College (Tōa Dōbun Shoin) decades before U.S. academics claimed credit for the idea.
Photo: Public domain

shadow intelligence and espionage service for the Japanese military.[18] Much like its affiliated Tenyūkyō, a paramilitary group organized by Genyōsha member Uchida Ryōhei, Genyōsha secretly received funds from the Japanese government to support its *agents provocateurs* in Korea, Manchuria, and China. Genyōsha operatives—some of whom were graduates of the Tōa Dōbun Shoin—operated as far away as the Philippines, and were the first to connect the Japanese military to the anticolonial revolutionaries in South and Southeast Asia. In their earliest known covert action, they had stimulated an uprising in Korea in 1884 that was used as a pretext for intervention by the Japanese military.[19] In October 1895, two Genyōsha members cooperated with the Japanese minister to Korea to provoke a pro-Japan military coup, during which Queen Min was assassinated.[20]

In 1901, with the help of the Japanese industrialists and the patronage of cabinet ministers, Uchida also created the Kokuryūkai (the Amur River Society, sometimes called the Black Dragon Society), perhaps Japan's most storied "unofficial" nationalist espionage group. Its goal was to keep the Russian Empire north of the Amur River and out of East Asia. The ambition and reach of the Kokuryūkai was extraordinary. It operated its own espionage training school, lobbied successfully for a more muscular Japanese military and foreign policy, supported Chinese revolutionaries such as Sun Yat-sen, and engaged in espionage and paramilitary sabotage of all sorts, including assassinations. Along the way, it produced some of its longest-lasting—and least acknowledged—contributions to Japan's intelligence community: accurate maps of the battlefields of Asia.[21]

The extent to which membership in these groups overlapped is not entirely clear, but it is apparent that these patriotic "secret societies" filled a niche for the Japanese military and Foreign Ministry. Konoe's Tōa Dōbunkai was funded with secret MOFA funds and enjoyed a close working relationship with MOFA from the start, but members of these groups—and their more transactional brethren, the so-called "continental adventurers"—often spied for the Japanese army "on contingency."[22] This worked for both sides. The "agents of chaos" could profiteer, but they could also be punished when it was convenient for the Japanese military to discard them, as in the previously mentioned 1884 incident when the Genyōsha was shut down after having been involved in preparations for the coup and invasion of Korea.[23] Foreign Minister Mutsu Munemitsu's account of this episode airbrushes out the disreputable hired hands. He reports that he had relied on MOFA's own intelligence source in Seoul, the special *chargé d'affaires* and Korea expert Sugimura Fukashi. Mutsu claimed that he "secretly ordered Sugimura to pay very careful attention to the movements of Donghak peasants and observe closely how the Korean government would deal with . . . Chinese representatives stationed in Korea." When Sugimura reported to him that the Korean government had requested Chinese reinforcements, Mutsu says that he asked the cabinet to authorize the dispatch of "forces of comparable size to prepare for any contingencies and maintain the current balance of influence over Korea between China and Japan."[24]

Relationships between the decorous state and the criminal patriots were more transparent at some times than at others. Uchida, who had honed his skills as an explosives expert for the ultranationalist Tenyūkyō (and likely also for the Genyōsha and the Foreign Ministry), was determined to undermine Chinese control of Korea. He moved to Vladivostok in 1895 as an unacknowledged operative for the Imperial Army. Two years later he crossed Siberia to map the terrain, and his maps famously aided Japanese troops during the Russo-Japanese War.[25] Uchida's government connections are more easily documented after 1906, when he joined Itō Hirobumi, who had just become the first Japanese resident general of Korea. Although Uchida's cover was as Itō's "research assistant," the central focus of his activities involved convincing Itō and Yamagata Aritomo that the Empire of Japan should annex Korea.[26]

Akashi Motojirō was probably Japan's most acclaimed spymaster and skilled covert operative before the Asia-Pacific War. He also was the personification of the connection between Japan's mainstream intelligence community and its less savory satellites. Akashi entered the Imperial Army College at the age of twenty-four in 1888, and four years later was assigned to the chief of the General Staff, General Kawakami Sōroku. He subsequently studied in Germany for a year and served as military attaché at the Japanese legations in Paris in 1901 and in St. Petersburg in 1902, where he initiated contacts with anti-tsarist revolutionaries through personal connections on campus, possibly including Lenin and his Bolsheviks during the Russo-Japanese War.[27] He also reportedly penetrated the Russian intelligence services and smuggled arms to Finnish nationalists.[28] Akashi was not a member of the Genyōsha, but his brother-in-law Tsukinari Isao was its seventh president, and his father-in-law, Kōri Toshi, was a leading member as well.[29] We also know that Akashi was in active correspondence with Tōyama Mitsuru and with Uchida Ryōhei, who was sent by the Genyōsha to Russia before Akashi began operations there.[30]

Dissatisfied with the quality of the dispatches from military attachés in St. Petersburg, Akashi took it upon himself to supervise the collection and analysis of intelligence regarding Russian opposition groups before the Russo-Japanese War erupted in 1904.[31] On the basis of this intelligence—and having been forced to move because of the war—Akashi decamped to Stockholm and persuaded the Japanese government that if revolutionaries were strengthened and enabled to foment disorder in Russia, a task that he could accomplish for 100,000 yen, the tsar might sue for peace. Upon receipt of that enormous sum—which would today be more than $1.2 million—he set up an intricate espionage network in major European cities, an effort that has been described as "the first and most ambitious Japanese attempt to intervene in the domestic affairs of a European country."[32] Although the Russian secret police (Okhrana) were surveilling him, Akashi paid off local merchants, workers, and anti-tsarist activists—as well as Russian military officers and Finnish, Estonian, and Latvian dissidents.[33] From Stockholm he also recruited Polish operatives who tried and failed to sabotage the Trans-Siberian Railway.[34] It has been reported too that Akashi paid Georges Clemenceau and Anatole France to produce anti-Russian propaganda in European newspapers and magazines.[35]

Akashi secured an additional fund of three thousand yen to organize a conference of revolutionary parties and anti-government activists from across different European countries in Paris in October 1904. Attendees, including representatives of the Russian Liberal Party, the Russian Socialist Revolutionary Party, the Finnish Constitutionalist Party, the Polish Nationalist Party, and the Polish Socialist Party, adopted a joint declaration expressing their solidarity and their intention to conduct and coordinate armed anti-government demonstrations and terrorist activities—including farmers' riots.[36] A few months later, in January 1905, Akashi funded a demonstration led by Father George Gapon, a popular Russian Orthodox priest and a working-class leader of the Assembly of Russian Factory and Mill Workers in St. Petersburg. Although it was designed as a peaceful rally to petition the tsar, the protest went awry when police opened fire on hundreds of thousands of demonstrators.[37] Forever after it was known as the Bloody Sunday Uprising, an event denounced by the global media that helped undermine the prestige of the Russian government to the advantage of Colonel Akashi and Japan. The deteriorating domestic political situation caused partly by Akashi-financed riots and rebellions reportedly made it difficult for the Russian army to deploy its most sophisticated divisions to Manchuria. In addition, rumors about revolutionary parties' movements may have sapped the morale of Russian troops.[38] In April 1905, during the Russo-Japanese War, some of his paid agents set to work generating unrest in Odessa, Kiev, and other major cities, and Akashi was rumored to be the conduit for the British "master spy" Sydney Reilly, who provided critical information about the Russian order of battle and, in particular, about the Russian Pacific Fleet to the Japanese General Staff.[39] Akashi also ran operations across the Asian continent, from Siberia and Central Asia to China and Manchuria, where he may have worked closely with the Kokuryūkai. He submitted a record of his wartime operations, including the expressively titled *Rakka Ryūsui* (Falling Flowers and Flowing Water), to the

General Staff in 1906, twelve years before he was appointed Japan's governor general in Taiwan. The entire record of Akashi's exceptional HUMINT work was classified top secret, and his field reports were used by the Imperial Army General Staff Office to train future intelligence officers.[40]

Many highly competent covert army operatives followed Akashi on much the same path, but none worked across such a vast range. In northern Europe in the mid-1930s, Colonel Manaki Takanobu, a military attaché at Japan's Berlin embassy, ran a special duty unit, the eponymous Manaki Kikan, with agents and operatives in Estonia, Finland, Lithuania, Poland, and Turkey, and cultivated relationships with émigrés from Georgia and Ukraine.[41] His unit continued energetic efforts to destabilize the USSR, and came to be led by Major Onodera Makoto, who claimed to be motivated by a sense of racial solidarity with the "Asiatic" Finns and Estonians. But cash helped. Onodera kept Estonian intelligence chief Richard Maasing on the payroll as he built the Imperial Army's Riga office into "the hub for Japanese military intelligence against the Soviet Union" by 1937.[42]

In China, the often insubordinate Colonel Kōmoto Daisaku, who assassinated the warlord and former Japanese ally Zhang Zuolin in 1928, also followed—and expanded—the Akashi covert action playbook. Another successor, Itagaki

FIGURE 2.2 Generations of Japanese intelligence officers were inspired by the exploits of Akashi Motojirō (1888–1919).
Photo: National Diet Library

FIGURE 2.3   A "Russian Fascist Party" was supported by Japanese intelligence. Akikusa Jun, who became the first commandant of the Nakano School (discussed in this chapter), is seated third from the right in the front row at its 1934 New Year's Eve banquet.
Photo: Public domain

Seishirō, contrived the Manchurian Incident in September 1931 with Ishiwara Kanji and Doihara Kenji when the three were Imperial Army colonels. Ishiwara became the more famous military strategist and political activist, but Doihara was known as "Lawrence of Manchuria" for effectively insinuating himself into Chinese society. In November he secretly exfiltrated former Qing emperor Pu Yi and helped anoint him head of Japan's puppet state Manchukuo.[43] Echoing Akashi, Doihara used local bandits to cause a public disturbance in Tianjin, where Pu Yi was under house arrest, to lure Chinese troops into suppressing it. Once the Chinese used violence, Doihara deployed his troops to "protect" Japanese citizens, and amidst the instability, his army-affiliated operatives were able to transport Pu Yi to Dalian without attracting public attention.[44]

Doihara plotted successfully and repeatedly to create pro-Japanese local governments in northern China. In one case, in June 1935, four Japanese soldiers were detained for not possessing the required travel permits from the local government in Chahar Province. The soldiers were soon released, but the local Japanese consul accused the Chinese authorities of treating those soldiers inhumanely by pointing rifles at them, thereby insulting the Japanese army. The IJA's elite Kwantung Army, stationed in southern Manchuria, then advanced into the province to force the Chinese side into an agreement with Doihara that stipulated the Chinese army's withdrawal and acceptance of a Japanese policy adviser in the local government.[45] In July 1938 Doihara, who was commander of the Fourteenth Army Division deployed in China, established his own special duty unit in Shanghai under the direct control of the Imperial Army chief of staff. In cooperation with local criminal organizations, he attempted (but failed) to establish a puppet government in Beijing to challenge Chiang Kai-shek's authority in Chongqing.[46]

FIGURE 2.4   Doihara Kenji was known as "Lawrence of Manchuria" for effectively insinuating himself into Chinese society.
Photo: Kyodo News

Diplomatic intelligence capacity also expanded in the first half of the twentieth century. It hadn't started well, though. In 1882, after MOFA failed to anticipate or prevent a military revolt by units of the Korean military in Seoul, some Japanese legation staff were killed in the so-called "Imo Incident."[47] Some in MOFA responded predictably by calling for enhanced intelligence collection and analysis on the continent. But apart from establishing four new consulates in China—which merely raised the total number of Japanese diplomats there to just seventeen—and apart from sending several employees to China to study Chinese culture and language in 1883, very little was accomplished. Worse, many of those trained as China experts were sent either to British Hong Kong or to Europe, presumably because MOFA's intelligence activities in the late nineteenth century focused on the revision of Japan's unequal treaties with Western powers and its funds for covert operations went either to Western officials or foreign intellectuals who advised and brought intelligence to the Japanese government.

One early example of the latter was Alexander von Siebold, a fluent Japanese-speaking German publisher whose father had advised the shogun. Von Siebold was paid by the Japanese government to plant positive stories about Japan and collect diplomatic and military information in Europe.[48] According to one source, the United States and European countries accounted for nearly 85 percent of the overseas payments from MOFA's secret funds at that time.[49] MOFA funds were made available to consuls in port cities for reporting on the movement of naval vessels, and Japanese embassies in Sweden and Austria ran agents under MOFA's guidance.[50] Still, diplomatic intelligence was a pale shadow of its military cousin, and would remain so throughout this period. Until the end of World War I, diplomatic intelligence was often an easily disregarded afterthought. Intelligence collection and analysis could not be the priority of Japan's limited number of foreign diplomats, who were consumed by day-to-day activities. Acting without strategic guidance or significant resources, legations and consulates often simply purchased information from locals and third-nation expatriates.[51]

MOFA control of the continental adventurers had begun to slip away by the time of the Sino- and Russo-Japanese wars.[52] But after its diplomats famously failed to be heard at the Paris Conference of 1919, MOFA concluded it needed a fuller understanding of international diplomacy and convened an internal discussion group, the Reform Association (Kakushin Dōshikai), to improve its intelligence operations.[53] The group called for creating a research bureau (Chōsabu), and in 1920, after extended deliberation, MOFA created a new Intelligence Bureau (Jōhōbu) with responsibilities for collecting and analyzing information on foreign affairs in general; editing and distributing diplomatic bulletins for propaganda purposes; communicating secretly with domestic and foreign newspapers and journals; funding domestic and foreign newspapers and news agencies; collecting and analyzing the foreign policies of other nations and the public opinion of their citizens; and performing analysis and communication of information regarding domestic and international situations. The new Intelligence Bureau would have two professional intelligence offices: one responsible for research on China, Hong Kong, and Macao, and the second to cover the rest of the world.

This had no impact on the growth of military intelligence, and MOFA became noticeably concerned about the army's reliance on covert action by undisciplined soldiers and adventurers on the continent. In late 1931, just after the Manchurian Incident, MOFA created another group to deliberate on ways to strengthen its intelligence capabilities vis-à-vis both national policy requirements and military competitors.[54] It concluded that a new Research Bureau, independent of its now robust regional bureaus, would be helpful. But plans for this Seichōbu were ill-conceived: in addition to research and analysis, it would also train diplomats and do policy planning. The Privy Council, also hoping to contain radical elements in the army, rejected this proposal in favor of undertaking government-wide research and policy coordination at a higher level. MOFA had to settle for a much smaller research-only bureau.

In January 1934, its new Chōsabu was established, comprising five offices. Only three did intelligence: the First Office conducted research on diplomatic history; the Second Office organized and managed diplomatic records; the Third Office was responsible for research on the politics, diplomacy, and economies of Manchuria and China; the Fourth Office covered Europe; and the Fifth Office was responsible for North and South America. MOFA's Jōhōbu was left to specialize in propaganda.[55] The only subsequent reform of diplomatic intelligence before the end of the Asia-Pacific War came in 1940, when MOFA transferred part of its Jōhōbu resources to a Cabinet Information Bureau (Naikaku Jōhōbu) created to integrate propaganda-related activities conducted by different government organizations. MOFA incorporated the remaining international propaganda and external intelligence-gathering responsibilities into its Chōsabu.[56] But by then it had long since ceded control of intelligence to the imperial military.

Military Intelligence on the Road to Total War

Japan kept its head down during the First World War. Its navy hunted German merchant ships on behalf of the British but risked little and benefited enormously from sales of materiel to the belligerents in Europe, while encroaching on their neglected Asian markets and focusing its strategic activities closer to home. In the process, Tokyo learned more about modern intelligence in the service of "total war."[57] One source was its British ally, which provided Tokyo access to wireless intercepts of German naval activity, including submarine traffic. This not only enabled the Japanese navy to arrange convoy/escort operations to protect merchant shipping but, as we shall see, also stimulated considerable interest in accelerating its SIGINT development.

Even then, like most support functions, military intelligence was not yet a fully accepted institutional fixture within the Japanese military. Army officers received only the most rudimentary training in intelligence tradecraft or analysis, although naval officers received a bit more.[58] The intelligence bureaus of the Imperial Japanese Army and Imperial Japanese Navy were staffed by collectors and analysts, many of whom had honed their skills during Japan's earlier conflicts with China and Russia. But two problems slowed the professionalization of the military intelligence function during this period. The first was that intelligence professionals were stuck in a lower-status role. One former intelligence officer recalls that senior military officials regarded intelligence staff as "messenger boys," and that the dominant view was that "anyone can do intelligence."[59] The standard joke was to ask intelligence officers if there was something wrong with their health. Intelligence officers were seen as professional administrators, not as professional specialists capable of contributing directly to the success of operations. It did not help their image that much of what they administered were newspaper clipping services.[60] As Michael Barnhart has pointed out, "It was considered more important to know how to run a ship than understand the character of a potential enemy."[61]

A second, equally serious problem was one the army and navy shared with foreign militaries of the era—the absence of an intelligence career track. As elsewhere, military and naval officers would take new assignments every two or three years on average. Even experienced intelligence officers often had to serve in unrelated staff positions between intelligence assignments.[62] So by the time of the Asia-Pacific War, only one senior officer on the Imperial Army General Staff, General Sugita Ichiji, had risen through assignments in the intelligence units.[63] And many who served as intelligence chiefs did so only for a very short duration, quickly rotating back out to operations.

This rapid turnover intensified when the war expanded to include the United States: three different major generals served as chief of the Second Bureau (intelligence) of the Imperial Japanese Army's General Staff from 1940 to 1942.[64] This disdain was reflected in the resources made available for intelligence in the years before the Asia-Pacific War. In 1941 the army General Staff's Second Bureau had only thirty-six officers above the rank of captain, and the Imperial Japanese Navy's Third Bureau had only twenty-three. In December 1940, the army established its Taiwan Military Research Institute to coordinate military intelligence for its southern operations and placed it under the control of the Operations Bureau rather than the Intelligence Bureau. And when the army's General Staff planned its move into French Indochina, it did not consult its own senior area expert.[65] Within decades, operations officers had such disdain for their intelligence staff that they began routinely to seize intelligence functions for their own commands.[66] The notorious Ishiwara Kanji did exactly this when he reorganized the General Staff Office in 1937. He raged against what he viewed as the inability of Japan's intelligence community to generate actionable tactical intelligence, and at one meeting with the chief of the Intelligence Bureau's China Section, Ishiwara denounced his analysts as "completely worthless," thundering at them for not doing "real work, just sit[ting] on your butts and theorizing."[67]

In Japan's evolving intelligence community, it was evident that dashing covert action was more highly valued than dreary desk-bound analysis. During World War I, Japan began experimenting with a particularly flexible variety of organization, the "special duty unit" (tokumu kikan), which would become the model for espionage and tactical intelligence collection through World War II.[68] Most were formally attached to the military hierarchy (see figure 2.5), but an uncertain number of these semidetached units, commanded by (and usually named after) military officers operating outside strict military hierarchy, became the nucleus of Japan's wide network of espionage activity across Asia.[69] One of the first special duty units was formed in 1917, when Japanese troops were deployed in Siberia. Another, formed in January 1918, was the Ishimitsu Kikan, led by the same Russian-speaking Ishimitsu Makiyo introduced earlier who served the Imperial Army from both inside and out. He had come to Siberia in 1917, when, on behalf of Tanaka Giichi, the deputy chief of the General Staff (and later prime minister), the Kwantung Army formally rehired him to monitor Soviet military activities in Siberia. Ishimitsu's assignment morphed when he was instructed to help local Cossacks fight Bolshevik forces to achieve political independence in both the Amur and Primorsky regions.[70] The Japanese military hoped for a friendly noncommunist state in Siberia that would serve as a buffer against Soviet threats.

The Ishimitsu Kikan used a local Japanese mining company, Hisahara Kōgyō, as its base of operations and hired several Japanese expats for translation, finance, and other administrative services.[71] The Cossacks were neither ready to fight Bolshevik forces on their own nor capable of protecting the life and property of Japanese residents; they requested that Tokyo arm its residents and support their joint fight against the Bolsheviks. Ishimitsu sent a telegram to the governor general's office in Liaoyang to request rifles for

Japanese residents' self-defense in February 1918. But the Japanese military was slow to respond, presumably concerned that such a joint force would risk escalation into a full-scale war with the young Soviet government. Bolshevik forces attacked the next month anyway, killing hundreds of Cossacks and nine Japanese residents. In August, when the Japanese government finally made a decision to send tens of thousands of troops to Siberia, Cossack leaders established a Republic of Siberia, and the Japanese General Staff made Ishimitsu Japan's putative ambassador.

This Siberian Expedition—or "intervention period"—lasted until 1922, at which point Soviet counterintelligence became more effective and collection became considerably more difficult for the Japanese. Tokyo's intelligence, assigned to the special duty units of frontline Kwantung field armies with virtually no oversight from the General Staff, came to be limited to border regions and relied primarily on a constricted flow of wireless intercepts, captured documents, interrogations of soldiers and refugees, and what it could collect from the simple observation of rail traffic from several hundred elevated observation posts on plateaus along the Soviet border.[72]

The Imperial Army's Second Bureau and the navy's Third Bureau were further enhanced after army field intelligence was bogged down in the Siberian Expedition and Tokyo was outmaneuvered by the United States and Great Britain at the 1921 Washington Naval Conference. Their efforts may have been retarded by the Imperial Army's excessive focus on Russia and China.[73] Indeed, from 1917 to 1937, the army sent only seventy-six officers to privately run English-language schools, compared to the 102 who were sent to study Chinese, seventy-four sent to study Russian, sixty-eight sent to study German, and sixty-three sent to study French. Oddly, the navy had similarly skewed priorities. During these same years, sixty-two officers studied German, but only twenty-two studied English, despite the global reach of the British Empire and the rise of the United States.[74] Each sent the top one quarter of its academy graduates abroad for three years of training, but the majority were stationed in Germany, France, and the Soviet Union.

Sugita Ichiji, the wartime intelligence officer introduced earlier, offered three reasons why Japan was slow to increase intelligence activities against the United States and Britain despite their prominence in the international system. First, neither the government nor the military fully appreciated the significant changes in the global balance of power—a strategic intelligence failure. Second, while the navy regarded the United States as a potential adversary, the army remained obsessed with the Soviet Union, and there was no policy coordination between the two branches of the military. Third, there was still limited awareness in the government of the importance of intelligence to national security. Indeed, the government established no organization dedicated to analysis of foreign countries' strategies until much later.[75]

Still, the U.S. Strategic Bombing Survey judged that Japan was developing a "vast" global intelligence network to collect tactical military and commercial information. As earlier, much of this depended on diplomats, civilians, businessmen, and a large number of "enthusiastic amateur spies" who provided maps and other documents.[76] But a growing share of the effort was professional—both in the diplomatic corps and in the military. That said, although Japan's interwar intelligence efforts were active and increasingly wide ranging, they were directed at actionable intelligence, not designed for policy planning, and remained more anchored in Asia and Europe than in the United States.

In Asia, the bulk of the effort was in China, of course. A postwar U.S. report judged the Foreign Service Intelligence Section in China to have been Japan's "most important prewar information gathering agency," evaluating it as "far superior to military or naval organizations."[77] This may have been hyperbolic, but it was the case that by the mid-1930s, MOFA had two dozen consulates across China.[78] Part of its "diplomatic" effort involved one of the oldest—and surest—techniques, setting "honey traps" to use evidence of illicit sexual engagements to blackmail credulous officials and extort information. One 1937 U.S. counterintelligence report describes a "Miss Kawashima, head of the Japanese intelligence on the Soviet-Manchukuo border," who arrived in "Peiping" accompanied by the French-educated "Misses Yuriko, Haruko, and Tokeko [who were] sent here for special duty . . . on the dance floors of the various hotels."[79] It seems that Japan's diplomatic corps was stepping up its game, but in the larger scheme of things, the Japanese remained too narrowly focused on HUMINT and operational matters.

Military intelligence was not to be outdone by the diplomats. Before 1931 there had been only six army special duty units targeting the Soviet Union. By 1934 there were fourteen, two of which were in Paris and Berlin. All were under the jurisdiction of the Harbin Intelligence Section of the Kwantung Army General Staff. At the same time, the army began deploying intelligence officers at nine consulates general in the Soviet Far East, in Europe, and in Manchukuo.[80] Indeed, the special duty units in Manchukuo that had been attached formally to the Kwantung Army in 1931 were now assigned responsibility for the puppet government's intelligence functions.[81] They had their hands full, since they had also been having difficulty controlling many of the former tsarist officers who had come to their side as intelligence assets and as fifth columnists during the Siberian Expedition.[82] For its part, the Imperial Japanese Navy deployed special duty units in Shanghai, Nanjing, Hankou, Qingdao, Tianjin, Guandong, and Fuzhou.

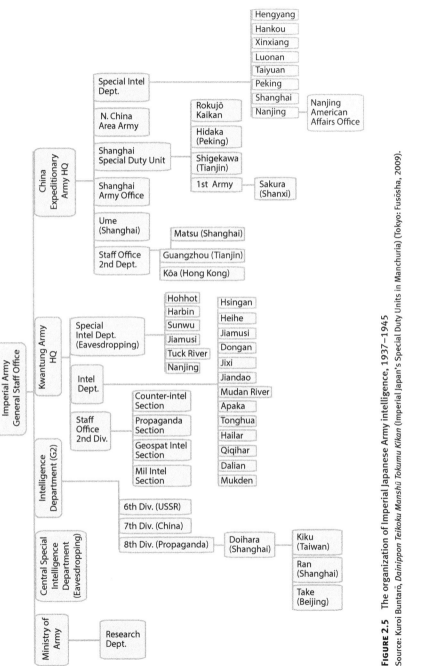

FIGURE 2.5 The organization of Imperial Japanese Army intelligence, 1937–1945

Source: Kuroi Buntarō, *Dainippon Teikoku Manshū Tokumu Kikan* (Imperial Japan's Special Duty Units in Manchuria) (Tokyo: Fusōsha, 2009).

Technological Enhancements

Japan's intelligence technologies, particularly military SIGINT, improved rapidly after World War I. But their paths were strewn with familiar organizational boulders. After the army, navy, MOFA, and the Ministry of Communications (MOC) decided to undertake joint diplomatic code research in the early 1920s, the project fell apart when familiar jurisdictional disputes shattered the collaboration.[83] In an outcome that highlights the deepest pathologies of the Japanese intelligence system, each thereupon struck out on its own. The Imperial Army's Second Bureau and the Imperial Navy's Third Bureau each collected and analyzed its own intelligence and reported exclusively to its own Operations Bureau.[84] Despite the absence of central coordination, they all made surprising progress for a time. In 1923 the army started learning how to decipher Soviet codes from the Polish military. A Polish army captain, Jan Kowalewski, came to Japan at the invitation of the Army General Staff, which also sent six Japanese officers to Poland to study code-breaking.[85] Moderately soon thereafter, in July 1930, the Imperial Army stood up its own code-breaking unit, the Second Bureau's Fifth Section, and began deciphering a U.S. "gray" code. In doing so, the army discovered that the U.S. military had been breaking Japanese codes for nearly a decade, leading an exasperated General Tōjō Hideki to declare that "the U.S. Ambassador knows more about Japanese internal affairs than I do!"[86] By 1935 the Imperial Army had broken lower-level Red Army codes, and more Polish cryptographers were recruited to Japan after the Polish General Staff collapsed in 1939. Indeed, it seems that Poland continued to help Japan "unofficially" throughout World War II, their conflicting alliance relationships notwithstanding.[87]

MOFA, for its part, continued to lag behind. It is not clear if the Foreign Ministry recognized just how transparent its own communications had become to the Allies, but recognizing that foreign intelligence communities were well ahead in cryptography and that it had too few experts to enable it to catch up, MOFA drafted a plan in mid-1935 to improve Japanese cryptographic capabilities. In a startling exception to their now familiar competition, MOFA even got some help from the army. Its plan included using random number codes the army had learned from Poland and dispatching cryptographic experts to Japanese embassies and legations abroad to devote time to studying cryptanalysis.[88] This seemed to have paid off. One postwar U.S. government analysis concluded that "the Japanese appear to have learned more about Soviet codes from liaison [with foreign governments] than through their own resources."[89] This did not include much intelligence sharing with Berlin, however. In 1941 and 1942, Berlin and Tokyo initialed two limited intelligence-sharing agreements, but despite weekly meetings, little intelligence was provided to the Japanese military attaché in Berlin or shared by the German military attaché in Tokyo. Nor was information on Japan's future operational plans passed on to the Germans.[90]

The Imperial Navy had been quicker off the mark. In 1924, the same year that the U.S. Navy established a Radio Intelligence Unit in its Codes and Signals Section, the Imperial Japanese Navy outfitted its first dedicated intelligence collection ships, the *Yucho* and the *Sata*, and deployed them to monitor U.S. naval exercises. In 1928 the navy established its own section for signals intelligence (with just nine staff) to break diplomatic codes of other great powers participating in naval arms control conferences.[91] By 1932 it deployed the *Erimo*, a tanker loaded with sophisticated electronics capable of intercepting U.S. Navy transmissions, off the Hawaiian Islands.[92] In May 1937, intelligence ships were off the continental U.S. coast listening to U.S. fleet radio transmissions. And in 1938, the Imperial Navy stood up the so-called "L Unit," an intercept site in Mexico from which it could listen in on the main Atlantic fleet transmitting facilities in New York and Washington, D.C. Two years earlier, it had begun operations at the signals intercept site in Ōwada, a small village twenty miles from Tokyo, that could monitor naval signals across the Pacific. This facility was also used to listen in on transmissions from U.S., British, French, Soviet, and even German military attachés based in Tokyo.[93] According to Edward Drea, during the 1930s the Japanese navy had "extended their collection capability dramatically. . . [and] had developed an arc of intercept sites [from Tokyo to Mexico at sea]. At the tactical level, the Imperial Navy's radio intelligence system was well prepared for World War II."[94] The larger problem was that without a central authority that might have forced them to cooperate, these facilities were replicated in Hokkaido and Manchuria by the Imperial Army, and in Tokyo by the Ministry of Communications.

Transpacific HUMINT

Although SIGINT had improved despite self-inflicted handicaps, HUMINT and covert action remained the primary foci of Japan's interwar military intelligence. The Imperial Japanese Navy ran an intelligence unit in London that funneled cash to British MPs and former military officers in the 1920s through the 1930s. One early recipient was a decorated carrier-based pilot, Frederick Joseph Rutland, who supplied both technological and strategic intelligence to the Imperial Navy in the early 1920s.[95] With Imperial Navy support, Rutland set up an office close to the Douglas Aircraft factory in southern California and, charming locals with his British accent, moved easily in West Coast society. Rutland may also have facilitated Japan's carrier development and its ability to launch naval attacks. He had been paid so handsomely by his handlers that by 1925 he was wealthy enough to build a home on Yokohama's bluffs, an elite residence for foreigners in Japan. But after they broke Japanese codes, MI5 and U.S. counterintelligence discovered Rutland and arrested him when he returned to Britain for a visit. The Rutland case seemed to generate a sort of intelligence security dilemma in which "poorly focused and insecure intelligence operations can create a vicious cycle of escalating suspicion and increasingly unrestrained intelligence gathering."[96] Indeed, some in the U.S. and British intelligence services became convinced there were traitors and Japanese spies everywhere, elevating fears and connecting espionage to the Japanese American community.

There is considerable debate as to whether or not such a connection existed—and not just in the United States. It is not clear why, but the Japanese military reportedly tried to exploit (or transform) the allegiances of some of the more than 200,000 Japanese Brazilians. Under the guise of supporting agricultural and commercial activities, covert operatives supervised the sabotage of crops and trained volunteers for other subversive activities.[97] There is evidence in the Magic intercepts that Japan's military and diplomats attempted to cultivate relationships with some Japanese Americans and with Japanese citizens living on or visiting the West Coast as early as the 1920s.[98] An intercepted cable in 1941 revealed that the Japanese consul general in Los Angeles, Nakauchi Kenji, was aware of his unit's efforts to recruit Japanese and Japanese Americans to obtain intelligence—particularly those working in aircraft plants, with whom he had regular contact.[99] In another, we learn that Ambassador Nomura Kichisaburō complained to the home office that they had made intelligence collection more difficult. Stephen Mercado concurs with David Daniel Lowman's controversial argument that "Washington's internment of individuals of Japanese descent on the West Coast deprived the imperial army of valuable intelligence on ship movements, U.S. industrial trends, aircraft production, and other information."[100] Another analyst has speculated that "the evidence that [the Imperial Japanese Navy] directed an extensive network among second-generation workers in airplane plants may have had an influence on the U.S. government decision to intern the Nisei population."[101]

But two separate reports to President Roosevelt after Pearl Harbor found no evidence of Japanese American espionage on behalf of imperial Japan.[102] It seems that these pressures were animated more by racism, hysteria, greed, and simple risk aversion than by accurate counterintelligence; but a full decade before Pearl Harbor, the entire Japanese American community was under surveillance on the West Coast.[103] This secret program, supervised by the FBI in collaboration with the army, the navy, and the Departments of Justice and Commerce, enabled the federal government to round up and jail more than two thousand Japanese Americans as "dangerous enemy aliens" immediately after Pearl Harbor.[104] Not one was ever convicted, and no subsequent investigation by the federal government turned up any Nisei spies.[105]

Japanese military intelligence relied on more conventional channels. The most famous cases of prewar infiltration in the United States involved Japanese naval officers who, having trained at the Imperial Japanese Navy's Intelligence Bureau, enrolled in U.S. universities as language students.[106] In addition to making contacts and learning English, they acted as couriers for the naval attaché in Washington. In 1935 a naval officer, Miyazawa Toshio, was caught running an espionage network on the West Coast which included paid U.S. informants who were either active in or retired from the

"... and here's the new Curtiss-Wright propeller plant, slightly to the left of Mrs. Togomatsu and the children."

FIGURE 2.6 It was widely assumed that Japanese Americans were spying for the Japanese in U.S. defense plants during the run-up to the Asia-Pacific War, but none was ever convicted of espionage. Image: Alain/*The New Yorker* © Condé Nast

U.S. military. Commander Tachibana Itaru ran an even more elaborate network. When he was discovered by the Office of Naval Intelligence in 1939, Secretary of State Cordell Hull and President Roosevelt intervened so as not to upset delicate talks they hoped would keep Japan from joining the Axis. Tachibana, one of Japan's most effective intelligence officers, was expelled without excessive fanfare.[107] At around this same time, MOFA's senior intelligence officer in the United States, Terasaki Hidenari, the same man who had attempted to organize the Nisei working in defense plants, began cultivating a heterogeneous group of pacifists, communists, union leaders, anti-Semites, isolationists, and aggrieved African Americans to gather information and mobilize their opposition to war with Japan.[108]

Before the beginning of the Asia-Pacific War, Japanese intelligence on the East Coast was organized primarily around two military attachés—one in Washington and one in New York. The Japanese embassy also had a separate intelligence section which "collated" open source reports from consular officials. Its political and commercial attachés collected, analyzed, and communicated directly to MOFA and, backchannel, to the ministries from which they were seconded, such as the Ministry of Finance. The military attaché in Washington had flag rank and supervised several technical analysts. With the help of Japanese company representatives in New York, the military attaché there focused on weapons production and the U.S. order of battle.[109] Some military intelligence officers came to the United States to refresh and enhance their networks, others to update their analyses of U.S. capabilities.

Shinjō Kenkichi was one of the latter. Under the cover of Mitsui & Company, the army colonel arrived in March 1940 in New York, where he received "valuable cooperation" from more than fifty Japanese companies. Shinjō was impressed with the depth of U.S. industrial capacity—some ten to twenty times larger than Japan's—and concluded that Japan would be seriously outgunned in a fight. But his reports were ignored by Imperial Army officers who remained certain that the United States would be defeated by its own spiritual deficiencies.[110] As often happens in intelligence communities everywhere, good analysis fell on deaf ears, the victim of a failure to eradicate the *idées fixes* of smug policy makers. And Japanese policy makers—particularly military officers with operational responsibilities who were convinced of Japan's spiritual advantages—were apparently more smug than most.

First, though, there was Pearl Harbor—surely America's greatest intelligence failure and Japan's most striking intelligence success. The U.S. Strategic Bombing Survey acknowledged that Japan's "careful planning based on nearly complete intelligence" contributed to the "shocking success" of the attack that brought the United States into World War II.[111] General Hoyt

Vandenberg, director of central intelligence, testifying before the Armed Services Committee of the U.S. Senate in April 1947, even credited Japan with having a more advanced intelligence capacity than the United States before the attack.[112] But as stunning as Pearl Harbor was tactically, and as capable as Japanese naval analysts were in gathering operational intelligence—much of it open sourced—and in protecting it while their colleagues planned the attack, Pearl Harbor would be better known as a profoundly costly failure of strategic intelligence.[113] Colonel Shinjō was right. The attack on the United States proved to be Japan's greatest and most costly strategic failure. In this case, effective collection and excellent analysis—both well protected—collapsed under the weight of wishful thinking.

Japan's Wartime Intelligence

Japan's tactical success at Pearl Harbor was actually the second major battlefield test of its military intelligence. It failed its first one, which occurred on the Soviet front in 1939. From Japan's perspective, the most important systemic change in Northeast Asia subsequent to its invasion of China in September 1931 was the rise of Soviet power in that region. Having moved decisively into the Soviet sphere of influence—and having established a continental border with the USSR for the first time—the army commanders felt compelled to enhance their intelligence capabilities. In addition to covert actions, the Kwantung Army's principal intelligence operations included propaganda, mapping, radio intercepts, border observation posts, interrogations, and, by mid-1933, aerial photography.[114] These operations were conducted by eight special duty units, most prominently by the Harbin Special Duty Unit, which ran White Russians, Chinese, and Korean locals across the border. It had some initial success intercepting and decrypting Soviet radio signals, and was able to learn the size and disposition of border garrisons and some air units—as well as to garner details about industrial conditions in the Soviet Far East.

By 1935, however, the Red Army had effectively secured its borders with Japan, and Japanese SIGINT, which was not well networked across the vast spaces of Outer Mongolia, was nearing its limits. Kwantung Army efforts to improve tradecraft, including forged documents, dress, and language, were proved of little avail, for the larger problem was that it had gained only limited insight into the Red Army order of battle. Within four years after Japan's arrival on its border, the USSR had increased its Far Eastern military presence from six to eleven divisions, while the Japanese Sixth Army maintained only five divisions. The two militaries squared off in a long series of skirmishes, the last, largest, and most decisive of which took place near Nomonhan, a small village along the Khalkhin River, which served as the border from May to August 1939.[115] It was the first use of airpower in a high-intensity battle in the Far East, and Japan lost more than eight thousand troops to the Red Army under the command of the future Hero of the Soviet Union Georgy Zhukov. It was also seen by Unit 731 commander Ishii Shirō as a "golden opportunity to test the possibilities of [biological weapons] on a large scale."[116]

Most analysts agree that Japan's defeat could be attributed to "conspicuous" intelligence failures in counterintelligence as well as at the strategic level.[117] In the case of the former—and well before the battle was joined—master spy Richard Sorge had already acquired and passed on to Moscow detailed information on Japan's Manchurian order of battle.[118] In the case of the latter, although MOFA was prepared for the August 1939 German-Soviet nonaggression pact which freed up Red Army troops for deployment to the Far East, the military (with which MOFA was not in effective contact) was caught flatfooted and missed both the German attack on Poland and the Soviet grab of Finland. Alvin Coox argues persuasively that "what passed for net assessment at the upper levels of the prewar Japanese high command [were] fuzzy prognostications and platitudinous exhortations."[119] It is clear there were other failures to communicate, even within the military itself. Reliable intelligence was often ignored. In June 1938, a senior Soviet secret police officer, Genrikh Samoilovich Lyushkov, sought asylum in Manchukuo and provided the Imperial Army up-to-date intelligence detailing how Soviet military capabilities in the region were clearly superior to Japan's. It came as news to the Imperial Army's General Staff that the USSR had deployed 2,000 aircraft while Japan had only 340, and that the Red Army had 1,900 tanks while Japan had just 170.[120] But the army would not allow inconvenient intelligence to undermine its strategic decisions.[121] It stuck to its original theory that the Soviet military did not have adequate capabilities.[122]

There is also debate about whether the army effectively collected, analyzed, and communicated tactical intelligence during the battle.[123] The Harbin Special Duty Unit did not coordinate effectively with the Kwantung Army's other special duty units or with the operations staff. In one case, Harbin failed to inform headquarters that it had learned a document it once judged to be a sensitive high-level Red Army communiqué was actually a Soviet deception.[124] After the war, U.S. interrogators learned from an army captain, Kawaguchi Takeo, how his counterintelligence unit set up a secret wireless detection squad to monitor radio frequencies and locate spies in Manchuria. Kawaguchi reported that in one case they captured a radio operator and handed him off to the local special duty unit, which in turn used the radio to send false signals back to the Soviets. The ploy backfired, as the Red Army immediately attacked, causing his unit "considerable embarrassment."[125] Kwantung radio operators were often unable to send even the sensitive information they did manage to acquire back to headquarters.[126] The larger embarrassment by far was the fact that the Red Army had amassed a force four times the size estimated by Japan's military intelligence.[127] The Imperial Army's tactical intelligence at Nomonhan was unclear about the size or disposition of the Red Army, failed to reconcile multiply sourced estimates, and neglected to communicate what it did learn to the General Staff. It even mistook an early August probe by the Red Army for a major offensive, which actually came when 57,000 Soviet troops attacked two weeks later.[128]

As we would expect, the Kwantung Army set up a Committee of Intelligence Experts for the Study of the Nomonhan Incident in order to diagnose the failure and study how to enhance the role of intelligence in military operations. The intelligence units took the brunt of the blame for the Nomonhan failure. The investigators determined that it was the operational staff's lack of confidence in their intelligence that led them to make decisions based on outdated pre-battle conditions. It also concluded that intelligence communications were weakest in the Kwantung Army, and that the special duty units should be placed under a single headquarters below the operations level. They should be relieved of operational duties and given responsibility for analysis only. Covert action, propaganda, interpreter training, and tradecraft education would be separated out and provided their own commanders and staff.[129] In a manner common to much intelligence reform everywhere, the Imperial Army's judgment remained largely unassailable, Japan's intelligence community remained splintered, and many of its analyses continued to be routinely ignored.[130] We have here an excellent case of the cloudy boundary between intelligence failure and policy failure discussed in chapter 1.

Getting Tradecraft Right

Military intelligence might not have failed so spectacularly at Nomonhan had the army been able to field better-trained intelligence officers with the sophisticated skills and equipment necessary to conduct risky covert action in enemy-controlled areas. Ironically, getting tradecraft right was a requirement that had already attracted the army's attention. The War Ministry established the Training Unit for Rear Duty Agents (Kōhō Kinmu Yōin Yōseijo) near the Yasukuni Shrine in central Tokyo in March 1938. A little more than a year later this unit was moved a few miles west, to Nakano, and was attached to the General Staff Office formally as the Army Communications Research Institute (Rikugunshō Tsūshin Kenkyūjo). The Nakano School—and its branch in Shizuoka—lasted until Japan's surrender, and trained more than 2,500 spies.[131]

Contrary to the notion that "anyone can do intelligence," the Nakano School was an elite institution from the beginning. Its first class matriculated six hundred, but only sixty sat for the exam, and just eighteen passed. Over time, it attracted increasing numbers of graduates from Japan's leading universities as well as many accomplished athletes—martial and otherwise. The underlying ethos was "to know the enemy, not simply fight him."[132] But indoctrination in Japanese values was also central. So the diverse curriculum ranged from "spiritual training"—including study of classics such as the fourteenth-century *Jinnō Shōtōki* and imperial rescripts—to military history, psychology, and foreign languages. Students were also expected to master practical problems of tradecraft: deception, disinformation, infiltration, reconnaissance, sabotage, propaganda, concealment, radioing, explosives, and codes.[133] They toured Manchurian factories, newspaper offices, and broadcasting stations. Just 2 percent of the students' time was allocated for leisure.[134] In order to emphasize the school's value to national security, General Tōjō Hideki attended the first cohort's graduation ceremony.

Original plans called for eighteen months of study, but the pressures of war forced the shortening of the curriculum to six months in 1941. By then the faculty had expanded from two instructors (one of whom was Itō Samata, a veteran of the "2/26 Incident," the failed ultranationalist coup d'état of February 1936), to sixty teachers in five departments and class cohorts of 120. As the prospect of defeat came into focus, the curriculum was expanded to include the principles of guerrilla war and agricultural self-sufficiency.[135] This came in handy for one of the most famous of all Nakano School graduates, Onoda Hirō, who emerged from the Philippine jungles in 1974, twenty-nine years after the war ended.[136]

Intensively trained and fully endorsed by the General Staff, Nakano School graduates fanned out across the empire and beyond. Their covert actions included infiltrating Soviet territory, running foreign journalists and businessmen, shipping arms to anticolonial insurgents, demolishing bridges, and counterfeiting currencies, often within the army's special duty units.[137] Working within Section Eight of the General Staff's Second Bureau under the label "Sea Transport," many gained traction in India, Malaya, the Philippines, and Indonesia by waving the banner of Japan's pan-Asian crusade.[138] Their appeal to the common cause of expelling European colonialism from Asia was accompanied by the provision of considerable material benefit to local freedom fighters.

Some of the better-known special duty units included the army's Matsu Kikan, which tried and failed to infiltrate spies on Australia's north coast, and the Kami Kikan, which was active in Borneo. The Kōa Kikan was based in Hong Kong to collect intelligence on U.S. forces in Asia and the Chinese order of battle; the Manwa Kikan used its privileged position as a "supplier" to the Imperial Navy in Singapore to generate funds for espionage across Southeast Asia. In Burma, the Minami Kikan assisted pro-independence guerrillas,

FIGURE 2.7   Nakano School graduate Onoda Hirō survived in the Philippine jungles for twenty-nine years after the war ended.
Photo: Mainichi Newspapers

including the storied 1940 rescue of Aung San, the father of the future Nobel Peace Prize laureate and Myanmar leader Aung San Suu Kyi.[139] And in December 1941, the Fujiwara Kikan and Iwakuro Kikan started operations in Malaya to help underground activists achieve their independence from Britain, operations that were taken over by the Hikari Kikan.[140] Later in the war, the Azuma Kikan was created by the Imperial Japanese Navy in Shanghai to collect intelligence on movements of the Chinese communists and on U.S.

FIGURE 2.8 Onoda returned home from the Philippine jungles in 1974 with a group of Nakano School classmates.
Photo: Asahi Shimbun

naval movements. U.S. intelligence regarded the Tonegi Kikan, the only Japanese intelligence unit based in Allied territory (Canton), as "by far the most active and aggressive espionage unit yet known to be operated by Japanese diplomatic intelligence in the Far East." Stood up in March 1942, it was still sending reports to Tokyo "in considerable volume" as late as July 1945.[141]

Perhaps most storied were the efforts of the Fujiwara, Iwakuro, and Hikari Kikan, the special duty units "responsible for gathering intelligence on British dispositions in India, spreading propaganda among the Indians, and controlling the Indian National Army" (INA), which was leading the fight against British colonialism on the subcontinent.[142] In February 1942, when the British surrendered in Singapore, they turned over 45,000 Indian officers and soldiers to Major Fujiwara Iwaichi, head of the Fujiwara (or F) Kikan. Fujiwara in turn assigned them to General Mohan Singh with an exhortation that they join the INA and help undermine Britain in South Asia. In his postwar memoirs, Fujiwara insisted that the "F" stood for "Fujiwara, Freedom, and Friendship," and insisted: "We were driven by a strong desire to help the Indians who, jeopardizing their own safety, were dedicating themselves to the cause of national independence. Our friendship knew no national barriers in helping them achieve their aspirations."[143] General Singh recalled that he and the INA had "functioned in close cooperation with the Japanese army as if we were part and parcel of the same force."[144]

But after Major Fujiwara was replaced by Colonel Iwakuro Hideo in late 1942, General Singh recalls that the Imperial Army's "attitude [toward the Imperial Navy] stiffened and they decided to cut us down to size and to impress upon us that the INA movement would get the shape and play the role that the Japanese desired."[145] After protesting an army decision to place the navy under the control of a Malayan group of South Asian nationalists, Singh was arrested and exiled until the end of the war. Meanwhile, the various special duty units struggled in their liaison with Indian nationalist leaders until they were able to engage with the charismatic Calcuttan Subhas Chandra Bose, who had split from Mahatma Gandhi's Indian National Congress and gone all in with the Axis powers.[146]

Japan's special duty units were energized by graduates from the Nakano School, though their success was limited geographically.[147] According to one postwar intelligence report, Soviet counterintelligence, strict border controls, the expulsion of Chinese and Koreans from the eastern provinces, and "anti-spy" instructions disseminated to the general population frustrated the army's best efforts to place officers inside the USSR. White Russians hired at great expense by Japanese intelligence to infiltrate the Soviet embassy in Harbin proved unreliable. And by the 1940s, Japanese operatives were reduced to having to rely on interrogation of deserters and refugees.[148] For a time, there were a great many of these. But they were a declining asset. When the Russo-German fighting began in 1941, some forty to fifty Red Army deserters per month came to the Japanese armed with Soviet magazines and Red Army infantry textbooks. By the time of the Battle of Stalingrad in early 1943, however, their number had dropped in half.

Netaji-ka-Swapna   356

FIGURE 2.9 Subhas Chandra Bose (1897–1945) was an Indian nationalist and anticolonialist who worked closely with Germany and Japan to undermine British rule on the subcontinent.
Photo: Offset chromolithograph by unidentified Calcutta press, 1940s. Courtesy of Dr. Christopher Pinney, University College London.

Meanwhile, the Tōa Dōbun Shoin remained productive throughout the war. Many of its graduates had been recruited by the central research office of the South Manchuria Railway Company, and a growing number of them supported military intelligence or served in the puppet government of Man-chukuo in an intelligence capacity.[149] A wartime report by the U.S. Office of Strategic Services (OSS) labeled the Tōa Dōbun Shoin an "agency of infiltration," and when the war ended, the school (by then located in Shanghai) was

FIGURE 2.10   Japan's "special duty units" (*tokumu kikan*) eventually became part of popular culture, as in this 2009 comic book.
Photo: By permission of *SPA! Komikku*, Fusōsha

shuttered by the Allies.[150] By the end of the war it had educated more than five thousand students, including Nezu Hajime and the "nine martyrs" who were executed by Chinese authorities for wartime spying.[151] In May 1946, in the first purge notice signed by the emperor, the Occupation targeted those who had advocated or cooperated in advocacy of militant nationalism, dictatorship or fascism, and racial supremacy. It specifically listed the Tōa Dōbun Shoin faculty and its post-1937 graduates as "nonacceptable persons for educational service."[152]

Intelligence in Decline

As the war progressed, the flow of intelligence from all sources declined. General Arisue Seizō, the chief of army intelligence from 1942 until the end of the war, recalls that by 1942, the flow of overseas intelligence reaching the General Staff had declined because so many military attachés at Japanese embassies and consulates general had been detained. The only exceptions were those stationed in Germany and Italy and in neutral states. Japan maintained only a small handful of diplomatic missions in the Western Hemisphere.[153] As it no longer had active attachés or diplomats in the United States, the General Staff created a section responsible for intercepting shortwave transmissions, and relied on the U.S. print media and published meeting minutes from Congress, much of which was supplied by the Federated News Agency (Dōmei Tsūshinsha), a propaganda and OSINT service created by the Ministry of Communications in 1936.[154] Deprived of direct access to U.S. citizens, MOFA turned to third-country nationals, such as the Spaniard Alcasar de Berasco, an agent in their employ who provided accurate intelligence regarding the capacity and disposition of U.S. naval forces in the South Pacific after July 1942.[155]

Japan did rather better with its wartime SIGINT. Five receivers and twenty listeners were deployed by the navy's Third Bureau to monitor Allied broadcasts from San Francisco, London, Australia, Chongqing, India, and Moscow. Japanese SIGINT was capable enough to support the attack on the U.S. landing at Leyte Gulf, to determine B-29 raid probabilities, and to assess the damage done by Japanese aircraft to the Allied fleet off Okinawa.[156] The army regularly intercepted Chinese battlefield transmissions, leading Lieutenant Colonel Taguchi Masazuki to claim that by 1942, fully 80 percent of the intelligence he received originated as intercepts. And some, such as advance knowledge of Chiang's March 1945 decision to delay his advance into Burma, were of particular value.[157] Cryptographers supervised by the Central Special Intelligence Department (Chūō Tokushu Jōhōbu) were never able to break the higher-grade U.S. or British military codes, but they did well with Allied diplomatic codes and, especially, reading Allied aircraft and ordinary radio traffic.[158]

The first important code broken by Japanese cryptographers was the one used by the U.S. Army Air Corps in Burma.[159] This, of course, provided Japanese intelligence with a window on what the Allies knew of their capabilities. And their decrypts of British and U.S. messages gave them considerable confidence that a Japanese advance in Indochina would not be met by resistance.[160] The Central Special Intelligence Department also supervised intelligence sections in army field units across all theaters of operation. Some were quite substantial, as in the case of the Special Intelligence Section of the Fourteenth Area Army in the Philippines, with three hundred staff divided into four groups: wireless (to monitor tactical ground circuits), broadcast (to record Allied broadcasts), air-ground liaison (to intercept Allied messaging), and task force designation (to monitor Allied naval movements).[161] As the war wound down, however, reports derived from signals intercepts accounted for only one quarter of the total stream of intelligence traffic.[162] Much of Japan's best equipment came from abroad, including a Swedish code machine similar to the one used by U.S. forces and IBM calculators commandeered from Japanese insurance companies for which cryptographers had to manufacture their own cards from Sakhalin pulp in Shizuoka mills.[163] Less amusing—indeed in what was a deeply ironic turn of events—Japanese code-breakers had success late in the war when, in July 1944, Colonel Onodera Makoto, having been promoted from his responsibilities in Riga to chief of Japan's military intelligence in Europe, acquired an M-209 mechanical encryption device. Sadly for Japan, the device successfully decoded a message referring to the nuclear bomb two days after the second one was dropped on Nagasaki.[164]

By war's end, Japan's intelligence community was riddled with the generic pathologies outlined in chapter 1. In the field, the different special duty units reported through different, uncoordinated channels—some in theater, others in Tokyo.[165] For example, successful communications intercepts by the nominally separate South Manchurian Railway Company led to the establishment of an East Asian Communications Investigation League in August 1940, with more than 370 personnel drawn from the Manchukuo state-owned telephone and telegraph company—including civilians dispatched from Tokyo—under the command of the Kwantung Army.[166] Although diplomatic and commercial intelligence efforts were nominally led by MOFA's Investigative Bureau (Chōsabu), much of the analysis was undertaken by competing agencies such as the Greater East Asia Ministry (Daitōashō) in Tokyo and the East Asia

Development Board (Kōain—EADB) in China until the latter was absorbed by the former in 1942. So while the functions of MOFA and the Greater East Asia Ministry were not sharply delineated, it seems that MOFA had been effectively boxed out of Asia for all but "purely diplomatic" affairs and forced by bureaucratic logic—that is, the "jealousy and frigid cooperation" with the military—to focus on Europe and North America.[167]

From April 1940 until October 1942, the EADB was effectively run by Lieutenant General Oikawa Genshichi, who claimed after the war that his formal responsibilities entailed coordination with other Japanese government ministries to "help improve economic, cultural, political and technological conditions in China."[168] But General Oikawa also testified before the International Military Tribunal for the Far East that the EADB was "mediating [the] opium trade."[169] It has been reported that the Kwantung Army and other military branches had been coordinating opium sales and smuggling in Manchukuo, Mongolia, and China since the early 1930s and that the EADB helped decide how to divide profits among them.[170] These activities involved many of the military's special duty units, such as the Amakasu Kikan and the Satomi Kikan, whose illicit profits were harvested by disreputable fortune hunters and the EADB.[171]

Clearly, the scope and scale of the imperial military's intelligence activities expanded rapidly during the war. Estimates vary, but according to Ken Kotani, an Imperial Army HUMINT budget that had been just 40 million yen in 1941 was ten times larger by war's end.[172] When the war with the United States began, the army General Staff had fewer than two dozen intelligence specialists and the navy fewer than thirty. When it ended, the army's Central Special Intelligence Department (Chūō Tokushu Jōhōbu) alone had more than one thousand staff.[173] Sugita Ichiji, an army intelligence officer who later became chief of staff for the postwar Self-Defense Force, puts the total number of communication and encryption staff during the late stages of the war at 25,000.[174] In April 1944, the Imperial Army established the Military Mathematical Research Association at Tokyo Imperial University, a late effort to enlist help from the nation's leading mathematicians and linguists.[175] Overall, however, the military intelligence budget never exceeded one half of 1 percent of the total military budget during the war.[176]

Increasing the size of the intelligence community was certainly not a solution for many other problems, one of which was the tendency toward bureaucratic puffery. General Arisue reported that army officers stationed in China routinely inflated their achievements, and that reports from Germany and Italy were excessively optimistic and triumphant.[177] The "crossed wires" described earlier regarding MOFA's Chōsabu after 1940—conflation of intelligence and propaganda functions—were now pervasive across the entire Japanese intelligence community. The General Affairs Section of the General Affairs Bureau in the Greater East Asia Ministry was responsible for both, as was the intelligence office in Japan's Nanking embassy. Likewise, the cultural and intelligence departments were merged in Canton. Even the weekly and daily army General Staff intelligence reports included "detailed descriptions" of military progress and "tributes to the indomitable fighting qualities of the Japanese soldier."[178] By the end of the war it became a standing joke that the Operations Bureau had reported the sinking of the USS *Lexington* six times and the USS *Saratoga* four times. But it could not have been funny when the emperor, in a moment of painful candor, complained to the Imperial Navy's chief of staff, Admiral Oikawa Koshirō, that "to the best of [his memory], this is the fourth report of the *Saratoga's* sinking."[179]

Wishful thinking based on stereotyping was prospective as well. Just as the Japanese evaluated the "fighting spirit" of Japan's armed forces more hopefully than analytically, they also reported the fighting capacity of forces of the British Empire and of the United States in similarly stereotypical terms. The Australians, for example were seen as "unemployed people, villains . . . known for their lack of military discipline and public morals," while Indian and Malay soldiers had "no desire to fight against Japan." U.S. soldiers, for their part, "are lacking in sincerity." They "would probably tire of a long term war. . . [and] would not be able to endure shortages and discomfort on the battlefield, unlike their Japanese counterparts."[180] This was hardly actionable intelligence.

Perhaps the most famous example of hopes and stereotypes substituting for professional analysis was the unwillingness of the General Staff to believe abundant multiply sourced reports of impending Soviet-German hostilities in the months ahead of Hitler's attack, Operation Barbarossa, in June 1941. Ambassador Ōshima Hiroshi first warned Tokyo of the possibility in April 1941, and a high-level Soviet defector, G. S. Lyushkov—a former chief of the NKVD in Siberia—warned his Japanese hosts of the German move a month in advance. The army's Second Bureau immediately issued a bulletin for the General Staff, but it was ignored. Tōjō insisted it was not a pressing matter. Having already decided on a southern advance, he calmly put off further discussion for another month. His General Staff even chose to ignore the clear and urgent warnings communicated to them from Berlin by Ambassador Ōshima based on his meetings with Hitler and Ribbentrop on 3 June.[181] Tōjō's indifference was met with a similar appraisal by Foreign Minister Matsuoka Yōsuke. Dismissing the prospects for a German invasion, and wishfully believing it was a bluff to mask German plans to mass forces

against Great Britain, Matsuoka told the emperor there was at best a 40 percent chance that the German-Soviet status quo would change. Ōshima was
"vexed. 'When the head of state [Hitler] says he will do something . . . he
will do just that.' "[182] And when Hitler did do what Ōshima warned he would
do, MOFA learned of it through the International News Service, and the
Kwantung Army heard through the Manchukuo National Press Agency.[183]

Analytical failure compounded the damage from failed communication.
After Operation Barbarossa got under way, Japanese intelligence underestimated Soviet resistance and accepted the prospect of the swift and pain-
less German victory the Germans were promising. Briefing Military Affairs
Bureau chief Mutō Akira and Operations Bureau chief Tanaka Shinichi on
22 June, the army's intelligence chief, Okamoto Kiyotomi, estimated that
Germany would prevail in a matter of months. He projected a German victory in which the USSR would lose 60 percent of its electric power capacity,
50 percent of its iron ore, 60 percent of its coal, 75 percent of its oil, and
75 percent of its population—all "rosy" figures that were wildly off.[184]

All this occurred just six months before Pearl Harbor, but the Japanese
military did not move to establish a standalone intelligence unit focused on
the United States until four months after the attack—and then with but three
permanent officers. Meanwhile, its considerably better resourced Soviet experts continued to make inexplicable mistakes.[185] In his review of Japan's intelligence miscalculations regarding when the Red Army might abrogate the
nonaggression pact and attack Japanese positions in China, and with what
size force, Drea finds that Japanese intelligence expected that the Soviets
would need forty-five divisions, a force it estimated could not be assembled
until the spring of 1946. But in 1945 the Red Army had already amassed well
over one hundred divisions along the USSR's border with Manchukuo, and
they easily overran the Japanese forces. It is possible that the intelligence estimates had been influenced by a desire to depict a manageable problem. But
whether Japan's military intelligence was politicized or just wrong, according to Drea, "After hostilities ended, a Soviet general merely snickered when
a Japanese operations officer showed him the Kwantung Army's intelligence
estimates of the Soviet order of battle."[186]

These failures were dramatic but hardly isolated. The U.S. Strategic
Bombing Survey concluded that Japan's intelligence consistently underestimated U.S. resilience and concomitantly overestimated the losses Japan
could inflict on U.S. expeditionary forces. As a consequence, the U.S. military was able to move sooner and with greater strength than the Japanese
anticipated—thereby inflicting greater losses of warships, merchant vessels, and, eventually, territory. Excessively optimistic tactical intelligence led

Tokyo "to overextend her conquests and lines of communications."[187] J. W. Bennett, W. A. Hobart, and J. B. Spitzer present it with even greater clarity: the Japanese were "unable to produce a substantively accurate order of battle list of American or British dispositions in any theater."[188]

Many of Japan's wartime intelligence failures were political and ideological. Recognizing the need for better coordination in the face of a possible U.S. invasion, in March 1944 the Imperial Army's operations and intelligence bureaus were directed to compile what they had learned about U.S. tactics for a textbook to be distributed to soldiers.[189] But the General Staff, worried that this *Quick Guide to Understanding Enemy Tactics (Tekigun Senpō Hayawakari)* would discourage Japanese troops confronting American forces on the front line, inserted guidelines instructing soldiers "not [to] overestimate the enemy's capabilities as even U.S. troops have various sorts of weakness and provide opportunities that we should take advantage of."[190] This was the same General Staff which ordered that intelligence estimates at odds with national policy be burned in 1941, even when the chief of staff could find nothing to argue with in the analysis.[191] In April, navy intelligence estimated U.S. forces would target Saipan within a month. But Operations thought the Allies would come later, via a different route. The intelligence analysts were right, but the policy makers chose Operations' estimate because it was a better fit with their extant plans.[192] By the end of the war, the Imperial Army's Operations Bureau was relying on "exaggerated" reports from frontline troops, while its Intelligence Bureau was using SIGINT and OSINT to generate reliable estimates that were ignored because the General Staff worried that doing otherwise "would affect the fighting spirit of the forces."[193] Once again, policy failures and intelligence failures converged with murderous consequences.

Silos

Communication across the services was the greatest—and costliest—problem facing Japan's intelligence community during the war. U.S. intelligence learned that the Foreign Ministry was even spying on the Imperial Army in China, and concluded without apparent irony that "for this type of intelligence collection it would be better to go through normal channels."[194] The largest bill for intelligence stovepiping and jurisdictional competition came due after Midway in June 1942, when, largely as a consequence of U.S. intelligence success, Japan lost four aircraft carriers, two cruisers, and one destroyer in addition to the lives of more than three thousand soldiers and sailors. According to one retired Japanese intelligence officer, the navy's leadership significantly misrepresented the results of the Midway battles in Japan's favor not only to the Japanese public but also to army and political leaders. Only a handful of top army high command leaders were informed of the decisive defeat; indeed, it was not until one month after the battle that Prime Minister Tōjō even learned of it.[195] Soldiers who survived and returned from the battle were kept in quarantine in order to keep the results secret, and nobody tried to hold Commander Yamamoto accountable for the defeat. As a consequence, intelligence sections in neither the army nor the navy seriously analyzed the implications of Japan's defeat at Midway on subsequent operations in the Pacific, including at Guadalcanal just months later.[196] Postwar U.S. analysis of Midway concluded that there was "almost a total lack of effective liaison between services."[197]

Another prominent stovepipe-induced intelligence failure—what U.S. intelligence later gently referred to as Japan's "policy of non-exchange"—came just ahead of the October 1944 battle of Leyte Gulf, when the Imperial Japanese Army failed to provide the Imperial Japanese Navy with current situation reports, and the navy wildly and irresponsibly overstated its situation to the army.[198] The navy falsely reported that it had sunk eleven Allied carriers, two battleships, and three cruisers, leading the army to shift operations to the south, where, they believed, Allied forces had been decimated. As a result, most of the army's main force was annihilated by Allied airstrikes while en route.[199] During his postwar interrogation, General Yamashita Tomoyuki, commanding general of the Fourteenth Area Army, acknowledged the difficulties he had with intelligence throughout the Philippines campaign, revealing that he had been compelled to fight "a blind war."[200] For his part, General Arisue railed at how the extreme sectionalism within the military, driven by a competition to claim credit for battlefield achievements, prevented the service branches from sharing realistic assessments of operational developments.[201]

Although this problem was hardly limited to Japan, it was woven very tightly into the fabric of the Japanese intelligence community. Notwithstanding recognition of the problem, efforts to reform the intelligence community during the war were episodic and rarely effective. Presaging the 2013 "whole of government" intelligence reforms that will be examined in chapter 6, a Cabinet Intelligence Committee, staffed in 1936 by personnel from the Home Ministry, MOFA, the Ministry of Communications, and both the army and navy ministries, was tasked with providing coordinated intelligence directly to the prime minister. But both the Imperial Army and Imperial Navy were unhappy with this arrangement, so when the cabinet announced plans in 1940 to establish a Cabinet Intelligence Bureau to facilitate intelligence

sharing, they pulled the plug.[202] In September 1940 the government established a National Institute for Total War Studies (Sōryokusen Kenkyūjo) to
conduct war games and model a southern advance. It concluded that Japan
had enough materiel to last only two years against the United States and
Great Britain, and warned that if the USSR were to enter the war, Japan
would be finished much sooner. When the results were presented to Prime
Minister Konoe and War Minister Tōjō, the latter rejected it as "armchair
theory."[203] Other efforts at intelligence reform came far too little and too
late. In 1944 arrangements were made for the exchange of liaison officers between the intelligence bureaus of the two service branches, but the plan was
never actualized.[204] Imperial Army and Navy intelligence chiefs finally had
their first formal meetings in mid-1943, but it was not until 1945 when army
cryptologists showed their navy counterparts how to break U.S. codes—and
even this had to be undertaken "unofficially" because of objections by some
in the army's General Staff.[205] Japan's self-destructive intelligence stovepiping
persisted until the war's end, the requirement for military attachés to report
through Foreign Ministry communications channels making it possible for
MOFA officials to see, handle, and even change or quash military intelligence
reports. From October 1944 to July 1945 the Imperial Navy received just two
reports from MOFA and only eleven from the Imperial Army.[206]

That Final Element

To this point we have reviewed the history of the early development of the
modern Japanese intelligence community, focusing on how the shifting strategic context, technological development, and failure influenced collection,
analysis, communication, and covert action. Since there was no democratic
oversight of authoritarian Japan's intelligence community—and, indeed,
since there was precious little political control of the military—only one element in the framework outlined in chapter 1 remains to be examined: protection. This, too, was connected with Japan's authoritarian politics.

   Japan's military police, the feared Kempetai, was established by the Imperial Army in January 1881.[207] Just as the Imperial Army was modeled on
the French army, the military police were modeled on the French Gendar-
merie.[208] Its original purpose was twofold: to protect Japanese military organizations and to maintain public safety.[209] At its origin the Kempetai had
fewer than 350 officers, but it tripled in size within three years.[210] It remained
a small elite force until the turbulent early 1920s, when it assumed an additional role—counterintelligence. In 1924, amidst the political uncertainties of late "Taishō democracy"—including the rise of mass politics—the

Imperial Army minister, Ugaki Kazunari, declared that in an era of total wars it had become impossible to distinguish peacetime from wartime preparation, and the Kempetai was assigned to monitor the home front line.[211] Its presence was expanded in each of Japan's regional cities, and, in addition to the classical remit of counterintelligence—protecting state secrets—the Kempetai now was told to focus on curbing ideas, movements, and organizations in Japanese society—particularly anarchists, socialists, communists, and social democrats—whose activism could impede efficient war mobilization.[212] It was ordered to repress dissent and thereby enforce ideological orthodoxy and conformity. It was also responsible for monitoring foreign embassies, residences, and workers in Japan, and disrupting foreign intelligence networks.[213] As the empire expanded, the Kempetai moved offshore.[214] By 1937 the Imperial Army had three Kempetai headquarters in China, covering seventeen different cities.[215] And by the war's end, there were twice as many Kempetai troops in the occupied areas across Asia as in Japan's home islands.[216]

Japan's Special Higher Police for Public Surveillance (Tokkō Keisatsu) was administered by the Home Ministry. It monitored anti-military, anti-war, and other political movements, and collected intelligence on Korean residents and intellectuals. It even monitored military officers on a watch list.[217] Moving beyond counterintelligence and into the realm of repression, one month after Japan's first general election with universal male suffrage in February 1928, the Tokkō Keisatsu made a mass arrest of 1,600 communist activists, and subsequent right-wing violence in 1932 led to action against ultranationalists. Then the Tokkō moved to surveil and repress citizens who were not politically active. Wielding the 1925 Peace Preservation Law (Chian Iji Hō), it began arresting intellectuals who supported liberal ideas and prohibited their publications.[218] The police had authority to arrest those with a view to altering the *kokutai*—a vaguely framed but spiritually infused reference to the "body politic." Anyone who had joined an association opposed to private property with full knowledge of its objectives was liable to imprisonment with or without hard labor for as much as ten years. And invoking the 1937 Military Secrets Security Law (Gunki Hogo Hō), the Special Higher Police reached directly into Japanese daily life, even banning photography clubs and suspending weather forecasts.[219]

But these laws and the repression they legitimated could not prevent leakage of some of the most closely held state secrets. The most prominent (and embarrassing) case in point was that of Richard Sorge, a German resident of Tokyo who posed as a Nazi and worked for the Soviet Union with Ozaki Hotsumi, a prominent journalist and China specialist with elite connections

FIGURE 2.11   Civilians were advised how to keep secrets during wartime state campaigns, such as during this "Counterintelligence Week" in 1944.
Photo: Provided by Jan Banning with permission of the Netherlands Institute for War Documentation

serving as an adviser to Prime Minister Konoe. Sorge, the son of a German oil engineer, joined the Communist Party in 1919 in Hamburg and became an active Soviet agent in 1927 in Scandinavia. Moscow then sent him to Britain before moving him on to Tokyo. His biographers describe him as dogmatic, intolerant, didactic, sarcastic, and bereft of any sense of humor—but also as resourceful and charismatic. By his own account he was "a man of consequence."[220]

From 1933 to 1941, Sorge was able to procure detailed information on Japanese military and industrial activities from the idealistic Ozaki (and from others in their circle, many of whom were Japanese journalists in China), which he passed along to Moscow using a concealed radio, special couriers, and (rarely) the Soviet embassy. Ozaki described himself as "affable," his sociability affording him a wide network of cherished and influential friends who felt sufficiently intimate to speak openly, even of state secrets.[221] As a result of Ozaki-generated leaks and other contacts, Sorge's reports included accurate information on the order of Japanese battle in Manchuria, German-Japanese relations, Japanese activities in China, and U.S.-Japan relations. Because Sorge had impeccable cover—including a desk in the German embassy—he was able not only to collect information but also to analyze it after vetting the information with senior officials at the German embassy and the Japanese War Ministry. Sorge's most prized dispatches were reliable intelligence regarding Japan's invasion of China in 1937 and the German invasion of the Soviet Union in 1941. Both reports reassured Moscow that Japan was not planning to invade the Soviet Union, allowing Moscow to move divisions from the Far East to meet the Germans in the West.[222] Sorge and Ozaki were arrested in October 1941 and executed in November 1944.

The colossal counterintelligence lapse generated by Sorge's and Ozaki's activities inspired promulgation of the draconian May 1941 National Defense Security Law (Kokubō Hoan Hō— NDSL), which expanded significantly the scope of classified state information.[223] Now anyone revealing or publishing state secrets to foreign nations or to anyone outside the government, and anyone seeking state secrets with a view to sharing them with foreign nations, or plotting to do these things, was subject to the death penalty. The House of Representatives spent only one week—and the House of Peers just two weeks—examining the draft legislation before approving it. Ministry of Home Affairs records show fifty-nine cases of NDSL violations in 1941, and while only a few were sentenced to death under the NDSL—Sorge and Ozaki being the most prominent—about two hundred were tortured to death during interrogation, and more than 1,500 died from illness in jail after arrest on suspicion of NDSL violations.[224]

The NDSL was also invoked to surveil some of Japan's most senior political leaders. The army's Military Administration Bureau Annex—informally known as the Yama Kikan—had been eavesdropping on Japanese politicians and diplomats since 1937.[225] Their most distinguished targets included Prime Minister Konoe and a future prime minister, Yoshida Shigeru. A Nakano School

FIGURE 2.12   Master spy Richard Sorge was executed by the Japanese for espionage and celebrated by the USSR as a "Hero of the Soviet Union."
Photo: Public domain

graduate serving undercover at the Yoshida home in Ōiso discovered that Yoshida had been actively trying to find a path to an early peace with the United States.[226] Yoshida was arrested in 1945 and remained in custody until war's end, an experience that would stand him in good stead with the Occupation.

There was one other front in the world of wartime counterintelligence: the protection of codes. Here, too, the Japanese encountered problems. The most famous—and, for the Japanese military, the most costly—operational intercept occurred when a U.S. signals unit decoded radio messages revealing Admiral Yamamoto Isoroku's location near the Solomon Islands in April 1943.[227] His plane was ambushed, and his death dealt a blow to the morale of the Japanese military and public. Japan's wartime signals counterintelligence failures were owed to U.S. success in breaking Japanese military and diplomatic codes that had begun bearing fruit well before Pearl Harbor.[228] But by January 1944, the U.S. Signals Security Agency had compromised eight of the Imperial Army's sixteen high-level cipher systems.[229] In addition to the Yamamoto ambush, other intercepts—derived from the Magic diplomatic code decryption—had enormous value. One was the Allied intercept of Ambassador Ōshima's cable informing Tokyo of Hitler's impending invasion of the Soviet Union in June 1941. But there were other gems as well. In January 1943, for example, Allied intelligence learned that Ōshima was planning to assemble all of Japan's European-based intelligence officers for a conference on how to improve their liaison and intelligence sharing. Magic decrypted Ōshima's entire account of the meeting and also learned that he was reluctant to report to Tokyo the full story of what he knew about Germany's impending disaster in Stalingrad.[230] Perhaps he thought that given their aversion to bad news, they would shoot the messenger.

The period reviewed in this chapter was one of massive political change, both at home, where democratic forces were crushed by authoritarian ones, and abroad, where geopolitics and technological change made new and challenging demands on Japan's intelligence community. It was also a period of rapid, often unmanageable expansion. Having to invent an intelligence bureaucracy that could function effectively in an unstable region that it claimed to champion and sought to lead—and having to make sure it functioned effectively within the rest of a global system it felt compelled to challenge—was surely part of the reason why the early development of Japan's intelligence community was more pocked by failure than garlanded by success.

Japan fought three major wars—with China, Russia, and China again (this time with China's American and British allies)—as well as two extended battles in Siberia and at Nomonhan. It did so bravely and often successfully. But as General Yamashita put it, too frequently it did so blindly. Although the Imperial Japanese Navy and Army often outmatched their opponents and achieved important victories, Tokyo misread regional and world politics. Japanese intelligence got Russia right during the tsarist period but consistently underestimated Soviet strength. As others have noted, Tokyo fought and sacrificed using the wrong theory of victory. Its intelligence system—like its grand strategy overall—assumed Germany would prevail in Europe and the United States would opt for passivity in the face of Japan's Asian expansion.[231] Delusions that spiritual power would prevail over material capabilities devalued intelligence. Notwithstanding the occasional tactical success, such as the stunning one at Pearl Harbor—and despite some impressive SIGINT coups—neither Japan's strategy nor its operational planning was supported consistently by adequate intelligence. As a result, the early twentieth century was littered with Japanese intelligence—and intelligence-starved policy—failures.[232]

These failures were evident in all six elements of our model. Across this period overall, collection, the first element, was intermittent and imbalanced. Tokyo relied to a surprising extent on OSINT and frequently did well with its SIGINT, but its military units relied too heavily on special duty units of questionable integrity for collection of HUMINT-based information. Then, when it came to the second element, analysis, the focus throughout the first half of the last century was weighted toward tactical and operational intelligence; strategic intelligence was underproduced and, when available, was too often discounted. No doubt because of the domination of military over political intelligence, this too cost Japan dearly.

The most stubborn problems for the Japanese intelligence community during this period were connected to the third element, communication. Operational assessments too often were fragmented, imprecise, wishful, qualified, and uncollated. Mutually insular, competing bureaucratic units refused to cooperate; indeed, they often surveilled one another, animated and undermined by parochial mistrust. Vertical communication was no more successful: analysts struggled to provide their judgment to policy makers who too often were demonstrably indifferent to them, and who too often were heedless of the need to be flexible in the face of facts that change. The indifference and inflexibility of the General Staff when confronted by intelligence that pointed them in directions contrary to extant plans were particularly vexatious during the Asia-Pacific War. In the absence of central coordination—indeed, in the presence of active turf-protecting hostility toward the very idea—Japanese intelligence services had no superordinate customer. Without civilian control and political oversight, the military was unprotected from its own misjudgments. The intelligence community would underprovide information, and the government would underprovide security.

Compounding these problems was Japan's failure to shield national secrets from the prying eyes and pricked ears of its enemies—despite an authoritarian state that ought to have been able to sustain effective counterintelligence capabilities. Japanese policy makers were not only remarkably vulnerable to Allied deception but also apparently unaware of the extent of their exposure. Finally, we have seen that Japan's covert actions during this period were more ambitious than they were successful, and often were counterproductive because of insufficient oversight.

No doubt because oversight was so underdeveloped in authoritarian Japan, the multiple intelligence failures of this period did not stimulate the course corrections anticipated in chapter 1. This chapter has documented how meager reform efforts by MOFA—and even by the cabinet—were blocked by the military. Thus, when reform finally occurred after the war, it would be overdetermined, forced on a conquered nation by a shift in the global balance of power that placed the United States alone at the top, and by technological change that left Japan needing to play catch-up—again. Total defeat in total war meant subordination to the United States for the next several generations and engendered a deep and sustained mistrust of the military among the Japanese public, both of which delayed construction of a robust Japanese intelligence community. The next chapter will explore how the accommodation by Japanese leaders to U.S. power and to the public's widespread aversion to security affairs shaped (and stunted) the Japanese intelligence community during the Cold War and beyond.

CHAPTER 3

Accommodating Defeat (1945–1991)

> There are no docile natives. . . . Every Japanese is an
> enemy. . . . All intelligence agencies must face this
> sinister background.
>
> —General Headquarters, United States Army
> Forces Pacific, Military Intelligence Section, General
> Staff, 1945

> In Japan we have been aiming at establishing a
> military intelligence system which can continue
> to operate effectively even after Japan becomes a
> sovereign nation.
>
> —General Matthew B. Ridgway, 14 April 1952

Japan's intelligence failures in the Asia-Pacific
War contributed to the new strategic environment that, in turn, drove the
subsequent transformation of each element of Japan's intelligence community. The subordination of Japanese foreign and security policy to U.S.
priorities set strict limits on the shape, pace, and direction of intelligence
reform. In the nearly half century from 1945 to 1991 during which Japan
was a junior partner to its conqueror, Japan's degenerated intelligence community became an undersized, compromised, and (still) organizationally
handicapped operation. Analysts have called Japan's Cold War intelligence
community "a stark transformation from the past" marked by sharp "discontinuity."[1] And a late Occupation period report by the CIA noted that "few
groups were as hard hit by the reversal in fortunes in 1945 as the intelligence
services."[2] Gotōda Masaharu, a powerful postwar advocate for strengthening
Japan's intelligence capabilities, recalled ruefully that when he was head of
the Analysis Department of the National Police Reserve (NPR), Japan's first
postwar military unit, "we did practically nothing [regarding intelligence].
It was natural to take guidance from the U.S. military."[3] Certainly Japan was
forced into an unprecedented position—accommodation to a foreign power
viewed by some intelligence professionals as capitulation.

Gotōda, who would become the central figure in Cold War Japan's intelligence community, helps us connect the dominance of U.S. intelligence and

the atrophy of Japan's capabilities to the fact that Japan's postwar intelligence community—like its political and bureaucratic classes more generally—also had to accommodate to another, equally powerful force: the emergence of antimilitarist norms in a restructured, democratic political system. In his memoirs, Gotōda remarks that throughout the Cold War, Japan remained "complacent about peace" (heiwa boke) and that "[without] rabbit ears [for listening at a great distance] . . . Japan would not survive the rough-and-tumble of international affairs."[4] He, and others who wished for a more muscular recovery from defeat, felt hamstrung by a postwar national discourse that placed blame on the military for dragging Japan into national catastrophe and placed hope on democracy to ensure there would be no revival of Japanese aggression abroad or surveillance at home. He was reacting to the popular consensus that quickly emerged in support of Japan's new pacifist constitution—even at the cost of relying on the United States for protection. Indeed, this became the central pillar of Japan's postwar national security strategy, the Yoshida doctrine.[5] What Gotōda and his allies viewed as Japan's "complacency" would change slowly. But as we shall see, this meant that for much of the Cold War the Japanese intelligence community had to keep a low profile—even by the standards of its own secretive profession.

But as in much else related to postwar Japan—and without understating how much changed—there was also considerable trans-war continuity in the intelligence community.[6] For one thing, many otherwise discredited intelligence professionals found ways to survive with the enthusiastic support of their conqueror, and many of the covert groups they led behaved in surprisingly familiar ways.[7] Although the targets for collectors and demands on analysts shifted after Japan's defeat, the most important single factor shaping the postwar evolution of the Japanese intelligence community was the robust anticommunism that predated the Cold War. It was not an impossible stretch for Japanese political and military elites to pivot and embrace—and offer their services to—U.S. Occupation officials who were obsessed with fighting Soviet and Chinese communism. Nor, of course, was domestic counterintelligence anything new for them. They had failed in war but were eager to reinvent themselves for a new postwar order in which, freed from international responsibilities, they could narrow and refocus their efforts on a consensus enemy. For decades there would be no urgent need for autonomous strategic intelligence, so even if their embrace of the Americans was between unequals, resilient intelligence officials found a common cause and rationally accepted what was on offer from Washington—a cheap ride on national security. Their accommodations paved the way for a (not entirely) new and (only partially) improved Japanese intelligence community.

Resilience in Japan's Early Postwar Intelligence Community

This road was pocked by considerable uncertainty at first. At the war's end, groups of Nakano School–trained agents spirited away members of a collateral branch of the imperial family to protect the imperial line in case the Allies began executing the emperor and his immediate family. Other Nakano School graduates harbored Ba Maw, the head of Japan's puppet government in "liberated" Burma, who had sought asylum in mid-1945.[8] And still others buried caches of arms for possible insurgency operations. One such group did so to prepare for an assassination attempt on General Douglas MacArthur, the Supreme Commander for the Allied Powers. Omata Yōzō, a Nakano School guerrilla warfare instructor, ordered a subordinate to file an official report of his death in late August 1945.[9] He then took a fake name and, with a fabricated résumé, applied for an administrative job at MacArthur's general headquarters (GHQ) in order to acquire information about his daily schedule. Omata and his associates, hoping to put an early end to the Occupation, hid as much as 6 million yen in Nakano School cash, but abandoned their plot once it became clear they were under suspicion by Occupation authorities.[10]

Some intelligence officers, such as Arisue Seizō, the wartime chief of Imperial Army intelligence, were much shrewder. Arisue buried 100 million yen and weapons for an insurgency, but he also concealed sensitive documents that he could dole out to voracious U.S. (and Soviet) intelligence officials.[11] Arisue—described as a "very clever turncoat" by some Occupation authorities—brazenly showed up to welcome General MacArthur's advance party when it landed at Atsugi on 28 August 1945, and was there again two days later when MacArthur himself arrived. Arisue and selected subordinates gained even more than their freedom.[12] Many newly unemployed senior military officers and intelligence operators enriched themselves in the black market while cultivating relations with Occupation officials who became dependent on them for the designation of war criminals. They built trust with their conquerors and avoided arrest while constructing a network of like-minded patriots determined from the very beginning to resurrect the Japanese military from behind the smokescreen of service to the Allies.[13]

Their first, and most successful, target was the military intelligence (G-2) section of the Supreme Command for Allied Power (SCAP) and its main operational unit, the 441st Counter Intelligence Corps (CIC) Detachment. The 441st was commanded by General Charles Willoughby, a MacArthur acolyte untrained in intelligence who fancied it "a sort of FBI" that could collect evidence for the purge of Japanese wartime officials and for the impending war crimes trials. And as a "prophylactic" for the coming Cold War, he used its "observation units in every prefecture. . . [to hunt] communist agitators, saboteurs, and foreign espionage agents."[14] Surely the equal of SCAP's most complicated personalities, Willoughby was born Adolf Karl Weidenbach in Heidelberg to an American mother and a German father. He had served as a U.S. Army pilot in World War I and as an impromptu intelligence officer in the Philippines. Willoughby hit the ground running after communists in Tokyo—and never stopped, even after retirement, when he worked as a publicist for Generalissimo Francisco Franco.[15] His papers contain florid communications to Senator Joseph McCarthy and J. Edgar Hoover, declaring his commitment to their anticommunist crusade and his determination to root out "reds" within the Occupation administration.[16] Facing off against General Courtney Whitney, head of SCAP's Government Section, whom he viewed as too soft on liberal Occupationaires, Willoughby even ordered Japanese police to spy on SCAP officials in Whitney's office and to keep their reports secret from other U.S. authorities.[17] The two generals also fought over how to organize Japan's postwar police and even about the wisdom of democratizing Japan.[18] British analysts characterized Willoughby as "[just] the kind of militarist the Occupation was dedicated to destroying in Japan."[19] MacArthur called him "my loveable fascist."[20]

In early September 1945, just days after the surrender, and even before the 441st was operating, Willoughby began debriefing General Arisue with SCAP communications specialists who were eager to unlock Japan's military codes. Within weeks, apparently satisfied of Arisue's value—and despite reports that he denied even knowing of the existence of the Nakano School—Willoughby secretly enlisted the former spy chief to serve as intelligence gatekeeper for the "credulous" occupying army.[21] One American officer, speaking of Willoughby, recalls that "only the most rabid American militarists dared to embrace the recently disgraced military men of Japan."[22] While assisting in the interrogation of returning soldiers, Arisue protected friends and redirected Allied attention during the demobilization. He is best understood as the Japanese counterpart of Reinhard Gehlen, the resilient Nazi intelligence chief who survived by making himself invaluable to U.S. forces in postwar Germany.[23]

The Arisue-Willoughby tie, which would ensure Arisue's "rehabilitation" until Willoughby turned his attention to Korea in 1950, was built on more than mutual convenience. Although no unclassified documents seem to have survived the meeting—and although Willoughby's own account never mentions Arisue by name—they first met at a hastily arranged conference in Manila on 19 August 1945, just four days after the emperor's declaration of defeat, to discuss surrender and occupation procedures.[24] They had both served as military attachés in Mussolini's Rome—Willoughby received a decoration from Mussolini—and neither made a secret of his admiration for Il Duce.[25] Even better, they could communicate with each other in German, Willoughby's native tongue. Arisue, who impressed upon Willoughby his control of a "vast spy network" and his personal ties to the imperial household, was joined in Manila by the intensely anticommunist Kawabe Torashirō, a former deputy chief of the IJA General Staff and spymaster who had supervised covert operations in northern Europe, and who also spoke fluent German.[26] The Arisue-Kawabe tie—enabled by Willoughby—would become a principal feature of Japan's early postwar intelligence community.[27]

Indeed, the Manila meeting could not have gone better for Arisue, Kawabe, and their associates. Arisue was invited on 5 September to create his own intelligence unit within Willoughby's G-2, an opportunity he seized "with alacrity."[28] He was given an office in the Nippon Yusen Kaisha building

FIGURE 3.1 Spymaster General Kawabe Torashirō meets General Charles A. Willoughby in Manila in August 1945 to discuss surrender procedures.
Photo: U.S. Army Signal Corps, Courtesy of Harry S. Truman Library

FIGURE 3.2 General Arisue Seizō, the head of Japanese military intelligence, seems oddly relaxed on 28 August 1945 at the handover of the Atsugi army base. (Note the cigar in his right hand.)
Photo: U.S. National Archives (80-G-490415)

and allowed to hire a staff of two hundred Japanese—mostly his former subordinates in the IJA intelligence section—to help write the history of the Asia-Pacific War.[29] In addition to Kawabe, with whom Arisue maintained close ties, his motley crew of so-called historians included Tsuji Masanobu, identified by one historian as the "fanatical ideologue and pathologically brutal staff officer" who ordered the Bataan Death March and massacred civilians in China, the Philippines, and Singapore, and Watanabe Wataru, the former administrator of Malaya, infamous for his harsh treatment of Chinese captives and imposition of stern military administration (*gunsei*). Also helping out was Kodama Yoshio, the ultranationalist gangster and "outright thief," and many other equally unsavory types.[30] The history project was a convenient cover for a Japanese-run counterintelligence unit inside G-2 that would eavesdrop on communists both in Japan and on the continent.[31]

Unsavory or not, these were foxes in the SCAP henhouse. The Occupation soon found itself in a "one-sided marriage of convenience" and became dependent on the services of the well-protected Arisue and his new special duty unit, the Arisue Kikan. Freshly decommissioned Japanese military officers had, after all, better maps and deeper contacts in China and the Soviet Far East than the Allies. Although SCAP had the authority to order the surrender of documents, it instead purchased intelligence reports from the officers and many of the thousands of special duty unit staffers who "had run countless agents—White Russians, Chinese, Koreans and others—against the Soviet Union" and who now were back in Japan. Some had served in the Special Higher Police and other counterintelligence units at home, and had an equally deep knowledge of Japan's revolutionary underground.[32] Willoughby approved and paid for a great many of Arisue's schemes, as well as those of his associates, and their competitors. Willoughby justified this modus operandi in his final report on the demobilization of the Japanese armed forces in December 1945:

> Already communism is stretching its claws at the disillusioned, defeated millions of soldiers, sailors, and airmen. . . . [T]he employment, under our direct control, of former officers . . . is the only method by which we can hope to influence and control, indirectly and without publicity, the actions, thoughts, and philosophy of former members of the Japanese armed forces, and guide them into proper, conservative, law abiding attitudes.[33]

His Master's Voice?

But who was manipulating whom in this "tangled, morally ambiguous world?"[34] Although Occupation intelligence focused at first on nearly two dozen "subversive" right-wing societies, it soon shifted most of its attention to the Soviet Union, "Red" China, and left-wing groups.[35] Willoughby's Japanese proxies aggressively surveilled the Korean community in Japan—both those with sympathies toward the authoritarian South (Mindan) and those with sympathies toward the communist North (Chōsensōren).[36] They also actively monitored the trade unions and politicians of all stripes.

The most storied intelligence operation funded by G-2 and operated by Arisue, Kawabe, and their associates was undertaken in April 1949. "Operation Takematsu" was aimed at both foreign and domestic targets, and

General Willoughby was nominally its "supervisor."[37] One covert action called for agents in the southwest to infiltrate existing smuggling networks operating between Tsushima and the Republic of Korea. Seamen and fishermen were recruited to gather intelligence on Soviet shipping out of Port Arthur and to smuggle Japanese agents into South Korea. G-2 provided nearly 4 million yen for the purchase of a speedboat and acquisition of U.S. radio equipment, but it is not clear if it responded positively to Arisue's smug demand that his captured maps be returned to him.[38] Arisue, who was close to Chinese nationalists, supplemented this effort with funds from Taiwan to support a "Japan Volunteer Army" (Nihon Giyūgun) to assist Chiang Kai-shek's Kuomintang in continuing its fight against communist troops.[39] Although it was conceived by General Ugaki Kazunari in April 1948, operational leadership resided in the Arisue Kikan, as part of the amalgam KATO Kikan—so named for the prominence of Kawabe, Arisue, Tanaka Ryūkichi (a former commandant of the Nakano School), and Oikawa Genshichi (commander of the IJA's Twenty-third Division in the Philippines from 1942 to 1944). They were joined in this unofficial, but hardly trivial, operation by the Hattori Kikan under the leadership of Hattori Takushirō, whom Arisue had introduced to Willoughby and who, as the Kwantung Army's senior operations officer, had been a trusted aide to two of America's most devoted enemies—Ishiwara Kanji and Tōjō Hideki.[40]

In the north, plans were laid to establish an intelligence headquarters in Hokkaido, where repatriated Japanese POWs could be interviewed and recruited to establish smuggling routes under the supervision of General Arisue's brother Arisue Sansaburō. Kawabe's 6 million yen budget was earmarked for equipment such as radios, cameras, film, and invisible ink and larded with audacious requests for detailed information on specific U.S. intelligence targets, for office space within G-2 headquarters, and for a black limousine. He insisted that he needed only start-up cash from U.S. intelligence because the operation would become self-supporting with revenue from smuggling operations and profits from phony trading companies.[41] In this sense, Takematsu was modeled on the wartime "commercial cover" special duty units but provided more than mere cover for intelligence activities. The most prominent example, playfully named Mitsuboshi Trading, was staffed by former military secret police (Kempeitai) officers. Stood up in 1948 in Korea, Taiwan, and North China by former General Watanabe Wataru, the much reviled administrator of Malaya, it was taken over by Arisue in 1949 with the cooperation of the deeply corrupt Kodama Yoshio and with the support of G-2.

Takematsu's tentacles stretched in many directions. Arisue and Kawabe—sometimes under the banner of the Arisue Kikan and other times under the banner of the Kawabe Kikan—planted agents inside the Indian and Pakistani governments; they established spy rings within Manchuria and North Korea, placed anticommunist Korean residents inside the North Korean military, and—as noted earlier—recruited "volunteers" (many former Kempetai officers) to work with Guomindang nationalists on Taiwan.[42] Takematsu sponsored similar operations to fight communists with G-2 support by infiltrating agents into the Philippines and Indochina and by exploiting commercial connections.[43] Although Japanese agents in Korea are properly credited with helping guide MacArthur's famous Inchon landing, the Takematsu operation generated limited actionable intelligence.[44] Indeed, little came of it beyond the enrichment of its operatives and their temporarily enhanced standing among crypto-militarists. Michael Petersen calls it "an elaborate scam . . . that deceived its U.S. paymasters," and one U.S. counterintelligence official dismissed it as "nothing more than a high level shakedown."[45]

It may have been that, but it also was more. Takematsu and other early Japanese intelligence operations were designed in part to serve as a cover for Japanese remilitarization.[46] A detailed report by the CIA in May 1951 concluded that the real goal of the various special duty unit leaders was "not intelligence operations nor even the establishment of a Japanese Intelligence Service, but a buildup of political power and re-creation of the Japanese armed forces."[47] Kimura Takeharu, a senior intelligence official in the postwar Ground Self-Defense Force (GSDF), recalled rather disingenuously that he and his Nakano School classmates met secretly during the Occupation "to protect and maintain the body politic" (kokutai wo goji suru). He also acknowledged membership in a pan-Asian political organization, a resurrection of imperial dreams, which he insisted unconvincingly was "neither left nor right, but a third peaceful way."[48] A declassified 1949 CIA report says that while Arisue was working for G-2, he was also guiding a so-called National Restoration Society (Minzoku Fukkokai) as part of his effort to restore the military. The CIA called the group a "terrorist organization" and said that while the Arisue Kikan developed plans for remilitarization and designed the National Police Reserve as a "constabulary Army" at G-2's request, it also actively collected intelligence on the United States and the Soviet Union.[49] A contemporaneous U.S. counterintelligence report of unspecified provenance declared, "It is doubtful whether General Willoughby's trust in Arisue is justified."[50]

Ironically for an operation designed around counterintelligence, Willoughby's activities were compromised in a great many ways, and it was not clear if he understood the extent to which all sides were being played by all players against a vanishingly small middle.[51] In October 1945, for example, when the

Soviet spies Max Klausen and his wife were released from jail, Willoughby remarked that "the unhappy thought that a Soviet spy who had worked against the Japanese might later work against the United States had not yet occurred to many Americans."[52] Yet it is hard to imagine that this same "unhappy thought" had not occurred to Willoughby regarding former Japanese spies on his own payroll. Or perhaps he willingly suspended disbelief. After all, recently defrocked Japanese intelligence officers in his employ knew of (and may have helped procure) Willoughby his mistress, Araki Mitsuko, the wife of a Tokyo University professor who was serving as liaison for GHQ to the Imperial Household Agency.[53] But the problem was much larger than that. According to Petersen: "Reliability problems plagued U.S.-financed Japanese intelligence operations throughout the Occupation. . . . Japanese operators regularly deceived their U.S. paymasters. . . . Arisue and Kawabe used their connections to Willoughby to funnel high level information about U.S. military interests not only to the Chinese, but also back into the Japanese underground."[54] And, he adds, although some of the information was valuable, a great deal of it included "outright fabrications," inaccurate assessments, and operations that "often degenerated into nothing more than theft from U.S. authorities."[55]

In May 1951, after Willoughby's and MacArthur's monumental failure to grasp the significance of entire Chinese divisions in Korea led to their dismissals, and as the resumption of Japanese sovereignty neared, the CIA—which had been distrusted and unwelcomed by MacArthur—took stock of Willoughby's nurturing of Japan's postwar intelligence community. Its first conclusion was harsh: Japan's early postwar intelligence was best understood as a valuable means of livelihood for a disparate collection of ideologically driven displaced agents whose "independent and often conflicting operations [were] chiefly concerned with plans for a nationalist (Rightist) resurgence." Little of the rest of the evaluation was any more positive. The report found that the same weaknesses that plagued wartime Japanese intelligence persisted: poor security, undisciplined personnel, political interference, and subversion by secret societies. The CIA also observed that there had been a decline in professionalism in the Japanese intelligence community due to the flood of opportunists eager to sell information to Occupation authorities who were eager and able to pay for it.[56]

Apart from several large, well-organized groups "supported by U.S. agencies"—such as the Maritime Safety Agency, precursor to the Japan Coast Guard, which was used by the U.S. military to surveil and photograph Soviet warships—little was coherent. Certainly nothing was centralized—either clandestine or open—in Japan's early postwar intelligence community.[57] Moreover, many of the U.S.-supported units were seen as collaborationist and hence lacked legitimacy. The report concludes pessimistically, but with surprising (if imperfect) prescience: it predicted that the Japanese government would not be able to build a centralized intelligence service and that it would have to rely on competing agencies run by the police, and by a future army and navy—services that would have to depend on "powerful unofficial groups, mostly unfriendly to us," that would serve as operations units. The "resultant official Japanese intelligence agencies will be . . . plagued by lack of funding, and have the organizational weaknesses of [their] prewar counterparts." And for good measure, the report concluded that these services would be "vulnerable to penetration and subversion."[58]

In short, early postwar intelligence provided a good living for some and a prospective power base for others. Survival, reinvention, and anticommunist agitation all met at—and were nurtured by—General Willoughby's G-2. For many, this turbulent and uncertain time provided little more than a flimsy cover for political ambition, the long-awaited chance to betray political competitors, the opportunity to profit from criminal activities, and the prospect of rebuilding Japan's military power on the regional—and global—stage. Willoughbitis had left the Japanese intelligence community badly in need of reconstructive surgery.

Recovering from Willoughbitis

Apart from sweeping up and replacing some broken china in Japan's already crowded—but still incoherent and unsanctioned—postwar intelligence cabinet, General Willoughby's reign had limited impact on the subsequent development of the Japanese intelligence community. After Willoughby and MacArthur turned their attention to Korea in 1950, Arisue and others whom G-2 had favored quickly fell from grace. Arisue had openly flaunted his connections to Willoughby and now could openly be condemned as a "comprador strategist" (*baiben seisakusha*) and ostracized by members of competing groups with similarly oversized nationalist ambitions.[59] One such ambition, his public call for Japanese rearmament was too much for his longtime comrade Kawabe, who disavowed the idea and broke from him.[60] Arisue's organization, meanwhile, had been penetrated by Chinese agents and was no longer of much use to the Occupation, which now labeled him an "Armyist-Bourbon Militarist" (as compared to so-called "Navy–Foreign Office Moderates").[61] In the event, only one of Willoughby's handpicked collaborators from the imperial Japanese military—Sugita Ichiji, who was appointed head of the GSDF guerrilla warfare training school—became a leader of the postwar Japanese intelligence community.[62]

Perhaps the most prominent case in point was that of Arisue's trusted deputy Hattori Takushirō. Much like Willoughby, Hattori had at best a spotty relationship to intelligence that did not seem to hurt him on the way up. After neglecting to take responsibility for his failures at Nomonhan in 1939, he became the chief of operations and was blamed by some for Japan's 25,000 casualties in the shattering defeat at Guadalcanal in 1942–43. He thereupon was again promoted, this time to serve as Prime Minister Tōjō's aide.[63] Willoughby made the ruthlessly ambitious (and famously fawning) Hattori head of his "hidden general staff," with responsibility for helping SCAP prepare for an imagined coming war with the Soviet Union and, later, for designing Japan's future military.[64] Hattori, who had been on the payroll of the Willoughby-Arisue "history" project, had "systematically withheld significant documents from the project. . . [which] he intended to use for his own 'true' history," a glorifying account of Japanese wartime heroism and virtue free of inconvenient facts which he hoped would inspire military recruits with Willoughby's support.[65] He left the Takematsu operation to Kawabe and Arisue, and focused instead on lobbying for the revival of the Japanese military.

In the summer of 1950, Willoughby asked Hattori to design the National Police Reserve, which would be the forerunner of Japan's Self-Defense Forces (SDF).[66] Hattori accepted the job but moved directly to create a new Japanese military instead, with a "shadow general staff" and thousands of pre-designated officers ready to take command of a well-equipped, reborn Japanese military with four divisions.[67] Already distracted by the war in Korea, Willoughby recommended eight former military officers for senior NPR posts (including Hattori as commander in chief). The U.S. Army colonel assigned to stand up the NPR recalled that Willoughby, who "may have imbibed too heavily of the heady wine of infallibility that flowed so freely [in SCAP]," threw a spanner into the works: "Completely out of sympathy with announced policy, Willoughby was determined from the very beginning to bring Imperial military officers into the NPR—purge or no purge."[68] But Chief Cabinet Secretary Okazaki Katsuo and Prime Minister Yoshida Shigeru rejected them all for having been confidants of Tōjō Hideki.[69] In subsequent testimony, Hattori reports having been disappointed when "as it happened I was not permitted to take the initiative in establishing the National Police Reserve and leading it myself, in spite of my efforts."[70]

But the politics were more complicated than this suggests. Hattori was a political ally of Hatoyama Ichirō, the purged rival of the former diplomat Yoshida Shigeru, who was then prime minister with strong U.S. support.

Yoshida had consolidated some power within the Occupation outside the Willoughby orbit and was not reticent in reaching out to him for help creating a Japanese CIA. By then, Willoughby was focused on Korea, and Hattori was out in the cold. Whether because Hattori blamed Yoshida for stymying his personal ambitions by shutting down the Hattori Kikan after General Willoughby's portfolio shifted, whether because Hattori was determined to clear the path for a Hatoyama premiership, or whether because Yoshida passed over him and made Tatsumi Eiichi his principal security adviser with instructions to break off all ties to Hattori, Hattori may have taken matters into his own hands.[71] According to a declassified CIA report, in July 1952 he organized a group of former military officers active in the rearmament movement and began plotting Yoshida's assassination and a coup d'état.[72] Petersen reports that the nefarious Tsuji Masanobu talked Hattori down from that ledge, noting the irony by which "America's staunchest political ally in Japan [was] being protected by one of Japan's most well-known alleged war criminals."[73]

The Japanese intelligence community evolved from a number of non-Willoughby-related, but vigorously competing, initiatives that got under way well before the end of the Occupation. Representatives of the former military, the Foreign Ministry, and the police each issued "detailed plans and compromise arrangements regarding the establishment of a future Japan Intelligence Service."[74] Each of the Japanese claimants vied with the others to reinvent itself as a—preferably *the*—Japanese government intelligence service.[75] But each proposal engendered a new round of competition and redesign, resulting in new levels of policy incoherence. During the Occupation the priority was counterintelligence, and three different police organizations—the National Rural Police, the metropolitan police of major cities, and the Special Investigations Bureau of the Ministry of Justice—directed their attention toward the Japan Communist Party (JCP), Chinese communists in Japan, and Korean residents. Nationalist groups lobbied for creation of a fourth, military counterintelligence unit within the NPR. In 1949 the government introduced a bill in the Diet that would amalgamate the first three of these units into a single FBI-like agency, but it was withdrawn in the face of concern by opponents that it would act like the wartime Kempetai. SCAP scrubbed the various police units of those who might be "ideologically unsafe," especially after members of the JCP's Central Committee were tipped off and disappeared ahead of their pending arrests in July 1950.[76] And in December the Japanese government moved—this time without seeking Diet approval—to create the Special Investigations Bureau within the Ministry of Justice.

Producing an Unproductive Cold War Intelligence Community

Given the vacuum created by the abolition of the imperial Japanese military and the post-Willoughby marginalization of some of its more ambitious survivors; given that counterintelligence and counterterrorism seemed far more urgent national security challenges than the collection and analysis of foreign information; and given that moderate Japanese leaders wanted to keep a lid on a right-wing military resurgence, it is easy to reconstruct a clear path for the National Police Agency (NPA) to prevail in the bureaucratic competition to lead Japan's postwar intelligence community.

The first institutional manifestation of the NPA's leadership was the creation of the Cabinet Research Chamber (Naikaku Sōridaijin Kanbō Chōsashitsu—CRC) with a small staff in April 1952, shortly before the end of the Occupation.[77] The basic idea was that an office be in place to collate and analyze the intelligence collected at home and abroad by the various line agencies of the Japanese government. But it was more important to Prime Minister Yoshida that it be ready for upgrading when the time was ripe.[78] With step one completed and sovereignty restored, Yoshida and his chief cabinet secretary, Ogata Taketora, wasted no time. They hatched an ambitious plan—a joint effort by Yoshida's government and the United States to create a Japanese CIA. After studying foreign intelligence organizations to identify an appropriate model, Ogata accepted the recommendation of Willoughby's shadowy deputies Jack Canon and Yeon Jeong and opted to establish the new unit under the direct management of the prime minister.[79] Ogata wanted Murai Jun, chief of the NPA's Security Section, to be its first director. The CIA would provide the financial assistance.[80]

Believing that a nation with a weak military ought at least to have long ears, Yoshida and Ogata sought to establish an intelligence unit that would not only integrate other agencies' raw data but also establish its own robust SIGINT, OSINT, and HUMINT capabilities.[81] This CIA-like apparatus would be staffed by three hundred technicians, including journalists recruited from the private media who could collect and analyze intelligence independently of the other services.[82] Yoshida asked Tatsumi Eiichi, who had been interrogating Japanese survivors of Soviet internment camps for General Willoughby, to secretly recruit veterans who would form the basis for this future "Intelligence Bureau" (Jōhō Kyoku).[83] Within two years, Tatsumi's secret wing in the CRC, code-named Rikurinkai or Miyako Kikan, had recruited fewer than thirty intelligence officers specializing either in the Soviet Union or in China, one of whom, Higure Nobunori, later was discovered to be a Soviet agent.[84]

Despite the considerable political muscle being applied to make this happen—and despite the influence that Yoshida still wielded within MOFA—the plan failed. Foreign Minister Sono Akira insisted that the CRC be limited to domestic intelligence activities, and both MOFA and the Ministry of Justice submitted their own counterproposals. Meanwhile, the media and the left also opposed the plan—especially one that would enhance HUMINT capacity provided by Nakano School graduates and run by former Home Ministry bureaucrats who had supervised the repressive Special Higher Police. In a harbinger of future confrontations between civil society and the intelligence community, they feared this would be the first step on the slippery slope to remilitarization and suppression of civil rights.[85] Yoshida's plan came unraveled just as his base within the Liberal Party was eroding as a result of the return to politics of his nemesis Hatoyama Ichirō. Nor were his ambitions helped when Arisue and Higure—likely on behalf of MOFA—helped bring down Murai in the so-called Black Market Dollar Incident, when he was found with $3,000 in cash under his shirt while visiting London at Yoshida's request in August 1953.[86] Without sufficient political capital to complete this ambitious intelligence reform, Yoshida abandoned collection and scaled back the CRC to focus on analysis alone.[87] Ogata reduced the CRC budget to one tenth of the initial request, ensuring that, as one analyst later remarked, a coherent, centralized intelligence function would be "conspicuously missing" in Cold War Japan.[88]

Given persistent bureaucratic and public resistance to empowering a full-service intelligence agency—and without national legislation that would legitimate it—this new Cabinet Research Office (Naikaku Jōhō Shitsu) had to operate at the whim of the chief cabinet secretary, which rendered it politically vulnerable. Indeed, it was also reportedly politically active on behalf of its current Liberal Democratic Party (LDP) overlords. The Cabinet Research Office was rumored to have spent time and resources investigating scandals involving politicians from rival party factions, and in that respect it may have been subordinating its national security function to a domestic political one. Its staff comprised mostly a token number of secondees from other agencies, and, despite several efforts to establish a "proper" (formal) career path for its own employees, neither it nor its successor after 1986, the Cabinet Intelligence and Research Office (Naikaku Jōhō Chōsa Shitsu—CIRO), would have permanent staff at the senior management level.[89] It did little more than collect OSINT and coordinate information supplied by line agencies—when they were willing to provide it. The NPA always supplied its director general, and along with MOFA and the Japan Defense Agency (today the Ministry of Defense), it dispatched intelligence officials to the cabinet. Each agency reserved the prerogative to bypass it when communicating with policy makers. The result was the all too familiar stovepipes in which directors of the cabinet intelligence office often could not even read MOFA cables.[90] Often referred to as "Japan's CIA," CIRO was anything but. It has also been referred to as "a laughing-stock" (*waraigusa*) and as "the world's worst intelligence unit" (*sekai saitei no jōhō kikakan*).[91]

While several powerful postwar political leaders had a hand in intelligence reform, it was Gotōda Masaharu, the former Home Ministry police official who was chief cabinet secretary for Nakasone Yasuhiro at the time of the 1986 reform (having earlier served as deputy director of cabinet intelligence), who worked hardest to create a comprehensive intelligence organization during and after the Cold War.[92] Gotōda was a skilled administrative infighter with a national vision who was implacably opposed to bureaucratic sectionalism and the LDP politicians who enabled it. He was widely respected for his toughness and for elevating national over bureaucratic or political interests. One of his lieutenants recalled using him as a "lion's skin"—threatening fractious ministry officials that he would bring their problems to Gotōda himself for resolution. Often the threat of doing so was enough to settle the bureaucratic infighting.[93] By the late 1980s, Gotōda was possibly the most powerful politician in Japan, and although he declared often that "policy coordination" was his greatest challenge, even he could not claim much success.[94] In his memoirs, Gotōda described Japan's underdeveloped intelligence community as "reckless" (*nonki*), "insubstantial" (*hinjyaku*), and "incompetent" (*muryoku*).[95]

A generation later, Machimura Nobutaka was Gotōda's successor as the leading politician advocating for intelligence reform. The son of a wartime director general of the Public Security Bureau of the Home Ministry who had been responsible for Japan's Special Higher Police, he too pulled no punches: "Compared to the CIA, CIRO was about the equal of a nursery school."[96] CIRO operated under considerable legal constraints—including a ban on the dispatch of HUMINT assets abroad—that rendered it "hollow" and "barely functional as an intelligence apparatus during the Cold War."[97] Instead of a centralized intelligence authority, an ineffectual Joint Intelligence Committee (Gōdō Jōhō Kaigi) was created in 1986 for intelligence coordination across the relevant units in the Japanese intelligence community. The committee—comprising vice minister– and deputy vice minister–class officials supported by their bureau chiefs—met only twice monthly. The prime minister would be briefed by the CIRO director just once weekly. Historian Kotani Ken bluntly labels this reform "clearly a case of design error."[98]

FIGURE 3.3 Chief Cabinet Secretary Gotōda Masaharu (right), who was determined to realign Japan's stovepiped intelligence community, with Prime Minister Nakasone in 1984.
Photo: The Mainichi Newspapers

Although the NPA won these early postwar bureaucratic turf wars, and was assigned expanded counterintelligence and counterterrorism functions, it never achieved CIA-like capabilities or status. It was authorized to hunt domestic terrorist groups as well as foreign-inspired ones in a target-rich environment. Although homegrown leftists were deemed the greater threat during the Cold War, there were still a great many right-wing conspiracies in the first decade after the end of the Occupation. So it was not too odd when, in December 1961, the NPA first invoked the Subversive Activities Prevention Law to disrupt a nascent coup d'état led by an ultranationalist Imperial Japanese Army veteran, Kawanami Toyosaku, who had first been arrested in the right-wing "May 15 Incident" in 1932. Now, Kawanami's ragtag group of Imperial Army veterans, students, and a small number of loosely affiliated SDF members dedicated themselves to "sav[ing] the nation from leftist plots" by assassinating Japan's political leaders and destroying the Diet building under the banner of "no taxes, no war, and no unemployment"—the so-called "Three Noes Incident" (*sanmu jiken*). The police confiscated a cache of rifles, grenades, swords, and armor, as well as printed materials related to the May 15 Incident. It may not have been a major threat to the commonweal, but twenty-two were arrested, twelve were indicted, and eight were convicted.[99]

From the start it was fixed that an NPA official would always sit atop CIRO, while a MOFA secondee could rise only to deputy director.[100] In fact, CIRO became one of several organizations supervised by senior NPA officers: a police officer is always second in command of the cabinet's Satellite Intelligence Center, another always directed the SIGINT unit inside the Japan Defense Agency (JDA), and a fourth has always been in charge of the Public Security and Investigation Agency's First Intelligence Department. Still, it would be twenty more years before the NPA would have its own Second Foreign Affairs and Intelligence Division.

The Public Security Intelligence Agency (Kōan Chōsachō—PSIA), an investigative unit in the Justice Ministry, was also in the bureaucratic scrum vying for a leading role in the postwar intelligence community. Inheriting the roles and mission of a series of counterintelligence units stood up by Occupation authorities (and their prewar progenitors), the PSIA was created in July 1952 under the terms of the same highly contested Subversive Activities Prevention Law.[101] Before then, as the Public Security and Investigation Bureau, it was charged with rooting out rightists by General Whitney and the socialist prime minister Katayama Tetsu. After becoming a full agency, however, the PSIA turned its attention to the communists at the direction of Prime Minister Yoshida. Following the Willoughby-Arisue model, it was staffed by returnees from across the former empire—including nearly two dozen Nakano School graduates with espionage experience who had somehow either avoided arrest or been de-purged.[102] As with the NPA, the PSIA's primary jobs were counterintelligence and counterterrorism—to monitor communists, Pyongyang-affiliated Korean residents, rightists, and labor unions at home. But unlike the NPA—and unlike the FBI, with which it is often compared, the PSIA was provided no authority to issue subpoenas or to make arrests.[103] And, like CIRO, it was thinly staffed—mostly with lawyers who had little experience interacting with senior policy makers rather than with intelligence professionals who had analytical skills. The PSIA training center in Tokyo eschewed both analytical and physical training, focusing instead on "law and some basic training in tradecraft."[104] This apparently came in handy when PSIA officials discovered that the CIA had stationed thirteen careless "non-official cover" agents in Japan who had to be repatriated.[105]

This success, having been directed in an embarrassing direction, did not likely count for much. The PSIA survived in large part thanks to powerful political advocates. The first director of its Soviet section was Hatano Akira, a future LDP strongman who was an ally of Gotōda Masaharu, with whom he served in the wartime Home Ministry, and who served as justice minister in the Nakasone administration. Their protection was helpful, since the PSIA periodically had to defend itself against administrative reforms that might have forced it to merge with the NPA. Its defense was that "every country separates law enforcement from intelligence and that even within the intelligence domain, duplication is normal and necessary."[106] Protected, but never fully respected, the PSIA limped along for several decades focused on leftists at home. Its small number of agents stationed abroad—mostly in eastern Europe, Southeast Asia, and Korea—were charged with monitoring connections between the international communist movement and domestic communists. According to one PSIA official, "the JCP has always criticized the PSIA, but we maintain that it was—and still is—dedicated to overturning our constitutional form of government."[107] As we shall see in the next chapter, this raison d'être began to fade after the Cold War, and after its very visible counterterrorism failure vis-à-vis the Aum Shinrikyō cult, the PSIA had to be reinvented. In a classic case of reform following (and rewarded for) failure—and with its political protection unfaded—the PSIA was assigned a broader international mandate.

As we have seen, the Foreign Ministry was also eager to get back into the game. During the Occupation, when intelligence was still a disreputable endeavor undertaken by many disreputable characters, a MOFA adviser, Horiuchi Ganjo, secretly ran an unofficial Far East Affairs Research Society involving ex-*zaibatsu*[108] officials and politicians associated with Yoshida's bête noire, the purged Hatoyama Ichirō. In the spring of 1950, while running for the Diet, Horiuchi secretly organized a group of section heads within MOFA's Research Bureau whom he identified as future leaders of Japan's intelligence community, as part of a plan to create a new CIA-like organization that he would direct on behalf of MOFA.[109] Hedging his bets, he also began to lobby friends in the former imperial military for campaign support. When he lost the election, he lost control of both the former military officers and the MOFA section heads.[110]

MOFA's postwar intelligence efforts were scaled back considerably after this false start and the creation of the CRC. During the Occupation, MOFA's intelligence activities had focused nearly entirely on analysis of open source information in its Research Department (Chōsakyoku).[111] To facilitate this, MOFA revived a widely used OSINT product called Radiopress that it first launched in 1941 as its Radio Intercept Unit. Spun off in 1946 as a formally independent company, Radiopress, Inc., collected, transcribed, and distributed the texts of foreign broadcasts from communist countries, particularly the Soviet Union and North Korea, for government subscribers.[112] Despite employing just several dozen collectors, Radiopress produced reliable and valuable information throughout the Cold War, including details on the movements of high-level North Korean officials and details on Soviet industrial production. After the Occupation, MOFA's intelligence-related activities were transferred to its regional affairs bureaus, which relied on diplomatic cables from reopened Japanese embassies abroad.[113] Blocked from overseeing a centralized intelligence service, MOFA implemented a series of low-profile organizational reforms to enhance its intelligence capacity. In 1960, for example, the foreign minister's secretariat added a new Research Division (Chōsaka), and three years later MOFA established an International Documents Department (Kokusai Shiryōbu), incorporating the Chōsaka and creating a new Document Division (Shiryōka) under its umbrella.[114] Echoing past errors, and presaging future ones, in 1970 MOFA transformed that department into a Research Department (Chōsabu) housing both policy and analysis divisions.[115]

As is so often the case, visible failures stimulated incomplete reform, and MOFA's intelligence capacity lurched slowly toward coherence. After MOFA failed to provide the cabinet with adequate intelligence during a series of high-profile international events, particularly the 1979 U.S. embassy hostage crisis in Iran and the 1980 Soviet invasion of Afghanistan, the government's Administrative Reform Council issued a report recommending that MOFA's intelligence capabilities be strengthened.[116] Prime Minister Nakasone Yasuhiro, Chief Cabinet Secretary Gotōda, and senior MOFA officials such as Okazaki Hisahiko and Murata Ryōhei were determined that Japan should be able to generate more and better intelligence of its own.[117] MOFA's Research Department was upgraded to become the Intelligence and Research Bureau (Jōhō Chōsa Kyoku) with four departments: Intelligence, Planning, Analysis, and Research. Once again there were conspicuous design flaws; the new bureau contained a National Security Policy Office (Anzen Hoshō Seisaku Shitsu) which overlapped with both the planning and intelligence units and crossed the policy-intelligence divide by treading upon the jurisdictions of other policy units in MOFA. This arrangement, which was supposed to be modeled on the State Department's Bureau of Intelligence and Research, did not last a decade. In 1993, the units responsible for policy were relocated to a Comprehensive Foreign Policy Bureau (Sōgō Gaikō Seisaku Kyoku) to enable more "objective intelligence and analysis."[118]

CIRO, NPA, PSIA, and MOFA were not the only civilian offices with aspirations to grow their intelligence functions during the Cold War. Given Japan's mercantile foreign and security policy and its voracious appetite for foreign technology, it was natural that the Ministry of International Trade and Industry (MITI, today the Ministry of Economy, Trade, and Industry, or METI) would develop significant intelligence capabilities as well. This took many forms, including the 1958 establishment of the Institute of Developing Economies (Ajia Keizai Kenkyūjo—IDE), which focused on the collection and analysis of political and economic data on Asian economies. IDE, which was built on the foundation of the wartime intelligence and research unit of the colonial South Manchuria Railway, soon became the largest social science research institute in Japan specialized on developing economies. In its new incarnation, IDE actively collected and analyzed data on countries with which Japan did not have diplomatic relations, engaging, for example, in exchanges with the North Korean Research Institute for Korean Trade and Economies.[119] While the IDE was never formally linked to government intelligence units, its analyses were widely used by government officials.

But the largest and most effective of METI's commercial intelligence operations was established in 1951 as the Japan Export Trade Research Organization at the initiative of Kansai-area business leaders. In 1954, after a bureaucratic wrangle with MOFA, which attempted to block it from establishing offices in foreign capitals, it became the Japan External Trade Recovery Organization, and in 1958 it was repackaged as the Japan External Trade and Research Organization (JETRO). Invoking a military metaphor, a retired JETRO CEO recalls that MOFA was chary in sharing economic data with MITI: "We [MITI] were not getting enough arms from MOFA to fight the United States and western Europe, and MOFA was uncomfortable with JETRO expansion. So we arrived at a special relationship."[120]

JETRO's economic intelligence contributed to (and grew along with) the remarkable expansion of the Japanese economy during the Cold War. In 1958 JETRO maintained thirty-eight foreign offices, and by the end of the Cold War the number had nearly doubled to seventy-three. Hundreds of its officials and an equal number of local hires collected mostly open source data on local conditions regarding the full range of commercial activities—intellectual property, regulatory regimes, market forecasting, product design, technological developments to share with private firms. Officials acknowledge that they collect, analyze, and communicate foreign economic information for the government and private firms but are uncomfortable when Western and Japanese analysts identify JETRO as an intelligence unit. They insist that its work is open source and therefore "not spying."[121]

JETRO was only the largest and most visible of six different MITI units that conducted commercial intelligence on behalf of Japanese firms and economic policy during this period. Among the others were the research section of the Industrial Policy Bureau and the International Economic Affairs Department of the International Trade Policy Bureau. Occasionally MITI was caught abetting industrial espionage, as in 1981 at the height of U.S.-Japan "trade frictions," when Hitachi was found to be using Japanese government communications links while illegally acquiring confidential documents from a former IBM employee. In other cases, MITI's counterintelligence sensibilities left a great deal to be desired. In one instance, its export licensing office approved sale to the Soviet Union by Ishikawajima-Harima Heavy Industries of a large floating dock, nominally for use by the commercial fleet. The JDA later discovered that the dry dock was servicing nuclear submarines and an aircraft carrier for the Soviet navy.[122] Even more embarrassing—and even more damaging to the U.S.-Japan relationship—was MITI's earlier approval in violation of international export control rules of Toshiba Machine Tool's sale of multi-axis milling machinery used by the Soviet navy to fabricate quiet propellers that would enable the fleet to evade detection by the U.S. Navy.[123]

Cold War Military Intelligence

Of course, the Japanese military was also a major player in this highly balkanized Cold War Japanese intelligence community. Military intelligence wasted little time creating space for itself after the National Police Reserve was stood up in July 1950 and large numbers of U.S. forces moved to the Korean theater. Soon thereafter—even before sovereignty was returned to Japan—the NPR Training School (Keisatsu Yobitai Sōtai Gakkō) opened in Kurihama, where an initial class of twelve junior officers received instruction from Nakano School–trained faculty in a nine-month course in tradecraft, signals, foreign language, psychology and other topics.[124] Immediately after the CRC was stood up and sovereignty was restored, the 75,000-man NPR morphed into the 110,000-man National Safety Force, and an intelligence department with the anodyne name Second Department of the School of Services (Gyōmu Gakkō Dainibu) was established at Camp Kurihama and transferred to Camp Kodaira in Tokyo soon thereafter.

When the Self-Defense Forces were established in July 1954, the Kodaira school became the GSDF Intelligence Training Academy (Jieitai Chōsa

Gakkō).[125] Although its existence would not be revealed for another decade, an early commandant of the academy, Matsumoto Shigeo, recalls that its aim was to train and stand up a special forces–like unit with full-spectrum capabilities, "from collection to special operations."[126] In 1957 the training program was renamed the Tai Shinri Katei (Counter-Psychological Intelligence Program—CPI). Like its precursors, the CPI program aimed to educate and train commandos capable of both intelligence collection and special operations.[127] Its curriculum expanded to include strategic information, aerial photograph analysis, psychological warfare, foreign languages, infiltration training, handling communication equipment, and encryption and decryption.[128] CPI had more than ten instructors at any given time, including the famous special duty unit commander Major General Fujiwara Iwaichi, and a former Nakano School commandant, Yamamoto Kiyokatsu.[129] The school used textbooks modeled on those developed for the Nakano School, and its graduates planted seedlings of the invasive Chinese parasol tree (aogiri), famous for surviving the atomic bombing of Hiroshima, at the end of the nine-month curriculum to celebrate their accomplishments and pray for their future success.[130]

The "Soldiers of Aogiri" were being prepared for two specific missions. One was to fight a guerrilla war alongside civilians to defend Japan in case of ground invasion until the arrival of the main SDF force. With the assumption that the most likely invader would be the Soviet Union, the CPI program's guerrilla warfare training was located in the Nayori Camp, Hokkaidō, the northern region of Japan closest to the USSR. Their other mission, based on the public security emergency provision in Article 78 of the Self-Defense Forces Law, was to suppress violent demonstrations in the capital and other major cities.[131] Both were domestic operations; its formal remit acknowledged no foreign activities.

In fact—and not surprisingly, given the nature of the enterprise—very little has ever been published about the GSDF's main intelligence unit, the Ground Staff Office Intelligence Department (Rikubaku Dainibu, or G-2), which supervised these activities. Nor does the public know much about the several other intelligence organizations within the staff offices, the civilian bureaus of the JDA, the counterintelligence corps, or the intelligence training school. In its early years, many senior officers in this new G-2 were former Home Ministry (police) officials, and the entire operation was overseen by the JDA's Internal Bureaus (Naikyoku) by officials seconded from the NPA.[132] The flow of intelligence professionals from the training academy was at first just a trickle, so the G-2 was established with only ten JDA/SDF professional analysts, only one of whom specialized in China.[133] According to one early G-2 chief, Tsukamoto Katsuichi, even by the end of the SDF's first decade, there were only forty or fifty analysts overall, and he laments that his unit was "forbidden from spying."[134] His colleague Hirajō Hiromichi reports that Russianists across the various agency-embedded intelligence services met just once a month to compare notes.[135] One of the analysts reports that his SIGINT unit was trained entirely on public broadcasts regarding industrial and agricultural production, infrastructure construction, and forestry in the Soviet Union.[136] Another retired G-2 officer, Kiyomizu Hiroshi, recalls that when he was a Soviet specialist in the Ground Staff Intelligence Department in the early 1960s, he and the one other specialist depended on information from the military attachés of third countries, as well as on OSINT and SIGINT data provided by the GSDF's Central Data Unit (Chūō Shiryōtai), which had an adequate number of collectors but precious few country experts.[137] Those analysts in the new G-2 with wartime intelligence and in-country experience aged out over time, and their replacements came with less contextual—and, of course, without war-fighting—experience.[138]

In one sense, this hardly mattered. The heads of Japan's military intelligence units did not share their intelligence estimates with any office beyond their chief of staff and rarely met with one another or with the intelligence officials in the JDA's internal intelligence section (Chōsaka). According to one participant, when they did come together in their monthly "intelligence bureau chiefs' meeting" (Chōsa Buchō Kaigi), "it was little more than an informal social gathering [*shinbokukai*]."[139] It was not clear to the participants whether or not the various streams of their intelligence reports ever converged at the top level of the JDA—the offices of the administrative vice minister and of the director general—much less if consolidated versions were ever presented to the policy community.[140] This—and the fact that communications with CIRO and with MOFA were imperfect—may help explain why JDA officials were "caught off guard" by how quickly Non-Proliferation Treaty negotiations were concluded in 1968. Recently declassified documents reveal that they believed that the United States and the Soviet Union would not agree quickly—if at all—and Japan was unprepared for the fait accompli that forced its reluctant hand and made it impossible not to sign the treaty.[141]

Counterintelligence

The SDF's postwar G-2, like the Japanese intelligence community overall, was more active in counterintelligence. Two largely HUMINT-based Cold War counterintelligence Central Intelligence Corps (Chūō Chōsatai—CIC)— one in the GSDF and one in the Maritime Self-Defense Force (MSDF)—were created to coordinate with the PSIA and the NPA's Security Bureau (Keisatsuchō Keibikyoku), as well as with the U.S. Central and Defense Intelligence Agencies.[142] Since recruitment efforts for the Chōsatai had to be conducted under absolute secrecy, many initial recruits were Nakano School graduates who could serve as immediate assets.[143] Matsumoto Shigeo, a former Chōsatai chief, says that he hired Nakano School veterans because "their situation was pitiable," adding that "they had sacrificed for Japan and the United States had forced the police to investigate them. They were at risk and many had been in hiding after the war."[144] He notes that unlike in the United States, where being a communist was cause for dismissal and arrest, "communist spies" in the upper echelons of the SDF during the early Cold War years could not be arrested because the JCP was legal.[145] One former KGB major active in Japan during the 1970s recalls in his memoir that there was a wide "scope of opportunity to exploit Japan [because] Japanese counterintelligence is very weak," and an understanding that "we can use Japan as a base from which we can get anything we need." He recalls too that Japanese counterintelligence was "so pitifully short-handed that they couldn't follow me or any other suspect on a regular or routine basis," and judged it to be "sloppy."[146]

So, while Japan's Cold War counterintelligence had a number of successes (see table 3.1), it also had more than its share of better-known failures. In between there were a great many arrests that were accompanied by lenient punishment.[147] Japan came to be known as "spy paradise" in part because the Subversive Activities Prevention Law that had been introduced to replace wartime anti-espionage laws had no teeth.[148] Japanese journalists, politicians, and officials could cooperate with the Soviets with near impunity.[149] One early postwar case in point, the 1954 "Rastvorov Affair," involved a deputy minister for foreign affairs who had been turned by an Interior Ministry operative with diplomatic cover in the Soviet embassy, Yuri Rastvorov. Rastvorov ran spy rings for five different Soviet organizations: the Ministry of Internal Affairs, the Ministry of Foreign Affairs, the Tass News Agency, the Red Army, and the Soviet trade mission to Japan. He also controlled members of the Military Committee of the JCP, which was, until the 1960s, the Soviet Union's "main intelligence asset" in Japan.[150] Rastvorov's agents could be prosecuted only under the very weak National Public Service Law, the top punishment for which was just one year in jail and a thirty-thousand-yen fine—less than $100 at that time—and many were identified only after Rastvorov defected to the United States.[151]

The highest-ranking Japanese military officer to be caught moonlighting for Soviet military intelligence during the Cold War was Major General Miyanaga Yukihisa, a GSDF Soviet expert who was turned in 1973 after visiting the Soviet embassy in Tokyo to seek post-retirement job opportunities. A Soviet military attaché in Tokyo recruited General Miyanaga to provide classified JDA documents through his former subordinates still on active duty. After Miyanaga and two subordinates were arrested in 1980 for violating the Self-Defense Forces Law, he acknowledged receiving about 3.1 million yen in compensation for his cooperation with the Soviet embassy over the previous four years. The Miyanaga incident sent shock waves through the government and led to the resignations of the JDA director general and the GSDF chief of staff.[152]

But surely the most storied postwar Japanese counterintelligence failure involved Stanislav Levchenko, a former Russian KGB officer who defected to the United States in 1979 and revealed Soviet espionage activities in Japan to the U.S. Congress in July 1982.[153] Levchenko, who had been running agents in Japan, provided the names of dozens of Japanese who had helped the KGB, including Ishida Hirohide, a former LDP labor minister; Yamane Takuji, deputy chief of the *Sankei Shimbun*'s editorial department; Katsumata Seiichi, former head of the Japan Socialist Party (JSP); and several other former Diet members. He revealed that the USSR also subsidized several JSP publications and controlled lower-level diplomats and cipher clerks, whom they snared in "honey traps." Levchenko even claimed that "the KGB in the 1970s had been able to effectively control the political platform of the JSP, having recruited more than 10 of its high-ranking leaders as agents of influence."[154] He also ran Japanese agents who held senior government positions, such as two Foreign Ministry officials who provided him with a large number of secret diplomatic cables, and he paid academics and journalists in major dailies to use their close contacts with government officials and members of the Diet to collect information for the Soviets.

By late 1979, Levchenko claimed, the USSR had thirty-one agents and twenty-four "confidential contacts" in Tokyo engaged in collection, disinformation, and espionage.[155] He recalls how easy it was to "consistently extract a wealth of scientific, economic, and political data from Japan for use against the Japanese government."[156] In his congressional testimony, Levchenko identified a number of Soviet objectives: to preclude creation of an anti-Soviet triangle among Washington, Beijing, and Tokyo; to undermine political and military cooperation between Japan and the United States; to provoke bilateral political, military, and economic distrust; to discourage improved ties between Japan and the People's Republic of China (PRC); to nurture a pro-Soviet lobby among prominent Japanese politicians, starting with the LDP and JSP; and to foster closer Japanese ties with Moscow. As in the Rastvorov case two decades earlier, the Japanese government was unable to punish Levchenko's collaborators very stiffly, leading Levchenko to "declare" that Japan badly needed an anti-espionage law.[157]

In the event, though, the KGB "was never able to compete financially with the kickbacks on offer" from the United States and "never truly penetrated the commanding heights of Japanese conservative politics."[158] This was an American monopoly about which much is still classified. Although the CIA began operations in Japan in 1948 without either a corresponding Japanese unit or even the prospect of one, it was able to identify reliable sources of intelligence regarding both foreign policy and, especially, domestic Japanese politics. There is surely a great deal more to the relationship of relevance to the development of the Japanese intelligence community, not least because the CIA is reputed to have underwritten an entire generation of LDP politicians. None of this has been declassified, possibly because that generation's children and grandchildren—including prime ministers, deputy prime ministers, and foreign ministers—are still governing Japan in alliance with the United States.[159]

Musashi Kikan

One direct connection that can be documented—at least partially—was a Ground Self-Defense Force G-2 sub-unit known formally as the Ground Staff Second Department Special Unit (Rikubaku Dainibu Beppan), and known to its Japanese staff as the Musashi Kikan, a nickname redolent of the Asia-Pacific War kept secret from U.S. colleagues.[160] In 1954, U.S. Army commander John Edwin Hull sent a note to Prime Minister Yoshida suggesting that the GSDF and the U.S. Army jointly train military intelligence agents. Toward that end, in 1955 Tokyo and Washington initialed their first temporary intelligence-sharing agreement (Jōhō Renraku Kyōtei). They secretly stood up the Musashi Kikan with some two to three dozen experienced American and Japanese personnel (including members of Aogiri Gurūpu) at the U.S. Army's Camp Drake in Saitama. It was jointly operated by the U.S. Army's Military Intelligence Unit 500 and the SDF's Ground Staff Intelligence Department, and 80 percent of its funding came from the CIA through the JDA Internal Bureau's Intelligence Section (Naikyoku Chōsaka).[161]

By 1961, U.S.-Japan military intelligence cooperation seemed to have progressed smoothly, and the two sides agreed formally that their collaboration would extend from training and collection to operations. Japan was promised equal standing, but the existence of its operations unit would remain secret even to other units in the SDF.[162] The official explanation why the Musashi Kikan could not exist as part of the Ground Staff Office was fiscal:

its budget was earmarked for education and training activities only. But a former G-2 commander, Tsukamoto Katsuichi, argues it should have been formally recognized because intelligence was "a normal part of public policy."[163] Another of its former senior officers reports that the reason for having the U.S. and Japanese operatives on the same teams was "educational."[164] Who was educating whom in the Musashi Kikan was contested, though. The U.S. side maintained its customary tutelary posture, but Kimura Takeharu, a former chief of the CIC, insists that the Americans learned more from the GSDF analysts than vice versa, particularly about China.[165] Its organization chart reflects the notionally equitable balance.

Although the Japanese side would continue to insist that none of the operations would be "directly" foreign, that was not the case. Working mostly off

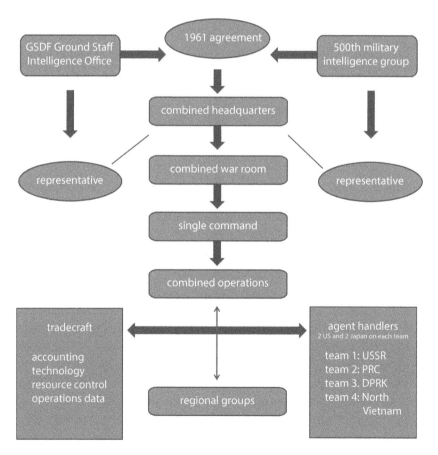

Figure 3.4 U.S.-Japan combined military intelligence operations after 1961
Source: Hirajō 2010. The original source used the term "joint" rather than "combined."

base in mufti, they monitored communists at home and across East Asia with a budget that became 50 percent Japanese in 1963.[166] The unit trained fishermen, trading company executives, travelers, and tourists. Musashi Kikan agents also collected intelligence—including photographs—from civilians whose foreign travel they subsidized, and from foreigners visiting Japan. It operated from "front offices," small photo studios and retail shops across Japan—six in Tokyo, three in Osaka, two in Sapporo, and one in Fukuoka. Its headquarters were in a nondescript building near Shinjuku Station, a nightlife district in Tokyo where the agents could indulge their nostalgia for wartime songs by frequenting "military cabarets."[167] At work they interviewed Japanese trading company employees and fishermen who had recently visited North Vietnam to learn of possible hostile activities against the United States or Japan. After Japan and the PRC normalized relations in 1972, agents went to the mainland to collect intelligence in cooperation with the Taiwanese government and its Ministry of National Defense.[168]

The personal account of one of its operatives, Ao Hiromasa, is particularly illuminating.[169] After graduating from the CPI program, Ao was assigned to the Musashi Kikan. Joining three colleagues, he began working from a residential apartment in Shinjuku, using employment at a Japanese think tank, the Uemura Economic Institute, as cover. His first mission was to investigate a small trading company called Shinten Bōeki (Progress Trading), a subsidiary of the large trading company Itōchū, suspected of having ties to the Soviet government through wartime connections of one of its directors, Sejima Ryūzō.[170] His second mission was to create a map of Nakhodka and Khabarovsk, which he accomplished by paying a Russian interpreter to travel there undercover on a lumber carrier. Ao also took advantage of a group of Japanese veterans headed to Khabarovsk to mourn for comrades who died in Soviet detention camps. Lying to her about his father's having died in Siberia, Ao asked a Japanese interpreter accompanying that group to snap photos of the graves and their surroundings.

Working in the Musashi Kikan, Ao grew increasingly skeptical about the virtue of sharing the information he collected with the U.S. military and CIA. In his view, continuing to do so would reinforce Japan's client status. Consequently, he petitioned his commander, Colonel Hirajō Hiromichi, for permission to create his own, independent service agency. Hirajō kicked the idea upstairs to the Ground Staff Office Intelligence Department. Six months later, Ao's petition was accepted. Ironically, however, creating a new special duty unit for the GSDF required him to resign as an officer and give up all benefits that would come with his military status, including salary, job security, and a pension. In July 1965, Ao officially left the GSDF and took responsibility for his Ao Kikan, which would report to the SDF Ground Staff Office.

Ao's first mission involved very delicate counterintelligence: he had to investigate the political leanings of high-ranking SDF officers. In order to enter their homes without arousing suspicion, he ran a small vegetable store inside a military housing complex. Ao claims that some of his most important work was political. In 1969 he and other retired military officers created an Association to Discuss National Defense, which organized exhibitions to support the GSDF and prevent the revival of anti-base demonstrations. With the endorsement of former prime minister Kishi Nobusuke and other high-level LDP politicians, including Finance Minister Fukuda Takeo, the LDP provided the group 10 million yen. The inaugural ceremony for its first exhibition was attended by Prime Minister Satō Eisaku, Finance Minister Fukuda, and Tanaka Kakuei, then LDP secretary general. It is not clear from where the LDP got these funds.

The Ao Kikan was also active in Thailand, China, and Taiwan. Ao's activities in Thailand from 1970 to 1971 were part of CIA-led anticommunism operations. In Taiwan, Ao was a member of a Japan Committee for the Assistance of the Republic of China, which was established in 1972 with thirty scholars and retired government officials to express their solidarity with Taiwan before Japan's diplomatic normalization with the People's Republic. Ao frequently visited China to collect intelligence. In Guangzhou, Guilin, and Hainan Island, for example, he verified which radio signals were reaching the mainland from Taiwan. While there he also collected local maps, train timetables, military publications, and statistical data. To support Ao's operations, the GSDF provided 2 million yen every month through a trading company called Yashima Bussan, run by a retired head of the Musashi Kikan, Uchijima Hiroshi. This was a small budget in absolute terms, but the budget of the Musashi Kikan during its heyday in the late 1960s amounted to just 1 million yen a month per agent, up from less than half that much earlier in the decade.[171] In all, Ao sent some 150 reports to the GSDF General Staff during thirty-seven years of service before his retirement in 1991.[172]

In April 1974 the JCP's daily newspaper, *Akahata*, revealed the existence of the Musashi Kikan, calling it a "shadow military" and generating Diet hearings and firm disavowals by the SDF and JDA.[173] The unit was renamed in 1978 and was moved out of Camp Drake to Camp Zama in Tokyo's western suburbs.[174] The exposé also stimulated a series of memoirs by Musashi Kikan principals, such as Hirajō, Matsumoto, and Ao, who wanted to justify their activities to the Japanese public.[175] The former CIC head Kimura Takeharu dismissed the suggestion that the secret *kikan* was a "shadow military," defending it rather curiously (and ineffectively) as more like a group of ninjas who had to remain in the shadows to be effective.[176]

Reports of the Musashi Kikan's secret activities were first discussed in the Diet during interpellations at the House of Councillors' Budgetary Committee in late April 1976, when a JCP representative, Ueda Kōichirō, attempted to gain confirmation of the *Akahata* scoop by asking why an SDF colonel, Uchijima Hiroshi, and his Japanese colleagues regularly worked at Camp Zama, a U.S. base, five days a week.[177] The JDA argued that Colonel Uchijima was simply a liaison officer who facilitated cooperation between the GSDF and U.S. military intelligence.[178] Following up in early May, Ueda again interrogated defense officials in the Diet, asking specifically why there were as many as twenty-six personnel assigned to the First Intelligence Section of the G-2 even though its officially declared (and legally sanctioned) staff size was only six. Ueda also pointed out that despite his senior rank, Colonel Uchijima was not leading the First Intelligence Section, which was taken as indicating that he was actually commanding another, secret section. Again the JDA maintained there was no such secret organization in the G-2.[179] After a year of further investigation, in March 1977 Ueda revealed the names of each of the Musashi Kikan's twenty-four members (as of November 1970) during a Diet session, drawing particular attention to connections between that group and the abduction of Korean politician Kim Dae-jung, which is explored in the next section of this chapter.[180] Again, his charges were met by official denials. Intensive debates on the same question followed at the House of Councillors' Budgetary Committee in April 1977, but Ueda was never able to elicit an official confirmation of the unit's existence.[181]

One of the more intriguing aspects of service in the Musashi Kikan was that it seemed to deepen anti-American sentiment in the Japanese intelligence community. Although Hirajō reports positively on the semiannual Japan-U.S. Intelligence Communication Conference (Nichibei Jōhō Renraku Kaigi), during which the U.S. side provided Japanese analysts with top secret U-2 IMINT on the Soviet Union that was kept secret from civilian officials, others were more negative.[182] Tsuboyama Kōzō, a former Musashi Kikan operative, resents that the unit was led by and for the U.S. military.[183] Kimura Takeharu, a former head of the CIC, claims that he refused repeated requests from Unit 500 at Camp Zama to cooperate because he "did not trust the Americans."[184] And, according to one former Musashi Kikan chief: "It would have been fine if the U.S. and Japanese agents had had good relations with each other, but the common fault of the Japanese was that they were deeply anti-American [*kenbei*]. There were many who said, 'I don't want to do this for America.'"[185] When asked about this, General Kunimi Masahiro, another retired GSDF intelligence officer and the first head of the Defense Intelligence Headquarters, refused to discuss the Musashi Kikan but allowed that "resentment of the United States varied by units. Those of us in uniform exercised with U.S. forces and had no problems."[186]

Technological Failures and Successes

There was much more to Cold War U.S.-Japanese intelligence sharing than covert operations. Technological collaboration was both more prominent and more consequential. The U.S. military began helping rebuild Japan's Cold War SIGINT capabilities as soon after the war as was practicable. GHQ created Japan's first postwar SIGINT unit in Ōi in Saitama Prefecture with members of the newly established National Police Reserve in 1950.[187] Soon after the Occupation ended and the CRC was stood up, Prime Minister Yoshida tasked its director, Murai Jun, to create "a special organization responsible for monitoring and deciphering encrypted communications of foreign countries including the Soviet Union and Communist China, in particular."[188] More sophisticated facilities were built in 1958, when the Ground Staff Office Intelligence Department Special Annex (Rikujō Bakuryō Kanbu Dainibu Besshitsu, or Nibetsu—G-2 Annex) was created with U.S. military assistance.[189]

With the aid of the U.S. Air Force, Nibetsu incorporated the GHQ-created SIGINT organization and used GSDF equipment to monitor Soviet, Chinese, and North Korean aero and maritime communications and to manage Japan's Base Air Defense Ground Environment (BADGE).[190] Effectively Japan's main SIGINT center, by the mid-1970s this unit operated nine listening posts, from Wakkanai in the north to Kikai Island in the south, with more than one thousand operators. According to one former commander of that unit, however, even that size was insufficient to monitor adequately all Soviet air traffic and ICBM tests.[191] As a result, Nibetsu/Chōbetsu staff—many of whom were cycled through CIRO, its nominal parent organization—often were forced to ignore the content of what they were intercepting in favor of simply counting the radio transmissions as a proxy for determining the location and intensity of Soviet activity.[192]

Japan's naval intelligence was also deeply connected to the U.S. military during the Cold War. After a U.S. submarine had an unfriendly encounter with a Chinese submarine in the Yellow Sea in the mid-1970s—fully four decades before the issue of collective self-defense came to wide public attention in Japan—the MSDF acceded to U.S. requests that it deploy an underwater sound surveillance system to monitor the mechanical noises produced by

Chinese ships and submarines.[193] Japanese sailors were trained in Hawaii, and MSDF submarines were provided American monitoring equipment. A few years later, in addition to monitoring Chinese naval activity, the MSDF began full-scale underwater operations against the Soviets. Areas for this activity included waters close to the Soviet coastline, leading a former chief of the naval staff to recall that "this was the riskiest operation we ever experienced." The submarine used for this operation returned to the headquarters of the U.S. Pacific Fleet every several weeks. In addition, airborne and surface naval surveillance was combined with underwater acoustic capabilities, and Japan's very able submarine fleet gave officers at the Ōwada communications facility in Kiyose—and at the U.S. Seventh Fleet—a clear "view" of Soviet traffic in neighboring waters.[194]

Japan's surveillance and SIGINT successes strengthened the alliance in substantive ways, while intelligence, surveillance, and reconnaissance failures predictably drove further reform of the Japanese intelligence community. Perhaps the best example involved yet another Soviet defector, who, in early September 1976, violated Japanese airspace and forcibly landed his MiG-25 jet fighter—the most advanced in the Soviet inventory—at a civilian airport in Hakodate, Hokkaido. Pilot Viktor Belenko, an elite military officer, immediately asked for political asylum in the United States. It was the first time a Soviet pilot had defected since 1945, and his doing so with a brand-new classified aircraft was an intelligence bonanza for the Allies. Washington approved the asylum request over Soviet protests, and Tokyo decided to dismantle the fighter to have its first close look at Soviet aeronautical technologies.

The MiG-25 incident revealed three major defects in Japan's air defense system. First, ground-based air defense radars could not see, much less identify, aircraft violating the Japanese airspace at low altitudes. Second, unlike the U.S. F-14 and F-15, the F-4, then Japan's top-of-the-line jet fighter, did not have look-down capabilities allowing it to search for lower-altitude aircraft from above. As a result, an F-4 scrambling from Chitose Air Base to warn the MiG-25 away completely lost the still unidentified fighter when it rapidly descended. Third, even if the Japanese air defense system had not lost track of the MiG-25, it still would have allowed the unidentified aircraft to land intact without anyone knowing its purposes for landing: Japan's defense personnel naïvely assumed that all air space violations were due either to mistakes or to emergency evacuation.

The incident also revealed several organizational defects in the Japanese intelligence and crisis management communities. First, the JDA director-general, Sakata Michita, received the initial report of the incident more than an hour and a half after the MiG-25 landed, and Prime Minister Miki Takeo only got the news a half hour later than that. These delays were compounded nearly to the point of a Keystone Kops parody by Japan's ubiquitous intelligence silos. Even though it was unclear whether the landing was hostile and constituted a threat to national security, when an air traffic controller at the Hakodate Airport notified the SDF of the landing, he was told that the incident fell within the Hokkaido Police Department's jurisdiction because it occurred at a civilian airport. Meanwhile, at the instruction of the NPA, the Hokkaido police denied SDF officers access to the scene.[195] The JDA soon changed its mind and declared this was its business because of the territorial violation; the Ministry of Justice claimed it was theirs as a matter of illegal immigration; the NPA insisted that it owned the issue because Belenko had fired his pistol into the air, making it a matter of public safety; and MOFA demanded control because Belenko was seeking to defect.

Then there was the matter of custody of the plane itself. The police wanted it under lost property laws; the Finance Ministry wanted it as a smuggled item; the Transport Ministry refused to take any jurisdiction because the MiG-25 was not a commercial aircraft; and MITI invoked the three military non-export regulations to decline Moscow's demands for its return. Perhaps most relevant, though, the entire Japanese government lacked the capability to transfer the MiG-25 to an SDF base for investigation and had to rely on a U.S. transport aircraft—but only after Satō Yukio, MOFA's Security Affairs Division director, steamrolled his MOFA colleagues who had declined to allow the U.S. military to inspect the plane out of a concern for relations with the Soviet Union.[196] In an attempt to conceal evidence of its widespread incompetence, the government ordered the SDF to dispose of all documents related to the MiG-25 incident. The chief of the ground staff, Miyoshi Hideo, resigned in protest, and the SDF in fact destroyed the documents in what has been called "one of the decade's most notorious events."[197]

Clearly this was not the finest hour for Japan's Cold War intelligence community, its command and control system, or its political leadership. But as we have seen repeatedly and as anticipated in chapter 1, failure stimulated reform. In the aftermath of the incident, the JDA decided to introduce airborne early warning aircraft as well as new fighters with look-down capabilities that can capture a full picture of aerial activity, evaluate it, and share it with all aircraft, surface vessels, and operations centers.[198] As one senior Ministry of Defense official explained: "The MiG-25 case taught us how good the Soviets were at knowing the blind spots in our air defenses. This led directly to the procurement of AWACS [Airborne Early Warning and Control System]."[199] According to Sassa Atsuyuki, a former director of cabinet security affairs, this incident also led to the purchase of over-the-horizon radar systems and the introduction of the F-15 to replace the F-4.[200] In addition, the Japanese government belatedly started discussions on whether to use force when, despite repeated warnings, unidentified military aircraft violate Japanese airspace.[201]

Japan's SIGINT capabilities were proven to be far more effective in an even more dramatic case, the 1983 Soviet fighter attack on a commercial jet that killed 240 passengers, 27 of whom were Japanese. Korean Airlines flight 007 was en route to Seoul from New York, via Anchorage, when it mistakenly entered Soviet airspace at about the same time that a U.S. RC-135 reconnaissance plane was in the area. Soviet Su-15 pilots were ordered to shoot it down without first confirming its identity. The Kremlin, which initially denied the attack, later insisted that the plane could not be identified with certainty as a commercial aircraft. What has been described as "a most retiring group of cryptologists" until then working secretly at the GSDF's G-2 Annex on the northern tip of Hokkaido, just across the Soya Strait from Sakhalin, intercepted and recorded the Soviet commands and their acknowledgment by the pilots—a conversation that transpired unencoded in natural language. After the intercepted communications were automatically shared with the U.S. Air Force, the tape was played at a meeting of the UN General Assembly, forcing Moscow to acknowledge its tragic error. Washington, for its part, insisted mistakenly that the Soviets knew they had ordered the downing of the commercial airliner.[202] As a measure of how sensitive Japanese intelligence cooperation with the United States was at that time, this decision—and the announcement by U.S. ambassador Jeane Kirkpatrick that she was releasing the communications "in cooperation with the government of Japan"—blew the cover of the G-2 Annex and apparently strained SDF's relations with the U.S. National Security Agency "for the better part of a decade."[203] Gotōda was furious that he had not been consulted.

Civilian SIGINT facilities were also expanded during the Cold War, for both collection and analysis. A section called "Yama"—homage to the Imperial Army's domestic surveillance unit after the invasion of China in 1937—in the NPA's Foreign Affairs Division operated multiple fixed monitoring facilities and also used mobile monitoring equipment loaded on trucks. Data collected by its foreign affairs technical investigators (gaiji gijutsu chōsakan) were analyzed in-house.[204] Although its existence and locations were never officially announced, Yama reportedly was headquartered in western Tokyo and served as the NPA's Second Radio Communication Center. There may have been at least fifteen NPA-run SIGINT facilities throughout Japan, including on SDF bases, and as many as four hundred technical officers monitoring

foreign ships operating near the coastlines.[205] It was these facilities that captured communications from a North Korean ship which provided evidence
that North Korea had been abducting young Japanese in the late 1970s, counterintelligence suppressed by both progressive and conservative politicians.[206]

Apart from its close connection to the NPA and its formal responsibility
for Chōbetsu's SIGINT activities, CIRO likely had its own Cold War SIGINT
capabilities, although their scale and scope remain largely unknown. According to a former Chōbetsu intelligence officer, for a time CIRO routinely deployed officials and eavesdropping equipment to the facility in Ōi to collect
non-military signals intelligence, but later ceased to do so for fear of public
criticism.[207] But it is known that it was one of CIRO's auxiliary organizations
that recorded the phone conversations in the hotel room from which Korean
opposition leader Kim Dae-jung was abducted by South Korean agents in
1973 (see the next section of this chapter).[208] MOFA is also believed to have
begun running a monitoring facility with four officials from its Information
and Communication Division in Funabashi City, near Tokyo.[209] For its part,
the PSIA also stood up a SIGINT monitoring facility disguised as a private
technology research institute called Terada Gijutsu Kenkyūjo.[210] In addition,
there have been a number of allegations that the PSIA was eavesdropping
on labor activists in the 1950s and 1960s.[211] Finally, the Cold War Ministry
of Posts and Telecommunications had eleven regional offices analyzing data
from hundreds of sensors scattered across Japan designed to detect and locate the origin of illegal terrestrial and spatial radio waves.[212]

Stains on the Uniform

This elaborate SIGINT network and technology-based intelligence successes
notwithstanding, there were two high-profile blemishes on the history of
Cold War Japan's intelligence community, neither ever having received
the attention it deserves. The first involved a notable failure in the chain
of command involving a senior intelligence officer and one of Japan's most
renowned novelists, Mishima Yukio. Mishima was a Nobel Literature Prize
nominee who had become deeply—indeed dangerously—patriotic in the
1960s.[213] Resisting widespread antimilitarist sentiment, he opposed the notion that the emperor became human in 1945, repudiated Article 9 of the
postwar Constitution, and argued that the Japanese people should make serious efforts to defend their nation by themselves.

Toward those ends, Mishima joined the SDF for a trial period in 1967 and
published a hortatory essay on the need for a Japan National Guard (Sokoku
Bōeitai). He wanted the populace to prepare to fight a guerrilla war in the

FIGURE 3.5 Hundreds of thousands of protesters opposed to the Japan-U.S. Security Treaty took to the streets in June 1960. Ten million signed petitions supporting them.
Photo: Hiroshi Hamaya, ©Keisuke Katano, courtesy of the Hiroshi Hamaya estate

event of infiltration by subversive communist elements into Japanese society. In his judgment, the SDF alone was too small to defend key fortifications and the gap had to be filled by civilian volunteers. In Mishima's view, participating in civilian defense would be a great opportunity for citizens to gain spiritual strength.

He had help. Yamamoto Kiyokatsu was a former Imperial Army intelligence officer and Nakano School instructor who joined the NPR in 1952 to design a curriculum for psychological warfare.[214] He also helped create the GSDF's Intelligence Institute in Kodaira a few years later. Yamamoto was attracted by Mishima's idea about civilian troops and was particularly moved by Mishima's regret that discussion of the emperor had become taboo within the SDF. So in December 1967, while still on active duty, Colonel Yamamoto met Mishima and offered to help train his Japan National Guard. In March 1968, Mishima and twenty of his followers spent one month training at an SDF facility in Shizuoka Prefecture. Then in May, Yamamoto began lecturing the group on psychological warfare, both at public venues and within SDF facilities. It is unclear if political leaders and the JDA approved Yamamoto's initiative, but the fact that Mishima's "troops" were trained at SDF bases and that Yamamoto's lectures took place at SDF facilities suggests that Yamamoto's superiors may have looked the other way. Moreover, it is clear from Yamamoto's own account that Mishima had political allies and received help from other Nakano School graduates, including Fujiwara Iwaichi, the storied leader of the "F Kikan," discussed in chapter 2.

In September, after he failed to secure financial support from the Japan Federation of Employers' Associations (Nikkeiren), from which he had hoped also to recruit members, Mishima changed the name of his civilian National Guard to the far more evocative Tatenokai (Shield Society). According to Yamamoto, this was the beginning of the end of their relationship and of his assistance to the group. In his view, Mishima was impatient and had become dangerously radicalized while waiting for the chance to mobilize his own "troops" to suppress anti-SDF demonstrations in Tokyo. Indeed, by late November 1970, Mishima could wait no longer. Wearing a homemade uniform, he burst into GSDF Camp Ichigaya in Tokyo and took the eastern district commandant, Masuda Kanetoshi, hostage. After delivering a fiery speech that failed to incite SDF troops to join him in a coup d'état, Mishima committed ritual suicide. It was only then that Yamamoto informed the head of the Ground Staff Office Intelligence Department that he had been helping Mishima by providing intelligence training *as an individual*, not in the capacity of vice president of the SDF Intelligence School. The police investigated Yamamoto's contacts with Mishima and indicted him in December 1970 for cooperating in the attempted coup. But the Ground Staff Office did not call on him to resign, and in fact Colonel Yamamoto was promoted to general in February 1972.

The second blemish was equally dramatic, if less theatrical. In August 1973 a former Musashi Kikan officer, Tsuboyama Kōzō, provided the South Korean Central Intelligence Agency (KCIA) with intelligence regarding the whereabouts of Kim Dae-jung, the main political foe of President Park Chung-hee, the ROK's Japanese-educated dictator. Kim was living as a fugitive in Tokyo, forced to use a false name and change hotels every few days. Relying on information provided by Major Tsuboyama—likely with the collusion of his former superior officer—KCIA agents abducted Kim from the Hotel Grand Palace in Tokyo and sent him back to Seoul.[215] The original plan, which was to kill Kim and dump his body at sea, was foiled when U.S. diplomats intervened with the assistance of the CIA and the U.S. Navy.[216]

It seems likely that Kim's abduction was orchestrated with the connivance of Japanese intelligence. Tsuboyama, an intelligence officer who specialized in Korea, retired early from the SDF in June 1973 to establish a private research firm, reportedly at the request of his commanding officer, Tsukamoto Katsuichi, the director general of the Ground Staff Office's Intelligence

FIGURE 3.6   Novelist Mishima Yukio exhorted indifferent Self-Defense Force troops in a dramatic, but failed, coup d'état in November 1970 that ended in his ritual suicide.
Photo: *Asahi Shimbun*

Department. Soon thereafter he was contacted by Kim Dong-un, a first secretary at the ROK embassy in Tokyo with whom he had collaborated in the past. Kim asked Tsuboyama to locate Kim Dae-jung.[217] Tsuboyama claims that he believed "Kim Dong-un wanted to talk to Kim Dae-jung because his idea for Korean democratization would risk communizing South Korea."[218] Now in mufti, he reached out to journalist contacts and was able to set up a meeting with Kim Dae-jung in early August. Kim Dong-un reportedly offered Tsuboyama 20 million yen to kidnap the opposition leader. After Tsuboyama declined, Kim Dong-un and other KCIA operatives took matters into their own hands.[219]

Ao Hiromasa, the intelligence officer introduced earlier, suggests in his memoir that the Musashi Kikan (likely Tsuboyama) provided the KCIA with intelligence regarding where Kim Dae-jung was hiding.[220] Indeed, Tsuboyama never disavowed the possibility that he was operating as a cut-out for his old boss and for the Musashi Kikan.[221] There were also press reports that Tsuboyama met with then Deputy Chief Cabinet Secretary Gotōda Masaharu in September 1973, and that the powerful former intelligence officer promised him future compensation, asking Tsuboyama to "disappear for a while, as the media are too noisy."[222] But the noise did not soon subside. Immediately after the incident, the NPA's director for foreign affairs, Sassa Atsuyuki, met with the head of the KCIA Tokyo office in an attempt to have Kim Dong-un interviewed by police authorities. When the KCIA refused, claiming diplomatic immunity, Sassa severed ties with the KCIA, and the Japanese government declared Kim Dong-un persona non grata and deported him.[223] For its part, the Japanese government not only denied any involvement in this incident but also continued to deny the very existence of the Musashi Kikan, even during Diet interpellations.

Oversight

The apparent complicity of Japanese intelligence in both the Mishima and Kim incidents raised serious concerns about civilian control of the military and about intelligence oversight in particular. Neither case generated sanctions that might reassure a public that remained concerned about slipping back into authoritarianism. But this period was not without some measure of oversight success. The variety that seemed to gain traction across the Cold War was mass-based rather than elite-based, and was less a matter of formal judicial or parliamentary oversight than of informal constraints generated by a mobilized public which prevented Japan's political leadership from establishing a more coherent intelligence community. As we have seen, SCAP and the government backed away from consolidating the national police in 1949, and in 1953 Prime Minister Yoshida was forced to retreat from plans for a Japanese CIA. In these and other cases, a population with vivid living memories of intrusive state power—and some for whom that memory had begun to fade or who were too young to know of it firsthand—mobilized to prevent Japan from stepping onto what they feared was a slippery slope back to wartime authoritarianism.

The downside of the Japanese public's persistent efforts to constrain the intelligence community was that throughout the Cold War, the Japanese government found itself unable to impose significant costs on leakers of classified information. It was also unable to consolidate and strengthen secrecy protection, despite embarrassing disclosures that may have compromised national security. These leaks were enabled when, during the democratization/demilitarization phase of the Occupation, GHQ abolished the draconian wartime state secrets laws. In December 1948, SCAP reversed course and had the Diet promulgate a Public Service Act. But it was a weak placeholder. When the Occupation ended and the alliance went into effect, Japanese government officials came under U.S. classification laws—the May 1952 Japan-U.S. Special Criminal Act (to protect against leaks from the NPR and interference with secret alliance activities), and the June 1954 Mutual Security Assistance Secrets Protection Law, the extraterritorial application of which was difficult—and rare.[224] So here was a moment when the two accommodations forced upon the Japanese intelligence community during this period were in conflict with each other: the Japanese government had formally agreed to use its courts to protect U.S. military secrets at a time when much of the public was inhospitable to the very idea of intelligence. Public opinion did not budge, and the government yielded.

Given clear public concerns, it was a long time before any Japanese government would again attempt to tighten its anti-espionage regime. It took nearly three decades after the restoration of Japanese sovereignty before the LDP even considered legislation to block leaks from the intelligence and defense communities. Its so-called "Spy Prevention Act" (formally the Bill Regarding Prevention of Espionage Activities to Acquire State Secrets, or Kokka Himitsu ni Kakaru Supai Kōi tō no Bōshi ni Kansuru Hōritsu An) was drafted in 1980, during the administration of Prime Minister Ōhira Masayoshi, when an LDP backbencher, Arima Motoharu, prepared legislation that would subject leakers of national security–related secrets to up to fifteen years' imprisonment.[225] After Ōhira and other pragmatic LDP leaders judged the measure too incendiary and refused to take it up, a second backbencher, Mori Kiyoshi, drafted an even harsher version that would have subjected leakers of diplomatic documents to the death penalty.

In June 1985, Prime Minister Nakasone Yasuhiro decided to submit the severe Mori draft, rather than the relatively benign Arima one, to the Diet.[226] But, anticipating strong opposition, Nakasone hedged his bets and refused to submit it as a government bill. He was right to be worried. Each of the opposition parties, led by a then still vigorous Japan Socialist Party, future alliance partner Kōmeitō, and the JCP refused even to discuss the bill in the Diet. A potent alliance of civil society groups, including pacifists and many of the same trade unions that Nakasone had been determined to undermine, mobilized with exceptional vigor against the bill. And even within the LDP, the moderate Kōchikai worked to kill it. More than one hundred local governments quickly passed resolutions opposed to the bill, and a pacifist group declared its "thorough opposition . . . out of respect for the atomic bomb survivors."[227] JCP leader Fuwa Tetsuzō minced no words: "This law is a serious crime . . . that reveals piece by piece Japan's military policies and the fattening alliance with the United States. It is fascism itself."[228] In December 1985, after an extended period of high-profile street demonstrations, Nakasone withdrew the bill. An effort to revive it two years later also died stillborn after being met by the same slippery slope rhetoric. At one rally in Tokyo festooned with banners declaring "Danger!" and "Block the Road to War!," an activist referred directly to wartime controls, proclaiming that this legislation would "trace the path of the Peace Preservation and Military Secrets Protection Laws." He urged the crowd not to allow the government to "rob the people of our freedoms and create a system that would lead to the darkness of war."[229]

Intelligence historian Kotani Ken has described this outcome as "a trauma for [Japan's] political leaders."[230] But it can also be coded as a victory for public oversight of the intelligence community. To be sure, this was not legal oversight in the sense outlined in chapter 1 of this volume, not least because no formal classification system had been introduced that could be overseen. But it is clear that the Japanese population was fearful of the excesses of unfettered state power and would not abide it. This extended battle, effectively a Cold War–long test of direct public (rather than judicial) oversight, left so many political scars that the next effort to introduce secrecy legislation would be delayed for nearly another two decades, well after the trade unions and leftist parties had lost much of their vigor—and after 9/11, when world affairs turned even more sinister.

As we have seen, the Japanese intelligence community during the Cold War was buffeted about, its development stunted by each of the political and organizational constraints outlined in chapter 1. The main driver was clearly the way in which Japan found itself embedded in the bipolar postwar security environment as a subordinate to the United States. During the Occupation—and even after Japan regained sovereignty—its intelligence function was derivative, underdeveloped, and aimed narrowly at domestic enemies and foreign firms. CIRO was dependent on the CIA, SDF intelligence largely served U.S. military stationed in Japan, and MOFA's intelligence bureau depended upon CIA and State Department intelligence sharing. The leading champion of intelligence reform, Gotōda Masaharu, felt this dependence keenly, remarking that "because we have delegated our entire national security to the Americans, we have become a vassal state [zokkoku]."[231]

As we have seen, his resentment of Japan's subordination to its U.S. partner—what one prominent intelligence journalist has called a persistent "master-servant relationship" (shujū kankei)—was widely felt in the intelligence community.[232] But as this chapter has also shown, accommodation by the Japanese intelligence community to U.S. power was only one problem, and may even have been the least significant. Japan's intelligence units were small, non-comprehensive, uncoordinated, underfunded, and, as a result of lingering political sensitivities (especially regarding HUMINT), unnecessarily baroque. The main players in Japan's Cold War intelligence community were former soldiers from the Imperial Japanese Army and the SDF, diplomats in MOFA, police in the NPA, economists in MITI, and lawyers in the PSIA. All operated in a highly politicized environment with limited central authority, insufficient political control, and meager public support. Indeed, it was this public opinion that was often mobilized to provide democratic oversight of the intelligence community.

The May 1951 CIA report reviewed earlier in this chapter anticipated many of these dynamics with remarkable clarity but missed others. It predicted that the political orientation of the evolving Japanese intelligence community would range from the "ultra-right to new style militarism."[233] This was evident in the way that former imperial military officers manipulated their U.S. paymasters while simultaneously competing for control of a renascent Japanese military during the Occupation, as well as a quarter century later, when military intelligence officers helped train the far-right minions of ultra-nationalist Mishima Yukio as he prepared his failed coup d'état. Throughout the Cold War, anticommunism and the Soviet threat dominated the intelligence agenda, while economic growth and technology attracted a growing share of the intelligence resources.

The CIA report also predicted that a centralized intelligence service would be "almost an impossibility" because neither the military nor

MOFA would be able to control the police. Coordination across intelligence units embedded in different ministries would, the report continued, be better than during wartime, but it anticipated that the intelligence community would be "burdened by sectionalism" and, therefore, inadequate. This, too, was accurate. We observed in the case of the Soviet MiG-25, when the NPA and SDF squared off, in the case of the GSDF's own G-2 that would not share intelligence even with the Defense Agency's internal bureaus, and repeatedly in the case of CIRO just how the "fierce rivalries" among these units handicapped policy.[234] One former senior intelligence official characterized communication among Japanese intelligence agencies simply as "awful."[235] We also observed how Japanese leaders tried repeatedly—but with limited results—to improve the vertical flow of communication between the intelligence and policy communities. In the event, as Nishihiro Seiki, a clearly exasperated JDA administrative vice minister, put it just at the end of the Cold War: "There is no system in Japan to raise intelligence experts. And once information is developed, there is no real system to bring it directly to the Prime Minister. It is all sent through various ministries and twisted to fit their own beliefs and interpretations."[236]

The 1951 CIA report also anticipated that the Japanese intelligence community would be compromised by its inherent susceptibility to penetration and manipulation by foreign and domestic political interests. Japan's intelligence personnel, it predicted, would be underpaid and have competing loyalties.[237] As we have seen, the subversion of Japan's intelligence community began soon after Japan regained sovereignty; it became a leaky "spy heaven" for foreign agents, who bought politicians, academics, journalists, and intelligence officers alike.[238] The CIA report did not anticipate the effect on the development of the Japanese intelligence community that would derive from the extent to which many in the Japanese political and professional classes may have been secretly assisting U.S. intelligence.

Kotani argues that Cold War antimilitarism and dependence on the United States "resulted in a vulnerable and late developing intelligence function within the Japanese government."[239] Kaneko Masafumi concurs, describing the Cold War intelligence community as "suppressed" and "incomplete," run by leaders who were excessively "cautious" and satisfied with merely "gradual" improvements.[240] Kaneko connected these conditions to a pragmatism bordering on moral hazard, born of necessity during the Cold War: "To the extent that the alliance with the United States was healthy, there was little chance of a direct attack on Japan. Japan's economic interests were expanding globally, but . . . Japan was entirely dependent on America. . . [so] from this perspective, there was no strong demand for foreign intelligence."[241] And indeed, this is a large part of what we have observed: subordination to American power converged with a dominant postwar aversion to the military—both derived from the unprecedented shift in Japan's strategic environment—to render accommodation the only choice available for Japan's Cold War intelligence community. But subordination does not necessarily mean the lack of capabilities.[242] As we have seen in the case of Cold War Japan, it also meant that Tokyo had to tailor—and upgrade—its intelligence skills to U.S. requirements. As a result, the Japanese intelligence community could become sophisticated at certain kinds of intelligence collection—SIGINT, for example—even if not at others, such as HUMINT, or in the ability to analyze raw intelligence and effectively communicate its findings to political leaders.

Moreover, subordination to U.S. power and—to an even greater extent— postwar antimilitarism also contributed to the one function least likely to be embraced by any intelligence community or its political leadership: oversight, another outcome unanticipated by the CIA report. Repeated efforts by the Japanese government to reintroduce secrecy laws and to enhance the reach of counterintelligence and counterterrorism authorities into the private lives of Japanese citizens were rebuffed by an agitated and mobilized public, many of whom had a personal memory of Japan's authoritarian past, and most of whom cared less about the costs of espionage than they feared the loss of their postwar freedoms.

So in closing, we return to the 1952 letter from General Matthew Ridgway to General Walter Bedell Smith that serves as an epigraph for this chapter.[243] As Ridgway prepared to hand Japan back to the Japanese, he insisted that the Occupation had pursued "a policy of forthright integrity, subordinating the acquisition of intelligence within Japan to the establishment of harmonious working relations with the embryo Japanese military forces." The general was preoccupied by the threat of "communist elements" who would seek to use "carryovers" from Occupation intervention as propaganda, suggesting the United States intended to continue controlling the Japanese government. So, not surprisingly, he focused on military intelligence rather than on the broader enterprise. And, equally predictably, he never expressed concern for the future of democratic or civilian control. But during the Cold War, clear democratic boundaries to Japan's jurisdictionally riven, uncoordinated, and underperforming intelligence community began to emerge for the first time. They, and the intelligence community itself, would be tested further as a new world order emerged.

Table 3.1 APPENDIX A: Selected Cold War Counterintelligence Incidents

INCIDENT	YEAR	COUNTRY	DESCRIPTION	CONSEQUENCE
Mitsuhashi Incident	1952	Soviet Union	A Japanese radio engineer detained in the USSR agreed to cooperate with the Soviets in exchange for his release. After U.S. intelligence detected his communications with the Soviets, he became a double agent.	The man was sentenced to four months in prison.
Seki Sanjirō Incident	1953	Soviet Union	A man who was born in Japan but later lost his Japanese citizenship became a Soviet agent and smuggled himself into Japan to purchase maps and uniforms for Soviet agents.	The man was sentenced to one year in prison with a two-year suspension.
Second Korea Spy Incident	1953	North Korea	A North Korean intelligence agent, Kim, smuggled himself into Fukuoka Prefecture to recruit Japanese agents and obtain information on Japanese and U.S. military capabilities.	The Japanese police authorities arrested Kim and seven colleagues. Kim was sentenced to one year in prison.
Pactbopob Incident	1954	Soviet Union	Yuri Pactbopob, a second secretary at the USSR Trade Office in Tokyo, cultivated MOFA and MITI officials. After seeking asylum in the United States, he revealed his activities in Tokyo, declaring that some 500 Japanese citizens promised to cooperate with Soviet intelligence and that more than 8,000 Japanese served as non-contract informants.	A MOFA officer was sentenced to eight months in prison and fined 1 million yen; a trading company president was sentenced to eight months in prison with a two-year suspension and a fine of 300,000 yen.
Third Korea Spy Incident	1955	North Korea	A North Korean intelligence agent, Kang, smuggled himself into Nagasaki Prefecture to collect trade intelligence and recruit Japanese agents for a network of intelligence agents in Japan.	Kang and two colleagues were arrested and sentenced to one and a half years in prison with a four-year suspension.
Kōshōmaru Incident	1957	North Korea	Two North Korean agents smuggled themselves into Hokkaidō to help other agents immigrate illegally.	The two agents were arrested and sentenced to one year in prison and to a fine of 30,000 yen, respectively.
Shinkōgan Incident	1957	North Korea	A North Korean agent, Quan, was smuggled into Japan to facilitate radio communications between North Korean operatives and Pyongyang. Shinkōgan is the name of the ship that Quan attempted to board for North Korea with radios and encryption codes.	Quan was arrested and sentenced to one year in prison.

Incident	Year	Country	Description	Outcome
Fourth Korea Spy Incident	1958	North Korea	A North Korean agent, Sho, smuggled himself into Ishikawa Prefecture to recruit agents, monitor activities of the Association of Korean Residents in Japan, and collect information regarding the SDF and U.S. troops in Japan.	Sho was arrested and sentenced to one year in prison with a four-year suspension and was fined 100,000 yen.
Taki Incident	1959	North Korea	A North Korean agent, Zhao, smuggled himself into Ishikawa Prefecture to deliver a random numbers table and funds for operations, obtain a safe house, and investigate smuggling locations.	Zhao was arrested and sentenced to two years in prison.
Hamasaka Incident	1960	North Korea	A North Korean agent, Kim, smuggled himself into Hyōgo Prefecture to recruit and train Korean residents in Japan as North Korean agents.	Kim was arrested and sentenced to one year in prison.
Daijumaru Incident	1962	North Korea	A North Korean agent, Choi, smuggled himself into Yamagata Prefecture disguised as a naturalized citizen to purchase a 20-ton ship, *Daijumaru*, to transport agents and materials between Japan and North Korea. Choi conducted covert operations in Japan for one year.	Choi was arrested and sentenced to one year in prison.
Kaihōgō Incident	1962	North Korea	A North Korean agent, Kim, smuggled himself into Niigata Prefecture on an operational ship named *Kaihōgō* to collect economic intelligence and data on policy makers' attitudes toward trade with North Korea.	Kim and his two collaborators from North Korea were arrested. Kim was sentenced to one year in prison with a three-year suspension.
First Noshiro Incident	1963	North Korea	Two North Korean agents attempting to smuggle themselves into Japan with pistols, radios, a random numbers table, and fake driver's licenses were found drowned on a beach in Akita Prefecture.	Prosecutors suspended indictment on account of the death of the suspects.
Second Noshiro Incident	1963	North Korea	Another North Korean agent attempting to smuggle himself into Japan with pistols, a random numbers table, and U.S. currency was found drowned on a beach in Akita Prefecture.	Prosecutors suspended indictment on account of the death of the suspect.
Sakata Incident	1963	North Korea	A North Korean agent, Ma, smuggled himself into Yamagata Prefecture to recruit Japanese agents and obtain a visa to stay in Japan.	Ma was arrested while waiting for a North Korean ship to leave Japan. He was sentenced to one year and four months in prison.

(Continued)

Table 3.1 (Continued)

INCIDENT	YEAR	COUNTRY	DESCRIPTION	CONSEQUENCE
Dong Group Incident	1964	North Korea	A North Korean agent, Dong, smuggled himself into Niigata Prefecture to recruit and train Korean residents in Japan as North Korean agents, investigate U.S. military cooperation with South Korea, and illegally obtain a Japanese certificate of residence.	Dong was arrested and sentenced to one year in prison.
Sanwa Incident	1964	North Korea	A North Korean agent, Li, smuggled himself into Yokohama to cultivate relations with Japanese and South Korean government officials to gather information on U.S. and Japanese relations with South Korea, Japanese remilitarization, and South Korean military capabilities. Li managed a network of a dozen agents in Japan.	Li was arrested and sentenced to a fine of 30,000 yen.
Honjōhama Incident	1964	North Korea	A North Korean agent, Jiang, smuggled himself into Kyoto Prefecture to recruit Korean residents in Japan for operations in South Korea and to collect intelligence on the Japanese military. Jiang disguised himself as a South Korean refugee seeking political asylum and status as a legal resident.	The Japanese police authorities saw through Jiang's disguise and arrested him. He was sentenced to six months in prison.
Ichimiya Incident	1964	North Korea	A North Korean agent, Park, smuggled himself into Akita Prefecture to collect intelligence about the SDF and the Japanese defense industry, and to recruit and train Korean residents in Japan as spies.	Park was arrested and sentenced to one year in prison.
Neyagawa Incident	1964	North Korea	A North Korean agent, Park, whose mother was Japanese, smuggled himself into Hyōgo Prefecture and sought to obtain Japanese citizenship by marrying a Japanese woman. He collected intelligence on South Korea and monitored the Association of Korean Residents in Japan.	Park was arrested and sentenced to one year in prison.
Kamata Incident	1964	North Korea	A North Korean agent, Quan, smuggled himself into Ishikawa Prefecture to collect intelligence on U.S. and Japanese military bases and the Japanese defense industry. He also recruited and trained agents for operations in South Korea.	Quan was arrested and sentenced to one year in prison.

Incident	Year	Country	Description	Outcome
Kanda Incident	1965	North Korea	A North Korean agent, Li, smuggled himself into Kyoto Prefecture to collect information on Japanese and South Korean political and military affairs and to recruit Korean residents in Japan for North Korean intelligence operations.	Li was arrested and sentenced to one year in prison.
Edogawa Incident	1965	North Korea	A North Korean agent, Song, smuggled himself into Ishikawa Prefecture to gather intelligence on South Korean political, economic, and military affairs and to recruit Korean elites living in Japan to be sent to South Korea as opinion leaders.	Song was arrested and sentenced to one year in prison with a two-year suspended sentence.
Nagata Incident	1965	North Korea	A North Korean agent, Choi, smuggled himself into Kyoto Prefecture to collect intelligence regarding U.S. military bases and assets deployed near ports in Kobe and Sasebo and to organize anti-American demonstrations in Japan.	Choi was arrested and sentenced to one year and two months in prison.
Suginami Incident	1966	North Korea	A North Korean agent, An, smuggled himself onto a Norwegian cargo ship visiting Nagoya to collect intelligence regarding U.S. troops and Japanese politics and the economy, and to recruit agents to be sent to South Korea.	An was arrested, but his indictment was suspended and he was expelled from Japan.
Foreign Ministry Spy Incident	1967	North Korea	A senior official of the Korean Merchants Association in Japan, Li, met a MOFA official regularly for one year to receive top secret documents in exchange for cash and entertainment at fine Japanese restaurants.	Li was sentenced to one year and six months in prison with a five-year suspension, and the diplomat faced one year in prison.
Higashi Ōsaka Incident	1968	North Korea	A North Korean agent, Han, hid in a cargo ship and smuggled himself into Osaka. Working out of his sister's apartment there for four years, he collected intelligence on Japanese politics, the economy, and the military, which he reported back to North Korea. Han illegally obtained a Japanese passport by using a copy of someone else's official family register.	Han was arrested and sentenced to one year in prison.
Sedov Incident	1969	Soviet Union	An Indonesian student in the USSR became a Soviet agent and was sent to Japan to work in Japanese firms in order to steal confidential documents. The agent was under the control of Sedov of the Soviet trade office in Tokyo.	The police authorities arrested the agent and summonsed Sedov, who refused to appear voluntarily and left Japan.

(Continued)

Table 3.1 (Continued)

INCIDENT	YEAR	COUNTRY	DESCRIPTION	CONSEQUENCE
Iwasaki Noshiro Incident	1969	North Korea	A South Korean, Kim, smuggled himself into Japan to find work, and became a North Korean agent working for the Pyongyang-affiliated General Association of Korean Residents in Japan. Kim left for North Korea for spy training and returned to Japan to start intelligence operations mainly targeting South Korea.	Kim was arrested and sentenced to one year in prison with a two-year suspension.
Kononov Incident	1971	Soviet Union	Two assistants to a Soviet military attaché at the Soviet embassy in Tokyo, Kononov and his predecessor Havinov, paid a Japanese broker dealing in communications equipment disposed of by U.S. troops in Yokota to steal U.S. missile and radar technology.	The Japanese broker was sentenced to two years in prison with a three-year suspended sentence, and Kononov left Japan under the protection of diplomatic immunity.
Ishihara Incident	1971	North Korea	A South Korean, Woo, smuggled himself into Japan and became a North Korean agent. He ran a network that collected intelligence regarding Japanese military capabilities and planted North Korean agents in South Korea. Woo obtained a Japanese passport by stealing a copy of an official Japanese family register.	Woo was arrested and sentenced to one year in prison.
Adachi Incident	1971	North Korea	A North Korean agent, Park, smuggled himself into Shimane Prefecture to gather intelligence regarding Japanese and U.S. military capabilities as well as South Korean political and military affairs. Park also recruited his brother-in-law in the South Korean military to defect to North Korea.	Park was arrested and sentenced to six months in prison with a two-year suspension.
Atsumi Incident	1973	North Korea	Two North Korean agents, Choi and Kim, attempted to smuggle themselves into Japan disguised as victims of a wrecked ship off the Yamagata coast.	The two were arrested immediately after they came onshore, and were sentenced to one year in prison with a three-year suspension.
Mizuyama Incident	1973	North Korea	A North Korean agent, Kim, smuggled himself into Aomori Prefecture. Disguised as a Japanese man named Mizuyama Yoshio, he obtained a Japanese passport and ran a Japan-based network of intelligence agents able to infiltrate South Korea.	Kim was arrested and sentenced to one year in prison.

Incident	Year	Country	Description	Outcome
Nakagawa Incident	1974	North Korea	A North Korean agent, Li, smuggled himself into Ishikawa Prefecture and obtained a safe house in Aichi to recruit and train Korean residents in Japan as North Korean agents.	Li was arrested and sentenced to ten months in prison.
Hokusō Incident	1974	North Korea	A Korean fugitive, M, ran a construction company, Hokusō Kensetsu, that served as a front for collecting intelligence regarding U.S. and Japanese military assets. He also recruited Korean residents in Japan with families in South Korea to be agents.	M was arrested and sentenced to one and a half years in prison with a three-year suspension.
Kirihama Incident	1974	North Korea	After two years of spy training in North Korea, a Korean resident in Japan attempted to begin covert operations in Kirihama.	The agent was arrested and sentenced to one year in prison with a three-year suspension.
Kublicki Incident	1974	Soviet Union	A stateless person, Kublicki, working for the USSR, came to Tokyo to collect Japanese defense industry secrets with instructions from a Soviet military attaché assistant, Fedorov. Kublicki surrendered to the police to seek protection.	Kublicki was sentenced to one year in prison with a three-year suspension.
Tsurumi Terao Incident	1975	North Korea	A North Korean agent, Kim, smuggled himself into Tottori Prefecture and created a safe house in Yokohama. He paid two Korean businessmen to investigate Korean businesses in Tokyo and attempted to cultivate South Korean government officials.	Kim was arrested and sentenced to eight months in prison.
Nigorigawa Incident	1975	North Korea	A North Korean agent, Li, smuggled himself into Kyoto Prefecture and hired a Korean resident in Japan to help him develop a pro–North Korean network in South Korea.	Li was arrested near Aomori Prefecture while attempting to leave for North Korea. He was sentenced to two years in prison with a three-year suspension.
Fuse Incident	1976	North Korea	A North Korean agent, Zhao, smuggled himself into Shimane Prefecture and hid in Osaka to collect intelligence regarding the SDF and to recruit Korean residents in Japan as North Korean agents. Zhao made several trips between Japan and North Korea hidden in ships.	Zhao was arrested and sentenced to six months in prison.
Wong Incident	1976	China	A Hong Kong–based Chinese merchant, Wong, stole Japanese industrial technologies—including regarding aircraft engines—under instructions from PRC intelligence.	Wong was arrested and fined 200,000 yen for violation of the Foreign Exchange and Foreign Trade Control Law.

(Continued)

Table 3.1 (Continued)

INCIDENT	YEAR	COUNTRY	DESCRIPTION	CONSEQUENCE
Machekin Incident	1976	Soviet Union	A Novosti Press Agency correspondent, Alexandre E. Machekin, attempted to steal confidential U.S. documents regarding electronic devices on the aircraft carrier *Midway* through contacts with an American crewman in Tokyo.	The Japanese police authorities arrested Machekin but suspended his indictment.
Drew and Gottlieb Incident	1976	Soviet Union	An Australian, W. F. Drew, came to Tokyo as part of the Allied Occupation and became a broker of used U.S. military engines. He provided aircraft manuals and other technological information to the Soviet embassy. A German, W. R. Gottlieb, came to Tokyo in 1964 as a salesman dealing with U.S. military officers. He provided intelligence regarding U.S. bases to the Soviet embassy.	Drew was sentenced to eight months in prison with a three-year suspension, whereas Gottlieb was sentenced to a fine of 30,000 yen.
Toshima Incident	1977	North Korea	A North Korean agent, Shin, smuggled himself into Kyoto Prefecture to collect intelligence regarding South Korea's politics, economy, and technology as well as Japanese military capabilities and defense industry. Shin paid a Korean resident in Tochigi Prefecture to acquire someone else's alien registration certificate for him to be able to operate safely in Japan.	Shin was arrested and sentenced to one year and six months in prison with a three-year suspension.
Ushitsu Incident	1977	North Korea	A Korean resident in Japan running a construction company became North Korean "Agent A" and attempted to recruit another agent operating in South Korea to collect intelligence regarding U.S. troops in Japan. With instructions from North Korea, Agent A abducted a Japanese man and handed him over to another North Korean, Agent B, in Ishikawa Prefecture.	The Japanese police authorities arrested Agent A and issued an arrest warrant for Agent B, notifying Interpol.
Research Data Leakage Incident	1978	China	A Nippon Telephone and Telegraph (NTT) employee stole documents and research data from governmental institutes and sold them to a Chinese-language bookstore in Tokyo, which in turn transferred the documents to the PRC.	The NTT employee was arrested and sentenced to two years in prison with a three-year suspension.

Incident	Year	Country	Description	Outcome
Mizuhashi Incident	1980	North Korea	Park, a Korean resident in Japan working for the General Association of Korean Residents in Japan, recruited another Korean resident who, after training in North Korea, was tasked to investigate the geography of the Sea of Japan coastline. Park also compiled a list of candidates for future recruitment.	Park was arrested and sentenced to one year in prison with a three-year suspension, while the agent faced four months in prison with a two-year suspension.
Isonomatsu Incident	1980	North Korea	Two North Korean agents living in Japan surveyed the Sea of Japan coast to identify suitable smuggling points for other agents coming to Japan.	The two agents were arrested and sentenced to six months in prison with a three-year suspension.
Kozlov Incident (also known as Miyanaga Incident)	1980	Soviet Union	A former GSDF major general, Miyanaga Yukihisa, became an agent for the GRU, a Soviet foreign military intelligence organization. Miyanaga collected classified JDA documents through former subordinates at the SDF, and handed them over to the Soviet embassy in Tokyo in exchange for 3.1 million yen.	Miyanaga was sentenced to one year in prison, and his two subordinates at SDF to eight months in prison.
Hyūga Incident	1981	North Korea	A North Korean agent, Huang, smuggled himself into Miyazaki Prefecture and disguised himself as a Korean resident, using a fake alien registration certificate to conduct intelligence operations in Japan, including recruitment of agents and collection of intelligence regarding the SDF and Japanese foreign policy.	The Japanese police authorities arrested Huang when he was about to board a North Korean ship. He was sentenced to four months in prison with a two-year suspension.
Oga Wakimoto Incident	1981	North Korea	A Korean resident in Japan became a North Korean agent and attempted to smuggle himself into Akita Prefecture after receiving intelligence training in North Korea.	The agent was arrested when he arrived onshore at the Wakimoto beach. He was sentenced to ten months in prison with a two-year suspension.
Levchenko Incident	1982	Soviet Union	A former Russian KGB officer, Stanislav Levchenko, defected to the United States, where he revealed KGB espionage activities against Japan. Levchenko had cultivated eleven Japanese agents working for him, including influential politicians and journalists with privileged access to high-level government officials.	Levchenko's testimony rocked the Japanese Diet and the government, but no one was held responsible for Japan's weak counterintelligence.

(Continued)

Table 3.1 (Continued)

INCIDENT	YEAR	COUNTRY	DESCRIPTION	CONSEQUENCE
Nishiarai Incident	1985	North Korea	A North Korean agent, Choi, conducted intelligence operations in Japan for 15 years by disguising himself as Japanese after acquiring a Japanese passport. Choi also managed two agents he recruited in Japan.	The Japanese police authorities issued an international arrest warrant for Choi. One of his agents was arrested and sentenced to one year in prison with a four-year suspension.
Shin Gwang-soo Incident	1985	North Korea	A North Korean agent, Shin Gwang-soo, smuggled himself into Ishikawa Prefecture to abduct a Japanese cook, Hara Tadaaki, in order for Shin to steal his identity and obtain a Japanese passport. Shin recruited Korean residents to go to South Korea to gather intelligence on the South Korean military.	Shin was arrested in South Korea and deported. The Japanese police authorities then issued an arrest warrant for Shin and asked the International Criminal Police Organization (Interpol) to circulate a notice.
Yokota Base Spy Incident	1987	Soviet Union and China	In cooperation with three others, a Japanese agent working for a Soviet intelligence organization stole technical orders for U.S. fighters and transport aircraft from the Yokota Air Base and sold them to both the USSR and PRC.	The agent and his collaborators were sentenced to imprisonment for varying periods between a year and a half and two and a half years.
Pokrovsky Incident	1987	Soviet Union	A deputy Soviet trade representative in Tokyo, Y. G. Pokrovsky, stole information regarding Japanese flight management systems and other aero-engineering technologies by cultivating an executive of a Japanese company in 1984.	Pokrovsky and his colleagues refused police interviews and left Japan with diplomatic immunity.
Preobrazhensky Incident	1987	Soviet Union	A Tass News Agency correspondent, Preobrazhensky, who was thought to be a KGB agent, cultivated a Chinese student studying in Japan as an agent to obtain information on the PRC for two years.	Preobrazhensky left Japan with diplomatic immunity, but later sought political asylum in the United States and revealed his intelligence activities in Japan.
Korean Air Flight 858 Incident	1987	North Korea	KAL Flight 858 exploded in mid-air when a bomb planted in the passenger cabin was detonated by two North Korean agents. One of the bombers, Kim Hyon Hui, revealed that she had lived for two years with a female Japanese abductee (believed to be Taguchi Yaeko) in North Korea to learn Japanese language and culture.	N/A

Incident	Year	Country	Description	Outcome
Yokosuka Incident	1988	North Korea	Five Japanese women living in Europe, recruited by a North Korean agent, returned to Japan to collect intelligence on Sea of Japan coastal conditions and on the SDF.	The women were issued an order to return their passports to the Japanese Foreign Ministry.
Mihama Incident	1990	North Korea	Two North Korean men were found dead on a wrecked North Korean ship washed ashore in Fukui Prefecture. The ship contained intelligence-related equipment such as a random numbers table and encryption codes.	Criminal papers were filed against these dead men from North Korea on suspicion of smuggling.

Source: Gaiji Jiken Kenkyūkai, ed., *Sengo no Gaiji Jiken: Supai, Rachi, to Fusei Yushutu* (Postwar Intelligence Incidents: Spy, Abduction, and Illicit Exports). Tokyo: Tōkyō Hōrei Shuppan, 2007.

CHAPTER 4

Tinkering with Failure (1991–2001)

> [In 1941] we knew almost nothing about the tens of thousands of things we were going to have to learn about in a hurry. . . . [W]e found ourselves all too reliant upon British intelligence.
>
> —Sherman Kent, Central Intelligence Agency, 1955

> In the Cold War era the world moved in teams, and as a member of the American-led team, our judgment was not so important. Now Japan needs its own [intelligence] ability.
>
> —Nishihiro Seiki, Japan Defense Agency, 1992

Like intelligence communities elsewhere, the Japanese intelligence community did not anticipate—and was not prepared for—the end of the Cold War. Neither monitoring Moscow nor identifying and rooting out communists at home seemed so important any longer. The "East" and "West" were realigning—in some cases even finding common ground—and triumphalism reigned in the "free world." How would Japan's intelligence community survive, much less expand, without political leadership or public support in a target-free environment? Where would the support come from, and for doing what? Did the Japanese intelligence community need better intelligence on whether the United States, on which it had long been dependent, would draw down in Asia? Was it capable of shifting toward collection and analysis of the effects on Japan of Washington's new strong-arm tactics related to technology and trade? What sorts of intelligence reform would have to be pursued? Whatever came to pass, the Japanese intelligence community (not unlike others, to be sure) would have to reinvent itself (or be reinvented) once more. If intelligence professionals were to resort to inflating threats, who would believe them? Perhaps they would first try to reduce the imbalance in its system favoring counterintelligence by building a capability to identify and anticipate novel threats in a new world order.

This was not going to happen overnight—nor even over a decade. Inchoate threats took time to percolate through the international system. And if past is prologue, inchoate solutions would have to precede robust ones. Since the United States was now by default (or by design) the world's overwhelming military power, some Japanese policy makers felt less urgency to develop a new, comprehensive intelligence formula to cope with this new world order. Like leaders elsewhere, most only dimly understood the implications of these many changes—and how America's "unipolar moment" might affect their strategic environment. If the slow emergence of an underspecified "new world order" had been the only driver of intelligence reform in the 1990s, however, this chapter would be a straightforward account of Japan's meek surrender to a decade of tentative, groping, half-measure reforms. And in part, it was that.

But as we shall see, post–Cold War intelligence reform was actually far more complicated. In an interesting parallel with the earlier U.S. experience described by Sherman Kent in an epigraph to this chapter, senior Japanese strategists dissatisfied with how Tokyo's unequal alliance with the United States was manifest in its dependence on Washington for actionable intelligence had already begun to seek change. So while the first post–Cold War decade became well known as the first of two "lost decades" in economic terms, it was more than a lost decade of unforced errors by the Japanese intelligence community. There were such errors, but during this extended moment of global power shift, political leaders began to tinker with Japan's intelligence community—testing changes they first conceived in the 1980s and tentatively enhancing intelligence capabilities in ways that could reduce U.S. dominion. The shift in the strategic environment and trade frictions with the United States gave greater purpose to their determination to do more and better on their own, and several highly conspicuous intelligence failures would provide the necessary political impetus for change. But in this first post–Cold War decade, imagination was still at a premium, public suspicion of the intelligence community remained stout, and demand pull from politicians for both comprehensive intelligence reform and intelligence estimates was in short supply. Experimentation was possible: it was a time for tinkering.

Political Leadership

Prime Minster Nakasone's failure in 1985 to create an anti-espionage law signaled to reformers that they could not attack the problem head-on. Not only was Japanese public opinion unlikely to support intelligence reform, but also, after the fall of the Berlin Wall in 1989, the once hegemonic political power of the conservative Liberal Democratic Party had become shaky. By 1993 the LDP was out of power for the first time in nearly half a century.[1]

Even if they were not knocking on an open door, however, a small number of determined intelligence reformers found a way in. Indeed, they entered through the side door of Japan's latest ambitious plan to overhaul its bureaucracy. In 1996, after confusion about how to respond to the first Gulf War weakened the LDP—and after a socialist premiership stalled intelligence reform for a few years—Prime Minister Hashimoto Ryūtarō kicked off a new round of administrative reform, led by an Administrative Reform Council (Gyōsei Kaikaku Kaigi) which he charged with rationalizing the form and function of central government ministries. Not only would his council discuss ways to overhaul ministries and agencies to reduce the number of government personnel, but also it would pick up where Gotōda Masaharu had left off during the Nakasone years and accomplish this by strengthening the Cabinet Secretariat's leadership across policy domains.[2]

Hashimoto's Administrative Reform Council was composed of leaders from different fields, including industry, trade unions, academia, and the media, who were comfortable with centralized power and who sought to enhance the political leadership of the bureaucracy.[3] Their ambitious agenda left no administrative rock unturned: it would reduce the inflated number of policy advisory councils (shingikai) under each ministry; promote the outsourcing and privatization of policy services; require policy evaluation by disinterested third parties; accelerate information disclosure; and reform the entire civil service system—including appointment, promotion, and retirement rules. One analyst called the effort "the zenith of 50 years of administrative reforms."[4]

It was also the apogee (in a much lower orbit) of years of unrewarded efforts by national security strategists to elevate intelligence to a central place in the national policy agenda. As we shall see in the case of military intelligence, two strategists in particular—Gotōda Masaharu, the powerful former chief cabinet secretary and implacable foe of "selfish bureaucrats," and Japan Defense Agency vice minister Nishihiro Seiki, the first career JDA official to have risen to the top of the agency—had been hard at work on intelligence reform for more than a decade and a half.[5] Now, with incipient new threats becoming visible on the horizon, they seized the opportunity created by a broad national consensus on comprehensive administrative reform to try to generate support for a more robust, effective, and independent intelligence system.[6] When the council's final report was issued in December 1997, intelligence reform was identified for the first time as a fundamental matter of national policy. In addition to calling for the creation of a Cabinet Secretariat with political appointees who would wrest control from turf-protecting bureaucrats, and in addition to staffing a powerful planning and coordinating body to provide direct support to the prime minister in matters of policy and legislation—the administrative reforms that attracted the most attention in the media—the report also called upon this new centralized unit to be responsible for "coordination within the government *as well as the intelligence community.*"[7] This was unprecedented in postwar Japan.

The council's report was explicit regarding the need to separate intelligence and policy functions—as we have seen, a cardinal rule for effective intelligence and a conspicuous failure in Japanese practice.[8] Cognizant of many of the long-standing problems afflicting the Japanese intelligence community, the Administrative Reform Council recommended a number of changes to strengthen Japan's intelligence infrastructure. The most prominent was its call for creation of a permanent independent intelligence organization within the Cabinet Secretariat because of "the importance of separation between intelligence and policy bureaus and the degree of specialization required for intelligence analysis." Concerned about how stovepipes had afflicted Japanese intelligence, the council also took direct aim at horizontal communication problems by promoting "the idea of [an] 'intelligence community' [comprising] all relevant ministries and agencies that would mutually review intelligence analyses and evaluations." It therefore proposed that "the current de facto intelligence meetings [be given] the status of official regular Cabinet Secretariat meetings." The report also called for strengthening CIRO's capabilities and enlarging its staff.[9]

Indeed, as often happens, particularly in intelligence reform, things turned out differently than planned. What might have been the beginnings of a strategic reform was reduced to tinkering by a politically weakened Hashimoto administration that responded to pressures from bureaucratic turf protectors by creating a new position, cabinet crisis management officer (*naikaku kikikanrikan*), and simply renaming the existing Cabinet Security Office the Cabinet Security and Crisis Management Office.[10] This was followed in October 1998 when Hashimoto's successor, Obuchi Keizō, created an unimaginative and strikingly passive biannual vice minister–level Cabinet Intelligence Committee (Naikaku Jōhō Kaigi) to be chaired by the chief cabinet secretary, beneath which a director general–level bimonthly Joint Intelligence Committee (Gōdō Jōhō Kaigi) would meet in the Cabinet Secretariat.[11] Problems derived from stovepipes and jurisdictional battles, and from crossed wires between the intelligence community and political class, went unaddressed.

Six months later, in April 1999, a "Guideline for Promoting the Restructuring of Central Government Organizations"—a decision by the Central Government Organizations Reform Promotion Headquarters—called for implementation of more of the council's recommendations, and intelligence received renewed attention. Without specifying exactly how it might be accomplished, the "Guideline" stipulated that the government would "reinforce the staff and capabilities of the current Cabinet Intelligence and Research Office [CIRO] . . . strengthen cabinet intelligence collection and analysis capabilities by pursuing more specialized and more sophisticated intelligence analysis, and [stimulate] cooperation with relevant ministries and agencies."[12] It also called upon "intelligence-related ministries and agencies [to] participate proactively in intelligence sharing with [one another] and the cabinet in particular . . . mutually reviewing intelligence analysis and evaluations based on the idea that they are all part of 'an intelligence community.'" In the spirit of this "Guideline," the head of CIRO was upgraded to director of cabinet intelligence in January 2001.[13] Nonetheless, as a senior non-CIRO intelligence official involved in the process later would recall, "There were still silos within silos with CIRO."[14]

So, despite drawing a direct bead on the intelligence community, the Administrative Reform Council and the subsequent "Guideline" amounted to little more than cosmetic, makeshift changes.[15] Political leadership was in shorter supply than needed, and intelligence sharing across administrative units remained limited. Indeed, according to one MOFA official, the JDA still did not share raw signals intelligence at the Joint Intelligence Committee, something one analyst blamed on "the sensitivity of U.S.-derived intelligence."[16] Moreover, no ministry or agency—certainly not CIRO—was given unambiguous authority to lead and coordinate the constituent organizations in the Japanese intelligence community.[17] According to Nakanishi Terumasa, the report identified the timeless problem of communication between analysts and policy makers that simply "resurfaced" when the resultant reforms, having been shaped by bureaucratic pushback, failed to fix the problem.[18]

Winners and Losers

Although comprehensive reform of the overall intelligence community would have to remain a work in progress—in part because the institutions of national security policy making and the military were left untouched—several individual intelligence units emerged as big winners. One was the Foreign Ministry, which benefited from the emergence of a powerful champion for intelligence reform from the business community, C. Itoh chairman Sejima Ryūzō, who also had impeccable credentials as an architect of administrative reform. After his career in military intelligence was cut short by the end of the war, and after more than a decade in the Soviet Union—some say in an internment camp, others say living in comfort in Moscow—Sejima joined the trading company in 1958 and, in what can only be seen as a peculiar and remarkable ascent, became a director within four years.[19] He was known to be a conduit to the Soviet Union, and managed the firm's strategy in the oil sector. Sejima also helped develop C. Itoh's strategy to become the first Japanese firm to enter China in 1972.[20] After becoming chairman in 1978, he turned to the political and policy world, participating in the very successful Second Administrative Reform Commission led by Nakasone Yasuhiro and Keidanren chairman Dokō Toshio. He later served as adviser to Prime Ministers Obuchi, Miyazawa, and Hashimoto.

Sejima, "a very mysterious gentleman" reputed to be a leader of the "actual, invisible Japanese intelligence community," was devoted to improving Japan's intelligence efforts, especially after the Cold War.[21] He had a keen sense of the limits to Japanese power but recognized that "no country in history that pursued defensive defense principles survived without having intelligence capabilities superior to its enemies'." Despite his commitment to streamlining government in general, Sejima advocated that MOFA train an additional ten thousand intelligence officers: "Japan needs to reinforce its diplomatic capabilities [gaikōryoku], and this requires strengthening intelligence capabilities." His diagnosis was remarkably specific:

> "Whether Japan aspires to be a great power or a small power, it will have to strengthen its intelligence capabilities. . . [mainly in three ways]: not being isolated internationally, but being part of a wide network of allies and friendly states; maintaining good coordination among intelligence organizations and other ministries and agencies; [and] having embassies that possess high-level intelligence capabilities supplemented by private-sector intelligence.[22]

In the early 1990s, Sejima chaired the Roundtable for Strengthening Diplomacy (Gaikō Kyōka Kondankai), a private advisory group created by Foreign Minister Nakayama Tarō in response to a report by Prime Minister Kaifu Toshiki's Provisional Administrative Reform Promotion Council (Rinji Gyōsei Kaikaku Suishin Shingikai). Sejima's Roundtable issued a report in 1991 that recognized the Foreign Ministry's shortage of collectors and analysts as well as its problem with stovepiped intelligence units.[23] The report stimulated more tinkering with MOFA's intelligence capabilities. In August 1993, when MOFA created a Foreign Policy Bureau (Sōgō Gaikō Seisaku Kyoku), the Planning Division and the Security Policy Office were both detached from the Intelligence and Research Bureau (Jōhō Chōsa Kyoku). As a result, for the first time in its postwar history, MOFA's intelligence unit would focus exclusively on collection and analysis.[24] Concurrently, the Intelligence and

Research Bureau was renamed the Intelligence Bureau—albeit with a Japanese name (Kokusai Jōhō Kyoku) that is more explicit about its international remit. The new bureau comprised two divisions with a staff of fifty-six (of whom twenty-two were intelligence analysts) responsible for collection, analysis, and communication of intelligence on all regions of the world.[25] MOFA's professional staff was slated to be increased by the addition of country and area specialists to enhance the intelligence functions of the home office as well as to augment the capabilities of its embassies and consulates around the world. Taoka Shunji, a journalist who specializes in security matters, was not impressed. He reports that despite the reforms, there remained "a strong tendency [for MOFA] to be dependent on the judgments of U.S. intelligence." Quoting a MOFA official who allowed as how "it was unavoidable for us to listen to the views of the U.S. embassy," Taoka concludes that MOFA's continued intelligence dependency meant that Japan "would receive only what advances and would not hinder [U.S.] interests."[26]

A review of MOFA's annual *Diplomatic Bluebook* reveals that renewed attention to intelligence affairs had been in the works for some time. During the last years of the Cold War, from 1980 to 1988, intelligence was barely mentioned except as a matter of internal organization. Once the Berlin Wall fell, however, the *Diplomatic Bluebook* stressed intelligence as a priority. And after the Soviet Union collapsed, it identified intelligence collection as "an instrument of foreign policy" and connected it to "the making of a new international order."[27] In the subsequent decade each edition referred to the priority MOFA was placing on "strengthening its ability to gather and analyze intelligence."[28]

But for MOFA, talk was relatively cheap, its reforms opportunistic, and its preferences parochial. Familiar organizational and political obstacles remained in the larger intelligence community. Despite the reform and bureaucratic rationalization, the roughly three dozen defense attachés serving in embassies abroad had no secure communications channels back to SDF or JDA headquarters, and were required to channel reports to them through MOFA.[29] One early chief of MOFA's new bureau, Magosaki Ukeru, insists that "Japan's intelligence capabilities shifted with its leaders," and recalls that Prime Minister Hashimoto regularly demanded intelligence briefings and used them as the basis for policy.[30] Hashimoto was particularly concerned about the possibility for war in the Taiwan Straits and insisted on strengthening Japanese intelligence as a preparatory measure. Ironically, the premiership of this leader duly credited with elevating intelligence was weakened in 1997, when rumors of a romantic liaison with a suspected Chinese agent—possibly a "honey trap" set by Chinese agents—became front-page news.[31] Other leaders seemed to care about intelligence much less—or were concerned about public opposition much more—and would not spend political capital on its reform. The result, as Shigeta Hiroshi, a former ambassador in charge of counterterrorism, explains, was that Japan "was not adequately equipped with an intelligence function," and that it was left "as always with an unfinished and incomplete" intelligence community.[32]

Frustration with Japan's leadership was well founded. In late 1990, for example, Prime Minister Kaifu Toshiki, unsure if he would receive domestic support and unable to judge foreign reactions (apart from those in Washington), responded lethargically to the 1991 Gulf War. Resorting to "checkbook diplomacy," his government supported the widely based "coalition of the willing" in Kuwait with $13 billion, a considerable cash transfer raised through a one-off tax of its citizens. But it did so only after considerable U.S. pressure and without placing any of its soldiers in harm's way in a region on which it depended for a very large proportion of its energy and, thereby, its economic vitality. It was an embarrassing miscalculation. Despite its magnitude, the Japanese cash transfer was not acknowledged when the Kuwaitis publicly thanked each of the members of the U.S.-led military coalition for its liberation in full-page advertisements in the *New York Times* and the *Washington Post*. The Japanese government vowed never to make that mistake again. Within months, CIRO took steps to improve both the quality of foreign intelligence and its situational awareness regarding the foreign political landscape.[33]

The extent to which the Gulf War had indirect ramifications for intelligence reform in Japan is not widely appreciated. Among the many difficult issues the Gulf War raised for Japanese security was whether or not Japanese military units could participate in United Nations–sanctioned activities. The refusal to do so on constitutional grounds by the timid Prime Minister Kaifu split the LDP and generated domestic and foreign demand for Japan to provide more tangible contributions to the international order. A hotly debated "PKO Law" (formally known as the Law Concerning Cooperation in UN Peacekeeping and Other Operations) was passed by the Diet in June 1992, well after the conflict had ended and the Kaifu government had given way.[34] Japanese forces were dispatched in September to Angola to monitor elections, and a larger force of 680 Japanese personnel—including fifty civilian police trainers and six hundred GSDF troops tasked with civil engineering, transported by four hundred MSDF sailors and 120 ASDF airmen—was dispatched to Cambodia to serve under UN auspices. Within seven months, a Japanese UN volunteer was killed, and a police officer was murdered shortly thereafter. Once the PKO Law passed, the overriding concern of the government and the SDF was to keep personnel out of harm's way, a concern that became an obsession in the aftermath of these deaths. This further intensified as the number of SDF missions abroad increased. But as one SDF flag officer explained, military intelligence would not be enhanced significantly for another decade, in part because of "discord between uniformed and civilian intelligence officers who competed with one another."[35]

Meanwhile, there was growing dissatisfaction with the consequences of slow and incomplete intelligence reform and continued excessive dependence on U.S. intelligence. Ōmori Yoshio was CIRO director, and Ishihara Nobuo was a deputy chief cabinet secretary in May 1993, when the United States shared intelligence with Japan that a North Korean Nodong missile had fallen into the Sea of Japan just 250 kilometers from the Noto Peninsula. Both were shocked that the Japanese government had no capacity to discover this information on its own or to verify it in a timely way.[36] Soon thereafter, in February 1994, Prime Minister Hosokawa Morihiro was surprised to learn that the United States had been making preparations to attack North Korea. And four months later, in June, Ōmori learned about the death of North Korean leader Kim Il-sung from the public media. He was unable to verify independently U.S. intelligence reports that the North Korean military showed no sign of mobilization and that there was no evidence of social unrest in Pyongyang. CIRO—and the Japanese intelligence community overall—still had wide room for improvement, and Ōmori and Ishihara added their voices to calls for reduced dependence on Washington.[37]

In October 1998, in yet another attempt to centralize policy making as prescribed by the Administrative Reform Council, a Cabinet Intelligence Committee (Naikaku Jōhō Kaigi) was created within the Cabinet Secretariat. The new organ, with CIRO serving as its secretariat, was designed to assemble all the relevant administrative vice ministers and the heads of each of their intelligence units in regular meetings chaired by the chief cabinet secretary. Its stated purpose was to consolidate and clarify the government's short- and medium-term intelligence requirements, which would be assigned to relevant intelligence units for the purpose of generating "all-source" estimates.[38] It seemed like a good idea. But the committee never met more than twice a year and, with no permanent secretariat of its own, was vulnerable to every variety of bureaucratic delay and obfuscation.[39] It was also as vulnerable as ever to the sorts of normal intelligence failures that plague every intelligence community and that, predictably, stimulate calls for reform.

High-Profile Failures and High-Profile Reforms

While the Administrative Reform Council was deliberating, two high-profile failures resulted in the reorganization of two intelligence units in 1995. This first was a failure in crisis management rather than in intelligence per se—the devastating Hanshin-Awaji (Kobe) earthquake in January, to that point the largest temblor in Japan since the Great Kanto (Tokyo) Earthquake of 1923. As in that earlier case, the human and economic costs were staggering. More than 6,400 persons perished, and rebuilding cost more than 2.5 percent of Japan's gross domestic product.[40] The government was criticized for acting too slowly, for being insufficiently prepared for a disaster, for placing excessive confidence in the mitigating capacity of the postwar infrastructure, and, in the words of one particularly acute critic, for having an "ossified administrative structure."[41]

This was manifest in the disconnect between the military and civilian authorities and in delayed communications from local officials and the central government. Since Prime Minister Murayama Tomiichi's office did not have a twenty-four-hour duty officer, he learned of the catastrophe on the broadcast news. By then, thousands of Kobe citizens already lay beneath the rubble of homes and offices, and the city was engulfed in flames. Demonstrating that policy silos are not the exclusive province of the intelligence community, the National Land Agency, which nominally owned disaster management responsibilities, busied itself squabbling with other ministries and agencies over control of the policy response. The inability of the government to assess the situation rapidly and accurately led to delays in the mobilization of critical resources that cost lives.[42]

According to a former high-level government official familiar with the Japanese intelligence community, this dark cloud of a disaster had a silver lining for what was still an underpowered CIRO, whose forty analysts operated in "a small household of only eight rooms" with a budget of under 2 billion yen before the Kobe quake.[43] Soon after, in May 1996, a Cabinet Intelligence Aggregation Center (Naikaku Jōhō Shūyaku Sentā) was established as an OSINT unit to compile and disseminate news reports and other public information to senior government officials in the Cabinet Secretariat on a daily basis. The center's staff would now be on twenty-four-hour duty, watching television and listening to news agency radio broadcasts in order to provide reports to the prime minister regarding any emergency in close to real time.

Ōmori Yoshio, the CIRO director at the time of the Kobe quake, adds that the lethargic performance of the government during the crisis stimulated reform in the wider intelligence community as well.[44] The Cabinet Secretariat assumed responsibility for the dispatch of ASDF reconnaissance aircraft to disaster sites in order to collect information. It also prepared a dedicated communications link between the cabinet and the utility companies to help it assess emergency situations. The downside, according to Ōmori, was that Kobe and other domestic natural disasters elevated to center stage what should have been his unit's side business, at the expense of foreign intelligence collection and analysis.[45] In the absence of comprehensive reform initiatives, and in an environment where bureaucratic tinkering was the most one could expect, CIRO was becoming a sort of ragbag for intelligence reform. To perform its notional central function, CIRO continued to rely on a small number of dispatchees abroad and secondees from competing ministries at home, and on information supplied by eleven contracted think tanks and external news organizations, such as Radiopress and the Kyodo and Jiji news agencies.[46] In a sense, there was less to that silver lining than imagined.

An even darker cloud seemed to have a more valuable silver lining for the Justice Ministry's Public Security Intelligence Agency. As reported in chapter 3, the PSIA was established in 1952 to monitor what were then deemed to be particularly violent and subversive organizations, such as the Japan Communist Party and, after 1955, the North Korea–affiliated General Association of Korean Residents in Japan (Chōsensōren).[47] After the Cold War, however, many government and political leaders questioned its raison d'être, and some suggested that the entire PSIA, or at least its external intelligence section, be disbanded and absorbed by either CIRO, the National Police Agency, or MOFA's Intelligence and Research Bureau.[48] In the event, however, Japan's most conspicuous postwar counterterrorism failure led to reform of the PSIA and to its rebirth as a foreign intelligence organization.

The PSIA was widely and vigorously condemned for failing to prevent devotees of the cult cum terrorist organization Aum Shinrikyō from murdering thirteen subway passengers and for leaving more than six thousand seriously ill or permanently disabled in its March 1995 sarin gas attack in central Tokyo. After the incident, when the PSIA shockingly declared that Aum "did not fall within its jurisdiction," it again found itself struggling to survive.[49] From a narrow bureaucratic and legal perspective, the PSIA failed to prevent Aum-related incidents between 1989 and 1995 because Aum was protected as a religion by the Subversive Activities Prevention Act (SAPA), which stipulates that investigations "shall not under any circumstances be carried out. . . [that] unreasonably restrict freedom of thought, freedom of religion, freedom of assembly and association, freedom of expression, academic freedom, the right of workers to organize and act collectively, or any other liberty or right of the citizens which is guaranteed by the Constitution of Japan."[50] As one PSIA official explained, "Because Aum claimed religious status, our senior officials who still suffered from the trauma of a severe controversy with [the Buddhist organization] Soka Gakkai in the 1960s judged them to be out of bounds."[51]

Moreover, since the PSIA did not have the power to arrest or interview suspects, it was unable to collect evidence required for an exemption to the SAPA requirements. This was a classic chicken-and-egg problem for the lawyers in the PSIA and the Justice Ministry: counterterrorism activities targeting a new and unknown organization required SAPA approval. Put differently, evidence that the organization in question was already involved in large-scale subversive activities was needed so that investigators could legally collect evidence on its subversive activities. So, since Aum was not formally labeled a subversive organization by the Public Security Examination Commission (Kōan Shinsa Iinkai—PSEC), the PSIA was stymied.[52] Still, PSIA officials acknowledge their failure. According to one official: "Aum should have been an easy case. We could identify its leader and we knew who handled its finances. But it was a religion, so when we tried to apply the law, we found there were no well-defined regulations for how to hold the required conferences with the accused. Their lawyers won delays and we lost momentum."[53]

So in May 1995 Aum's leader, Matsumoto Chizuo, was arrested, but only after perpetrating the most deadly terrorist act in postwar Japanese history, an act that many—including intelligence professionals—believe could have been prevented.[54] And even after the incident and Matsumoto's arrest, the PSIA continued to encounter what by some lights seem petty legal problems. In January 1997, PSEC officially rejected the PSIA's request for SAPA approval to dismantle Aum Shinrikyō on the grounds that this religious organization did not meet the required SAPA conditions for being designated a subversive organization to be disbanded.[55] Finally, in December 1999, when it was clear that Aum remained active—and possibly violent—the Diet passed a Subversive Organizations Control Law that relaxed SAPA conditions for the designation of subversive organizations.[56] As a result, the PSIA gained a new legally justified responsibility: inspecting Aum Shinrikyō and its related organizations.[57]

In the meantime, however, the PSIA had been resized and reauthorized. The Administrative Reform Council, possibly under pressure from PSIA supporters in the LDP like the influential Mizuno Kiyoshi, decided to keep the PSIA in existence.[58] In its final report, the council acknowledged that the agency was responsible for regulating organizations in order "to maintain our Constitution-abiding society."[59] The PSIA would survive but could not avoid entirely the wave of governmental restructuring that affected most ministries and agencies in the late 1990s. With the Aum trauma still fresh in people's mind, the council's final report also required the PSIA to close an entire division in its Second Research Bureau, which was monitoring right-wing organizations; to close twenty-nine of its forty-three regional offices within three years; and to "streamline" its organization by "adjusting to recent changes in international and domestic environments."[60]

Here, then, was the silver lining for the post-Aum PSIA. Thanks to this bit of political and bureaucratic legerdemain, the council called on the PSIA to assign additional "manpower for overseas intelligence gathering activities as well as for the strengthening of cabinet intelligence capabilities."[61] That is, it directed the PSIA to second more personnel to CIRO and to MOFA. Accordingly, there were twenty secondees from the PSIA in CIRO by 2005. Since seconded officials are not counted as part of a Japanese administrative unit's personnel size, this appeared on the books as a downsizing, even though most of the PSIA officials who were seconded to MOFA and CIRO returned after three years.[62] Moreover, the pain of downsizing was further mitigated in April 1999 when the Central Government Organizations Reform Promotion Headquarters ordered the PSIA to reduce its head count by only two hundred, just 11 percent of its nearly 1,750 staff.[63] Up to fifty-eight of these two hundred could be reassigned to overseas intelligence activities, and forty could be used "to strengthen the intelligence collection and analysis capabilities of the cabinet."[64] This was a textbook case of failure-induced enriching reform identified in chapter 1: the PSIA now had a broader and better-funded lease on life despite its conspicuous and tragic failure with Aum.

Once formally limited to domestic HUMINT for counterintelligence and counterterrorism, and allowed only a minimal presence abroad—mostly in eastern Europe to monitor communists— the PSIA was now being propelled in the direction it had already mapped out for itself, a direction that took it overseas. This was an unintended consequence of the administrative reforms and likely an intended consequence of political intervention; tinkering reduced its size temporarily but enabled the PSIA to expand its original mandate.[65] In fact, there is evidence that this was not only just where the PSIA had wished to move but also where it had already set up shop: in 1993, even before the administrative reforms, it had produced more than 6,800 intelligence reports, over half of which covered foreign affairs, including 528 on North Korea.[66]

So the PSIA not only *sur*vived but was *re*vived in the first decade after the Cold War. Although it was still denied subpoena power, was not allowed to collect electronically, and lacked its own intelligence customer, its officials now could focus more broadly on cults and others deemed subversive at home while expanding its reach to include more foreign intelligence collection than ever before, mainly in Russia, China, and South Korea.[67]

Military Intelligence

The structure of Japan's military intelligence had remained unchanged for most of the last two Cold War decades. It operated within a microcosm of the silo system that afflicted the Japanese intelligence community overall: the internal bureaus in the civilian defense bureaucracy, the Joint Staff Council, and the staff offices of each service branch handled their own intelligence collection and analysis.[68] Moreover, as documented in chapter 3, Japanese analysts depended disproportionately on U.S. estimates and on U.S. data, including images—when they were shared. And when they were not shared, Japanese analysts grumbled about their dependence. With public opinion still largely inhospitable to military affairs, the government made only intermittent efforts to persuade skeptics of the utility of SDF intelligence activities.

This would now begin to change, but not all at once. Editors of "The Defense of Japan," the annual statement of Japanese defense policy produced by the National Institute for Defense Studies were compelled to provide abbreviated descriptions of Japanese surveillance activities in language that conformed explicitly to official (sometimes tortured) interpretations of Article 9 of the postwar Constitution. They depicted SDF intelligence as limited to the routine collection of military signals from neighboring countries. The following paragraph appeared with virtually no changes in "The Defense of Japan" between 1984 and 1990:

> Embracing strictly defensive self-defense [*senshu bōei*] as its principle, it is extremely important for Japan to maintain constant warning and surveillance as well as the collection of information necessary for our defense in our territory and its periphery whether in peacetime or in emergencies. To this end, the SDF is constantly conducting warning and surveillance activities with its radar sites, coast surveillance troops, and security guard offices, aircraft, and vessels. In addition, it also collects information regarding the movements and equipment of foreign vessels and aircrafts. The Air Self-Defense Force is monitoring all flights flying over Japan's territory and its periphery with twenty-eight radar sites located across Japan and its early warning aircraft.[69]

Then, during the first eight years after the Cold War, "The Defense of Japan" referred very little to either intelligence or surveillance activities, perhaps because its editors felt they had less to boast about in the new threat environment. Other than noting that the SDF regularly engaged in (now mostly unspecified) surveillance activities, the annual report began to focus on intelligence for international security cooperation to deal with regional conflicts and humanitarian crises in the Middle East and Africa.[70] One retired senior military intelligence officer recalled that "SDF intelligence activities quite naturally stagnated" during this period.[71]

That would change in January 1997, when the government undertook its most ambitious intelligence overhaul to that point—its creation of the

Defense Intelligence Headquarters (Bōei Jōhō Honbu—DIH). Unlike most of the reforms reviewed in this volume, the DIH—the military's largest, most centralized technical intelligence operation ever—was neither the direct consequence of an intelligence failure nor connected directly to the transformation of the strategic environment. It was the long-simmering product of extended strategic planning in response to technological change and was seasoned by frustration with U.S. domination of the Japanese intelligence community.

The DIH emerged after the Cold War from discussions between a pair of farsighted policy entrepreneurs determined that the Japanese intelligence community must not fall behind technologically at the moment when it most needed to enhance its own capabilities. As far back as the summer of 1984, Nishihiro Seiki, then director general of the Defense Policy Bureau, coaxed support from Chief Cabinet Secretary Gotōda Masaharu for an integrated military intelligence unit modeled on the U.S. Defense Intelligence Agency. Gotōda, the ex-police and intelligence official who became the champion for political control of the bureaucracy and the enemy of parochialism in government, welcomed the idea that barriers to communication across the military services should be reduced.[72] In 1988, after rising to vice minister of defense, a post that gave him the tacit license to do so, Nishihiro began actively "lobbying" Diet members for a DIH with Gotōda's support.[73]

Nishihiro was responding to two sources of internal discontent as well. The first was domestic. By the 1980s, frustration had been mounting among military officers unhappy with CIRO's (and thereby the police agency's) nominal leadership of the Ground Staff Office Intelligence Department Special Annex (Chōbetsu), the 1,300-person unit described in chapter 3, where they, not civilians, actually performed the collection and analysis of signals data.[74] Chōbetsu was never part of the official CIRO or NPA organizational charts, and unlike CIRO, it had the capability to collect and analyze signals intelligence on its own. But it fell under CIRO's control because officials seconded from the police agency dominated the leadership positions in both Chōbetsu and CIRO, and because Chōbetsu's military officials were required to report intelligence to CIRO before reporting to the leadership of the Japan Defense Agency.

To add insult to injury, it was CIRO's head, not a military officer or JDA official, who reported signals-derived intelligence to the prime minister. To mollify his troops, Nishihiro proposed placing the new DIH under military leadership, a move he justified by arguing that a reformed Chōbetsu would be its core organization. But he knew that his plan would not succeed without consent from the NPA, and was concerned that seconded police officials within the JDA's internal bureaus would veto the plan. So the wily bureaucrat Nishihiro consulted Gotōda, the former bureaucrat but now powerful LDP leader, who, as we saw earlier, was familiar with Japanese intelligence organizations and respected by senior police officials. After extended deliberation, Nishihiro coaxed a solution from the shrewd Gotōda. The JDA could stand up a DIH under an SDF commander if its deputy were a civilian officer seconded from the cabinet and if the leadership of Chōbetsu—now subsumed within the larger DIH—continued to be commanded by a civilian NPA official. For his part, Gotōda got Nishihiro to agree that all intelligence handled by the DIH would have to be reported to the cabinet.[75]

Gotōda insisted that these conditions were not designed to help the NPA maintain its influence but that he was motivated by concern for civilian control of the military and by his desire to ensure Japan's control of its own intelligence community. He had been chief cabinet secretary when Korean Airlines flight 007 was shot down by the Soviets in September 1983. Natsume Haruo, the Defense Agency's vice minister who brought the JDA intelligence report about the incident to Gotōda's office, reportedly had been as unaware as Gotōda that the SDF had already shared its intelligence with the United States. Indeed, as reported in chapter 3, Gotōda had been unaware that for decades U.S. officers had been embedded in the SDF signals intelligence monitoring facility in Hokkaidō, which had intercepted the Soviet transmissions. He feared that if SDF officers were to monopolize military intelligence under the new arrangement, they might again use it without authorization and override the will of the civilian authorities.[76] Accompanying this was the now widespread concern about U.S. control of Japanese intelligence. An enraged Gotōda, who had once been forced into accepting this fait accompli, fumed: "The U.S. got the intelligence first, and we were second in line. We don't need the SDF subordinated to the United States."[77] Even before the KAL 007 dust settled, Natsume and Gotōda changed procedures to require prior approval for all military intelligence transfers to the United States.[78]

This was the second, equally difficult problem that Nishihiro had to solve—and the one highlighted in the epigraph at the beginning of this chapter. While his implicit bureaucratic goal for the DIH was to improve the status of both the Defense Agency and the SDF relative to other intelligence organizations, including the National Police Agency, he understood the long-standing and widespread discomfort within the Japanese intelligence community regarding accommodation to the United States. So the new, integrated DIH was designed to improve Japanese intelligence capacity not only relative to the civilian agencies but also relative to the United States. Sugiyama Shigeru, chairman of the Joint Staff Council when the DIH was established, channeled the preferences of Gotōda and other senior Japanese leaders when he recalled that the effort to increase defense intelligence collection and analysis capabilities was undertaken in part to "reduce its dependence on the U.S. forces."[79]

So for these reasons, and above all because technological advancement was for many the Holy Grail of national security, Nishihiro and Gotōda found themselves pushing on an open door—at least within the ruling LDP.[80] In 1989, less than a year after becoming administrative vice minister, Nishihiro had a DIH in mind when he announced that the JDA would integrate Japan's military signals and image capabilities within a decade.[81] In July 1992, he directed the formation of a precursor body that he would chair, the Defense Agency Intelligence Committee, with responsibility for communication and coordination between the ground, maritime, and air self-defense forces. In November 1995, the government issued the long-awaited "National Defense Program Guidelines," which explicitly addressed the need for improving Japan's "warning and intelligence capabilities."[82] Then, in January 1997, the DIH came into being—ahead of schedule—with a staff of 1,600 assembled from the intelligence-related organizations of the ground, maritime, and air self-defense forces under the Joint Staff Council at JDA headquarters in Ichigaya. The unit included the more than 1,300 intelligence professionals stationed at six SIGINT reception facilities across Japan: Ōi in Saitama, Shibata-Kofunato in Niigata, Tachiarai in Fukuoka, Kikaichō in Kagoshima, Higashi Chitose in Hokkaidō, and Miho in Tottori.[83] Each monitoring facility was given responsibility for recording transmissions, locating their origin, and, when necessary, decrypting them.[84]

Per the Nishihiro-Gotōda agreement, the head of the DIH would be an SDF flag officer supported by four senior analysts, including one civilian official who would be deputy vice minister for defense affairs—second in command. The section responsible for signals intelligence, which inherited the work of the Chōbetsu, was now called the Radio Wave Bureau (Denpabu); under the agreement, its chief would be an official seconded from the police agency.[85] But it is not clear that the military's relationship to the NPA in the intelligence domain was set on an entirely new course once SIGINT data and analyses were reported to the prime minister and the cabinet by the head of the Defense Intelligence Headquarters rather than by CIRO.[86]

Along the model of the U.S. Defense Intelligence Agency, each of the separate service branch–embedded military SIGINT units, internal bureau intelligence units, and joint staff units were consolidated and now had to report directly to the military's Joint Staff Council (Tōgō Bakuryō Kaigi). The idea was that this broader unit would be able to produce fully integrated image, signals, and open source analyses. And, as noted earlier, it also was designed to provide the Japanese intelligence community greater independence from the U.S. intelligence community. As Gotōda declared when the DIH was established, Japan should be more rabbit-like: "Rabbits aren't dependent on other animals because they have long ears."[87]

The DIH was a significant—but still flawed—investment. It was capable of both "policy support" and "operational support" using SIGINT and IMINT, and it was an important step toward engaging a shifting geostrategic environment. But neither of the two internal problems that had animated Nishihiro—the pervasive sense within the intelligence community that it had second-class status within the Japanese government and resentment that the intelligence community was excessively dependent on the United States—was entirely ameliorated.[88] Nor were the stovepipes blocking communication between military intelligence and CIRO eliminated.[89] Part of the problem was legal: Japanese military intelligence was still formally barred by a 1969 decree banning military use of space, and thus, despite Gotōda's and Nishihiro's best efforts, Japan remained "effectively a client of U.S. space-based surveillance and intelligence collection."[90] Moreover, despite the elimination of silos within the military intelligence community, many of those in the civilian intelligence community were grandfathered into the new organization. And while three of the first four DIH directors had served as commanders of the GSDF's Intelligence Department (Rikubaku Chōsabu), the decision to allow NPA and CIRO officials to command the SIGINT-focused Radio Wave Bureau continued to "generate strong resentment from defense and military officials."[91] Thus, despite the forethought and political bargaining that gave birth to the DIH, one former high-level government official familiar with the Japanese intelligence community not usually given to hyperbole could remain skeptical. The DIH, he explained, was essentially the product of tinkering; it was set up "only after eight years of procrastination" and in the wake of "a chain of intelligence failures and subsequent public criticism after several catastrophic events such as the Kobe earthquake, and the Aum sarin gas attack . . . caused humiliation for political leaders and government officials."[92]

More Failure

The humiliation continued even after the DIH got under way, when—just as in the 1993 Nodong missile case—the Defense Agency conspicuously failed to anticipate or detect the launch by North Korea of a Taepodong missile that flew through Japanese airspace in August 1998—despite early warnings from U.S. intelligence.[93] Former director of cabinet security affairs Sassa Atsuyuki called this Japan's "first national security shock since the MiG-25 incident in 1976" and blamed it on poor communication between uniformed command and the JDA internal bureaus and between the internal bureaus and the prime minister's office.[94] To its credit, the Denpabu's Miura Radio Wave Monitoring Center was able to verify immediately that Pyongyang had lied in asserting that it had launched a satellite.[95]

But accurate identification after the fact did not reassure the unsettled Japanese public. Unlike in 1993, the media and politicians instantly issued full-throated calls for improved intelligence capabilities. With the eager assistance of the defense industry, politicians embraced proposals for an indigenous (kokusan) Japanese military satellite system that they had been considering since 1992.[96] Former foreign minister Nakayama Tarō immediately convened the LDP's Foreign Affairs Research Council (Gaikō Mondai Chōsakai) to discuss the issue. The JDA and CIRO, which had also been formally studying how best to proceed with spy satellites, were also newly energized. With all parties aware of the need for enhanced intelligence, surveillance, and reconnaissance—and with a public that had begun to appreciate the threat more clearly than before—plans for an indigenous program were accelerated. It took barely two months for an agreement to be reached among cabinet members on a research and development budget for indigenous satellites, and less than four months before a formal cabinet decision was made to introduce an indigenous intelligence satellite.[97]

Sassa also recalls that everyone agreed, just as in the case of the MiG-25 incursion which triggered procurement of early warning aircraft, that the Taepodong incident provided a compelling reason to enhance the Japanese intelligence system—in this case its imaging capacity.[98] In March 1999, without even pretending to undo the thirty-year-old proscription on the military use of space, the government and Diet approved a budget that included a system designed by Mitsubishi Electric Corporation (MELCO) in the early 1990s.[99] Magosaki Ukeru, then chief of MOFA's Intelligence and Analysis Service, recalls that one reason for the quick decision to go forward with the new program was that the Japanese government did not trust the Clinton administration, which it suspected of harboring a "conciliatory policy" toward North Korea.[100] Others saw an opportunity for Japanese defense manufacturers. After all, the U.S. government had been actively pressing Tokyo to buy U.S. satellites and had been thwarting Japanese plans to develop indigenous ones.[101] Some in the Japanese government suspected that Washington was doing so, among other reasons, in the hope of maintaining "shutter control."[102] The Taepodong failure simply made what had been "politically untouchable" politically viable.[103] This mistrust and the conflation of security and defense industrial motives came during a very difficult period in U.S.-Japanese relations. According to one former NSC official, the Japanese response to Washington's advance warning was " 'You're just trying to sell us missile defense systems.' Actionable intelligence was rejected because trust was degraded."[104]

It seems clear that the time for this enhancement was coming soon in any event, more likely the consequence of the shift in the strategic environment and Japan's voracious appetite for advanced technology than of the Taepodong intelligence failure or alliance frictions alone. Science and Technology Agency and National Space Development Agency remote sensing satellites had been operating since the late 1980s, and images produced by their "research observation satellites" were provided regularly to military analysts—an "open secret" first revealed in August 1993, just ahead of the Taepodong launch, when the *Yomiuri Shimbun* published images showing Chinese port and airstrip construction on Woody Island in the Paracel Archipelago in the South China Sea.[105] CIRO, for its part, had been studying reconnaissance satellites since 1991, and before the Taepodong missile sailed through, the JDA had already issued a classified "Outline for Photo-Reconnaissance Satellites" with the help of the defense contractors MELCO, Nippon Electric Corporation, Mitsubishi Heavy Industries, and Toshiba.[106] MOFA had even included a line item for a spysat system in its 1997 budget request.[107] Appreciating lingering public sensitivity to bulking up intelligence and surveillance—and well aware that the Japanese government had been allowing the JDA to buy commercial satellite images (mostly from U.S. firms) since 1983—Nakayama contrived a particularly ingenious euphemism to sell this move: Japan should have what he dubbed "its own so-called *diplomatic satellite* [*gaikō eisei*]."[108] In the event, and without regard for what it was labeled, the decision was hailed as a "turning point" for a "vigorous new space policy."[109]

But it was difficult to proceed with unbridled vigor at a time when the LDP's once broad-based dominance of Japanese politics was coming apart, especially while Socialist Party leader Murayama Tomiichi was prime minister. Murayama took office in June 1994, just in time to obstruct implementation of the August recommendations of a high-level private sector panel calling for development of indigenous reconnaissance satellites, missile defense, and other defense systems that had already proved politically dicey. In January 1996, once his tenure—and the oddly coupled LDP-Socialist government—ended, the LDP's Hashimoto Ryūtarō became prime minister and revived these plans.

Still, it took more time than many hoped. Even though the "peaceful use of space" restriction had been compromised years earlier by the JDA's deployment of dual-use transponders on commercial satellites and by its acquisition of images from the Science and Technology Agency and National Space Development Agency—and notwithstanding a December 1998 cabinet order that specifically greenlighted "intelligence for crisis management for diplomacy and defense/national security"—a Cabinet Satellite Intelligence Center (CSIC) was not established until April 2001. And as if to poke the military intelligence community in the eye, it was stood up within CIRO. In yet another indication of the importance LDP politicians placed on maintaining civilian control of the military, Japan's defense-related space activities would have to be budgeted through civilian offices and justified as dual use.[110]

A retired senior CIRO official has a more benign interpretation as to why the CSIC was put inside the Cabinet Office under CIRO's control rather than directly inside the Defense Agency or SDF. He recalled that it was a time of fiscal austerity and observed that neither the JDA nor MOFA was willing to divert its own resources for this very expensive new activity. Invoking a baseball metaphor, he explained that "it was like when two outfielders are next to each other, but neither calls for the ball and it drops between them. If the funding had been attached, both players would have called for the ball."[111] CIRO's jurisdictional victory notwithstanding, CSIC began operations as a de facto part of the DIH's Imagery/Geography Department, and was initially directed by General Kunimi Masahiro, who was called out of retirement.[112] At first he supervised a staff of more than two hundred, fewer than two dozen of whom were SDF personnel. The others were all seconded from other ministries and agencies.[113] General Kunimi and his successors, all active duty military officers, would have to maintain appearances by reporting to an NPA official or a MOFA diplomat serving as deputy director and chief analyst.

Like DIH, the new satellite program was plagued by problems very nearly from its inception. Despite the enthusiasm for an indigenous satellite program from business and the strategic community, the launch of the first of Japan's four planned post-Taepodong satellites was delayed until March 2003, five years after the decision to go forward. Then, with subsequent program delays, it took nearly nine years to complete all four planned launches, by which time the second of the satellites (launched in February 2007) was already blind on account of a failure of its aging componentry.[114] But even the satellites that were generating images could not see as clearly as commercially available "off the shelf" (and therefore much cheaper) satellites. Operating with just one-meter resolution, the Japanese satellites could not be nearly as effective as the sixty-centimeter resolution of the best available commercial ones, and were a far cry in capability from the fifteen-centimeter resolution attributed publicly to U.S. military satellites.[115] Analyst Matsuura Shinya has argued that the snap decision to proceed with the indigenous program in 1998 was made by panicked politicians and by bureaucrats with limited technical expertise who tinkered with the system to reassure a concerned public. It was the elevation of politics over planning, he argues, that ensured the poor performance of the Japanese program in its early years.[116] Years later, one cynical, but unnamed, "individual with ties to the government" declared in the *Asahi Shimbun* that Japan "still relies on the United States for satellite intelligence. Japan's satellites have been virtually useless."[117]

This sort of hyperbole notwithstanding, the satellite program was very useful from the perspective of bureaucratic politics. Jury-rigged in familiar fashion, each unit negotiated its own piece of a new, high-priced and high-profile activity. The Cabinet Satellite Intelligence Center was housed physically at Defense Agency facilities, supervised by a uniformed officer whose deputy director and chief analyst were seconded from the National Police Agency in Kasumigaseki, and located administratively in the Cabinet Intelligence Research Office, but staffed overwhelmingly by secondees from the Defense Intelligence Headquarters.[118] One analyst of the Japanese satellite program was especially cynical about this arrangement: "All the data collected by Japan's information-gathering satellites are kept [in the Defense Agency] in Ichigaya. . . . They claim that the data are available to other agencies and ministries, but that requires these others to have the same level of clearance. The result is that no one else is using the data."[119]

Kidnapping Politics

For all the intense, albeit episodic, contestation about how to fix the Japanese intelligence system in the face of new threats after the Cold War, no matter involving national intelligence was more momentous, more sustained, or more consequential than the one known as the "abductee problem" (*ratchi mondai*). Different in kind from the others examined here, this was not a failure to collect or to analyze critical intelligence accurately or to manage a crisis. Neither was it a case of politicians ignoring intelligence reports. It was a failure to act upon uncomfortable truths—effectively a politicization of intelligence—that provides an important window on the porous boundary between intelligence and policy in Japan.

Many of the basic facts of this matter, equal to the most rancorous issue in postwar Japanese politics, are well known.[120] Starting in the 1970s, North Korean agents secretly entered Japan and abducted more than a dozen Japanese youths—one as young as thirteen—in a cynical program to bring native speakers to Pyongyang to train its spies. More than a decade of heartrending pleas for a full accounting of their children's fates by the abductees' families went unanswered by the government, despite leaks from North Korea as early as 1980 confirming that the youths had been kidnapped and that Japanese sovereignty had been violated. As normalization talks between Tokyo and Pyongyang proceeded, conservative groups in civil society stepped in to press for answers, working closely with the abductee families, for whom they became especially effective advocates.

FIGURE 4.1   Yokota Megumi was just thirteen years old when she was abducted off a Niigata street and spirited away to North Korea by North Korean agents.
Photo: *Asahi Shimbun*

A ferocious outpouring of public emotion—including anger directed at both North Korea and the Japanese government—was set off by the admission of North Korean leader Kim Jong-il during the visit of Prime Minister Koizumi Junichirō to Pyongyang in October 2002 that freelancers had abducted thirteen Japanese youths. Kim's promise to return the five who had survived shocked the Japanese public, which rejected the possibility that so many could have died from illness or accident in the prime of their lives. Meanwhile, activist groups roiled the political waters by insisting there had been as many as five hundred abductions. The cause was embraced by conservative politicians, most notably by an ambitious deputy chief cabinet secretary, Abe Shinzō, who used it to consolidate the LDP electoral base and secure his future as party leader and prime minister.

At a minimum, it seems that the Japanese state, designated protector of national sovereignty and provider of security to its citizens, remained willfully ignorant of actionable intelligence. Abductee families who had complained for years of the "unhelpfulness," "arrogance," and "callousness" of local and national bureaucrats were deprecated by haughty government officials who insisted that "young people often disappear into new lives in Europe."[121] Surely they knew better, as one retired former senior GSDF officer

FIGURE 4.2   Future prime minister Abe Shinzō (in background) was present at the historic meeting between Kim Jong-il and Koizumi Junichirō in Pyongyang in October 2002.
Photo: Kyodo via AP Images

familiar with the case has suggested.[122] After all, as early as January 1980, the *Sankei Shimbun* had connected the dots in a front-page story suggesting that young couples who mysteriously disappeared from Japanese beaches in the late 1970s had been abducted by foreign agents.[123] The *Sankei* report was dismissed by authorities as speculation, even after it was confirmed by evidence pried out of the intelligence community by the Japan Communist Party.

Indeed, the JCP was the first to bring up the abduction issue in the Diet— and it did so in the form of an extended critique of Japanese counterintelligence.[124] In March 1988, JCP Diet member Hashimoto Atsushi, using information supplied to his aide Hyōmoto Tatsukichi by abductee families, grilled the government regarding the revelation by North Korean agent Kim Hyon-hui that her Japanese instructor in Pyongyang, Li Eun-hye, was Japanese. Representative Hashimoto forced Japanese police officials to acknowledge that this woman with the Korean name Li had been abducted from Japan.[125] He also forced the authorities to acknowledge that citizens who went missing in July and August 1978 were likely to have been abducted as well.[126] He closed his questioning by urging the government to take action, but the issue was never taken up on the bilateral agenda during normalization talks. Then in early 1997, in an effort to understand the contours of the counterintelligence failure, the diligent Hyōmoto reached out to MOFA's Asia-Pacific Bureau chief to arrange a meeting with a contact in the Korean Workers' Party to discuss the abductees.[127] Hyōmoto was not aware that at the time the JCP was engaged in its own normalization negotiations with the Korean Workers' Party. Concerned that Hyōmoto's collaboration with MOFA would jeopardize their talks, party leaders accused Hyōmoto of plotting to spy for the Japanese police and stripped him of his party membership. The JCP was not interested in pursuing this matter any further.

This seemed to suit both MOFA and the NPA, which knew of—and was investigating—infiltration of Japan by North Korean agents at the time the *Sankei* article was published.[128] Harada Takeo, who served as the Foreign Ministry's North Korean desk officer in 2004, insists that the first reliable intelligence that abductions had taken place was received by MOFA in late 1993 and early 1994, but he believes that the local police and the NPA first became aware of the kidnappings more than a decade earlier and were complicit in covering them up. According to the intelligence historian Kotani Ken: "The NPA would like to forget about their failure. They had a listening post in northern Tokyo that ought to have captured SIGINT from DPRK agents."[129] But it is not clear if the North Korean agents were in radio contact with their home base, and in any event it seems just as likely that local police in Niigata and the Foreign Ministry were forced off the case by powerful politicians. In the meantime, MOFA claimed disingenuously that it had not actively pursued the issue at first so as not to endanger the abductees.

But MOFA did more than fail to act upon the information it had in hand. It repeatedly urged the families of suspected abductees to keep quiet for the sake of diplomacy. Many have come to suspect that the underlying reason it sat on its intelligence was that it feared reprisals from LDP soft-liners such as the powerful Kanemaru Shin, who, like the JCP, were engaged in sensitive talks with their North Korean counterparts.[130] Kanemaru may have kept a lid on the abductee issue in order to clear a path to normalization of diplomatic relations and to generate financial benefits for his faction and political allies in other parties, including the Japan Socialist Party (JSP).[131] Harada, the former MOFA official, sums up the government's response as a "conspiracy of silence" led by LDP power brokers, while others have attributed it in part to a fear among bureaucrats that the pro-Pyongyang Korean community and the JSP could hurt them by inflaming unrelated issues, for example, those related to the legal status of Korean residents or to wartime compensation for forced labor.[132] At that time, according to an NPA official, "the JSP was still powerful enough to keep the bureaucrats in line."[133]

An experienced PSIA official grudgingly acknowledged that unspecified "mistakes were made by the intelligence community and by law enforcement."[134] One retired diplomat, being more tactful and slightly more specific, explained that Japanese politicians "wanted to get credit in the history books for normalizing relations with North Korea and did not even want to see the intelligence."[135] But Tanaka Hitoshi, Prime Minister Koizumi's emissary to North Korea, reconnects the abduction case to our larger question of intelligence with characteristic incisiveness. As he sees it, the abductee issue was built not directly on an intelligence failure but on "a policy failure derived from our not having been willing to generate better intelligence."[136] Politicians, it seemed, did not want to know, and some were powerful enough to make sure others would not either. Here was a case in which policy makers failed the intelligence community, not vice versa.

We have learned that a limited number of imaginative leaders, like Hashimoto Ryūtarō, Gotōda Masaharu, and Nishihiro Seiki, felt the urgency to create a more robust intelligence system even before the strategic implications of the end of the Cold War became apparent to others—and that they did so without a major intelligence failure forcing their hand. They creatively seized upon the opportunity provided by the widely embraced enthusiasm of Japan's political class for "administrative reform," and were determined to integrate Japan's military intelligence capacity even before the collapse of the Soviet Union.

But in retrospect they would seem more like tinkerers than grand strategists. Even the most ambitious and successful intelligence reform of the first decade after the Cold War—creation of Japan's largest, and first integrated, military intelligence unit, the DIH—was insufficiently comprehensive to optimize military intelligence, much less to confront shifting geostrategic challenges adequately and to address the problems of the intelligence community overall. So the result described here—the admixture of persistent sectionalism, unremitting miscommunication, political narrow-mindedness, continued dependence on the United States, and resentment of that dependence—remained. Japan's leaders knew they had fallen short and that the shifting regional environment would require them to do much more; the problem was that only some in the political class cared. There was little that reform-minded bureaucrats could do unless and until political leaders asked for what the intelligence community had to offer. Without political leadership, the intelligence bureaucracy simply reverted to long-standing entrenched practices—the intelligence community's suboptimal mean.

The structure of the Japanese intelligence community at the end of the twentieth century thus remained a clutter of intelligence services connected with curved and straight lines of uncertain authority. CIRO became a catchment area for the flotsam and jetsam of the intelligence community that flowed its way, and remained colonized at the highest level by the National Police Agency. Hardly the "Japanese CIA" depicted by some novelists and journalists—Taoka Shunji frames it as the difference between a tiger and a house cat—CIRO continued to have no significant staff and only limited capabilities of its own.[137] It, in turn, colonized line agencies that became possessed by the desire to find workarounds. Often they could not. Military officers serving in foreign embassies as military attachés could not report directly to their uniformed superiors, but only through MOFA. The JDA, still a decade away from becoming a full ministry with a policy remit, reported directly to the prime minister, and not through the cabinet. Its newest high-tech imaging unit, supervised by a senior military officer, was formally housed in the Cabinet Intelligence and Research Office. And neither METI officials, its deputies in JETRO, nor officials in the Ministry of Finance's International Finance Bureau stationed abroad had any formal direct link to the intelligence community at all.

The inadequate intelligence reforms documented in this chapter were enabled by two factors beyond the demonstrated shrewdness of a few political leaders and beyond the opportunity presented to them by administrative reform. First, the Japanese public slowly but clearly began to understand national security threats and to appreciate the importance of intelligence. Whereas there had been virtually no public reaction in 1993 to North Korea's

Nodong missile launch, the Taepodong test five years later touched off a post-Sputnik-like uproar that breached the political dam that had been obstructing creation of the CSIC.[138] And second, Japan's U.S. ally—the continuing source of much of its most detailed intelligence—began to press openly for Japanese intelligence reform to enhance cooperation between Tokyo and Washington. A hortatory report by Richard Armitage and Joseph Nye in 2000 highlighted the need to enhance U.S.-Japan intelligence cooperation. Their high-profile study group compared U.S.-Japan intelligence sharing unfavorably to U.S.-NATO practices and argued that "a strategic vision of intelligence cooperation with Japan is long overdue. . . . The time has come to bring our intelligence cooperation out of the closet."[139]

Despite lingering exasperation with dependence on U.S. intelligence within the Japanese intelligence community, this appeal was met with enthusiasm there and in the security policy community as well. After all, many Japanese intelligence professionals were of two minds about intelligence cooperation with the United States. On the one hand, as we have seen, it was resented. But on the other, it meant enhanced capabilities that, ironically, could pave the way for more independent Japanese intelligence capabilities. Robert Henderson captures these dynamics well. On his account, Japanese leaders knew after the Cold War that they had "to face up to the country's dependency on American-generated intelligence as well as the weaknesses in [Japan's] own internal processes for collection, assessment, and distribution of intelligence for strategic policy decision-making and for national crisis management."[140]

This long-standing and widely acknowledged problem was finally coming into sharp focus. Post–Cold War reform of the Japanese intelligence community had no doubt been slowed by the powerful idée fixe widely held by the public and even by many policy elites that Washington would take care of East Asian security and protect Japan's interests abroad. That perception seemed to weaken with the rise of China, the relative decline of the United States, and the unremitting provocations of North Korea—factors that did not come to the fore until after the twenty-first century dawned. Only then did the Japanese public seem willing to accept proposals for an expanded and comprehensively reformed intelligence community. And only then did the same media that had once penalized politicians for discussing security begin wondering why intelligence was inadequate.[141] As we shall see in chapter 5, the world and, in particular, the regional balance of power were about to change once again and close the deal that made comprehensive intelligence reform imaginable for the first time. The immediate precipitant for this reimagining arrived after a conspicuous U.S. intelligence failure one sunny late summer morning in September 2001.

CHAPTER 5

Reimagining Possibilities (2001–2013)

> All intelligence organizations the world over
> experience painful failures and tribulations, reflect on
> and learn from them, and then rebuild.
>
> —Ōmori Yoshio, 2008

As we have seen, repeated tinkering by bureaucrats without consistent political support during the first post–Cold War decade generated only limited intelligence reform. Creation of the Defense Intelligence Headquarters was no small matter, but rearranging the units of military intelligence could not adequately address the full range of problems afflicting the Japanese intelligence bureaucracies facing a new world order loaded with complexities requiring more comprehensive and better-coordinated intelligence. Small states and non-state actors with high-technology weapons now could pose direct and serious threats to Japan. Civil and religious wars that the superpowers had once contained in their own interests now widened to destabilize states and regions with which Japan traded but about which Tokyo had insufficient information. Moreover, for the first time in its modern history, Japan had to contend with the economic and military challenges from neighbors besides the Soviet Union. These all added up to radical changes in Japan's security environment that demanded a more thorough reimagining of Japan's intelligence community than any before.

Indeed, senior Japanese policy makers realized that substantive, coherent, and strategic intelligence reform was now essential, and they knew that making this happen would require amassing and spending significant political capital. It seemed that this realization—not yet fully embraced by the public—might be galvanized after 9/11, when terrorism emerged as a global threat and when China began to position itself to surge past Japan economically and threaten it militarily. These developments pushed Japanese strategists to begin producing more comprehensive proposals. As we shall see, for nearly the next decade and a half the emphasis would be on proposals, not on action. The tinkering that characterized the first post–Cold War decade would be displaced by a cascade of schemes, some more ambitious than others, but none of which would be adequately comprehensive until after the Chinese economy had already surpassed Japan's, North Korea had demonstrated nightmarish offensive capabilities, and cyber insecurity had risen to nearly the top of the security agenda, and not until after the United States, notwithstanding its immense absolute power, was plainly in relative decline.

The Drivers

Orphaned Offspring of the Cold War

The 9/11 attacks were not the first time that non-state actors had terrorized mass publics and challenged the security communities dedicated to defending them, of course. In Europe, Italy had struggled with the Red Brigades and Germany with the Baader-Meinhof Gang in the 1970s. Japan had its own experiences with its Red Army Faction in the 1970s and the terrorist bombing by Aum Shinrikyō in 1995.[1] But al-Qaeda's highly visible murderous successes in New York and at the Pentagon raised the stakes. Suddenly terrorism by "non-state actors"—the orphaned offspring of the Cold War— were the greatest global threat. As the Koizumi government moved to support the United States in its war against the Taliban in Afghanistan, the prime minister declared foreign intelligence—particularly enhanced HUMINT—a matter of national policy.[2]

Several terrorist acts directed at Japanese targets after 9/11 made headlines and stimulated reform. In April 2004, three NGO volunteers were kidnapped by Saraya al-Mujahideen in Iraq. In October 2004, a twenty-four-year-old Japanese tourist who had ignored advice not to travel to Iraq was abducted and beheaded by an Islamist group led by Abu Musab al-Zarqawi after Prime Minister Koizumi refused to withdraw an SDF contingent from Iraq. In October 2007, a Yokohama National University student was kidnapped and released in Iran.[3] But the threat expanded palpably when, in January 2013, ten Japanese were among the foreign workers taken hostage and murdered at a Japanese-owned gas plant in In Amenas, Algeria. Now the larger economy was the target, and it was clear Japan still lacked the capability to anticipate and respond effectively to such challenges on its own.[4]

FIGURE 5.1   Koda Shōsei was murdered in October 2004 by an Islamist group led by Abu Musab al-Zarqawi which had demanded Japan withdraw its small military contingent from Iraq.
Photo: Screen grab by AFP/Getty Images

The United States immediately dispatched transport aircraft with medical teams to Algeria and then used these planes to fly released hostages to German hospitals. Likewise, the British deployed a team of MI6 agents to In Amenas. Norway brought in its army special forces' medical team. But it took Japan four days to act. News that Japan had to beg France and the United States for intelligence about its hostages (to no avail); that it had tried and failed to pay ransom for the hostages; that the Algerian government provided faulty intelligence on the situation; that Prime Minister Abe's personal intervention came too late to dissuade the Algerian government from attempting a flawed rescue operation resulting in the Japanese workers' deaths; and news that both the United States and the UK had made arrangements to airlift rescued hostages to safety without consulting Japan all underlined Japan's inability to gain independent and timely access to intelligence as well as its inability to intervene on its own to rescue the hostages. Abe blamed the Algerian government: "It is regrettable that precious Japanese lives were lost as a result of the Algerian military's operations." The Algerian government argued that it had abandoned negotiations with the terrorists and attacked them to avert a larger catastrophe, the demolition of the natural gas plant, which might have claimed hundreds of lives. Algerian troops freed 107 foreigners and 685 Algerian hostages.[5]

Abe, who had returned to office just days earlier, was able to leverage unflattering comparisons to other countries' capabilities to justify a renewed effort to reconstruct Japan's security policy and its intelligence infrastructure. In his first policy speech to the Diet just days later, the prime minister highlighted Japan's intelligence deficiencies, insisting ruefully that his government had done everything it could "to collect information and rescue the hostages in Algeria," but acknowledging that Japanese capabilities were limited.[6] In a widely read review of the first year of the Abe cabinet, Chief Cabinet Secretary Suga Yoshihide recalled: "The turning point for this administration . . . was the Algerian hostage crisis. . . . It was extremely difficult to get any intelligence after the crisis started. . . . Even though some was obtained, it was often contradictory and the situation was very confused. . . . At that time, intelligence was more vital than anything else."[7] Privately, one of Suga's former deputies went further, stating that "after the Algeria crisis, the Japanese government put a team together to improve intelligence. We always respond, but fail to anticipate."[8] In the wake of the crisis—at a time when the Japanese had only two military attachés on the entire African continent—the demand to do more and better was growing. The ruling LDP and its Komeitō coalition partner pressed for deployment of additional SDF personnel abroad to protect Japanese citizens, and former defense minister Ishiba Shigeru called for relaxation of restrictions on the use of force abroad.[9] Machimura Nobutaka, the son of a wartime supervisor of the Special Higher Police counterespionage unit and himself a former MITI/JETRO official, would inherit Gotōda Masaharu's mantle as the leading intelligence reformer within Japan's political class, and he engaged the intelligence debate from very close range. He recalled that Prime Minister Koizumi, whom he served as foreign minister, and Fukuda Yasuo, whom he served as chief cabinet secretary, each paid lip service to enhancing the intelligence community after 9/11, but that "neither was very forward looking with regard to organizational reform."[10] In fact, as we shall see, Fukuda slowed the entire process and declared himself satisfied with adding a mere five cabinet intelligence analyst positions.[11]

The rise in global terrorism after 9/11 brought the deficiencies of Japan's intelligence community into focus through the lens of concerns about dependence on flawed U.S. intelligence. Many Japanese leaders now wondered: If U.S. intelligence could not anticipate a direct strike on its own homeland,

and if it could err on Iraqi WMD so consequentially, how could Japan count on Washington for a timely warning of an attack on Japan? As one leading historian of intelligence aptly put it, a perception emerged that the U.S. "intelligence umbrella" could not be counted on to keep Japan dry.[12] A former CIRO chief who had played a major role in redesigning the Japanese intelligence community remarked in 2008 that "Japan has become accustomed to depending on the United States for key national security functions, such as security and intelligence, and our own capabilities in this regard have become impoverished."[13] One of his subordinates in CIRO admitted sheepishly, "We watch for failures abroad to determine if we need to make change at home."[14]

Concern about dependence and the desire for intelligence reform were suprapartisan. Opposition party representatives argued strongly for a strengthened, autonomous Japanese intelligence system. Democratic Party of Japan leader Maehara Seiji called upon the government to develop a robust HUMINT capability to "enable Japan to develop its strategic diplomacy." His DPJ colleague Haraguchi Kazuhiro was even more straightforward: "We need our own collection, analysis, and strategy." The DPJ maintained its support for intelligence reform after taking the reins of government. In 2012, while foreign minister in the DPJ cabinet, Genba Kōichirō testified in the Diet that enhancing Japan's intelligence capabilities was "one of the greatest challenges facing Japan."[15]

The End of U.S. Primacy

Japanese and American vulnerability to the rise of non-state actors was connected to a second shift in the security environment—the end of U.S. primacy, especially in Japan's Northeast Asian neighborhood, where the balance of power was shifting dramatically and in an undesirable direction. Japan's GDP had been roughly twice that of China in 2005, but within a decade China's GDP had grown to more than two and a half times that of Japan. Although Japan's GDP per capita remained more than four times China's, sharply differential economic growth rates impinged directly on Japanese security. In step with economic expansion, Chinese military budgets grew from under $20 billion to over $100 billion in the decade after 9/11. Japan's defense budget, in contrast, declined by 7 percent during this same period and remained at less than $50 billion.[16] The loss of primacy, diffusion of global power, and proliferation of weapons of mass destruction left Japan allied with a still immensely powerful, but effectively deterred, United States—and with limited resources of its own.

The implications of these shifts for intelligence were recognized early on by Japan's defense and intelligence professionals. In 2006 a private think tank report argued that new threats and the need to make intelligence reform a matter of "urgent business" were direct consequences of the regional power shift.[17] Magosaki Ukeru, a former chief of the MOFA Intelligence and Analysis Service, argued bluntly in 2009 that Japan could not afford to continue to rely on U.S. intelligence. Invoking the cases of Palestine, Iran, Cambodia, Myanmar, and China after Tiananmen, he pointed out that U.S. interests and Japanese interests had often been misaligned, and therefore if Japan was to pursue its own interests, it needed to enhance its own intelligence capacity.[18]

But it was not just that U.S. intelligence seemed ineffective and unreliable. After repeated failures managing disasters at home, and after suffering their own painful crisis management lapses abroad, other responsible Japanese strategists began to wonder openly about U.S. abandonment. How long would the United States, its population tiring of foreign wars and fiscal constraints, continue to be willing and able to maintain its overall defense commitments to Japan? Editorialists, politicians, and academics started asking if Washington would remain capable of defending Japan, and even if so, how much more would it require of Japan itself? By 2015 a consensus had formed that reconstructing Tokyo's security policy-making and intelligence infrastructure might help hedge against the relative decline of Japan's U.S. ally. In one particularly revealing exchange, after a former MSDF chief of staff, Sugimoto Masahiko, remarked that "the Chinese navy will outstrip the combined capability of the MSDF and the U.S. Navy in the Western Pacific by 2020," a former ASDF chief of staff, Hokazono Kenichiro, associated China's growing power with deficiencies in Japanese intelligence: "China has superior espionage capabilities in space and the cyberspace domains compared to Japan's inadequate intelligence-gathering ability. In an age of increased threats in these areas, this could prove fatal unless the situation is remedied."[19]

Japan had begun to question whether the United States would (or even could) really double down on its Cold War dominance even before the 2016 U.S. presidential campaign and the election of Donald Trump forced these concerns to the top of the agenda of every U.S. ally.[20] Tanaka Hitoshi, the retired diplomat who helped negotiate the 2002 Pyongyang Declaration, wrote in 2008 of "the gradual evaporation of U.S. leadership," and a senior Japanese defense and intelligence official connected the dots between the loss of U.S. primacy and Japanese intelligence reform, recalling that "the relative decline of the United States was clearly a factor in the reconstruction of the Japanese intelligence community."[21] A consensus had been forming for change, and there were plenty of ideas about how best to respond.

Cascading Recommendations

In 2008 Kaneko Masafumi, a leading analyst of—and think tank–based adviser to—the Japanese intelligence community, reviewed a raft of formal reports regarding Japan's intelligence community, distilling from them six endemic problems that track closely with the elements that frame this volume. He found a consensus that Japanese intelligence units are insufficient collectors, mediocre analysts, and poor communicators. Critical intelligence was not flowing up to the policy makers except through sclerotic ministry-specific channels; the Japanese policy community was not always clear about what intelligence it required and did a poor job of overseeing and coordinating collection and analysis in any event. This consensus may have been due in part to the limited number of government and think tank specialists who overlapped on the commissions that issued these various reports. But the process by which post–Cold War intelligence reforms worked their way from concept to practice provides considerable insight into Japanese policy making in general, and to the politics that impede intelligence reform in particular. This section provides a review of that process—both administrative and political.[22]

As noted, Machimura Nobutaka credited the Algerian hostage crisis with driving home the importance of intelligence reform for Prime Minister Abe, but Machimura actually took up the cause much earlier, right after 9/11, when he was LDP deputy secretary general. Although his formal remit in that post was domestic, Machimura pressed the party to create a project team to study intelligence reform, then led this Intelligence Collection and Analysis Team to the UK to study MI6, the British Foreign Office, and its police in 2002.[23] In 2004 Machimura became foreign minister, and the center of gravity for intelligence reform shifted to the government. In October, the prime minister's Council on Security and Defense Capabilities submitted a report, "Japan's Vision for Future Security and Defense Capabilities" ("Mirai e no Anzen Hoshō to Bōeiryoku Bijon"), which called for a highly controversial Emergency Basic Law (Yuji Kihon Hō) and for several intelligence reforms, including improved alignment of intelligence analysis with policy needs, enhancement of CIRO's role as coordinator of intelligence across ministries and agencies, cultivation of intelligence specialists—especially HUMINT collectors, establishment of a classification regime, and improved international intelligence sharing. Soon thereafter, the LDP, Kōmeitō, and the opposition DPJ formally agreed on the need for intelligence reform. As we shall see, there was considerable bureaucratic and political infighting ahead, but this so-called Araki Report (named after its chair, Araki Hiroshi, a private sector

CEO) became the mannequin on which numerous subsequent intelligence reform proposals would be fit.[24] Within months of the Araki Report, MOFA formally reorganized its main intelligence unit, the Foreign Intelligence Bureau (Kokusai Jōhōkyoku), into an Intelligence and Analysis Service (Kokusai Jōhō Tōkatsukan Soshiki).[25] Despite Machimura's best efforts, the shift was met with some derision. A former chief of the MOFA Intelligence and Analysis Service, Magosaki Ukeru, called this change a downgrade that reflected both Japan's dependence on the United States and the disregard MOFA truly had for intelligence. Shinoda Tomohito, an academic expert, notes that even after the reform, MOFA's intelligence function remained understaffed and there was still no clear career path for intelligence professionals to rise in Japan's Foreign Service.[26] One former high-level government official familiar with the Japanese intelligence community was even more critical. In his view, MOFA's subsequent redesignation of diplomats who had been trained to be policy staff to positions as "intelligence officers" (jōhō tantōkan) suggested clearly that "MOFA did not understand what intelligence activities are all about [and were] putting their officers at risk."[27]

Machimura was not finished trying to reform Japan's intelligence bureaucracies, but he found himself unable to generate sufficient support from senior LDP leaders. In September 2005, while he was still minister of foreign affairs, his private study group issued the report of its Roundtable on the Strengthening of External Intelligence Capabilities (Taigai Jōhō Kinō Kyōka ni kansuru Kondankai)—what came to be known as the Ōmori Report—calling for creation of an independent HUMINT unit within the Foreign Ministry, a "Foreign Intelligence Agency" (Taigai Jōhō Chō) modeled on the British Secret Intelligence Service.[28] Ōmori Yoshio, a former CIRO director, who chaired the study team and who provided the epigraph at the beginning of this chapter, argued that this unit would work closely with the Cabinet Office and across the entire government. Its head would have legal authority to require other ministries and agencies to submit relevant information and would lead the Japanese intelligence community. One hundred new collector and analyst slots would be created, but the reforms were met with the same awkward competition that reformers had grown used to dealing with. Even an exasperated Machimura noted that every ministry and agency had the same idea, and each was busy jockeying for leadership of an enhanced Japanese intelligence community.[29]

Then an external event—complicated in part by this competition—accelerated the pace of change. A Japanese diplomat, reportedly the head of the encrypted communications section of Japan's consulate general in Shanghai, became ensnared in a "honey trap" scandal. He committed suicide after MOFA was unable to prevent Chinese agents from blackmailing him. CIRO never reported the incident to the prime minister's office because it was never reported to CIRO by the Foreign Ministry.[30] An embarrassed MOFA reacted in the usual way: it created an internal commission to study how to safeguard official secrets.[31] For his part, Machimura cycled out of the Foreign Ministry and took leadership of intelligence reform out of the hands of MOFA and the bureaucracy. He moved it back to the LDP, where he had become head of the Policy Research Council.[32]

No longer burdened by acres of MOFA turf to defend, Machimura chaired a group that issued an ambitious plan for structural reform of the Japanese intelligence community. This Machimura Report—formally "Proposals Regarding Strengthening National Intelligence Capabilities" ("Kokka no Jōhō Kinō Kyōka ni kansuru Teigen")—called for an Intelligence Committee (Jōhō Kaigi) at the ministerial level where intelligence would be shared across ministries and agencies. It would upgrade the CIRO director from assistant deputy chief cabinet secretary to deputy chief cabinet secretary to enable him to attend meetings when the prime minister and the chief cabinet secretary receive intelligence briefs and to present CIRO's national intelligence estimates (NIEs). The proposals represented another step toward a consensus for comprehensive reform, but since the CIRO NIEs did not necessarily represent the consensus of the Japanese intelligence community, they did not yet add up to a complete overhaul of Japan's intelligence apparatus.[33]

The report also called for a new organization specialized in HUMINT activities under the jurisdiction of the CIRO director and staffed by trained secondees from both the ministries and agencies of the Japanese intelligence community as well as from outside the government. It took care to stipulate that its proposed reforms would protect against contradictory tasking instructions from MOFA and CIRO and included a call for a new secrets classification system. Finally—and remarkably—the Machimura Report proposed Diet oversight via creation of a new Intelligence Committee (Jōhō Iinkai) to discuss what information needed classification and to examine measures to ensure information security. Machimura had wanted its members to be appointed by the prime minister and to swear an oath to uphold a national secrecy law. In his view, this would ensure that "popular control would extend to intelligence activities at home and abroad."[34] This never came to pass. When asked why, one senior Japanese intelligence official suggested that "oversight is seen as too radical for Japan by most senior officials." Former defense minister Morimoto Satoshi went further, suggesting that "the NPA was reluctant to allow it and Prime Minister Abe was reluctant to cede power to the Diet."[35] Still, Machimura's program embraced an ambitious menu of proposals.

The Machimura Report was issued in June 2006 by the LDP's Policy Research Council at the same time that the PHP Research Institute, a private think tank, produced its own detailed—and similarly ambitious—blueprint for intelligence reform. The private study, "Japanese Intelligence: A Roadmap to Its Transformation" ("Nihon no Interijensu Taisei Henkaku e no Rōdomappu"), referred to and reinforced the Ōmori Report and anticipated closely the Machimura Report.[36] It argued unsparingly that Japan's intelligence community was "malfunctioning," and that because the nation's top political leaders were "insufficiently committed" to fixing the problem, at least three (by now widely recognized) roadblocks remained. The first was the Cabinet Office's weak capacity for collection and analysis. The second was the underdeveloped collaboration and sharing across the units constituting the Japanese intelligence community. And the third was the government's inability to protect state secrets and prevent leaks.[37]

Machimura and the think tank analysts were right about the vigorous battles among competing ministries for leadership of the intelligence community. Before the ink had even dried on the Ōmori, Machimura, and PHP reports, the National Police Agency upgraded its own Foreign Affairs and Intelligence Division to bureau level. Apparently it was not satisfied with its reserved seat atop CIRO, nor with its partial victory in the Machimura Report reversing the 2005 Ōmori Report stipulating that a new HUMINT organization should be under the jurisdiction of the foreign minister. In the wake of the report, the NPA reassigned 1,200 law enforcement officers to its Foreign Affairs Intelligence Division (Kokusai Keibi Kyoku Gaiji Jōhōbu). They would now act as "foreign affairs police" with responsibility for covering foreign nationals nationwide, mostly in prefectures with large foreign populations such as Osaka, Aichi, Saitama, and Fukuoka.[38]

Machimura was frustrated, noting how this change reflected "a battle under the surface between MOFA and the NPA."[39] Each agency eyed the chance to enlarge its own bureaucratic footprint, and neither wished the other to enjoy special prerogatives. For its part, MOFA was wary of how a new HUMINT organization under CIRO might require MOFA to dispatch its regional analysts, all trained at great cost, to CIRO in service of the NPA. Magosaki Ukeru, a former chief of MOFA's Intelligence and Analysis Service, was a particularly outspoken critic of efforts to reform Japanese intelligence that fail to first significantly reform CIRO. He noted that all the competing models revolve around CIRO, and argued for moving the remit for intelligence to the MOD and MOFA, predicting that "attempts to strengthen intelligence . . . while maintaining the dominance of the police will not go well."[40]

Table 5.1   A Guide to the Cascading Recommendations for Intelligence Reform

DATE	ORGANIZATION	REPORT TITLE	AKA
October 2004	Prime Minister's Council on Security and Defense Capabilities (Cabinet Secretariat)	"Japan's Visions for Future Security and Defense Capabilities" (*Mirai e no Anzen Hoshō Bōeiryoku Bijon*)	"Araki Report"
September 2005	MOFA's "Roundtable on the Strengthening of External Intelligence Capabilities" (Taigai Jōhō Kinō Kyōka ni kansuru Kondankai)	"Toward the Strengthening of External Intelligence Capabilities" (*Taigai Jōhō Kinō no Kyōka ni mukete*)	"Ōmori Report"
June 2006	LDP Policy Research Council	"Proposals Regarding Strengthening National Intelligence Capabilities" (*Kokka no Jōhō Kinō Kyōka ni kansuru Teigen*)	"Machimura Report"
June 2006	PHP Research Institute	"Japanese Intelligence: A Roadmap to Its Transformation" (*Nihon no Interijensu Taisei Henkaku e no Rōdomappu*)	"PHP Report"
February 2008	Prime Minister's "Council for Discussing the Strengthening of Intelligence Capabilities" (Jōhō Kinō Kyōka Kentō Kaigi) (Cabinet Secretariat)	"Policy Measures to Improve Cabinet Intelligence Capabilities" (*Kantei ni okeru Jōhō Kinō no Kyōka no Hōshin*)	"Cabinet Report"

Machimura was determined to change a situation in which "Japanese intelligence ha[d] been generally forsaken by political leaders" willing to ignore analyses that might complicate domestic politics.[41] He knew that he needed the prime minister to make a political decision to achieve effective intelligence reform, and found his chance when his most important ally, Abe Shinzō, succeeded Koizumi as prime minister in September 2006 and Machimura returned to the cabinet. Together they were determined to create an entirely new security policy decision-making infrastructure—including a Japanese National Security Council. Now leader of the largest faction within the LDP, Machimura would work with Abe to ensure that comprehensive intelligence reform would gain some traction. But the window afforded by that first, short-lived Abe administration (September 2006–September 2007) would prove too narrow for them to complete the task.[42]

In December 2007, when Machimura was chief cabinet secretary for Abe's cautious successor, Fukuda Yasuo, he chaired a Council for Discussing the Strengthening of Intelligence Capabilities in the Cabinet Office. The government stood up a Counterintelligence Implementation Council simultaneously and announced a "Basic Plan to Strengthen Counterintelligence Functions" the following August.[43] In February 2008, the council produced a final official report calling for intelligence reform, titled "Policy Measures to Improve Cabinet Intelligence Capabilities." It was filled with language and recommendations borrowed from the academic literature on intelligence reviewed in chapter 1—for example, the "intelligence cycle," "all-source analysis," and "silos"—and echoed widely much that had been written in the PHP and Machimura reports.[44] After this cascade of government, party, and private sector analyses, the elements of the intelligence community needing change were well known to the stakeholders: policy and intelligence functions called for better balance, collection had to be enhanced, intelligence sharing needed facilitation, and the state secrets classification system had to be overhauled.[45] By March, a cabinet decision was issued ordering reform, but the political leaders flinched. There was still no comprehensive overhaul of the architecture for intelligence and national security policy making.

Instead, reform focused narrowly on the elements of intelligence— specifically collection, analysis, and communication. Collection would be improved by enhancing HUMINT capabilities at Japanese diplomatic missions worldwide and by allowing agents to be hired for longer than three-year terms. But creation of a more specialized organization for HUMINT activities was set aside because of persistent jurisdictional battles between MOFA and the NPA. On the analysis front, six new posts were created for "cabinet intelligence analysts" (*naikaku jōhō bunsekikan*) modeled on the CIA's national intelligence officers, and a counterintelligence center was established in CIRO.[46] The government also strengthened IMINT by upgrading imagery analysis capabilities and enhanced OSINT by providing a roadmap for how the intelligence community might make better use of reports from Radiopress, the former wartime signals section within MOFA's Intelligence Bureau, which became an independent news agency under MOFA's oversight in 1946.[47]

To enhance horizontal communication, the Japanese intelligence community was formally expanded in 2008 to include four more ministries: Finance, METI, the Japan Coast Guard, and the Financial Services Agency (FSA), which would meet in an "Extended Intelligence Conference" (Kakudai Jōhō Kaigi) on a regular basis.[48] The FSA had been formed in 2001 during the Hashimoto administrative reforms reviewed in chapter 4. It was split from the Ministry of Finance and given responsibility to protect users of financial instruments and services. Doing so required it to examine the internal controls of financial institutions to ensure information security, prevent abuse of electronic banking, protect against cyberattacks and money laundering, and gather intelligence on the financing of terrorism.[49] In 2007, before its designation as a member of the expanded intelligence community,

FSA moved some of these responsibilities to the National Police Agency's Financial Intelligence Center (Keisatsuchō Keiji Kyoku Soshiki Hanzai Tai-sakubu Hanzai Shūeki Iten Bōshi Kanrikan). In this way, the NPA's intelligence role was further expanded, while at the same time, its ward, CIRO, would now coordinate production of quarterly intelligence estimates based on a community-wide intelligence consensus—without footnotes or dissenting opinions.[50] A Joint Intelligence Council (Gōdō Jōhō Kaigi), based on a new government-wide security clearance system, was established to enhance intelligence sharing.[51] Michael Green, a former senior director for Asia at the National Security Council, credits the effort to break down stovepipes to U.S. pressure—specifically the exhortations by Richard Armitage and Joseph Nye—and to the determination of CIRO chief Kanemoto Toshinori, who led the charge to create this new unit.[52] A former senior U.S. intelligence official recalls that after 2007, "we encouraged the Japanese government to break down their silos and to facilitate interagency cooperation. It was a time that we were going through the same process."[53]

The need to improve vertical communication was also addressed. The cabinet issued new guidelines for relations between analysts and policy makers. Analytical units (jōhō bumon) would now collect and analyze information independently from the policy units (seisaku bumon). But the firewall would not prevent intelligence sections from responding to clearly communicated information needs of policy makers who would seek "all source analyses" prepared by the new cabinet intelligence analysts.[54] To facilitate this, Cabinet Intelligence Committee (Naikaku Jōhō Kaigi) meetings would include participants from policy-making units from the Cabinet Office at which the director of cabinet intelligence (naikaku jōhō kan) would brief out intelligence estimates based on all source analyses. Likewise, this official would now attend policy-making meetings of the cabinet in order to get an accurate grasp of the cabinet's information needs. It was also stipulated that while individual intelligence bureaus would still report directly through their ministers and vice ministers to the cabinet leadership, they now would have the right—and obligation—to communicate directly with the director of cabinet intelligence.

Significant reform seemed within the government's grasp, but the timing was inauspicious. When the Machimura Report was issued in June 2006, the supportive Abe Shinzō had not yet come to power; and when the Cabinet Report was issued in early 2008, it came months after the first Abe cabinet had collapsed. Although Abe had been eager to stand up an even more ambitious Japanese National Security Council, for which strengthened intelligence capabilities and a new secrecy law would be essential, "serious disagreements" between the NPA and MOFA delayed the Cabinet Council's report.[55] Chief Cabinet Secretary Machimura tried to coax the Japanese intelligence bureaucracies to reach consensus on limited intelligence reform. But he was frustrated by Prime Minister Fukuda's unwillingness to enforce a lasting political solution to the bureaucratic competition.[56] Years later, the frustrated Machimura publicly denounced how the MOFA-NPA rivalry had not only choked off any immediate plans for a new HUMINT organization but also stifled progress toward legislation to establish the new secrets classification regime that Abe had sought to create.[57]

There was curiously little discussion of the 2008 Cabinet Report in the Diet, perhaps because the new enabling legislation had been put on ice. The exception was in a session of the House of Councillors Committee on the Cabinet in March, where a DPJ representative, Yamane Ryūji, encouraged the government to get moving to improve intelligence capabilities. In response, Chief Cabinet Secretary Machimura acknowledged that bureaucratic turf battles had slowed progress. Ōmori Yoshio, chair of the 2005 study group, joined in as a particularly vocal critic, arguing that the proposals were still too vague and opaque. Ōmori expressed particular concern about the absence of plans for a new National Security Council.[58] In the meantime, MOFA continued to lobby behind the scenes against its creation, and Japan's Cabinet Intelligence Committee met rarely and only very perfunctorily.[59] Although CIRO chief Mitani Hideshi was not misleading visiting U.S. intelligence officials when he told them in October 2008 that "progress was being made" toward development of a robust Japanese intelligence community, the elusive National Security Council and its associated Designated State Secrets Law—what advocates saw as the crown jewels of intelligence reform—were still several years, and a second Abe cabinet, away.[60]

The Slowly Evolving Post–Cold War Intelligence Community

Although political support for intelligence reform broadened during the first decade of the new century, the Japanese intelligence community still lacked the central administrative machinery that might have offset the centrifugal effects of bureaucratic competition. Note, for example, how, despite creation of the Intelligence Coordination Committee, individual ministries each had access to the prime minister, and how little connection they had to one another—or to CIRO—in figure 5.2, an organizational chart from 2006.

Even during the half decade after the cabinet acted in 2008, each of the various ministries and agencies in Japan's intelligence community moved independently to strengthen its own intelligence portfolio. We have seen how

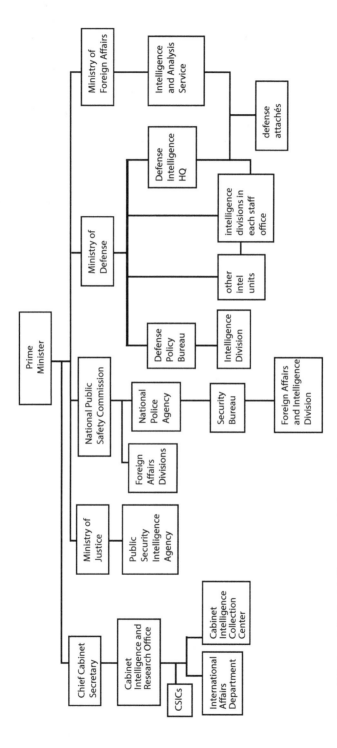

FIGURE 5.2 Japan's foreign intelligence organizations, 2006
Source: Adapted from *Gunji Kenkyū*, 1 September 2006

this worked to the advantage of the NPA and CIRO. The Foreign Ministry offers another good case in point. Sensitive to anti-militarist public opinion and hampered by Japan's diplomatic failure during the 1991 Gulf War, the ministry barely referred to intelligence in its *Diplomatic Bluebook* in the 1990s; and when it did, it used the ambiguous term *jōhō*, which it translated variously as either "intelligence" or "information," depending presumably on the political climate and the expected audience.[61] By the mid-2000s, with a consensus forming about the legitimacy of the intelligence enterprise, MOFA began to emphasize "intelligence for security" rather than "information for crisis management." In contrast to the 2005 *Bluebook*'s section headed "Strengthening Information Gathering and Analysis," the 2006 version addressed "Strengthening Intelligence Collection and Analysis Capabilities," and each subsequent edition of the *Bluebook* spoke of "intelligence collection." A separate section on intelligence first appeared in 2008.

Emboldened by the acceptance of intelligence as a valid function of government, but frustrated by the fact that personnel in its core foreign intelligence unit, the Intelligence and Analysis Service, were still formally prohibited from engaging in covert intelligence operations abroad, MOFA began designating dozens of its foreign-deployed diplomats as "intelligence officers" (*jōhō tantōkan*) in 2008.[62] There was, however, a self-defeating norm in operation—in effect an internal silo: embassies and consulates would bypass the MOFA intelligence office and communicate directly to the ministry's policy offices. So the service remained "a backwater in the ministry."[63] Its budget for the 2012 fiscal year was just $5 million for a staff of approximately eighty professionals.[64]

The most prominent among Japan's civilian intelligence units, CIRO, tried to seize upon the opportunity to do more.[65] As noted in chapter 4, CIRO had become a catchment area following intelligence failures: its "Cabinet Intelligence Aggregation Center" (Naikaku Jōhō Shūyaku Sentā) was created after the government's inept response to the 1995 Kobe earthquake, and its 370-person IMINT-oriented Cabinet Satellite Intelligence Center (Naikaku Eisei Jōhō Sentā—CSIC) was established after the 1998 Taepodong flyover.[66] A former CIRO director explained that although CIRO sought a more coherent set of roles and missions, much of its responsibility—and that of the CSIC in particular—was created "on account of a budgetary logic," not on the basis of a strategic plan.[67] In 2003, for example, CIRO informally explored the possibility of collecting non-military signals intelligence through antennas to be set up at Japanese embassies, but abandoned this idea because of the lack of budget and a legal basis.[68] CIRO still was allowed to collect only open source information and could not maintain officers of its own abroad "except in special circumstances."[69] In 2008 CIRO's director, Mitani Hideshi, explained to U.S. intelligence officials that CIRO was trying to address its human resource problem by beginning a training program, presumably focused on tradecraft, for new recruits. It is not clear what became of this initiative.[70]

As late as 2012, just before another round of major reforms, CIRO's budget was only $20 million, and some one hundred of its core staff of 170 persons had been seconded from (and presumably had career-based loyalties to) other ministries and agencies, including forty from the NPA alone. Many sent to CIRO had no background in intelligence.[71] Undersized and understaffed, CIRO attempted to enhance the training of its staff and to engage with Japan's political leadership on a more sustained basis. As recently as 2005, the CIRO chief briefed the prime minister only once a week for no more than a half hour each time.[72] A former CIRO director confirmed this and described "a silo at the very top" with just three persons inside: the prime minister, the chief cabinet secretary, and himself. He recalled, moreover, a "Catch-22" of near perfect proportions in which he was "prohibited from sharing [his] briefs with officials who could not share [their] briefs."[73] Meanwhile, his CIRO domain was divided into some one dozen "teams" (han), organized both geographically (Europe, the Americas, Russia, China, etc.) and functionally (military affairs, counterterrorism, IMINT, etc.). And in an apparent workaround of its ban on HUMINT activities, CIRO also housed a Trading Company Team (Shōsha han) to collect and analyze commercial information provided by private Japanese firms abroad.[74]

In contrast to the amply documented duplication and jurisdictional bickering in the Japanese intelligence community, Hayashi Yasuo, a former chairman and CEO of JETRO, Japan's leading economic intelligence agency, reports that JETRO and CIRO never crossed wires, and insists he never had any contact with CIRO. Hayashi attributed this to a sharp separation of roles and missions: he insisted that CIRO's relations to Japan's trading companies focused on security, while JETRO's were limited to commerce.[75] Whether or not this was formally the case, JETRO dwarfed CIRO in size by the mid-2000s. It had more than 1,500 staff in 2013, half of whom worked abroad in a network of more than seventy offices across nearly sixty countries and regions. Meanwhile, CIRO's budget that year—2.2 billion yen—was lower than it had been in 2011.[76] METI had long been dispatching several hundred of its officials to foreign posts annually—including embassies, consulates, international organizations, and public corporations. For decades, more than a quarter of these dispatches worked in JETRO offices around the world.[77] While JETRO had depended largely on OSINT, its officials also cultivated relationships with local businesspersons and government officials worldwide. One former JETRO official explained its non-OSINT intelligence collection in the eastern United States, where "JETRO New York has two high-level officers seconded from METI who collect a wide range of information through meeting in person with academics, journalists, U.S. government officials in Washington, D.C., who also write informal, unpublished reports exclusively for high-ranking METI political appointees and officers."[78] Despite JETRO's growth and METI's ambitions, the overall number of METI's overseas dispatches actually declined by more than 10 percent during the "lost decades" of the 1990s and 2000s.[79]

The NPA, which continued to enjoy a reserved seat for one of its senior officers atop CIRO, had more success expanding during this period. In April 2004 it established its own Foreign Affairs and Intelligence Bureau (Gaiji Jōhōbu). This elite counterintelligence unit, a "foreign affairs police," was created to monitor foreigners—mostly Korean and Chinese residents, but also Russians and Muslims—across Japan. Half its professional staff were said to be assigned from the "top secret" unit code-named "Yama"—a discomfiting nod to the Yama Agency, the wartime police counterintelligence unit discussed in chapter 3. At least in the beginning, the new bureau's director enjoyed the same direct access to the prime minister as the CIRO chief.[80]

All this was evolving at the same time that Japan's vulnerability to cyberattack was being exposed on a regular basis. And once again, the government responded with characteristic centrifugality in reaction to serial failures. The cyber threat first came into focus when Japanese investigators learned in early 2000 that nearly one hundred private firms, the MOD, and a dozen other government units had been using software developed by the terrorist sect Aum Shinrikyō.[81] The Ministry of Posts and Telecommunications was the first to create a counter-cyber action plan, which, in the event, did little more than identify vulnerable industries and exhort firms to take voluntary measures and improve communication with the government. The first military cyber surveillance unit was stood up by the ASDF in December 2000, after which each of the other service branches quickly followed suit.[82] The Cabinet Secretariat moved at the same time to establish an Information Security Measures Promotion Office (Jōhō Sekyuritī Taisaku Suishin Shitsu).[83] Before the end of the year, the NPA created a Cyberforce Center to manage emergency response to cyberattacks on key infrastructure.[84] In April 2002, the government created a National Incident Response Team (Kinkyū Taiō Shien Chīmu) at its Cabinet Secretariat with fifteen computer security experts recruited from both inside and outside the government who would be responsible for collecting and analyzing information in case of cyberattacks and suggesting measures to prevent their recurrence.[85]

Three years later, after the ASDF's Intelligence Data Group (Jōhō Shiryō Han) was hit in August 2003 by "Blaster," an early computer virus, the government upgraded its Information Security Measures Promotion Office to a National Information Security Center (Jōhō Sekyuritī Sentā—NISC) in the Cabinet Secretariat with nearly thirty personnel seconded from relevant ministries.[86] While the earlier cabinet units were no more than administrative secretariats for government meetings on the topic, the NISC now had authorization to inspect information security measures on a government-wide basis.[87]

Then, in 2005, government cyber-related measures were expanded to include standardization of IT systems across the prefectural level of government.[88] By early 2007, the U.S. National Security Agency (NSA) was providing training to GSDF personnel as part of its larger project to align the development of cyber network defenses in order to enable sharing of sensitive and classified intelligence among allies.[89] In July 2009, cyberattacks abroad became a Japanese problem when it was discovered that eight Japanese private servers had been used, along with more than four hundred servers across fifty-nine countries, to launch distributed denial-of-services attacks on U.S. and ROK websites simultaneously. The Japanese government responded by formally designating cyberattack as a domain that could activate its national security/crisis management protocol (although it left the role of the SDF undefined).[90] When the hacker group Anonymous threatened to attack the Japanese government in June 2012, the administration of Noda Yoshihiko created an emergency response team within the NISC called the Cyber Incident Mobile Assistance Team (Saibā Kidōtai) with forty personnel to be first responder to cyber incidents involving governmental organizations.[91] In September, just as the Noda administration began receiving U.S. intelligence on hackers and guidance on malicious software from the NSA, it authorized MOD to define cyberspace as an element of national territory, just like land, sea, air, and outer space, and announced plans to create a Cyber Defense Unit (Saibā Kūkan Bōeitai) with one hundred personnel.[92] Japan remained as vulnerable to cyberattack as any other country—and perhaps more than most.

These inchoate responses amidst competing bureaucratic ambitions within a weak counterintelligence environment—some of which came to naught—ensured that Japan's civilian intelligence community would remain inefficient, uncoordinated, underfunded, and understaffed, even after the 2008 cabinet order. One senior government intelligence official derisively characterized Japan's civilian intelligence in this period as engaged in three highly suboptimal activities: "collect, hog, and leak."[93] There were no more than five thousand intelligence officials in 2009, most of whom were on the defense side, which evolved separately after the Cold War.[94]

Military Intelligence

As examined in chapter 3 of this volume, CIRO's rather odd situation originated in highly charged debates over civilian control in the 1950s. So, despite quietly standing up its own Military Affairs Unit, and despite being assigned nominal responsibility to supervise the CSIC, CIRO had little military expertise well into the 2010s.[95] In the intervening years, however, proper military intelligence was enhanced considerably.

HUMINT

We can begin to review Japan's military intelligence during this period with Japan's widely acknowledged lack of HUMINT resources—particularly the sorts of foreign area experts discussed in chapter 2 who were so numerous and skilled before and during the Asia-Pacific War. It was not only CIRO and MOFA that had to play catch-up in this domain. The military's own language and analytic skills training program also had to be reorganized in March 2001, when two smaller training centers were combined in western Tokyo to create a successor to the Nakano School—the Kodaira School.[96] This was a delicate problem because, as one senior MOD intelligence officer uncomfortable with transparency explained: "The almost complete lack of clandestine collection overseas has been criticized by the LDP—first by Machimura. . . . But a bill authorizing such HUMINT would invite a very active political circus and would likely produce an intrusive accountability mechanism that would stifle any new intelligence organization. So on HUMINT we needed to start small and evolve over time."[97] Even if on a small scale, experience accumulated for military intelligence. There were unconfirmed press reports in 2013 that the GSDF was funding agents run by Kodaira School–trained handlers in Russia, China, and elsewhere.[98]

But the largest and fastest-growing number of active foreign area intelligence collectors were the military attachés of the SDF—mostly officials from the Second Section of the Investigation Division of the Ground Self-Defense Force who operated in the open.

After the Kodaira School was initiated and the supply of foreign area officers began to increase, the SDF broadened its reach. It began placing military attachés in such nations as Saudi Arabia, Vietnam, Ukraine, Syria, Afghanistan, Kuwait, Sudan, Kazakhstan, Lebanon, Algeria, Ethiopia, Kenya, Djibouti, Nigeria, and Morocco. Since many of these were sites of multinational peacekeeping missions, it was relatively easy to justify the increased attention. Nor, given the shift in the regional balance of power, were increases in

Table 5.2   Japan's Intelligence Attachés Abroad

	1995	2005	2015
Number of missions abroad with Japanese military attachés	32	37	43
Uniformed military attachés in missions abroad	42	48	61
MOJ (mostly PSIA) attachés in missions abroad	15	16	19
NPA attachés in missions abroad	19	21	25

Sources: *Defense of Japan [Bōei Hakusho]* (various years) and MOFA HR Division, 5 July 2015. These figures do not include non-uniformed JDA officials who are stationed in embassies, studying abroad, or serving as liaisons with allied forces.

the number of military attachés sent to China and South Korea hard to explain to budget examiners or the general public. The government also found it useful to take advantage of defense attachés and liaison officers dispatched to the U.S. Pacific Fleet, the Pentagon, or other billets as resources.[99] During the compilation of the 2015 budget, amid editorials calling for enhanced intelligence capabilities, MOD announced plans to send additional defense attachés to Mongolia, the UAE, and Jordan. In an uncanny echo of Nomonhan (see chapter 2), Mongolia was described by an unnamed official as a "particularly important platform for intelligence gathering" because of its borders with Russia and China and its diplomatic relations with North Korea.[100]

Predictably, the major problem for these well-trained attachés was that they had to be assigned to MOFA in order to take up embassy posts. This meant their reports had to be conveyed through diplomatic channels by way of MOFA in Tokyo before being forwarded to JDA's Defense Intelligence Headquarters (DIH). According to one analysis, while this may have taken a day or so in most cases, in extreme cases their reports could be delayed by a week or more. A former head of DIH recalls how MOFA prevented him from installing fax equipment so that both ministries could simultaneously receive cables from his attachés. MOFA rejected the request on the self-serving grounds that if MOD were to get this convenience, all of the other ministries with specialists in diplomatic missions abroad would want the same treatment.[101] Defense officials were unimpressed with the intelligence skills of their MOFA colleagues. One senior military intelligence official complained that "the SDF has agent-handling skills necessary for force protection and exfiltration, but MOFA has none. Its officers are limited to interviewing host nation nationals and Japanese living abroad. . . . Interviewing our nationals abroad who are willing to talk is not the same as a robust HUMINT function that can run agents below the radar of host nations."[102] A uniformed colleague working in the Cabinet Office agreed, linking the weakness of Japanese HUMINT to the fact that "we have to rely on embassy people who are policy oriented, and we are not allowed to go undercover."[103]

SIGINT

While the HUMINT situation may have been far from ideal from the perspective of some practitioners, the Japanese military also moved sooner and farther than the civilian agencies in both SIGINT and IMINT collection and analysis. The creation of DIH in 1997 consolidated most of the service-based intelligence assets and provided an enormous boost in both domains.[104] Here the bureaucratic bêtes noires for uniformed intelligence officials were CIRO and the NPA—as well as the civilians who occupy the so-called "internal bureaus" (naikyoku) in MOD— not MOFA. Although DIH was created to consolidate Japan's technology-based military intelligence, it struggled to operate as the MOD's intelligence center for several reasons. Its major obstacle was bureaucratic. Before its analyses are passed along to the defense minister or administrative vice minister, they first must pass through a separate division dedicated to supervision of military intelligence (Chōsaka) which operates within the "internal bureaus" that famously oversee Japan's uniformed military.[105] For many years, the section chief of the bureau hosting this division briefed the prime minister along with the CIRO director, but he was cut out from attending the weekly meetings of the Joint Intelligence Committee (Gōdō Jōhō Kaigi) in the mid-2000s, and the commander of the DIH rarely participated in prime ministerial briefs in its early years.[106] A former director of the U.S. Defense Intelligence Agency with intelligence experience in the Pacific Command and the office of the Joint Chiefs of Staff recalls:

> On occasion we had access to Japanese-collected SIGINT that was shared with the U.S. through SIGINT exchange agreements. But the JSDF may not have had access to that same Japanese-collected SIGINT because it was withheld from them by their collectors. The last thing the U.S. wanted to do in one of our exchanges was to reveal to our counterparts things that their Japanese counterparts had not shared with them. Part of the [reason for the] enthusiasm they had for the exchanges was that our all-source approaches to intelligence and assessments offered them insights that their vertically stovepiped structures and rules imposed by their collectors did not offer. Regularly you could tell from the discussion that we had raised something that was new for our counterparts. Just as regularly we knew that the information had been in the hands of Japanese intelligence and that the issue was lack of sharing on their side. Talk about walking on eggshells.[107]

Still, military SIGINT became more robust and more seamless over time. During most of the Cold War, the SDF operated fewer than ten SIGINT stations, but after DIH was established, these capabilities were rapidly expanded. By its fourth year, DIH had a staff of more than 1,500, and a decade later it had grown to nearly 2,500, some two thirds of whom were signals officers.[108] In March 2006, when the Joint Staff Council was replaced by a Joint Staff Office, the DIH created a sixth division for integrated intelligence, called Tōgō Jōhōbu, to provide real-time intelligence support during crises and to allow for integrated operations of the three service branches.[109] When North Korea tested its missiles in July 2006, the SDF was able to detect significant increases in radio communications over a North Korean missile base as well as government announcements addressed to North Korean fishermen.[110] By the mid-2010s, there were seventeen SIGINT stations operated by DIH, GSDF, or ASDF. Eight of these were operated by the GSDF's Second Intelligence Division Detachment, and many had more than one hundred personnel.[111]

Even if their technical level had improved, stovepiping within the SDF persisted. This was due in no small part to the fact that despite plans for DIH to integrate the intelligence sections of all SDF forces, individual service branches continued to maintain their own intelligence units.[112] Ironically, this meant that Japanese service branches were better able to coordinate with their U.S. counterparts than with one another—and indeed, retired U.S. officials report that secure communications between U.S. and Japanese military services was well developed long before it was established between the White House and the prime minister's office.[113] Nor did legal arrangements facilitate matters. For example, when the Maritime Staff Office C4I Systems Department of the MSDF received sensitive tactical intelligence from the U.S. Navy during U.S.-Japan joint anti-submarine operations in 2005, legal arrangements with the U.S. Navy precluded its sharing it either with DIH or even with the leadership of the Defense Ministry.[114]

In the case of SIGINT, DIH reportedly managed just six listening posts across the archipelago well into the mid-2000s.[115] By the mid-2010s, however, Japan's SIGINT capability had expanded dramatically, eleven stations had been added, mostly to the south in Kyushu and Okinawa, and several more were constructed in Yonaguni—the westernmost Japanese island, in sight of Taiwan—as well as on Iwo Jima some 1,200 miles to the east in the Pacific Ocean.[116] Japan's overall SIGINT capacity—including facilities operated by civilian agencies such as the NPA, MOFA, and the Ministry of Internal Affairs (with widely dispersed facilities inherited from the former Ministry of Posts and Telecommunications)—had the ability to intercept transmissions up to five thousand kilometers from Japanese territory in all directions and was estimated in 2015 to be third or fourth in the world after the United States and the United Kingdom, but possibly ahead of Russia and China.[117] Widely recognized and stubborn organizational problems aside, the capacity to analyze this volume of data, of course, lagged behind the capacity to collect it.

IMINT

As noted in chapter 4, in 1969, a time of near peak Japanese "antimilitarism," Japan's conservative leadership issued its famous "Peaceful Purposes" resolution, nominally blocking military use of space. Like other self-imposed constraints of that period—such as on arms exports, defense spending, and nuclear weapons—the ban on the military use of space was not formally a matter of law. But unlike the others, it was invoked only in the breach, and was the first to come undone when the Cabinet Satellite Intelligence Center was stood up in April 2001 in the wake of the Taepodong crisis.[118]

Indeed, Japan's various civilian space agencies and geographic information systems offices never seemed to take the ban on the military use of space seriously. Satellites launched in the 1960s by the Science and Technology Agency and the National Space Development Agency cooperated with the JDA from the beginning. Most famously, "civilian" images of Chinese port and airstrip construction on the Paracel Islands in the South China Sea were leaked to the press in 1993.[119] In addition to collecting and analyzing images from Japan's first earth observation satellite, defense analysts were provided images from the NTT communication satellite Sakura-2, the navigation satellite TRANSIT, and Japanese weather satellites before and after the "peaceful purposes" resolution was issued. Moreover, the SDF had also been purchasing and analyzing imagery data from foreign earth-observation satellites to monitor foreign military bases and other sites of military importance.[120] It is clear then why "by the time Tokyo launched its own reconnaissance satellites in 2003, it had more than a decade of experience using overhead imagery."[121]

Japan's first indigenous military "information-gathering" satellite—with a remit that included natural disasters for political cover—was launched by the Japan Aerospace Exploration Agency in March 2003, and the JDA increased the number of its imagery analysts from 120 to 160.[122] Its capabilities received positive public attention when, in April 2004, the government released images of a North Korean rail line that had been bombed moments after Kim Jong-il's train had passed through. Successes such as this were met by frustrations, however, as MOD often had to depend on the United States for IMINT on the whereabouts of North Korean cargo transports carrying sensitive materials and Pyongyang's preparations for missile launches.[123] Perhaps the most prominent such example was in January 2009, when Washington informed Tokyo that trains with large containers which had left a North Korean munitions factory arrived by truck several days later at the Tonghae Satellite Launching Ground. In March, U.S. reconnaissance satellites confirmed that a missile was mounted on the launching pad there, and in April, U.S. and South Korean intelligence confirmed that North Korea had begun fueling it.[124]

In 2008 the Japanese Diet, with the support of all three major parties, caught up with reality and declared that the development of space was necessary for national defense. It formally adjusted the legal interpretation of "peaceful use" by substituting the term "non-aggressive" for "non-military" when it issued its Basic Space Law (Uchū Kihonhō).[125] Given how long the Japanese military had been using space for signals intelligence, and given its long experience with both Japanese and commercially available foreign IMINT, this was merely a de jure acknowledgment of de facto policy. It was followed the next year by publication of MOD's first military space document, which called for accelerated indigenous development as well as cooperation with the United States in such areas as satellite navigation, space-based maritime domain awareness, and the development of new sensor technology.

Following that plan, in November 2009 Tokyo successfully added a third-generation optical satellite, reportedly with 0.6-meter resolution.[126] Nine months later, however, Japan's second, and sole operational, radar satellite stopped working less than four years after launch, leaving the Japanese IMINT system with three optical satellites but without the radar imaging that can see through cloud cover and some vegetation.[127] It was more than two years later, in December 2011, when Japan successfully launched and was able to operate its third radar satellite. And it was not until April 2013, when it successfully put into orbit its fourth radar satellite, that Japan finally achieved its planned system: it now had two optical and two radar satellites in full operation, allowing analysts to observe any target on earth at least once a day.[128] While complete, this was still a relatively small set of satellites, and the package lacked redundancy. Still, it was successful enough for Washington to ask Tokyo to provide surveillance data to the U.S. Strategic Command.[129]

Service Branch Units

While defense-centered HUMINT, SIGINT, and IMINT continued to evolve, each service branch in the Japan Self-Defense Forces continued to maintain and enhance its own intelligence units tailored to its specific roles and missions.

The Ground Self-Defense Force's first overseas wartime field experience in Iraq stimulated organizational changes soon after soldiers arrived in Samawah in January 2004. Later that year, when the cabinet updated the "National Defense Program Guidelines" (Bōei Taikō) and the "Midterm Defense Buildup Plan" (Chūki Bōeiryoku Seibi Keikaku), it made explicit reference to the need to upgrade field unit intelligence capabilities. General Ichikawa Takuji, a commander of the GSDF's primary intelligence unit, provided a now familiar explanation: it was awkward for Japanese forces to have to rely on allied troops for field intelligence reports during their mission in Iraq.[130] The key to the reorganization was integration of formerly separate intelligence and the geospatial units into a single "unified intelligence support *for the GSDF*."[131]

The changes were relatively ambitious. A Military Intelligence Command (Chūō Jōhōtai) with six hundred personnel was stood up in March 2007 when two existing intelligence-related units were renamed: the Central Document Unit (Chūō Shiryōtai) became the Basic Intelligence Unit (Kiso Jōhōtai), and the Central Mapping Unit (Chūō Chiritai) became the Geospatial Intelligence Unit (Chiri Jōhōtai). They were joined by two new units, an Intelligence Analysis Unit (Jōhō Shoritai) and a Local Intelligence Unit (Genchi Jōhōtai), to facilitate collection and analysis deemed important for SDF overseas activities.[132] For a decade this new Military Intelligence Command was located at MOD headquarters under the direct (civilian) control of the minister of defense. But in what could be seen as a move back toward internal stovepiping, the unit was transferred in 2018 to the Ground Component Command (Rikujō Sōtai) in Saitama on the site of a former imperial military installation that had been used as a U.S. base during the Occupation.[133]

The Central Mapping Unit, predecessor of the Geospatial Intelligence Unit, was originally created as the 101st Surveying Battalion in 1954. It was (and remains) the only unit in the SDF focused on geospatial intelligence, and is staffed by an estimated four hundred personnel with responsibility for surveying, analyzing aerial photos, drawing and printing maps, and creating electronic maps.[134] Often relying on shared intelligence from friendly nations and on images purchased from U.S. commercial satellites, it has produced detailed local maps of areas where the GSDF has conducted disaster relief, reconstruction, and peacekeeping operations, including in Iraq and the Golan Heights.[135] Between 2005 and 2009, each of the five GSDF regional armies stood up its own Intelligence Analysis Unit to enhance the flow of operational intelligence collected by the smallest field units—at the company and platoon levels.[136] The newly unified Military Intelligence Command began to provide infrastructure for each of the five regional armies to generate and share a tactical intelligence database on a real-time basis and to integrate, analyze, and share intelligence.[137]

Perhaps the most notable piece of the 2007 GSDF intelligence reform was the establishment of the Local Intelligence Unit, the first officially recognized HUMINT unit in GSDF history. As reported in chapter 3, GSDF operated an unofficial HUMINT unit, the Rikubaku Dainibu Beppan (or Musashi Kikan), whose existence was never formally acknowledged.[138] The Local Intelligence Unit now was designated as the first contingent of advance scouts to be sent abroad to collect tactical intelligence and do reconnaissance ahead of possible peacekeeping or reconstruction activities.[139] To bolster HUMINT and analytical capabilities, the GSDF followed up in March 2010 with the creation of its first new recruitment category since its establishment in 1954: "intelligence officer" (jōhōka). These officers would be recruited and trained in foreign languages and, possibly, tradecraft. The initial (and clearly aspirational) personnel target for jōhōka was 3,200 officers.[140]

In the MOD organizational structure, the Military Intelligence Command is neither part of DIH nor under the direct control of the Ground Staff Office. It is a GSDF unit focused on gathering, processing, analyzing, and disseminating tactical intelligence for the GSDF. Thus, while ambitious, these intelligence functions were consolidated only for the GSDF, and the reorganization largely elided the hoary problem of inter-service silos. One notable exception was in the counterintelligence domain. In an effort to address the stovepipe problem and to plug leaks after an MSDF lieutenant commander was discovered to have provided secret documents to a Russian military attaché in the so-called Bogatenkov Affair, the individual intelligence security commands (Jōhō Hozentai) of all service branches were combined in March 2009 to form a joint force, the SDF Intelligence Security Command (Jieitai Jōhō Hozentai), with about one thousand personnel at MOD headquarters under the direct control of the defense minister.[141] Each of the five SDF regional armies now would host a unit of the command comprising officers from all three service branches.[142]

It is important to note that this reform was animated by more than stovepipe-derived intelligence failures, by the need to fix damage from leaks, or even by the dependence-induced shortcomings of GSDF intelligence in Iraq. It was also the result of a failure to protect citizens and journalists from illegal surveillance. It seems that in 2003, as the Japanese government was contemplating support for the U.S.-led invasion of Iraq, military counterintelligence—specifically the GSDF's Tōhoku Army Corps—was surveilling large numbers of ordinary Japanese citizens and journalists who opposed the war.[143] The Japan Communist Party (JCP) had obtained SDF surveillance reports of events and demonstrations organized by 290 civil groups in forty-one prefectures, touching off an intense debate in the Diet, the courts, and the media regarding the legality of SDF domestic surveillance.[144]

The JCP reminded the public that the government had promised that domestic surveillance by military intelligence would be limited to those handling defense secrets, thus exempting ordinary citizens as targets. But the DPJ government vigorously defended the military's right to do so, maintaining rather wanly that it was important for MOD to understand citizens' opinions about the SDF.[145] After a bruising fight in the Diet, the MOD was directed to centralize control of its counterintelligence units as described earlier. And in 2012, the Sendai district court ruled that the gathering of information about private individuals by the GSDF was unconstitutional. It ordered the government to cease and to pay compensation for infringing on citizens' privacy.[146] Notwithstanding that this constitutional dispute originated in a leak of classified documents, which could be judged an intelligence failure, it might also be coded an ad hoc (and rare) *oversight success*, because opposition politicians had fought and won an unprecedented legal battle to preserve citizens' privacy. Ironically, at about the same time that the court was ruling in favor of Communist Party members, the press learned that military intelligence operatives had also been attending and recording the names of attendees at town meetings featuring the discharged nationalist ASDF chief of staff Tamogami Toshio.[147]

The Air Self-Defense Force's intelligence, surveillance, and reconnaissance (ISR) capabilities are typically divided into three categories of remote sensing: ground-based radar systems, ground-based electronic collection stations using either sensors or communication intercepts (ELINT / COMINT), and airborne collection using all of the above. Use of each by the ASDF was improved considerably after the Cold War. In 1989 it began operating a Base Air Defense Ground Environment (BADGE), its first integrated network of radar sites, patrol aircraft, and naval vessels that could process long-range detection, tracking, and identification data of incoming aircraft.[148] Under the BADGE system, air defense command and control functions were provided by four regional Air Defense Control Centers (Bōkū Shireijo) under the management of the Air Defense Command (Kōkū Sōtai). In 1991 the ASDF began to install three-dimensional active phased array radar (the Active Electronically Scanned Array, or AESA) with improved detection and tracking capabilities with a search range of 370 kilometers, at seven sites.[149] By the 2000s, ASDF's AESA radars had a search range of several hundreds of kilometers and some had a search range of several thousand kilometers.[150] The management of this system, including the Electronic Flight Surveillance Center and Air Reconnaissance Squadron, with signals interceptors and imaging reconnaissance aircraft, was directed from the Air Defense Command's Tactical Intelligence Center in suburban Tokyo.[151]

Amid increasing concerns about the threat of North Korean missiles and the rise of Chinese military power—a classic case of the shifting strategic environment that drives so much intelligence reform—Japan upgraded its BADGE in 2009. The successor, the new Japan Aerospace Defense Ground Environment (JADGE), would more efficiently integrate, at higher speed, ballistic missile sensors and interception systems across the three service branches—including its own radars and reconnaissance aircraft, as well as the GSDF's missile interceptors and the Aegis-equipped destroyers of the MSDF.[152] The JADGE system, comprising twenty-eight command and control ground stations in four sectors from Hokkaido to Okinawa, also would enable coordinated air defense operations covering a wider geographic area—and a greater distance (250 nm)—than before. Its most advanced airborne active phased array radar, with a search range of several thousand kilometers and a search altitude of thirty thousand meters, was first deployed in Kagoshima in 2008.[153]

After 9/11, the ASDF introduced a comprehensive architecture of ground-based ELINT systems equipped with a variety of antennas to detect and analyze electronic emissions and provide airspace early warning and surveillance.[154] By 2012, the ASDF was believed to have at least seven ELINT/COMINT stations operated by its Radiowave Collection Group (Denpa Jōhō Shūshū Gun) under the Air Intelligence Wing (Sakusen Jōhōtai), its largest intelligence unit, based at the ASDF's Air Defense Command Headquarters at Yokota Air Base, also in suburban Tokyo. These ELINT stations are different from SIGINT stations under DIH management. Some stations also have jamming and other countermeasure systems for electronic warfare fighting capabilities.[155] Whereas the ASDF's early ELINT collection stations were established in Hokkaido to focus on Soviet military activities and communications, the Air Staff had by the 2010s shifted ELINT/COMINT collection operations southward in order to monitor Chinese military activities more effectively.[156] And by 2013, the ASDF was operating more than two dozen facilities scattered across the country, each utilizing the most advanced radar technology available—with priority given to domestic manufacturers such as Toshiba, NEC, and Mitsubishi Electric (MELCO), domestic firms with considerable experience in this area.[157]

Unlike the indigenous ground-based tracking systems, ASDF airborne sensing operations have relied on imported equipment, including remotely piloted

Global Hawk drones manufactured by Northrop Grumman that patrol Japan's airspace in the East China Sea and elsewhere.[158] It also has deployed Northrop Grumman's E-2C Hawkeye aircraft, which entered service with the Airborne Early Warning Group at the Misawa Air Base as early as January 1987, and the AWACS E-767—a Boeing platform—first deployed in 1998.[159] ASDF Air Defense Command Headquarters Flight Group's Electronic Monitoring Group has been operating the indigenous YS-11EB, a YS-11-converted ELINT-capable aircraft, which has been used to monitor North Korean missile launches since the 1990s.[160] It has also converted vintage F-4Es and F-4EJs by adding optical camera and reconnaissance radars as well as ELINT capabilities.[161] As of 2013, the ASDF possessed four E-767s and fourteen E-2Cs.[162]

The Maritime Self-Defense Force (MSDF) has different requirements, of course. It has fashioned a "comprehensive architecture" for ocean surveillance that includes submarine detection and surface tracking systems, as well as airborne and ocean-based vessels.[163] The MSDF accelerated the enhancement of these capabilities after the Cold War. In August 1991 it began to procure SH-60J anti-submarine patrol helicopters equipped with dipping sonar to improve anti-submarine ISR.[164] The MSDF had acquired 103 SH-60J helicopters by August 2005, when the SH-60J's successor, the Mitsubishi SH-60K, entered service.[165] By March 2016, the MSDF had forty-nine SH-60Ks in service (some deployed on destroyers) with plans to acquire fifty more.[166] It also operates P-3 and EP-3, optimized for low-altitude and long-loiter patrols, and took first delivery of the indigenous P-1 in March 2013.

In 1993, the MSDF commissioned the first of its Kongō-class destroyers, equipped with sophisticated command and control and combat capabilities and the Aegis fire control system that significantly enhanced ISR capabilities at vastly greater ranges at sea.[167] Its phased arrays eliminated the need for a rotating antenna and incorporated stealth features to reduce the radar cross-section of the ship.[168] In March 2007 the MSDF acquired its first Atago-class destroyer, which is also equipped with SPY-1D phased array radars.[169]

In March 1998, MSDF ISR capabilities were further enhanced by the introduction of Oyashio-class submarines, which use the entire hull as a sensor, packing the sonar in the bow and a towed-array sonar system in the tail.[170] From March 1999 to March 2008, the MSDF added one Oyashio-class submarine to its fleet annually.[171] In 2009 the MSDF commissioned the first of its Sōryū-class submarines, which are more ISR capable than the Oyashio-class submarines because they can remain underwater for up to two weeks.[172]

MSDF ISR got its greatest boost when, in March 2009, after more than thirty years of R&D and testing, the MSDF commissioned the helicopter destroyer Hyūga with Japan's indigenous multi-function active phased array

C-band radar, the FCS-3.[173] Integrated with the Advanced Combat Direction System, the FCS-3 significantly reduced reaction time between the detection of enemy missiles and the launching of interceptors.[174] Hyūga-class ships also increased MSDF maritime patrol capabilities by carrying as many as four times more patrol helicopters than its predecessor.[175] In March 2013, the MSDF began replacing its aging Lockheed P3-C patrol aircraft with the indigenous P-1, built by Kawasaki Aerospace. The P-1 is the first to make use of an optical "fly-by-light" control system, which operates at a higher data transfer rate, is immune to electromagnetic interference, and is lighter weight.[176] With more on-board signal processing power and a 20 percent longer loiter time in the air, the P-1 is also more ISR capable than its predecessor. Moreover, its quieter engines make it more difficult for submerged submarines to detect its presence.[177] Meanwhile, a squadron of five EP-3 patrol aircraft, co-located with the U.S. Marine Corps in Iwakuni, continues to monitor the East China Sea. Analysis of the data collected by this unit is done in situ at the Iwakuni base and sent on to the Fleet Intelligence Center, and then to the DIH.[178]

In addition to these sophisticated sea- and air-based ISR capabilities, the MSDF built some dozen listening stations that serve as shore terminals for passive underwater hydrophone arrays—which integrate with marine surveillance radars sites, ELINT collection systems, and optical observation equipment.[179] Furthermore, magnetic measurement systems have been deployed on the sea floor across the Tsugaru and Tsushima straits that are linked to measurement stations in Osaka and Sasebo. Information from these systems is integrated into the MSDF Ocean Surveillance Information System Evolutionary Development system at its Oceanographic Command at Fleet Headquarters at Yokosuka, providing a 24/7 undersea surveillance and listening capability.[180]

It is important to note that there are offices apart from the services and outside the MOD that contribute to the Japanese intelligence effort. Two are located in the Ministry of Land, Infrastructure, Transport, and Tourism. The more prominent is the Japan Coast Guard (JCG), which, as mentioned earlier, formally became part of the intelligence community in 2008.[181] In September 2017, the JCG announced that it would set aside 240 million yen to create its own "maritime surveillance system" and purchase satellite images of a 2.2 million square kilometer area—stretching from the Japanese archipelago to coastal China, Korea, and Russia—to locate "vessels in need of rescue and to counter frequent intrusions by Chinese government ships."[182] A former chief of the DIH and the CSIC was not surprised that JCG opted to acquire its own images, acknowledging that the JCG was always a "low priority" for DIH and CSIC images.[183]

The other is the Geospatial Information Authority (GIA), which was established as the Cadastral Map Section of the Ministry of Civil Services in 1869. Its Intelligence Group was created just two years later to conduct surveys and produce maps, and the entire section was transferred to the General Staff Office of the Imperial Army Ministry in 1884. These functions were moved to the Home Ministry in 1945, and after the Asia-Pacific War to the Construction Ministry, forerunner of the Ministry of Land, Infrastructure, Transport, and Tourism, where it is located today.[184] Not a formal member of the intelligence community, GIA is tasked with "developing, updating, and providing geospatial information," and, unlike those of the GSDF's Geospatial Intelligence Unit, its activities are predominantly domestic. But in July 2007 it was tasked with "specify[ing] Japanese territory and territorial waters precisely" and "contributing to the management and maintenance of remote islands." Its budget was more than doubled in 2012.[185]

The JCG and the GIA contribute to the intelligence infrastructure both substantively and fiscally—by maintaining accounts apart from the formal defense budget. But in so doing, they call attention to the persistence of stovepipes in the Japanese intelligence community. The JCG decision to acquire region-wide images was partly a response to delays in receiving IMINT from MOD. It would share the images with "other entities" but indicated it had not been receiving images in a timely manner.[186] And when the SDF announced plans in 2016 to develop a new, indigenous GSI intelligence system, the stated purpose of which was "to rescue Japanese nationals trapped abroad . . . and to help them find hospitals and safe roads more easily," it bypassed the GIA and grudgingly allowed that it would share intelligence with MOFA "if necessary."[187]

What We Have Here Is a Failure to Communicate

As we have seen, long-standing problems of horizontal and vertical communication within the Japanese intelligence community—both across units in different agencies and ministries, and upward to the policy community—which existed from the beginning of Japanese engagement with the rest of the world persisted well past the reforms that got under way just after the Cold War. Although there was considerable improvement in the organization of Japan's military intelligence—as in the enhancement of communication between consolidated staff offices and the field military—parallel reform on the civilian side lagged. Competition between the NPA and MOFA continued, and spilled over into the military domain and other intelligence units. Even after the Machimura reforms, police officials continued to occupy senior posts across the intelligence community, including in CIRO, the SIGINT section of the Defense Intelligence Headquarters, the Cabinet Satellite Intelligence Center, and the First Intelligence Department at the Public Security Intelligence Agency.[188] Reporting channels between analysts and policy makers remained narrow and personalistic.

But there was an elephant in Japan's intelligence drawing room—Washington. All had not been well in U.S.-Japan intelligence cooperation for a very long time. As we saw in chapter 3, allied intelligence cooperation during the Cold War was close but lopsided. From the U.S. perspective it apparently remained so.[189] "Close cooperation" as judged by the U.S. National Security Agency referred mostly to the fact that it could maintain its Far East Headquarters in Japan, from which it supported more than a dozen SIGINT facilities, and that it could continue to refuse to share intelligence except on a "need to know" basis that it alone could determine.[190] NSA had good reason to be pleased. Despite the formal ban on collective self-defense, the Japanese government paid all relocation and construction costs—more than $500 million—to relocate NSA's high frequency remote collection facility to Camp Hansen in Okinawa in 1996.[191] It also provided nearly $7 million—14 percent of the total costs for the construction of a SIGINT antenna repair and fabrication facility (plus annual salaries of $375,000 for machinists and designers) that began operation in July 2004 at the Yokota Air Base, where equipment was prepped for use in Korea and Thailand, and for posts as far away as Afghanistan, Iraq, and the Balkans.[192] Admiral Otsuka Umio, a former head of Japanese naval intelligence, has a more generous view of intelligence sharing between the United States and Japanese militaries. He insists that "after 9/11, the U.S. attitude toward Japanese intelligence shifted from a 'need to know' to a 'need to share' basis."[193]

However lopsided the extensive relationship between the U.S. and Japanese intelligence communities may have been after 9/11, the United States had formal intelligence-sharing agreements with more than sixty nations but none with Japan until 2007. And what it had was opaque, leading one apparently exasperated former government official to insist, "We deserve to know how much we spend" to support U.S. SIGINT in Japan.[194] After 9/11, the United States stepped up pressure on Japan to adopt a classification system that would be a prerequisite for such a General Security of Military Information Agreement (GSOMIA), which establishes rules for how allies protect classified military information they share with one another.[195] It also pressed Japan to consolidate its intelligence community by eliminating sectionalism, a goal that one Japanese flag officer who resented U.S. domination of the Japanese intelligence community pointed out was a reversal of U.S. policy toward the SDF during the Cold War.[196] Machimura Nobutaka, the leading champion of intelligence reform after 9/11, heard it from both sides. He understood the frustrations of his intelligence professionals but also recognized that for decades Japan had what he referred to as a "take-take" intelligence-sharing relationship with the United States. He believed that the flow of intelligence—already constricted—would slow to a trickle without modification.[197] One part of that modification was installation of a secure telephone line connecting the White House and the prime minister's office in 2003, at a time when the U.S. government believed it had actionable intelligence that al-Qaeda was targeting Americans in Japan.[198] One retired U.S. intelligence official recalls: "One of the major hurdles we faced was to promote greater intelligence security. The Japanese government was leaky, and we tried to tighten it up."[199] The view in Washington was that the Japanese intelligence system had become inefficient not only for Japan but also for Washington. Indeed, it was viewed in some quarters as a risk for the United States.[200]

FIGURE 5.3 Deputy Secretary of State Richard Armitage and Foreign Minister Machimura Nobutaka, seen here in October 2004, were on the same page regarding Japanese intelligence reform after 9/11.
Photo: Kazuhiro Nogi/AFP/Getty Images

The problem was easier to identify than to fix, because Washington was not pushing on an open door—at least not at first. Although, as reported earlier, Prime Minister Koizumi's CIRO chief responded enthusiastically to these exhortations, other Japanese officials were reluctant to further subordinate their intelligence community to Washington. But a bigger obstacle was that many Japanese politicians remained cautious and judged public opinion to be unprepared for wholesale intelligence reform—especially one involving new secrecy laws. Meanwhile, Japanese defense firms did not wish to be further constrained regarding what they could acquire and the conditions under which it could be transferred from U.S. contractors. So, as often happens, policy converged on a case-by-case approach on defense technology exchange and, more generally, on intelligence sharing.[201] By the mid-2000s, however, China's rise and North Korea's provocations had driven bilateral military cooperation to a level that rendered these ad hoc arrangements unworkable. In order to integrate a bilateral missile defense system in response to North Korean missile tests, Japan and the United States now needed to share large amounts of sensitive information and technology on an ongoing basis. According to one Japanese analyst, "The need to share information grew dramatically as the U.S. and Japan coordinated policies on North Korea, missile defense contingency planning, and the global war on terror."[202]

The first public indication of a diplomatic effort to sign a bilateral GSO-MIA appeared in October 2005, when the joint statement from the "2 + 2" meeting of Secretary of State Condoleezza Rice and Secretary of Defense Donald Rumsfeld with Minister of Foreign Affairs Machimura and Minister of Defense Ohno Yoshinori endorsed increased intelligence cooperation. The statement bears hints of U.S. pressure on Japan for better information security: "Both sides will take additional necessary measures to protect shared classified information so that broader information sharing is promoted among pertinent authorities."[203] In the subsequent year or more, negotiations proceeded at the services level to establish a new channel for SIGINT exchange from reconnaissance aircraft across East Asia, including "all four mission areas"—the East China Sea, the South China Sea, the Korean Peninsula, and the Sea of Japan. The first exchanges began in February 2007 and came to include exchanges of Preliminary Mission Summary Reports from the most sophisticated U.S. and Japanese intelligence-gathering aircraft.[204]

Negotiations also quietly progressed at the diplomatic level, as Japan's domestic politics shifted in a direction that favored intelligence reform—the same direction in which U.S. policy was headed. In September 2006, just one day before Abe Shinzō became prime minister for the first time, CIA and CIRO officials met in Tokyo and agreed that it was a propitious moment for a "strategic dialogue" on intelligence cooperation.[205] Two months later, the U.S. embassy in Tokyo reported that both sides had agreed on the text of a GSOMIA. The U.S. ambassador to Japan, Tom Schieffer, celebrated the breakthrough while alluding to previous Japanese bureaucratic opposition to an agreement: "Progress on the [GSOMIA] text indicates Japan has overcome inter-agency differences that caused resistance to a GSOMIA for 25 years, and made it the only major U.S. ally without such an agreement."[206] At last, Schieffer wrote, all the major agencies endorsed the agreement: "Inter-agency buy-in was evident in the broad representation in the Japanese delegation at the talks. Japanese representatives included the Japan Defense Agency, Cabinet Intelligence and Research Office, Public Security Information Agency, Cabinet Satellite Office, National Police Agency, and Japan Coast Guard."[207]

The path to this agreement was paved by all three "drivers" addressed in this volume. To be sure, the regional security environment shifted in a direction unfavorable to Japan, and the introduction of new technology to counter new North Korean and Chinese capabilities required intelligence reform. But it was Japan's failure to protect information that was the most immediate precipitant. A number of damaging leaks by the Japanese government pertaining to North Korea's testing and the Aegis naval missile defense system foregrounded Japan's insecure information security arrangements. As Ambassador Schieffer would later reflect, Japan faced a systematic problem with handling classified information, "both in terms of Japan's structures for protecting information, and in terms of Japan's lack of appreciation for the counter-intelligence problem it faces."[208] His embassy's cables had explicitly mentioned several leaks, including one in the aftermath of North Korea's July 2006 ballistic missile tests after the United States shared sensitive information with Japan about the launches. Two months later, in a meeting with Japan's top defense official, JDA Vice Minister Moriya Takemasa, the deputy chief of mission at the U.S. embassy "stressed the importance of protecting sensitive sources and methods," according to a U.S. cable recounting the meeting. The cable goes on:

> While the United States sees expanded intelligence sharing as in the interests of both countries, recent leaks on North Korea–related intelligence to the Japanese press have *damaged our collection activities against the DPRK*. It is critical that the United States and Japan share intelligence and that Japanese policymakers get access to relevant intelligence data, [the deputy chief of mission] added, but there needs to be a wider understanding of the real consequences of disclosures.[209]

Vice Minister Moriya—an experienced bureaucratic infighter and reputedly prodigious leaker—passed the buck in an entirely predictable way. He claimed that neither the JDA nor the Japanese military was responsible for the leak and insisted it "resulted from expanded intel sharing with other agencies less experienced in the field."[210]

In January 2007, a new leak involving Aegis naval missile defense technology became front-page news. According to another U.S. embassy cable:

> The most troubling recent episode relates to classified Aegis operational data found in the home of an uncleared Maritime Self-Defense Force (MSDF) member in January whose spouse is a PRC [Chinese] citizen found to be residing illegally in Japan. . . . The U.S. government has registered our concerns about the case at senior Japanese political levels. This has resulted in Japan taking policy-level steps to assuage our concerns, including by committing to participate in a Bilateral Information Assurance Task Force.[211]

The cable makes clear that a GSOMIA would be only the beginning of a larger effort to overhaul the Japanese system: "Finalizing a GSOMIA is a good first step towards creating a common system to protect sensitive data, [and] that institutionalizes access, transparency, and accountability."[212]

These leaks accelerated progress toward the GSOMIA agreement by strengthening the leverage of both U.S. and Japanese proponents. At the next "2 + 2" meeting, in May 2007, the two sides officially announced their intention to sign a GSOMIA to "facilitate information exchange and establish a common basis of information security contributing to sharing of intelligence and defense program and operational information."[213] Ambassador Schieffer and Foreign Minister Asō Tarō formally signed the agreement in a ceremony at the Japanese Foreign Ministry in August. The new agreement superseded dated (and demonstratively inadequate) legal structures, specifically the 1952 Security Treaty and subsequent agreements that had served as flimsy guidelines for decades.[214] In the view of one NSA analyst, Japan had now transitioned "to the next level as an intelligence partner with the United States."[215] It would share intelligence according to "American standards."[216]

There is some ambiguity regarding just what this next level and these standards are. The press often refers to "Five Eyes," a postwar set of memoranda of understanding and exchanges of letters negotiated first by Washington and London, and then expanded to "Second Parties"—Australia, Canada, and New Zealand—whereby global SIGINT responsibilities were allocated and shared. While never considered a partner at the level of these countries— a level that one senior U.S. military officer refers to as "clubbiness"—the

Japanese government is occasionally reported to be a "Third Party" to the "UKUSA Agreement," along with dozens of other allied states such as Austria, Thailand, South Korea, Norway, Denmark, Germany, Italy, Greece, and Turkey.[217] But Japan does not formally acknowledge this status. Indeed, two former heads of the DIH insisted flatly that Japan has never been a party to Five Eyes, while a former deputy director of CIRO says he "does not know for sure," explaining that while Japan is aware of and follows Five Eyes protocols, it "is not likely a formal signatory as a 'Third Party.'" And a former CIRO head insists, "Officially Japan was not part of Five Eyes, but since my departure I would guess that Japanese cooperation with Five Eyes has made great progress."[218] A senior U.S. military officer insists there has been no such "progress" and confirms both Japan's denials and ambitions: "It is commonly understood that Japan has a broad interest in being included in the Five Eyes protocol, and indeed there has been reach out to counterparts seeking advocacy for their inclusion. But Japan does not do a good job of being allegiant even to bilateral protocols."[219] Likewise, a former senior policy adviser to President George W. Bush concurs: "Japan is not part of Five Eyes because it brings nothing to the table that the others can all rely upon. Each Five Eyes partner is assigned separate missions, but while Japan has gained considerable strength in military intelligence—and especially geo-spatial imaging—it is not yet up to that level."[220] That said, the adviser added that in some cases the U.S. Pacific Command sought limited exceptions to Five Eyes restrictions—"carve-outs" for Japanese intelligence on anti-submarine warfare, missile defense, and imagery.

These claims notwithstanding, leaked NSA documents refer obliquely to Japan as a "Third Party." And at the risk of obscuring the fact that there is an enormous gap between what is shared among the Five Eyes and others, Japan is often rumored to be one of the Forty-one-Eyes, the allied coalition in Afghanistan, as well as the Ten-Eyes, which is composed of the Five Eyes plus NATO as an organization, and four Pacific Rim nations such as Japan, South Korea, Thailand, and Singapore.[221] To the extent it is reported in the public domain, its SIGINT exchanges are all bilateral, involving liaison between the Department of Defense Special Representative Japan, the headquarters of the Fifth Air Force at Yokota Air Base, the MSDF Fleet HQ, and the headquarters of the U.S. Navy's Commander Naval Forces Japan, co-located at Yokosuka Naval Base.[222] Compared to the Second Parties, which participate in high-level strategic deliberations with the United States and the UK and enjoy privileged access to the most sophisticated defense and intelligence technologies, Third Parties are restricted to more limited and discretionary access to the Five Eyes resources—at best on an ad hoc, one-off basis.[223]

Reflecting on these and other arrangements, one former senior intelligence official explained: "Both sides are condemned to cooperate. The U.S. side needs Japan and Japan needs the U.S., and will for years to come."[224] But this mutual dependence hardly eliminated long-standing incentives for the Japanese intelligence community to seek additional intelligence partners. As a senior Japanese national security official observes:

> During the Cold War, Japan didn't need to be engaged in overseas [intelligence] activity. So intelligence was naturally linked to operations rather than to strategic analysis. After the Cold War, Japanese decision makers began to ask for more analysis, but the United States was not ready to share because it lacked confidence in Japan's ability to protect intelligence. . . . Since we did not get what we wanted from the United States, we began to speak to other friendly countries.[225]

Although it is rarely acknowledged, Japan did have other (far more limited) options that did not interfere with its main alliance relationship. Intelligence cooperation with "other friendly countries" actually was under way on a limited scale during the Cold War, but many of the bilateral exchanges between Japanese intelligence and other friendly services was intermediated—indeed managed—by the United States.[226]

Given this, it is no surprise that Japan did not sign GSOMIA with "other friendly countries" until the U.S.-Japan GSOMIA was concluded. Then, similar accords were concluded in short order with NATO (June 2010), France (October 2011), Australia (May 2012), the UK (2013), India (2015), and Italy (2016).[227] Agreement was most difficult to reach, however, with Japan's most important (and difficult) strategic partner after the United States—the Republic of Korea. In June 2012, under public pressure, and despite the strong support of his national security adviser, President Lee Myung-bak canceled the scheduled signing of a "direct and comprehensive" bilateral GSOMIA with Japan at the eleventh hour.[228] As we will see in chapter 6, negotiations would be revived, but only four years later—and only after considerable pressure from the United States and use of an inefficient "bypass" through Washington. Overall, however, Japan's intelligence sharing was now considerably more extensive than ever before. Like analysts elsewhere, Japanese intelligence officers often do not know the origin of the raw intelligence that crosses their desks and screens. But according to one, it is clear that the raw intelligence he reviews originates from more sources than Japanese collectors can access alone. He concludes that "overall, coordination with our foreign counterparts has advanced."[229]

Japan has also pursued intelligence cooperation of a very different, far more awkward nature. In 2007 Tokyo joined the first annual Asia-Pacific

Intelligence Chiefs' Conference, convened by the U.S. Navy's Pacific Command in Kuala Lumpur, and has participated each year since. Since this meeting is open to a wide range of states, including Australia, Bangladesh, Indonesia, Cambodia, South Korea, Laos, Malaysia, Singapore, Thailand, Vietnam, the UK, and, several times after 2014, China, the plenary sessions are limited to relatively anodyne topics such as humanitarian assistance and disaster relief and the more constabulary aspects of maritime security. The more important conversations reportedly take place on the sidelines in bilateral and trilateral settings.[230]

According to a leaked NSA assessment, intimate multilateral intelligence cooperation is difficult for the Japanese intelligence community: "Since they treat SIGINT in such a close-hold manner, it's very hard to engage them in multinational forums or even to get them to collaborate across Japanese governmental lanes. Bilaterally they are a good partner but they are very reluctant to participate with mixed or larger groups."[231] There are several publicly reported examples of this. The NSA participates with Australia, Canada, New Zealand, Thailand, the ROK, France, India, and Singapore in a "SIGINT Seniors Pacific" group. Japan was offered membership in the early 2000s but declined, expressing "concerns that unintended disclosure of its participation would be too high a risk."[232] The Japanese government—when not under the control of the more conservative wing of the LDP—also has pushed back on what was perceived as unwelcome U.S. pressure for intelligence reform. For example, in 2009 Japan withdrew from a sixteen-nation "Third Party Partner" project to maintain an NSA-led global high-frequency direction finding capability code-named CROSSHAIR after—on NSA's account—it "mistakenly perceived" that NSA was trying to impose its technical standards on the SDF. NSA claimed it was merely attempting to establish "system interoperability."[233]

This chapter has examined how the civilian and military institutions of the Japanese intelligence community were actively reimagined in the first decade of this century. The ruling party and the government—as well as the think tank community—all were motivated by shifts in the strategic environment to undertake extended deliberations regarding reform of the intelligence community. They outlined and debated how best to rearrange its roles and missions, how to introduce and optimize new technological capacity, and in what ways international collaboration might be enhanced. As one participant recalled, "Given the continued parade of difficult security problems, such as terrorism, the Iraq War, and the illegal behavior of North Korea, Japan was compelled to take foreign policy ever more seriously, and recognized that foreign intelligence had to be strengthened."[234] As with the proverbial tanker in port, however, it would take considerable time to turn the Japanese intelligence community around. And even after it was facing in the right direction, there would remain a great deal of distance for it to cover.

Kaneko Masafumi, a particularly astute student of the Japanese intelligence community—and the lead author of the influential PHP think tank study mentioned earlier—assessed the state of Japanese intelligence at precisely this moment. Writing just months before the fundamental reengineering that would take place in 2013, he listed several of its distinguishing features. On his account, despite changes in the Northeast Asian security environment, Japan's intelligence community was still inhibited by a pacifist public and riven by competing units that rendered it a "community" in name only. Kaneko attributed this to the absence of an explicit legal foundation and relatively insufficient collection and analytical capabilities, among other deficiencies.[235] Other experts also piled on. Magosaki Ukeru, the former chief of the MOFA Intelligence and Analysis Service who was quoted earlier, said that a central problem was that Japan remained "overwhelmingly weak in intelligence collection [attōteki ni yowai]."[236] Yonemura Toshirō, a former deputy chief cabinet secretary for crisis management, agreed and expressed his disappointment in the intelligence community's analytic capacity as well. His view at the time was that Japan's intelligence community still "has problems summarizing and analyzing collected data."[237] Three members of the Diet, each representing a different political party, jointly concluded that "unfortunately, there has still been nothing concrete accomplished."[238] So, however much the intelligence community was the object of strategic reimagining during this period, Kaneko aptly refers to its "germination" (hōga). It had been reimagined, but certainly had not yet been reinvented.[239]

Even if some of these criticisms were excessive, they were not far off the mark and represented a consensus view among cognoscenti that more work needed to be done before Japan would have an adequate intelligence capacity. It seems clear that well into the second decade of the twenty-first century, Tokyo still lacked the broad-based legal framework required for effective and sustained intelligence reform, that political leaders advocating change took the bit in their mouths only intermittently, and that Japanese intelligence remained more dependent on the United States than some could abide.

The main advocate for more significant structural change—what I refer to as "reengineering"—was Prime Minister Abe Shinzō, who fell ill and left office suddenly in September 2007. Once he returned to power in December 2012—and only after a period of relative indifference from his successors—Abe expended considerable political capital to create an entirely new security policy and intelligence apparatus based on new legislation, what one former CIRO chief has spoken of as "pillars [providing] structural integrity" for the Japanese intelligence community for the first time.[240] We turn next to an examination of these "pillars," and to the ways in which determined political leaders finally, and for the first time, reengineered each of the elements of the Japanese intelligence community. We will also explore the reaction of a public, its recalcitrance worn away by Chinese and North Korean provocations, that demanded (and to some extent received) fuller oversight in exchange for accepting intelligence reform.

CHAPTER 6

Reengineering the Intelligence Community (2013–)

> We have no objection to the alliance with the United States as the foundation of Japanese national security, but insist that if Japan is to be able to survive as a nation with keen senses amidst the sudden shifts in the strategic environment, it must establish its own non-military intelligence agency as a matter of national security.
>
> —Future foreign minister Kōno Tarō and two Diet colleagues, 2013

As we have seen, soon after the Cold War the Japanese government enhanced military intelligence—particularly imaging at the Defense Intelligence Headquarters and service-specific tactical surveillance/reconnaissance. But further shifts in the strategic environment after 9/11, technological change, and consequent intelligence failures—including by the DIH—illuminated the insufficiencies of the tinkering and reimagining examined in chapters 4 and 5. Chary leaders therefore had to prepare themselves to spend political capital on more expansive modifications—what one former military intelligence chief called "epochal" (*kakki-teki*) reforms—the "keys that would unlock the potential of the Japanese intelligence community."[1]

In this chapter we examine what was at this writing the most recent—and most ambitious—reengineering of the Japanese intelligence community. This round—beginning with the 2013 passage of a Designated State Secrets Law (DSSL) and creation of the National Security Council (NSC)—surely would not be the final word in Japanese intelligence reform. After all, we know that intelligence communities everywhere are in constant motion, and the ruling Liberal Democratic Party's Policy Research Council had already drafted even more ambitious plans by late 2015. But the scope and scale of the 2013 reforms suggest that political leaders anticipated—and were determined to get out ahead of—new security challenges by addressing many of

Japan's most difficult endemic intelligence problems. Examining how and why they did so provides us a window into understanding how Japan might resolve the inherent tension between enhancing alliance management and reducing the dependence on the United States identified in the epigraph to this chapter.

The Crown Jewels of Intelligence Reform

The Designated State Secrets Law

The previous chapter documented how Washington pressed the Japanese government to seal leaks and to take measures to improve intelligence sharing. We saw how those efforts accompanied a bilateral GSOMIA in 2007—a long-awaited, formal readjustment to the way U.S.-Japan intelligence cooperation would proceed. The willing embrace of these pressures by Abe Shinzō and his conservative allies was next expressed in a more ambitious set of structural changes in the way Japan collects, analyzes, communicates, and protects intelligence.

The first step in this reengineering of Japan's intelligence community was drafting of a Designated State Secrets Law (DSSL), prepared by the cabinet's Intelligence Research Office and approved by Prime Minister Abe's government in October 2013. Its primary formal justification, as stated in Article 1, was the need to establish a system to protect state secrets in an "increasingly complex international situation."[2] A year later, the law passed the Diet with multiparty support, but only after generating significant protest, undergoing considerable public discussion, and, ultimately, being amended to reflect popular concerns. Postwar Japan's first comprehensive state secrets regime got under way in December 2014, and limited legislative oversight began soon thereafter. Within one year nearly 100,000 government officials—90,000 of whom were in MOD—were certified by virtue of background checks to handle classified documents.[3]

The DSSL replaced a diverse and uncoordinated collection of ministry/agency-specific practices with uniform guidelines across nineteen government units for the classification of information in the areas of defense, diplomacy, counterespionage, and counterterrorism. These categories were further specified in more than fifty sub-classifications, such as military plans, weapons performance data, communications codes, details of negotiations, and specifics relating to intelligence collection and anti-terrorism preparations. The law also stipulated an initial thirty-year period of designation, with the possibility of renewal for an additional thirty years—its most controversial provision. Indeed, a third period of thirty years could be designated by cabinet order if the information concerned weapons systems, was relevant to ongoing negotiations, contained information on collection cryptography, or had been supplied by another country or international organization in which it was subject to a longer designation. In addition, the law established a system for background checks of government employees. Violators of the law—malicious leakers and whistle-blowers alike—would now face up to ten years in jail. And in yet another particularly controversial legal stipulation, those who came to learn a designated secret by accident, even in the course of official duties, faced up to five years in prison. Diet members remained exempt from any penalties.

The Abe government championed this legislation with unusual speed and determination. It was debated in the Diet for far less time than is normally allotted for major legislation, engendering impassioned criticism of legislative "steamrolling" (*kyōkō saiketsu*), including by some who supported the legislation. The *Asahi Shimbun* editorialized that "the ruling coalition railroaded the DSSL through the House of Representatives . . . in blatant disregard of the will of the people and the opposition camp's call for further deliberation."[4] Even Abe's chief cabinet secretary allowed as how "we should have shown more humility" and acknowledged that an additional sixty hours for public examination could have been added.[5]

In the event, however, the legislation remained the object of vigorous debate well beyond the legislative process, a debate that was strikingly different from any before it in this sensitive domain—at least in Japan. And there had been precedent: Japan had as much experience with spirited public debate regarding the right balance between protecting personal freedoms and control of information, between transparency and secrecy, as nearly any other industrial democracy. As we have seen, it often engaged the issue with vigor in the postwar era, as it did in 1985, when Prime Minister Nakasone fought and lost a public battle to introduce the anti-espionage law discussed in chapter 3. But the government had repeatedly failed to enact a comprehensive classification regime to provide an effective mechanism for intelligence collection or intelligence sharing with friendly states, in large measure because the public repeatedly was persuaded that such a measure would be the first step down a "slippery slope" back to prewar militarism.

By the time he returned to power in 2013, Abe was more determined than ever to upgrade Japan's security and intelligence infrastructure. And this time he was better situated. Abe enjoyed an overwhelming majority in the lower house and, with the support of coalition partner Kōmeitō, a majority in the upper house as well. He was keen to establish a system that would "keep a firm protective lid on information in order to be able to receive high-quality information [from allies]"—his primary public justification for the DSSL.[6] Indirectly acknowledging U.S. pressure, Abe frequently declared that "without rules on managing classified information, we cannot obtain intelligence from other countries."[7] The DSSL would be—along with the establishment of a new NSC—a critical building block for enhancing Japan's still underdeveloped intelligence community and constructing an entirely new national security policy-making architecture.

Although the Japanese public was not pleased with the Abe government's Diet management of the secrecy law, the opposition adopted a new tone. A number of familiar, Japan-specific, and long-prevailing "slippery slope" objections faded before more universal concerns about how to ensure that secrecy would be used to advance national security rather than to conceal abuse of power. Transparency, arbitrary application, press freedoms, whistle-blower protection, and even human rights dominated the discourse. Opponents of the law as drafted, including freedom of information activists, sought to make the law more acceptable and to reassert political control of the bureaucracy. In the process, Japan's discourse on state secrets migrated from its past preoccupation with the experience of wartime authoritarianism to a more universal concern for the preservation and health of democratic norms. Japanese civil society appeared to have abandoned the "slippery slope" to find solid footing for vigilant and engaged citizens, many of whom seemed to come to trust that they had a government that heard them. After the bill's passage, but before it went into effect—the period during which public comments were collected—the implementing rules of the DSSL were amended to address, if not to entirely ameliorate, public concern.

Japan's pragmatic leaders cared most openly about paving the way for better intelligence sharing. Across the Pacific, U.S. officials who had pressed hard for this change celebrated this "big step forward [that increases] confidence in our ally's ability to protect information [and] allows [us] to share more."[8] At home, Nakatani Gen, a former defense minister and deputy chair of the LDP's Intelligence and Information Protection Project Team, agreed. Rather than reflect on how far Japanese civil society and conservative politicians had come, he insisted that the most important aspect of the DSSL was that it would facilitate Japan's acquisition of foreign and domestic intelligence.[9] Chief Cabinet Secretary Suga Yoshihide was equally straightforward. He declared that the DSSL "will have absolutely no impact on the daily lives of ordinary citizens," and, like Nakatani, he discounted any negative effects DSSL might have by further increasing Japan's dependence on U.S. intelligence: "If

Japan can keep a firm protective lid on the intelligence it obtains, it should be able to receive highly accurate intelligence from the U.S. side."[10]

The National Security Council

As the several adjustments to the DSSL demonstrate, Prime Minister Abe heard—and was willing to nod in the direction of—citizens' concerns. Beyond the typical incumbent's passion for popular approval, however, it was clear that his primary focus in guiding intelligence reforms was national security. Abe expended significant political capital getting them through—even allowing his approval ratings to take a hit. But once the DSSL was in place, he declared with conviction that "it is vital to strengthen the government's intelligence functions and gather more accurate information that will be reflected in the state's strategic decision-making."[11]

It had been a long time since the process of national security decision making had been addressed in a serious way. In July 1954, as part of the reestablishment of the Japanese military under the banner of a Self-Defense Force, formal authority for strategic decision making was assigned to a National Defense Council (Kokubō Kaigi—NDC) in the prime minister's Cabinet Office.[12] The new organ, comprising five cabinet ministers, was assigned nominal responsibility for developing a "Basic Policy" for national defense, defense industrial mobilization, and other matters. Born in the shadow of Japan's defeat in the Asia-Pacific War and U.S. occupation, it was riven with problems from the beginning. Debates over civilian control of the military and the advisability of using the defense industrial base to power postwar reindustrialization distracted the NDC from its main tasks.[13] In July 1986 the NDC was reinvented as an equally inadequate Security Council of Japan (SCJ). Meanwhile, as we have seen, many in the intelligence community resented how Japan's Cold War alignment with the United States was accompanied by accommodation to Washington's priorities.[14]

Prime Minister Abe, long an advocate of "ending the postwar" and "taking Japan back," first recognized the need for an integrated organization to support national security decision making and an integrated intelligence capability when, as chief cabinet secretary to Prime Minister Koizumi during the July 2006 North Korean missile crisis, he had daily contact with U.S. national security adviser Stephen Hadley.[15] In subsequent speeches, Abe tied the two reforms together repeatedly, as when he introduced the plan for a new NSC to the Diet in the fall of 2013 by announcing that "[for the NSC] to function we need to protect secrets."[16] He did so knowing that this would require political and bureaucratic support from trusted allies. In the case of the

DSSL, Abe enjoyed unstinting assistance from Japan's leading champion for intelligence reform, LDP elder and foreign minister Machimura Nobutaka. Political leadership was paramount, but Abe also needed considerable support from within the bureaucracy, and received it from Yachi Shōtarō, Japan's top professional diplomat during the first Abe administration in 2006–7.[17] Yachi would become Japan's first secretary general of the National Security Secretariat (NSS), the centralized intelligence and policy coordination unit under the new NSC system.

Centralizing Japan's national security policy making proved no small task and faced obstacles both great and small. In late 2006, during his first administration, Abe asked his special adviser for national security Koike Yuriko to serve as deputy chair of a Council on the Strengthening of Cabinet Capabilities for National Security Decision Making (Kokka Anzen Hoshō ni Kansuru Kantei Kinō Kyōka Kaigi), a commission charged with generating a plan for creating an NSC that he would chair. Koike subsequently visited Washington to meet Hadley, to the consternation of Chief Cabinet Secretary Shiozaki Yasuhisa, who then took pains to remind Hadley on the phone that he, not Koike, was Hadley's Japanese counterpart.[18] Such seemingly minor political

FIGURE 6.1   Prime Minister Abe Shinzō and Foreign Minister Machimura Nobutaka in September 2008.
Photo: © *The Nikkan Gendai*

Figure 6.2   NSS Secretary General Yachi Shōtarō and Prime Minister Abe Shinzō in January 2014, soon after the creation of the National Security Council.
Photo: *Asahi Shimbun*

thumb wrestling provided maneuvering room for bureaucrats determined to protect their prerogatives, which they did with some success.[19] The Abe-Koike council concluded in its February 2007 report that a newly engineered NSC "will be the prime minister's advisory organ just like the current Security Council of Japan and will not change jurisdictions of relevant ministries such as MOFA and the MOD."[20] The bureaucrats' clear victory seemed assured when Abe suddenly resigned in September 2007 and political leadership for national security policy reform lost momentum. Abe's successor, the more cautious Fukuda Yasuo, withdrew the draft legislation altogether.[21]

But perhaps to Fukuda's surprise, reengineering the security policy-making process under enhanced political leadership actually had broad, supra-partisan support. The short-lived and weak DPJ governments of 2009–2012 also pressed for the change. The LDP was compelled to oppose DPJ initiatives, but immediately upon his return to power in December 2012, Abe called upon Yachi, who had retired to the private sector, to help resurrect his plans to establish an NSC.[22] He appointed Yachi to both the Council on Security and Defense Capabilities (Anzen Hoshō to Bōeiryoku ni Kansuru Kondankai) and the Advisory Council on the Establishment of a

National Security Council (Kokka Anzenhoshō Kaigi no Sōsetsu ni Kansuru Yūshikisha Kaigi), commissions tasked to study U.S. and British security policy decision making.[23] Yachi's councils developed a hybrid model in which a U.S.-style National Security Council would be supported by a British-style intelligence and policy coordination unit, the National Security Secretariat, staffed predominantly by secondees from relevant ministries located within the Cabinet Secretariat.

Reflecting in 2015 on his nearly decade-long effort to create the NSC, Abe acknowledged in the Diet that the government had had persistent difficulty coordinating and communicating intelligence analyses: "Until now, the various intelligence units have not been coordinated centrally in the service of a jointly shared policy decision."[24] This is why, after considerable study and debate, a formal cabinet decision in June 2013 called for an NSC that would implement an "all Japan" policy process that would maximize communication of intelligence to policy makers on the topics they requested, and that would be designed to minimize debilitating competition across ministries.

This time it seemed that the frustrated political class meant business. Improved intelligence coordination would be more clearly in service to the policy function. As one government document envisioned it, "Policy and intelligence have to be independent of each other and separated under cabinet leadership."[25] Strengthening the connection between intelligence and policy functions was to be a top priority for the NSC, but the former was always conceived as subordinate to the latter.[26] The "cabinet intelligence analysis officer" positions created in CIRO in 2008 would be used to strengthen further the capacity for "all-source analysis," and new guidelines were issued to improve intelligence collection, analysis, and communication.

Designs for the new system evolved through iterative deliberative council reports until final legislation was passed by the Diet in December 2013. The result was a reengineered structure involving three layers of ministerial meetings. The first, a biweekly "four-minister meeting," would be chaired by the prime minister and attended by the minister of foreign affairs, the minister of defense, and the chief cabinet secretary. It was tasked with giving fundamental direction for a broad range of foreign and defense policies. The second was a "nine-minister meeting," to be attended by the four ministers plus five other ministers, to deliberate on the basic principles of national defense and other issues previously under SCJ jurisdiction.[27] And the third was an "emergency situations ministerial meeting," which would involve the prime minister, the chief cabinet secretary, and any number of relevant ministries selected by the prime minister on a case-by-case basis, depending on the nature of the crisis. In a particularly significant shift, top uniformed officers could now participate in emergency situations meetings at the invitation of the prime minister.[28]

NSC meetings are supported by the NSS, the new gatekeeping interagency unit responsible for collecting and assessing intelligence from across the government on topics assigned by the NSC and then for presenting policy options to the political leadership. The NSS is led by a secretary general who reports directly to the prime minister, two deputy secretaries general (concurrently assistant chief cabinet secretaries), and three cabinet councillors. When the NSS was inaugurated, these councillors were recruited from MOFA, MOD, and the Air Self-Defense Force (ASDF). Six policy units/teams were organized to supervise policy coordination and planning, including one unit for overall management, three regional teams, one for strategic planning, and one for communication with the intelligence community.[29] None of these units had more than nineteen professionals, and most had fewer than ten. The entire operation involved just sixty professionals (forty policy analysts and twenty intelligence analysts) with twenty support staff, remarkably trim by U.S. or British standards.[30] Kanehara Nobukatsu, one of the first deputy secretaries general, has used terms associated with the Tokugawa shogunate to characterize the talented officials recruited to serve the new secretariat. He describes them as a sort of prime ministerial "elite guard" (*chokkatsu butai*) with "direct retainers" (*jikisan hatamoto*) dedicated to serving the political leadership in the comprehensive national interest, above the parochial interests of their home ministries and agencies.[31]

Even if this description is a bit fanciful, there is no question that the reform was meant to mitigate the abiding problem of stovepiped jurisdictions. The NSS was assigned formal authority to gather intelligence for the prime minister once kept closely within ministerial silos.[32] This measure was designed not only to promote intelligence sharing across "the whole of government" but also to restrict back channels for the delivery of raw intelligence to the prime minister via the various line ministries and agencies. One former CIRO director insists (wistfully, perhaps) that "until the creation of the NSC, there were stovepipes at every level of the intelligence community. Then it all changed 180 degrees."[33]

Not even Prime Minister Abe was so sure, however. Ignoring the long history of past failures to solve this debilitating and perennial problem, he testified wanly to the House of Councillors in February 2015 that the NSS would generate a "wide network" of intelligence officials with the experience of operating in an environment of trust, and with confidence in the security of the information they share. He lauded each of the component agencies whose analyses would be shared with, and consolidated and coordinated in, the new NSS.[34] In a system famously handicapped by jurisdictional competition—and in a domain in which secrecy is paramount—establishing norms of trust and cooperation was a nontrivial challenge. Anyone familiar with the Japanese intelligence community was well aware of the intransigence and self-regard of key elements in the system, but few until Abe were willing to spend scarce political capital to attempt reforming them comprehensively.

One early move was the creation of a common storage system accessible to each of Japan's various intelligence units. Using what they labeled a "first responder model" of distributed reporting, individual collectors could now feed the intelligence community with raw intelligence from wherever they are located.[35] One senior NSS official, a secondee from MOFA, describes this as "a positive Pandora's Box," suggesting that "a virtuous cycle has been established":

> We at NSS now have the authority to request raw intelligence and analysis from every unit in the intelligence community, and we do so constantly. We sit in the middle of the resulting traffic and, without sharing what we receive from one unit with the others, we provide feedback to each. The quality of their reports has improved because no unit wants to be compared unfavourably with the others. And because representatives of each unit sit within the NSS, they talk to one another more than ever.[36]

Given the history of the Japanese intelligence community, it is remarkable that intelligence officers consistently report high levels of cooperation across administrative jurisdictions.[37]

A major test of the efficacy of the new system is the extent to which the relationship between MOFA and MOD has become more open and cooperative. Although it seems that MOFA had come to accept a policy role for MOD and that both have attempted to find more productive ways to engage the NPA (and vice versa), some organization charts continue to show direct lines between ministries and the senior political leadership. This suggests that each of Japan's powerful sub-ministerial intelligence units—within the NPA, MOFA, PSIA, and MOD, as well as METI, the Financial Services Agency (FSA), and the Japan Coast Guard—continue to report directly to top cabinet officials, enabling them potentially to circumvent and weaken the NSS by transmitting their raw data to policy makers.[38]

The relationship between CIRO, whose director has always been an NPA secondee recognized as director of cabinet intelligence, and the new NSS, which has assumed many of CIRO's collection and communication functions, became yet another potential locus of bureaucratic infighting. Under

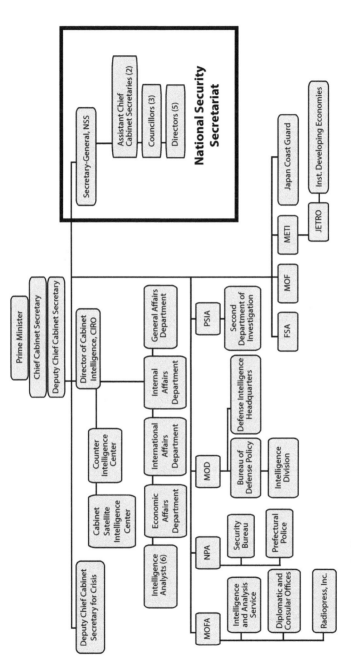

Figure 6.3 Japan's intelligence community, 2018

Source: Naikaku Kanbō (Cabinet Secretariat), "Jōhō to Jōhō Hozen (Information and Information Security)," May 2010, p. 4, http://www.kantei.go.jp/jp/singi/shin-ampobouei2010/dai7/siryou1.pdf; Naikaku Kanbō Kokka Anzenhoshō Kaigi Secchi Junbishitsu (Cabinet Secretariat Preparatory Office for the Creation of a National Security Council, 28 May 2013,), "Kokka Anzen Hoshō Kaigi ni tsuite Setsumei Shiryō (Explaining The National Security Council)," p. 3, http://www.kantei.go.jp/jp/singi/ka_yusiki/dai6/siryou1.pdf.

the new arrangement, the NSS is responsible for the flow of information between the political leadership and the intelligence community. NSS relays NSC requests to CIRO and other members of the intelligence community and integrates CIRO reports with information from other agencies and ministries.[39] Yet elements of ambiguity remain. As noted earlier, NSS officials claim to have large numbers of analysts on staff, but senior intelligence officials insist that the NSS role is limited to collection, assembly, review, and presentation of the analyses of constituent intelligence units. Moreover, CIRO and NSS are placed alongside each other in the Cabinet Secretariat's organizational chart, and CIRO maintains formal responsibility for intelligence collection and all-source analysis. It reports directly to the political leadership if necessary.[40]

One senior NSS official, a MOFA secondee who acknowledges that he is "sure that CIRO presents foreign intelligence separately to the prime minister," adds that "it would be a bridge too far for us to try to oppose that. We think it is better for us to consolidate our own capabilities."[41] This invites additional confusion that is compounded by reports that NSS staff members actively cultivate foreign intelligence sources themselves instead of relying on CIRO and other intelligence organizations, such as MOFA's Intelligence and Analysis Service.[42] In fact, it was NSS, not CIRO, which received intelligence reports directly from the United States regarding North Korea's alleged cyberattack on Sony Pictures Entertainment in November 2014.[43] Meanwhile, in at least the first two years of NSC operation, the CIRO chief may have spent more time with the prime minister than the NSS head did.[44] Their relative positions are reflected in budgetary terms as well: in the years since the NSC was created, the NSS budget has remained flat—0.7 billion yen in 2014 and 0.8 billion yen in 2018—while the CIRO budget nearly doubled from 2.2 billion yen to 3.9 billion yen during the same period.[45] The NSS is primarily a policy coordination unit, so the fact that it is collecting intelligence from other ministries and agencies suggests the Japanese government has not yet succeeded in its attempt to separate policy from intelligence functions, much less establish a central intelligence agency.

Familiar problems associated with bureaucratic turf battles and unclarified channels of communication between politicians and bureaucrats confirm this. Given the legacy of mistrust and the competition across units, it may be difficult for the NSS, where MOFA officials constitute one of the dominant groups in its management positions, to have full confidence in intelligence reports from CIRO, which is still dominated by the NPA. The way this section is staffed—with personnel seconded from the NPA, MOFA, MOD, and PSIA—suggests there exist plenty of opportunities (and incentives) to bypass

CIRO, which is itself a composite of secondees from these and other agencies. In practice, according to a senior government official, most analysis, including military intelligence, is reported to the NSS through each ministry's policy bureau.[46] Only in rare cases where intelligence reports include extremely sensitive information, such as unmasked intelligence sources or data that undermine current policy that no ministry has incentive to report, could the heads of intelligence organizations bypass the NSS and report directly to the political leadership.[47] Should this occur—or should other independent "pipelines" be activated—the system will be undermined, especially when, as is likely, the raw intelligence data are contradictory.

Uneasy Lay the Heads

Although the jewels of intelligence reform were now set in the Abe administration's crown, uneasy lay the heads that wore it. After focusing immediately on mid-range projects, such as issuing a new national security strategy and generating an ambitious update to the National Defense Program Guidelines that prioritized enhancing intelligence, Abe's reengineered intelligence community faced immediate challenges in most of the six elements under analysis here.

Collection

Improving collection was a priority for the new NSC. Just one year earlier, in January 2013, the Strategic Headquarters for Space Policy had adopted a five-year "Basic Space Plan." But Prime Minister Abe, concerned that the plan—which reiterated the already archaic (but politically safer) term "peaceful use"—was too ambiguous for his government's new national security strategy, instructed his policy staff to change it in September 2014.[48] Within three months, the relentlessly focused prime minister had in hand a revised ten-year Basic Space Plan "fully based on Japan's new security policies."[49] The updated plan, calling for 5 trillion yen in public and private funding, made it clear that the Japanese government would "engage in space development to directly utilize it for Japan's diplomatic and security policies, as well as for the Self-Defense Forces."[50] It identified three security-related purposes for Japanese space activities: (1) to defend satellites from space debris and hostile action; (2) to collect and communicate positioning information and intelligence for national security; and (3) to strengthen the U.S.-Japan alliance by upgrading coordination of space-based assets. The upgraded plan, now explicitly linked to Japan's national security strategy and anchored to the alliance, would double the number of reconnaissance satellites, improve space-based maritime awareness, and reinforce Japan's indigenous defense industrial base. Paul Kallender, an analyst of the Japanese space program, summarizes the changes at an operational level: (1) Japan would bulk up regional GPS capacity in a manner that complements the U.S. system; (2) MOD would take the lead from the Japan Aerospace Exploration Agency (JAXA) with the support and encouragement of the cabinet; and (3) Japan would double the number of intelligence satellites that monitor Chinese and North Korean activities.[51] He called this "a remarkable achievement . . . the culmination of a 20-year process of unknitting an increasingly unworkable policy and institutional framework . . . committed to strictly non-military use of space."[52] JAXA, the Cabinet Satellite Intelligence Center, and Mitsubishi Heavy Industries continued to collaborate on launches of intelligence satellites through 2018.[53]

More surprising perhaps even than this sudden and dramatic turnaround in national policy was the relative absence of opposition. A *Mainichi Shimbun* editorial reviewed an early draft and expressed concern that it was "lopsided" in favor of security and industrial development.[54] An *Asahi Shimbun* editorial criticized the plan for focusing excessively on military technologies but did not oppose the military use of outer space per se.[55] And when the Cabinet Office invited public comment on the draft plan, 90 percent of responses were positive.[56] While this is hardly dispositive evidence that there was broad-based popular support for the shift, when combined with the absence of organized opposition, it does suggest that the general public had become acclimated to the idea that space could be used for national security purposes. But even if more of the public had come to accept the military use of space, there remained some uncertainty among advocates about how to characterize it, even a half decade later. In 2017, despite public recognition of a palpable North Korean missile threat, a group of distinguished security specialists, speaking of what they acknowledged to be "Japan's de facto domestic spy satellites," still felt compelled to use the euphemism "information gathering satellites."[57]

As in the past, vertical battle lines were drawn within the Japanese government, including predictable opposition from the Ministry of Education, Science, and Technology (MEXT), which for decades had played a leading role in Japan's efforts to develop "peaceful" space technologies.[58] MEXT was able to maintain primary jurisdiction over JAXA and kept more than half the budget related to space activities, but it was made clear that administrative control was shifting in favor of the Cabinet Space Strategy Office (Naikakufu Uchū Senryaku Shitsu), which was working closely with the MOD.[59] Silos notwithstanding, there were prominent successes. In one case, Kim Jong-un had made a show of taking his missile off the launching pad ahead of a test launch in February 2016. Kim then waited until the Japanese satellite went blind to put it back on the pad. But a senior MOD official explained that his staff "detected it through other means and reported the imminent launch to the prime minister."[60]

Despite the implementation of these and other measures to improve intelligence collection by technical means, LDP elder and intelligence reform architect Machimura was still not satisfied. In his view, "there is still no clear roadmap toward the establishment of a new HUMINT organization."[61] A senior government official traced Machimura's discontent to the domination of CIRO by NPA officials who had minimal experience abroad and did not deal with international politics.[62] Without complaining about his home ministry, a former CIRO director seemed to agree: "Russia was our most important subject, but we were hampered by not having any HUMINT-generated intelligence of our own."[63] Besides, even MOFA diplomats could seem inept. For example, Tarumi Hideo, a political minister in Japan's Beijing embassy was expelled for intelligence collection. He was found to have acquired a Communist Party telephone directory—not exactly high-end espionage.[64] As one retired flag officer explained, "HUMINT comes last in the Japanese intelligence community," and as another added, "We do HUMINT, but not a lot of it, and not as covert action."[65]

Perhaps sensing an opportunity for organizational advantage, the Justice Ministry's Public Security Intelligence Agency, the Cold War (mostly) domestic HUMINT unit, which had been revived after the administrative reforms of the late 1990s, now seemed to spread its wings.[66] According to one CIRO official, PSIA has no choice but to continually reinvent itself because politicians regularly question why separate counterintelligence agencies are even necessary.[67] A former chief desk officer for North Korea at the Foreign Ministry confirmed that PSIA has indeed operated abroad, as in the early 2000s, when its agents enthusiastically distributed flyers at the North Korean border with China asking residents to help identify abductees.[68] A PSIA official stopped short of confirming its overseas covert action but acknowledged that PSIA officials had always "traveled abroad" in the course of their collection activities, supporting this with a copy of the "Review of International Terrorism" that PSIA had begun publishing biannually in 1993, well before the reforms under review here.[69] Although the number of its senior officials was stable, the PSIA budget and head count began to grow, and exceeded 1,600 for the first time in nearly two decades.[70] While PSIA is restricted by the Subversive Activities Prevention Act to hunting for violent or subversive activities in Japan, it seems to have larger ambitions, and has been actively recruiting nationwide.[71] In July 2015 PSIA announced that it would offer a one-day spycraft simulation for first- and second-year college students, who would learn and practice collecting, analyzing, and reporting foreign information to the NSS. The Okinawa press reported in January 2017 that PSIA had targeted Okinawan independence and anti-base groups, reprising its Cold War–era determination that they enjoy support from China, which is trying to divide Japan.[72]

PSIA's enthusiasm for HUMINT was rumored to have led it to engage in covert activities in China. Notwithstanding formal restrictions on HUMINT and denials of covert action abroad, press reports of PSIA activities there began raising neighbors' eyebrows well before the 2013 reforms were consolidated. Most seemed merely cases of individual ineptitude rather than of larger-scale espionage. According to a Chinese analyst, the majority of Japanese engaged in this activity in the first decade after the Cold War were either employees of small and medium-sized firms who were accused of mapping Chinese military installations or else Japanese-credentialed military attachés.[73] In 2005, China expelled two Japanese men for conducting unauthorized surveying activities and for collecting other data "precise enough for military use."[74] In March 2007, two more Japanese were arrested for illegally surveying in southern Jiangxi in the guise of archaeologists. In 2008 and 2010, Japanese nationals were detained for spying near a military base, both times in Heibei Province.

Whether or not the pace of Japanese covert activity abroad accelerated after the intelligence reforms—and whether or not this was authorized by PSIA—these arrests began to attract attention. From spring 2015 to summer 2016, at least five Japanese nationals were arrested in China on espionage charges. Although PSIA denied any involvement in HUMINT collection in China, the Japanese press connected several of the cases to the PSIA.[75] An NPA official familiar with these cases did not go that far, but did confirm that the four who were arrested as "spies" in China in 2015 were likely expatriates serving as "informants." An MOD official confirmed this: "They were probably interviewees who believed that they were tacitly tasked; but they had no training in tradecraft."[76] All this was met, of course, with acute Chinese sensitivity. One military outlet insisted that "Japanese intelligence activities have reached new heights." Japanese in China are, it claimed, "intelligence vacuum cleaners," and "once Japan wants to bomb strategically important targets in China, the positioning information collected by their professional and amateur spies . . . will cost China immense losses."[77] Of course it is difficult to separate propaganda from paranoia in this matter—or to ignore how this Chinese pot may be calling the Japanese kettle black—but in June 2017, with twelve Japanese nationals held on espionage charges, the Japanese government began warning travelers to China not to snap photos of airports, bridges, and other transport infrastructure.[78] One month later, China returned four of the detainees after a Chinese firm confirmed they had been employed to do geological research for a hot springs development.[79] But soon thereafter, another Japanese national was arrested in Dalian by the Chinese authorities on espionage charges.[80] And in July 2018, a Chinese court sentenced a Japanese national, Iwase Takahiro, to twelve years' hard labor for spying.[81] In any event, one NPA official concluded, "If the reports are true about PSIA agents in China, it proves their incompetence."[82]

It was particularly notable, therefore when Chinese State Security Minister Chen Wenqing, secretly visited the PSIA in Tokyo in October 2018 to discuss antiterrorism cooperation ahead of the 2020 Tokyo Olympics. The two sides agreed to institute exchanges between their intelligence authorities. During the meetings, the Japanese side raised the issue of China's arrest of the twelve Japanese—and indictment of eight—citizens on suspicion of spying. Chen insisted that their cases would be handled on the basis of domestic law.[83]

Analysis

External events continued to stimulate the Japanese government to further upgrade its intelligence analysis capacity. In one proactive move, the PSIA opened a new Immigrant Intelligence Center in October 2015 to collect and analyze information on foreign visitors in order to screen out terrorists ahead of the 2020 Tokyo Olympics.[84] But one particularly dramatic event that seized the attention of the Japanese people and focused them anew on intelligence occurred immediately after the NSC and NSS were in place. In January 2015, Gotō Kenji, a journalist, and Yukawa Haruna, a self-styled security consultant, were put on display by ISIS, which had kidnapped them months earlier in Syria. ISIS, enraged by Prime Minister Abe's offer of $200 million to states that would combat the terrorist organization, demanded that a ransom in the same amount be delivered within seventy-two hours for the release of Gotō and Yukawa. Abe responded by denouncing ISIS's acts as "outrageous and unforgivable."[85] Days later, brandishing a knife on video, their captor, "Jihadi John," issued a chilling declaration: "Abe, because of your reckless decision to take part in an unwinnable war, this knife will also carry on and cause carnage wherever your people are found. So let the nightmare for Japan begin."[86]

After the murders of Gotō and Yukawa, the debate on intelligence reform resumed—particularly a call for better analysis. Foreign Minister Kishida Fumio anticipated this in Diet interpellations immediately after the executions, declaring: "I am acutely reminded of the importance of training analysts on the Middle East. We will work harder to improve, including strengthening our intelligence and analysis organizations."[87] A few days later, an opposition Diet member, Matsuzawa Shigefumi, targeted CIRO. Possibly confusing HUMINT with OSINT, he complained that the bureau had "merely 500 plus staff, more than half of whom study satellite images and only 220 or so does HUMINT."[88]

A government report on the response to the ISIS beheadings, issued in May, found that Abe was not at fault for traveling to the Middle East to offer nonmilitary assistance in the fight against Islamic fundamentalism. But it acknowledged that Japanese intelligence analysis—based as it was on an ad hoc assembly of diplomats, academics, and tribal leaders in Jordan—could not be sufficient.[89] In a marked shift from their positions of just a decade earlier, editorials agreed and demanded better intelligence. The *Yomiuri Shimbun* editorialized that "every time a Japanese national has been involved in a terrorist attack overseas, there have been calls for better gathering, analyzing, and dissemination of intelligence—but they were soon forgotten. It is essential to break this pattern of behavior."[90] The *Mainichi Shimbun* declared that "it is probably necessary, as the report states, to improve Japan's information-gathering ability and train specialists in Arabic and other fields."[91]

Even a year later, senior intelligence officials were frustrated by the limited scale and scope of even the post-reform, reengineered intelligence community. As one senior government official explained, the NSS's job was to take stock of and analyze the flow of information across the "whole of government." The problem, he said, was that the NSS did not have sufficient staff to do the required analysis, and he was hoping that the government could upgrade it by at least dozens of additional analysts.[92] This obtains at the tactical level as well. As one Japanese military intelligence official noted, "We collect far more than can possibly be analyzed in real time."[93]

Communication

Beyond limits to the size and scope of the intelligence community, the larger test of the reengineered intelligence community is whether or not its analysis now reaches policy makers in coherent and actionable form. Many observers and participants have noted positive changes in the way units within the community came to coordinate and communicate their intelligence after the NSC/NSS system was stood up. One high-ranking official observed that "with the advent of the NSC Secretariat as its important client since January 2014, the Japanese intelligence community has become more active, and there has been a much-strengthened linkage [*renkei*] between the intelligence sections and the policy-making sections within the government."[94] Another senior government official reported that the establishment of the NSC caused a dramatic change in relations between MOFA and MOD. "For a half century," he said, "they had been unable to smoothly coordinate policies regarding security and intelligence. Now they communicate much better at all levels, and with less formality about who is whose counterpart. Coordination between the two is getting much speedier as well."[95] A former Defense Ministry intelligence chief reports that "working relations among the intelligence agencies has markedly improved. We are all awakened to the huge benefits that accrue to us by sharing . . . in a system designed to be fed by a wide range of classified intelligence."[96]

But this same official also allowed that CIRO and MOFA continued to struggle with each other. And there are episodic reports that bureaucratic competition and silos remain problems for all the participants in the reformed intelligence community. According to Nishi Masanori, the former administrative vice minister for defense, "there are still tribal conflicts" across the intelligence community, and, as noted earlier, many top intelligence officials continue to enjoy direct access to the prime minister.[97] Yonemura Toshirō, a former NPA official who had served as deputy chief cabinet secretary for crisis management, fired a preemptive shot at MOFA in December 2015 just as discussions were getting under way for the creation of a new counterterrorism unit: "The Foreign Affairs and Intelligence Department of the NPA should play a central role in summarizing and analyzing intelligence on terrorism. Terrorism cannot be prevented unless information gathering and investigations are done in a unified manner."[98] Easier said than done. MOFA and the NPA reportedly competed in a "stupid tug-of-war" to have responsibility for counterterrorism at the 2016 G7 summit in Iseshima.[99] Likewise, MOD and MOFA exchanged mutual recriminations in January 2016 regarding how the *Asahi Shimbun* learned of secret U.S.-Japan joint operational plans for a contingency in the East China Sea.[100] In typical (retro) fashion, when the Counterterrorism Unit of Japan (CTUJ) was finally stood up in December 2015 (discussed shortly), it had four deputy directors general, two from MOFA and two from NPA, which, in the view of one government official, were "three too many."[101]

There seemed fewer residual problems regarding communication between the intelligence community and the policy makers. The new cabinet intelligence analysts provide daily briefings to top cabinet officials, and each of the top officials of Japan's intelligence units meets regularly with the prime minister, leading one former senior intelligence official to boast that "the most important development under Prime Minister Abe is that policy and analysis are now seamless."[102] Seamless or not, public records confirm that the number of visits by the CIRO chief, either individually or with senior colleagues across the intelligence community, sharply increased after the 2008 reform, and increased again after the new NSC was established.[103] One cabinet intelligence analyst noted that he and his colleagues were now able to deliver national intelligence estimates (jōhō hyōkasho—NIEs) tailored to the formal requests of policy makers after full vetting across intelligence units. He suggested that this was a big change, an observation confirmed by a former CIRO director who could not recall ever having been tasked to produce an NIE.[104] Indeed, according to the leading historian of the Japanese intelligence community, "until 2013 only Prime Ministers Yoshida, Kishi, Nakasone, and Abe ever provided formal requirements to the intelligence community for an intelligence estimate. Others relied on lectures from silo-bound ministry officials—from METI, MOFA, etcetera—who had a direct pipeline."[105] In the reengineered NSC/NSS system, NIEs are primary instruments of communication between the intelligence community and policy makers. Interestingly, however, analysts report that they often discuss the requests they wish to receive among themselves before suggesting the topic to policy makers at the joint intelligence meetings that were created in the aftermath of 9/11 (see chapter 5). "Seeding" the NIEs in this way may be a collateral benefit from improved trust and communication; and even if not, it seems entirely consistent with the "bottom-up" ringi system that Japanese bureaucrats have practiced for years.[106]

Communication with U.S. intelligence also benefited from the reengineering of the Japanese intelligence community. In its first order of business, the NSC produced the 2013 National Defense Program Guidelines calling for deepened intelligence sharing with Washington. This was formalized bilaterally in new "Alliance Guidelines" issued in April 2015. Extending and expanding a long history of service-level intelligence cooperation, the MSDF and the U.S. Navy would now jointly operate a sea floor submarine detection system on the Pacific side of the southwest island chain, the civilian JAXA space agency would now share images with the U.S. military, and the two militaries would openly deploy unmanned aerial vehicles with broad area maritime surveillance sensors—"long dwell, high altitude surveillance platforms"—from bases in Japan.[107] U.S. combat pilots now often exercise under the guidance of ground- and air-based Japanese flight controllers, and although there is no combined command as in the U.S.–South Korean alliance—and although not everything is always transparent to each side—the U.S. and Japanese militaries operate multiple bilateral integrated tactical intelligence units.[108] The commander of an MSDF intelligence unit that monitors the entire East China Sea with naval air assets—including five EP-3 patrol aircraft—explains why he is eager to extend intelligence and warning to U.S. ships and planes in the region: "We can share the same intelligence because we face the same threats."[109] Admiral (ret.) Dennis Blair, a former director of U.S. national intelligence, concurs with this positive view of U.S.-Japan intelligence cooperation but acknowledges that it was neither monolithic nor always strategic: "American encouragement and assistance to Japan in developing its intelligence varied by agency. It was not guided by some overall plan for improvement." He singles out the U.S. Navy as being the "most forward leaning" and recalls the NSA as having close relations with Japanese SIGINT units, but that other U.S. intelligence units, themselves stovepiped, have "less intimate relations with their Japanese counterparts for a variety of legal and operational reasons."[110]

But Tokyo's difficulties sharing intelligence with the Republic of Korea did not improve significantly. As noted in chapter 5, Washington stepped in to persuade its East Asian allies to initial a trilateral defense intelligence agreement in December 2014.[111] To avoid having to deal with each other directly, Seoul and Tokyo channeled a video conferencing link through the Pentagon to share intelligence regarding North Korean nuclear and missile testing. Even the agreements setting up this contrivance were initialed separately with the United States by each country. The Korean press referred to this as a "bypass" for ROK-Japan intelligence sharing and characteristically reminded readers that this was the first military cooperation between Japan and Korea since Japan's colonial rule ended in 1945.[112] But there remained limits, even on the U.S. side. Even after this arrangement was imposed on Seoul and Tokyo, intelligence sharing by the United States with its two Asian allies itself remained stovepiped, operated on separate computers for "Secret Releasable—Japan" and "Secret Releasable—Korea."[113]

In late December 2015, what appeared to be a breakthrough in Korean-Japanese relations on a far more prickly issue, regarding what the Koreans consider wartime sex slaves of the Japanese military and the Japanese refer to as "comfort women," seemed to pave the way to renewed discussion of a bilateral GSOMIA.[114] Escalating provocations by Pyongyang—including its fourth nuclear test—seemed to force South Korea and Japan to acknowledge (at least to themselves) that their "bypass" was dangerously inefficient. At the same time, Washington ratcheted up pressure—including whispers that the bilateral U.S.-ROK agreement on the deployment of Terminal High-Altitude

Area Defense was at risk. So with the comfort women seemingly set aside amid concerns about regional instability, the Korean government announced in January that it would set up a new military data link to share text and satellite imagery on the DPRK nuclear program with U.S. Forces Korea (USFK). It did so knowing that this would effectively connect with U.S. Forces Japan (USFJ) and, thereby, to the Japanese SDF with its own direct link to USFJ.[115] In a multilateral crisis game held weeks later, Japan and the ROK reportedly worked together directly to share information regarding a simulated ballistic missile launch by North Korea.[116]

Weeks later, in early February, when South Korea's defense minister, Han Min-koo, testified in Parliament that the government was considering reopening GSOMIA talks with Japan, he was met by vigorous editorial opposition. Han quickly backed off, saying that he meant simply that "various factors should be taken into consideration before a GSOMIA deal could be reached."[117] Apparently they were, for Japan's defense minister, Nakatani Gen, took up the dormant GSOMIA issue at a meeting in April with President Park Geun-hye.[118] This overture was met with official support—again, as reported by the Japanese media. Han now declared that a bilateral GSOMIA "is necessary from a military perspective."[119] But it was not until Pyongyang's fifth nuclear test in September that Korea's MOD called upon the public to support a bilateral intelligence-sharing agreement with Japan.[120] Soon thereafter, the ROK government announced it would resume GSOMIA talks with Japan. Washington welcomed the announcement.

The opposition in Korea began to get traction on the issue almost immediately. The center-left press continued to remind readers that this would be "the first military pact between Seoul and Tokyo since Korea's liberation from Japan's colonial rule in 1945."[121] As pressure mounted, MOD was forced to insist that the shared intelligence would be limited to helping rescue Japanese residents in Korea, and would not include information about troop deployments. To appease the opposition, the (apparently desperate) government even proposed a GSOMIA to Beijing.[122] Still, all three opposition parties vowed to block the agreement and called for Han's resignation.

But there was a much bigger game afoot. Intelligence sharing was now taking a backseat to unrest generated by an influence-peddling scandal that led to President Park's impeachment. Although opposition politicians and newspapers tried to continue shining a spotlight on GSOMIA, the impeachment sucked the political oxygen out of Seoul's lungs, and the GSOMIA—which did not require legislative ratification—was signed in November, just three weeks after the talks were restarted. The two militaries directly exchanged classified intelligence for the first time in mid-December 2016. In May 2017, President Park was succeeded by Moon Jae-in, who had expressed reservations about the agreement during the election campaign. Prospects for the bilateral GSOMIA—the object of characteristically blistering attacks by North Korea—remained uncertain, even after it was extended for one year just before Pyongyang's sixth nuclear test in August.[123] Clearly, changes in the strategic environment stimulated and sustained intelligence sharing— but only at minimal levels—between South Korea and Japan. When the extension was signed, Seoul made clear it would limit sharing to intelligence regarding North Korean missile and nuclear programs, and refused all requests from Japan for information about Chinese activities in the South China Sea.[124] The agreement was extended for another year in 2018 because, according to one South Korean defense official, it was "needed during North Korea's denuclearization and peace consolidation process."[125]

Protection

After ISIS beheaded Gotō and Yukawa, a retired GSDF flag officer explained the challenges such occurrences presented to the newly revamped Japanese intelligence community: "Algeria and ISIS are both cases of intelligence failure. But they also point to another challenge—counterintelligence and counterterrorism. Gathering is not enough. We also have to deal with psychological warfare like ISIS's use of websites to intimidate and recruit. There is much more to be done."[126]

Indeed, the NSC got right to work on the counterterrorism front. In May 2015, just a few months after the new security and intelligence system began operating, a cabinet task force—the Joint Intelligence Committee for Counterterrorism under Deputy Chief Cabinet Secretary Sugita Kazuhiro (a career NPA official), announced plans to create an International Terrorism Intelligence-Gathering Unit within MOFA to oversee collection of terrorism-related intelligence. It was to be staffed by the now familiar potpourri of NPA, CIRO, and MOD officials inter alia, who would liaise with foreign intelligence services.[127] The new unit—the CTUJ introduced earlier—started up in December with forty staff, a number that was doubled to eighty within months. Half the staff were assigned to regional desks in Tokyo, and the other half were posted to Japanese government missions abroad, where they would focus on the Taliban from an office in New Delhi, on ISIS from posts in Cairo and Amman, and on Jemaah Islamiyah from Jakarta.[128]

This CTUJ was yet another small step in the direction of enhanced HU-MINT and merely the latest imperfect product of bureaucratic competition. Although it was located administratively within MOFA, its chief and deputy chief both came from the police agency, where presumably they had experience with the Yama unit, discussed in chapter 5.[129] But as in so many previous cases, administrative lines remained unclear. The CTUJ would be led by a director general–level official with four deputies, two from NPA and two from MOFA. The director general would report *both* to the minister of foreign affairs as well as to a Cabinet Counterterrorism Intelligence Coordination Center, directed by an NPA official, which would report to a Joint Intelligence Committee for Counterterrorism, which in turn would report to the chief cabinet secretary. The Japanese press reported grumblings within MOFA that Sugita, who had made no secret of his wish to create an MI6-like unit, was "acting like James Bond."[130] Former defense minister Morimoto Satoshi welcomed the creation of the new unit but acknowledged, "We still do not yet have a comprehensive structure."[131] A former senior defense intelligence official expressed regret that the "the new counterterrorism unit cannot run agents overseas yet, and has no capacity for extraction, either."[132] A CIRO analyst who relies on what the CTUJ collects and supplies reported that much of its raw intelligence comes from liaison with foreign intelligence agencies.[133] The CTUJ remained an excessively baroque work in progress.

Part of the reason for this was owed to the haste with which it was stood up and to the grim demands on its staff that soon followed. While plans for the unit were still being hashed out in November 2015, coordinated ISIS terrorists murdered 130 Parisians at six locations. Then yet another ISIS-inspired event demonstrated just how difficult the counterterrorism business would be for the Japanese government. After seven Japanese nationals—all foreign aid workers at the Japan International Cooperation Agency—were taken hostage in an ISIS terrorist attack in July 2016 in Bangladesh, Prime Minister Abe convened an emergency NSC meeting. The government quickly set up an emergency response headquarters in Dhaka and dispatched administrative, counterterror, and intelligence units to the scene. It was an uncharacteristically proactive response using the government's new apparatus. But the outcome was no different. The aid workers were murdered. In what was surely an unfair early test, Japan's counterintelligence and counterterrorism capacity seemed no better than those of other nations, and only little better than it had been before the Japanese intelligence community was reengineered.

The cyber threat—equal to the greatest challenge for peacetime Japanese (or any other nation's) counterintelligence—was little different. It first came into focus when Japanese investigators learned in early 2000 that nearly one hundred private firms, the MOD, and a dozen other government units had been using software developed by the terrorist sect Aum Shinrikyō.[134] The Ministry of Posts and Telecommunications was the first to create a counter-cyber action plan, which, in the event, did little more than identify vulnerable industries and exhort firms to take voluntary measures and improve communication with the government. The Cabinet Secretariat moved at the same time to establish an Information Security Measures Promotion Office (Jōhō Sekyuritī Taisaku Suishin Shitsu).[135] Before the end of the year, the NPA created a Cyberforce Center to manage emergency response to cyberattacks on key infrastructure.[136] In April 2002, the government created a National Incident Response Team (Kinkyū Taiō Shien Chīmu) at its Cabinet Secretariat with fifteen computer security experts recruited from both inside and outside the government who would be responsible for collecting and analyzing intelligence in the event of cyberattacks.[137]

Three years later, after the ASDF's Intelligence Data Group (Jōhō Shiryō Han) was hit in August 2003 by "Blaster," an early computer virus, the government upgraded its Information Security Measures Promotion Office to a National Information Security Center (Jōhō Sekyuritī Sentā—NISC) in the Cabinet Secretariat with nearly thirty personnel seconded from relevant ministries.[138] While the earlier cabinet units were no more than administrative secretariats for government meetings on the topic, the NISC now had authorization to inspect information security measures on a government-wide basis.[139]

Then, in 2005, government cyber-related measures were expanded to include standardization of information systems across local governments at the prefectural level.[140] By early 2007, the U.S. National Security Agency was providing training to GSDF personnel as part of its larger project to align the development of cyber network defenses and enable sharing of sensitive and classified intelligence among allies.[141] In July 2009, cyberattacks abroad became a Japanese problem when it was discovered that eight Japanese private servers had been used, along with more than four hundred servers across fifty-nine countries, to launch distributed denial-of-services attack on U.S. and ROK websites simultaneously. The Japanese government responded by formally designating cyberattack as a domain that could activate its national security/crisis management protocol (although it left the role of the military undefined).[142] When the hacker group Anonymous threatened to attack the Japanese government in June 2012, the Noda administration created an emergency response team within the NISC called Cyber Incident Mobile Assistance Team (Saibā Kidōtai-CYMAT) with forty personnel to be first responder to cyber incidents involving governmental organizations.[143] In September, just as the Noda administration began receiving U.S. intelligence on hackers and guidance on malicious software from the NSA, it authorized $1.2 billion for MOD to define cyberspace as an element of national territory, just like land, sea, air, and outer space, and announced plans to create a Cyber Defense Unit (Saibā Kūkan Bōeitai) with one hundred personnel.[144] Japan remained as vulnerable to cyberattack as any other country—and perhaps more than most.

It was only after a decade of high-profile and costly cyberattacks to which the government's responses proved inadequate—counterintelligence failures—and only after the NSC/NSS system was in place, that the Japanese government connected the reengineered intelligence community to protection in the cyber domain. It was facing a rapidly escalating threat: in 2013 alone, there were more than 5 million unauthorized attempts to access Japanese government systems, five times more than in 2012, more than 95 percent of which originated in China.[145] In January 2013, senior CIRO officials were briefed by visitors from the NSA regarding how it handles Chinese cyber threats. The impending 2016 G7 summit of world leaders and the 2020 Tokyo Olympics easily justified a range of new cybersecurity initiatives.[146] In November 2014, a Cybersecurity Basic Law (Saibā Sekyuritī Kihon Hō) was passed creating a Cybersecurity Headquarters (Saibā Sekyuritī Senryaku Honbu) in the Cabinet Office under the chief cabinet secretary. It was linked to the NSC and to the existing Information Technology General Strategy Headquarters (IT Sōgō Senryaku Honbu) to develop anti-cyberattack policies with the participation of electric utilities, banks, and other businesses that were vulnerable. All this was almost just in time: the National Institute of Information and Communication Technology reported 128 billion cases of cyberattack in Japan in 2016, ten times more than just three years earlier.[147]

From the perspective of industry, however, this all adds up to more silos and stovepipes—the wrong structures at the wrong time. In 2015 a Cybersecurity Working Group was created by Keidanren's Information Technology Committee to encourage sharing across firms that otherwise have been prone to conceal cyber intrusions from one another, and from customers, in order to avoid their disapprobation.[148] This working group, dominated by large information technology vendors such as Hitachi, NTT, NEC, Fujitsu, and Toshiba, collaborates with NISC but wishes the government had provided it more authority and a larger budget. It is particularly critical of the NISC for "merely coordinating and never leading." It also works with METI, which is determined to promote Japanese firms in this sector, and with the Sōmushō, which "has not been much of a presence." Its staff report that they interact with a large number of government-affiliated private sector nonprofit associations but claim to have no formal ties to MOD or to the NPA. The working group thus represented the alphabet soup of connections and disconnections depicted in figure 6.4.

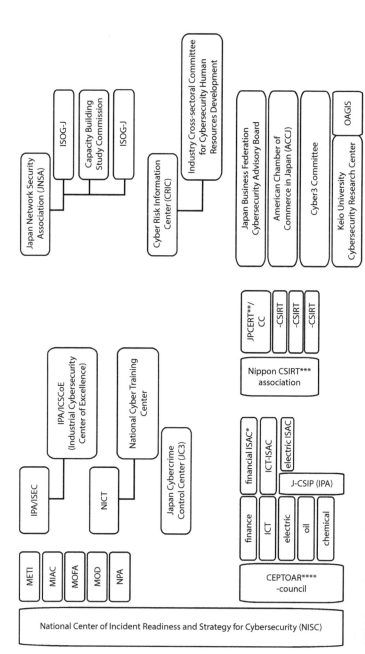

FIGURE 6.4 Cybersecurity-related organizations

Source: Nippon Keidanren Cybersecurity Working Group, October 2017

*ISAC: Information Sharing and Analysis Center

**CERT: Computer Emergency Response Team

***CSIRT: Computer Security Incident Response Team (each firm has its own CSIRT)

****CEPTOAR: Capability for Engineering of Protection, Technical Operation, Analysis and Response

The second Abe administration enacted a Cybersecurity Basic Act in November 2014, renamed the NISC a National Center of Incident Readiness and Strategy for Cybersecurity (still known as NISC, or Naikaku Saibā Sekyuritī Sentā), and established a Cybersecurity Strategic Headquarters (Saibā Sekyuritī Senryaku Honbu) in the Cabinet Secretariat chaired by the prime minister to discuss Japan's basic cybersecurity policies.[149] Abe repackaged the Noda administration's Cyber Defense Unit under a slightly different Japanese name, Saibā Bōeitai, and issued a paper in 2015 titled "The Cyber Security Strategy" (or "Saibā Sekyuritī Senryaku"), which, alarmingly, underscored that extensions of the previous measures would not be sufficient but outlined no alternative policy course.[150] One senior NPA official with experience in intelligence was not impressed. In his view: "Our leaders are not technologically proficient. Government officials are good at drafting laws, but weak on technology, so we rely on private firms."[151] Indeed, different intelligence units resorted to the now familiar default option—centrifugality: the NPA helped stand up an organization, Japan Cybercrime Control Center (Nihon Saibā Hanzai Taisaku Sentā), in November 2014 as a bridge between public and private organizations trying to defend against cyberattacks.[152] In December 2015, the government announced it would create twelve new director general positions with responsibility for cybersecurity in each of the ministries and agencies in the intelligence community.[153]

When the Cyber Security Basic Act was enacted, the Financial Services Agency was assigned responsibility to protect financial institutions against cyberattacks. Its policy statement set several goals, including enhanced information sharing among financial institutions with regard to cyber incidents, tutelage on best practices to protect against cyber intrusions, and supervision of industry-wide cybersecurity exercises in the financial sector. Since 2016, the FSA has organized annual industry-wide cybersecurity exercises dubbed "Delta Wall," which involve more than one hundred financial institutions. And of course, after FSA set up a new office to collect intelligence and coordinate across the agency, the government announced plans in January 2018 to create with the private sector yet another consultative body on cybersecurity to share information on cyberattacks. This one would be within the Cabinet Office.[154]

Japan was still groping to solve a problem common to rich nations. A widely circulated 2016 consultant's report included Japan in a group it called the "Cyber Five"—along with South Korea, Australia, New Zealand, and Singapore—countries that were nine times more vulnerable to cyberattack than other Asian economies.[155] The NISC had been staffed by secondees from other ministries who lacked technical sophistication, and there were no plans to initiate reforms that would strengthen the government's technical expertise.[156] To the contrary, the government's initial budget (*tōsho yosan*) for information security R&D declined during the decade after the cyber problem first surfaced, and the total counter-cyber budget remained less than one eighth of U.S. federal spending on cybersecurity R&D, which, by contrast, had been steadily increasing.[157] As a result, the NISC could not become the primary defender of government information systems: cyberattack defense was outsourced to a private nonprofit organization, and both the SDF and the NPA had to send staff in charge of cyber defense to private corporations for technical training.[158] Expressing confidence that increased funding would solve the problems, Japan's ministries and agencies reached aggressively for greater cyber budget shares. Their total request in fiscal year 2019 was 85.2 billion yen, up sharply from the 62.1 billion yen allocated the previous year, and more than double what the government spent in 2015. MOD staked a claim to more than a quarter of the total, a share that accounted for half the prospective increase. The Ministry of Internal Affairs and Communications and METI laid claim to 17 percent and 15 percent respectively.[159]

There was one further threat to the Japanese government that would require additional counterintelligence muscle, and it came from a particularly uncomfortable place: Washington—the NSA in particular. It turned out that the NSA has long had a "complicated relationship" with Japan. As noted in chapters 4 and 5, it had been permitted to maintain "listening posts paid for by the Japanese government to the tune of $500 million" to collect SIGINT from Russia and China—but also from as far away as the Middle East and North Africa.[160] The Japanese government also paid the salaries of staff working at NSA facilities in Japan. The NSA claims that it has "in return . . . kitted out Japanese spies with powerful surveillance tools and shared intelligence with them."[161] Despite occasional dustups, as in 2009, when the Japanese side pulled out of an NSA surveillance-sharing program code-named "CROSSHAIR" to protest what it viewed as efforts by the NSA to impose its own technical standards, the NSA singled out "two surveillance partners" in particular—the NPA and the GSDF—and, in documents leaked by Edward Snowden, claimed that Japan was one of its "strategically . . . most valuable partners."[162] This was reinforced in 2013, immediately after Prime Minister Abe returned to power, when the NSA and DIH agreed to begin a SIGINT-enabled cyber initiative that would allow DIH to peer into its "anonymous Internet." This was followed in April by DIH's provision to NSA of eleven malware signatures, seven of which were new to the U.S. intelligence community. Internal NSA documents during this period referred to Japan's

Directorate for Signals as a "sister organization" and an "important partner for more than fifty years.[163]

This is why it was so awkward when, in July 2015, Wikileaks revealed thirty-five "top secret" NSA targets, including the Japanese Cabinet Office, the Bank of Japan, the Ministry of Economy, Trade, and Industry, JETRO, and the energy divisions of major Japanese trading firms, all of whose phones the agency had tapped.[164] The NSA was also revealed to have been surveilling Japan's UN mission and had placed bugs on thousands of its ally's computers.[165] Prime Minister Abe and Chief Cabinet Secretary Suga each called it "regrettable," and the Japanese editorial pages had a field day excoriating the government for putting up with such a "subordinate and unproductive diplomatic relationship."[166] Vice President Biden apologized, no formal protest was filed, and the alliance moved on.

Covert Action

In testimony before the Diet in February 2015 just after the Gotō and Yukawa murders, Prime Minister Abe insisted that "Japan does not undertake [intelligence] operations abroad," but acknowledged former defense minister Ishiba's suggestion that it should. He also acknowledged that the creation of such a capacity was being debated within the LDP.[167] But there has been limited evidence of Japanese covert action since the Asia-Pacific War, and very little of what has made its way to the public domain—such as the PSIA leaflets at the North Korean border with China—was particularly ambitious. As one former MOFA official suggested without going into detail: "Japanese covert action since [the war] has been passive. It is collection oriented, and not disruptive or aggressive."[168] Another, a retired ambassador, insists that "a Japanese diplomat engaged in illegal collection is unimaginable."[169] And even those, such as the future Foreign Minister Kōno Tarō, who advocated enhancements to intelligence that would go beyond the NSC/NSS reforms, made sure to distance themselves from "the assassinations and espionage . . . evoked by action movies."[170] The consensus was that any future independent Japanese intelligence capability should be dedicated to collecting and analyzing the intentions of adversaries by civilian as well as military professionals.

The explanation for Japan's continued allergy to covert action and special operations seems straightforward and is linked to lingering antimilitarist public opinion and U.S. domination, the two elements to which the Japanese intelligence community accommodated during the Cold War. As one intelligence officer explained: "Given the high political cost of covert operations, no political leader would take the risk. If something difficult were to come up, they knew they could ask Washington to handle it."[171] This speaks to the ambivalence felt in Japan regarding its decades-long dependence on U.S. intelligence, the "capitulation" explored in chapter 3 of this volume and captured in the epigraph to this chapter. Although this book has documented a long undercurrent of resentment of Japan's subordination to its U.S. partner within the postwar Japanese intelligence community—such as in the case of the Musashi Kikan in the 1950s–1960s, SIGINT sharing after the KAL incident in the 1980s, creation of the DIH in the 1990s, and the impetus for post–Cold War intelligence reforms in the 1990s–2000s—a former CIRO chief expressed the dominant view of the limits on Japan's political and professional capacities: "Even in multilateral settings, the United States always dealt with other countries bilaterally to keep control. It would be a waste of energy to be resentful. After all, what else could we do?"[172]

This aligns with the views of U.S. officials, active and retired, who do not believe that resentment of Washington's power significantly affected the bilateral intelligence flow. According to Admiral (ret.) Lowell E. Jacoby, a former director of the U.S. Defense Intelligence Agency: "I didn't have any indication of dissatisfaction with U.S.-supplied intelligence content. On the contrary, [Japanese] counterparts were eager and enthusiastic with respect to engagement, although both sides chafed a bit at the classification restrictions that often interfered with the level of sharing and detail that could be exchanged."[173] A former director of national intelligence, Admiral (ret.) Dennis Blair, concurred, assessing resentment within the Japanese intelligence community as "an understandable chafing at dependence combined with the standing strain of Japanese paranoia at being left behind by the United States."[174] One retired U.S. intelligence official adds that "the rise of China and the North Korea nuclear program helped the Japanese intelligence community overcome their doubts about dependence on their U.S. ally."[175]

Thus, the view from the U.S. side seems to have been that four factors—two objective and two judgmental—converged to keep the Japanese and U.S intelligence communities' relationship on an even keel. The two objective facts were indisputable: the shifting security environment converged with the harsh reality that without a robust HUMINT capability, Japan had no alternative to relying on its U.S ally. These in turn forced Tokyo to make a judgment on two key issues: that there remained considerable benefits from cooperation with the United States, and that gains from intelligence sharing outweighed the risks (and rising costs) of a premature shift toward developing an active covert intelligence capacity. As we have seen, this has not prevented Japanese leaders from continuing to hedge their bets on U.S.

dependence and to enhance their own capabilities. Thus, covert action remains a risky, but not unlikely, next frontier for Japanese intelligence reform.

Oversight

Citizens in liberal democracies are used to calls for oversight from groups in civil society dedicated to preservation of privacy and to transparency of government, but we are not accustomed to hearing support for these values from within the intelligence community or its political boosters. Indeed, a former deputy director of CIRO pointed out that since Diet members never eliminated their exemption from penalties for disclosure of secrets, "they were, in a way, helping us."[176] Yet, as we have seen, there have been important exceptions in Japan. Machimura Nobutaka, for example, was an early and avid supporter of enhanced oversight. And even the chair of his 2005 MOFA panel, the former CIRO chief Ōmori Yoshio, advocated Diet oversight nearly a decade before the DSSL went into effect.[177] Several years later, he even argued that Japan should adopt an Intelligence Service Civil Service Law (Jōhō Kōmuin Hō) that would punish infringement on citizens' privacy and oblige agents to keep at a distance from politics.[178] In the months ahead of the passage of the DSSL, three Diet members of different parties—one of whom would later become foreign minister—published a call for a stout, independent intelligence unit, stipulating that "above all" it be placed under civilian control and Diet oversight.[179]

Support for robust oversight came from other, unexpected quarters as well. Kobayashi Yoshiki, an NPA official who studies intelligence closely and who served in the NSS, has observed that intelligence reform in democratic systems is always associated with oversight, and that oversight of Japan's reformed intelligence community is especially important for Japan, where abusive police and intelligence services had once neutralized political parties. He has published academic papers calling for a politically independent oversight committee to monitor the reformed intelligence community, and warned that as the intelligence community becomes stronger, the nature of the oversight system will become more prominent in national debate.[180] He has argued that oversight is an essential intelligence function, and that without it the intelligence community could never be legitimate.

Kobayashi was correct. The most widely embraced objection to the original draft of the DSSL concerned the lack of independent oversight and raised questions about its legitimacy. Concern about whether the DSSL would be monitored adequately attracted the attention of all the opposition parties, as well as the LDP's coalition partner, the Kōmeitō. After all, Prime Minister

Abe rejected establishment of a nongovernmental independent panel to oversee the implementation of the law. But within a month of the DSSL's passage, his government announced formation of an Information Protection Advisory Council (Jōhō Hozen Shimon Kaigi) in the Cabinet Office chaired by Watanabe Tsuneo, the publisher of Japan's largest newspaper, the conservative *Yomiuri Shimbun*. Watanabe's council was charged with advising the government as it developed guidelines for implementation of the DSSL. Seizing upon Watanabe's longtime support for Abe, some critics immediately declared this to be a case of the foxes guarding the henhouse.[181]

But the appointment of Shimizu Tsutomu, the secretary general of the Japan Federation of Bar Associations, who was "in the vanguard of the opposition to the bill," seemed to go some way toward neutralizing the "rubber stamp" critique.[182] Shimizu had criticized the DSSL for being "a law of the bureaucrat, by the bureaucrat, and for the bureaucrat."[183] He was joined by specialists on information management, U.S. classification practices, and other legal experts and insisted that he would be committed to making the system work properly: "One can be opposed to the law but work to make it the best law possible. Not expressing one's opinion because one is opposed is nonsense. One has to explain why one is opposed."[184] This was not convincing to the *Asahi Shimbun*, which editorialized that "it is impossible . . . to compensate for serious flaws in a law in any fundamental way only through smart administration."[185] The Watanabe Commission issued its first report in July 2014, stipulating that the government should designate the minimum number of secrets for the shortest possible period of time. Although none of its members were cleared to handle classified documents, they continued throughout 2014 to advise on operational guidelines—including how to classify documents and how to protect whistle-blowers.

Cheap talk, perhaps, but in the period between the law's passage and its enactment, the government responded to critics by changing twenty-seven of the DSSL's implementation guidelines and by adding a requirement that the law be reviewed after five years. No fully independent oversight body would be established, but each house of the Diet appointed an oversight committee (Jōhō Kanshi Shinsakai), and hearings began within three months of the law's implementation.[186] Meanwhile, new senior deputy vice minister posts (independent public records management secretaries) were created to manage the classification process in each ministry, to oversee the whistle-blower process, and to allay concerns about arbitrary classification by self-interested bureaucrats. Their remit also included the authority to request and review classified documents, demand declassification, and inspect all records.[187] In the Cabinet Office itself, a twenty-person Security Oversight Division was stood up with the vice minister as its direct supervisor. In all, the revised guidelines stressed respect for the public's right to know, limited classification to the "minimum amount of information for the minimum amount of time," ruled out broad interpretations beyond fifty-five specific categories of classification, banned classification of illegal acts by government officials, set up a hotline for whistle-blowers, and created posts for "independent archive management officials."[188]

The number of classified documents rose by about 25 percent from 2014 to 2015, and no journalists were arrested or claimed intimidation. Neither were there any whistle-blowers. In the first review of documents a year after the law went into effect, the Independent Public Records Management Committee, the cabinet's oversight commission, reviewed 165 documents and called for revision of three that had been classified by MOFA and the Japan Coast Guard without much public explanation.[189] For their part, the Diet committees charged with oversight under the DSSL have pressed the government to improve its accountability and provide more detailed information.[190]

The liveliest debate about oversight was injected from the outside in April 2016, when David Kaye, the United Nations special rapporteur on the promotion and protection of the right to freedom of opinion and expression, came to Japan to study the implementation of the DSSL. He found that the new law, combined with weak legal protections and constant government monitoring, "goes further than necessary in protecting information from disclosure, putting in peril the public's right to know in areas of immense public interest."[191] The Japanese government wasted no time responding to the UN Human Rights Council with a formal rebuttal to Kaye's findings and a defense of the DSSL.[192] The battle over the DSSL quieted for a time, until January 2018 when, in response to a citizens' group petition, the Japanese Supreme Court ordered the release of administrative documents related to a secret 1.4 billion yen Cabinet Secretariat Compensation Expense Fund, used for intelligence collection at the discretion of the chief cabinet secretary. And later that month, the chair of the House of Representatives' DSSL Oversight Committee, Nukaga Fukushirō, invoking the "citizens' right to know," pressed for an end to the disposal of classified documents held less than one year.[193] And there may be more to come on the oversight horizon. In March 2017 the Supreme Court ruled that police must obtain a warrant before installing GPS devices on suspects' vehicles. Although this ruling dealt with a criminal investigation and not with counterintelligence or counterterrorism, intelligence officials suggested it was likely to have an impact in these domains as well.[194] Even if intelligence oversight is not yet fully institutionalized in Japan, it has not been ignored in either the public discourse or the policy realm.

By the late 2010s, the Japanese intelligence community was finally the object of comprehensive institutional reform. Within five years of the reengineering that created the NSC/NSS system, the number of senior officials working on foreign intelligence within the Cabinet Office alone ballooned from 77 to 150.[195] However imperfectly, each of its generic elements—the working parts identified and examined in this volume—were adjusted and enhanced. By most accounts, constituent units that had historically kept their distance (and information) from one another began cooperating within the new framework. As a result, analysts acknowledge they have access to a wider range of raw intelligence than ever before, and senior policy professionals report that communication between them and the intelligence community has improved considerably. Oversight is being tested, and, while covert action apparently remains a bridge too far, there are indications that this could be the next object of intelligence reform. After all, as was stipulated at the beginning of this volume, the intelligence communities everywhere always are works in progress, so long as the strategic environment and technology change, and failures occur. There is no reason to imagine Japan being different.

Nonetheless, there remains a long road ahead before Japan has an intelligence system commensurate with its foreign and security policy aspirations. And there are many stakeholders ready to press for more. In December 2015, with the ink barely dry on the legislation creating the NSC/NSS system— and dissatisfied with the new Counterterrorism Unit patched together ahead of the 2016 Iseshima G7 meeting—policy entrepreneurs on an Intelligence and Secrets Project Team in the LDP's Policy Research Council submitted a plan to the government calling for an even more ambitious consolidation of the Japanese intelligence community. Modeling it on the British MI6 and the Australian Office of National Assessments, because the U.S. Central Intelligence Agency was deemed "too big," the party sought to further consolidate the Japanese intelligence community and provide the Diet with wider oversight authority.[196] Their ambitions for standing this up ahead of the 2020 Tokyo Olympics were rejected by the government as premature. "We are still studying it, but at this pace," says its leading proponent in the LDP, Iwaya Takeshi, "it will take several more years before we succeed—and that will depend on how severe the security environment becomes for Japan."[197]

While Japan's intelligence community no longer seems hamstrung by sustained and widespread public distrust of intelligence as a legitimate function of government or by the lack of interest of senior political leaders—even prime ministers—that shaped and limited policy earlier in the postwar period, even the most ambitious reformers, like Representative Iwaya, remain cautious. As a result, a reengineered Japanese intelligence community without wartime experience trains very few foreign agents (at least explicitly) and operates without any known remit for covert action. Likewise, although to a lesser extent than before, it continues to be weighed down by bureaucratic competition.[198] Former defense minister Morimoto Satoshi added all of this up and offered a blunt assessment of a handicapped Japanese intelligence community: "Intelligence management improved after the NSC was established, but we still have no single intelligence organization and no minister responsible for national intelligence. And we still won't have one even a decade from now because our bureaucracy has more than 150 years of experience managing careers in their own separate domains. We continue to think about national security in a narrow-minded way."[199] A former chief of the Defense Intelligence Headquarters, a GSDF flag officer, calls this a bureaucratic "loyalty problem."[200]

Beyond these structural features, moreover, there is concern that the effectiveness of the NSC/NSS system depends ultimately on the personal rapport between the prime minister and his national security adviser. Thus, there was apprehension in government circles when it was reported that NSS Secretary General Yachi threatened to resign in September 2017 because of what he viewed as diplomatic freelancing by another of Prime Minister Abe's senior advisers, Imai Takaya. Referring to this, Yachi was quoted as saying that "if things don't change, the NSC's raison d'être would be at risk, and I will not take responsibility for that."[201]

In a sense, then, the Japanese intelligence community is in a race against time. By the late 2010s, in the face of Chinese and North Korean provocations and (despite protestations to the contrary) an uncertain U.S. posture in northeast Asia, it seemed that the singular lingering issue for many in the intelligence community was whether, for how long, and to what extent Japan would continue to accommodate its intelligence functions to Washington's preferences. So it was not surprising to hear one former chief of the Defense Intelligence Headquarters say: "It is important for the Japanese people and government to feel they are defending their own country. It is essential to enhance the strength of the military and the capacity of our intelligence, even though truly 'autonomous defense' is *fiscally* a nonstarter."[202] Nor was it odd to hear another former DIH chief declare bluntly that "the United States is in decline and Japan should step up and do more."[203]

Both of these practitioners accept the need for—and appreciate the benefits of—Japan-U.S. intelligence cooperation. But given what we have learned about the history of the stubbornly sub-optimal Japanese intelligence community and about Japanese views of the trajectory of relative U.S. power, one is compelled to speculate about the future of Japanese intelligence. The final chapter of this volume measures the Japanese intelligence community against likely shifts in the security environment, technological change, and the costs of intelligence failure.

CHAPTER 7

The Past and Future of Japanese Intelligence

> To become a "normal country," an intelligence
> agency is vital.
>
> —Retired diplomat Kawakami Takashi, 2015

Heraclitus famously maintained that "no man ever steps in the same river twice, for it is not the same river and he is not the same man." This classical insight has infused this volume's analysis of the evolution of the Japanese intelligence community. Like Heraclitus's river, neither the strategic environment, nor technology, nor failure—the three drivers that frame this book—was ever at rest in Japan. And, like his river's forder, neither was the Japanese intelligence community. I have documented five discrete periods in the flow of Japan's modern intelligence history: periods of expansion, accommodation, tinkering, reimagining, and reengineering. While many structural pathologies—most notably the stovepipes that frustrate efficient communication—persisted, the intelligence community in each era had its own mix of strengths and weaknesses, its own characteristics, and its own share of success and failure. During each it was buffeted by a different mix of external forces and domestic politics. In this concluding chapter I review these dynamics, taking each period in turn, before speculating about the future of the Japanese intelligence community. I do so because one of the clearest lessons from this analysis is that there can be no period at the end of any history of intelligence reform. An ellipsis always has to suffice. . . .

Expansion (1895–1945)

The expansion of the Japanese intelligence community in the first half of the twentieth century was overdetermined. Although dramatic shifts in the security environment and technological change deserve pride of place as primary factors, intelligence failure and intelligence-related policy failures were never far behind, often serving as the proximate drivers of reform. These failures accelerated in the 1920s after the Japanese military intervened in Japan's increasingly dysfunctional politics and, coming to believe in its own invincibility, diminished the role and status of all but combat officers. As failures mounted, institutional adaptation became more difficult, and what had been a competent intelligence community became more fragmented and less effectual.

It is well known that Japan emerged suddenly on the world scene in the late nineteenth century when modernizing leaders, concerned about the designs of rapacious foreign powers, orchestrated a forced march to industrialization that transformed an isolated agrarian society into a regional and then a world power. Taking great pains to endow itself with a technologically sophisticated military industrial base, Japan defeated first a weak China and then a more powerful Russia to secure its northern and western flanks. Its young oligarchs were determined to meet the imperial ambitions of the great powers' designs on Asia head-on. They understood that the future of Asia was in play, and mastered a steep strategic learning curve. Indeed, few rising powers have ever been as adept at knowing what they needed. This, of course, was a function of effective intelligence.

But knowing and learning were not always in sync. As the words of Field Marshal Yamagata Aritomo which serve as an epigraph to chapter 2 indicate, it was clear early on that Japan's modernizing elite knew they needed to nurture a coherent intelligence capacity. But, in contrast to the success with which Japan adapted foreign models to reorganize its industry, military, police, and education, its intelligence community developed only in fits and starts. Japan had early successes with covert action and was an early adopter of technology-intensive signals (SIGINT) and image (IMINT) intelligence, but its intelligence community was infected from the beginning by the same debilitating structural and behavioral pathologies discussed in chapter 1 that afflict intelligence communities everywhere. Whether because Japan's bureaucracy was more entrenched and more privileged, because its political class was more distant, because its military was often delusional, or because oversight was more underdeveloped, the problems of the Japanese intelligence community seem to have been more widespread and persistent than those elsewhere.

As we have seen, what there was of a civilian foreign intelligence community was limited at first to a rather inept Ministry of Foreign Affairs whose connections to the military were inconsistent and sometimes counterproductive. Even though Japan's senior diplomats and general officers both understood and pioneered "area studies" in the service of intelligence collection and analysis by nurturing the careers of deeply knowledgeable area specialists—and even though they each developed impressive open source intelligence capabilities—both relegated the intelligence function to second-class status, impeding the career advancement of intelligence professionals and undermining the discipline itself. At just the moment when European states were beginning to professionalize their intelligence services, Japan was consigning its officers to a backbench.

At the same time, both the military and the Foreign Ministry came to depend on disreputable and self-serving ruffians known as "continental adventurers" (*tairiku ronin*), who provided information and generated instability in equal measure. They each ran agents abroad, including some—like (the earlier and far more decorous) Akashi Motojirō—whose services they seem to have shared. Indeed, it was often hard to separate the military and civilian role in supporting the covert activity of the innumerable "special duty units" (*tokumu kikan*) that, along with Graham Greene, inspired the title of this book. They were charged with destabilizing imperial Russia, supporting coups d'état in Korea, assassinating warlords and exfiltrating emperors in China, practicing espionage in Latin America and on the West Coast of the United States, and nurturing nationalist resistance movements in colonial South and Southeast Asia. In the main, however, civilian-military intelligence cooperation was limited—and to a detrimental extent. Surely the more familiar—and likely the most costly—of all mutual insularities was the one fed by competition within the imperial Japanese military itself. The bill for the inability of the Imperial Army and Navy to coordinate intelligence collection and analysis through the use of common facilities and technology came due after Midway in June 1942 and during the battle of Leyte Gulf in October 1944, when each actively sabotaged—or at a minimum ignored—the other's intelligence.

But the problems encountered and created by Japanese intelligence during the first half of the twentieth century cannot be attributed only to stovepiped competition or to the relegation of intelligence professionals to inferior status within their respective bureaucracies. Japan's military and political leaders—as everywhere else the most direct agents of intelligence reform—deserve their share of the blame. Chapter 2 documented the many ways in which the willful ignorance of top decision makers, who, unconstrained by oversight of any kind, ignored intelligence, sabotaged the nation itself. In one striking example at the tactical level, the General Staff of the Imperial Army had no one but itself to blame for its failure to appreciate the full extent of the Soviet buildup at the China-Mongolia border ahead of the extended battle at Nomonhan in the summer of 1939. The Red Army had amassed four times more troops than the Imperial Army had estimated, and its several thousand tanks and planes easily overpowered the several hundred Japanese ones.

At the strategic level, this was most clearly evident in the unwillingness of Tōjō Hideki to suspend disbelief when confronted by clear and credible evidence—reported by his own ambassador after direct conversations with Hitler and Ribbentrop—that Nazi Germany was about to invade the Soviet Union in June 1941 in its fateful Operation Barbarossa. Failures were also owed to an inability—surprising for an authoritarian state—to operate an effective counterintelligence organization. The standard HUMINT example, of course, is that of the Soviet spy Richard Sorge's infiltration of the highest levels of the government and the imperial household, a costly counterintelligence failure discovered only when the Special Higher Police were investigating a different matter, and only after his extractions had already compromised wartime Japanese national policy.

The standard example from the world of signals intelligence is another counterintelligence failure: the inability of otherwise highly competent Japanese cryptographers to prevent wartime codes from being compromised by the Allies and to fix those that had been breached. This connects, at least indirectly, to the preferences of Japanese leaders for essentialist stereotyping and wishful thinking—especially within the military's overconfident Imperial Way faction, whose leaders convinced themselves that the Japanese spirit could overcome an enemy's superior material strength. Thus, failure was not far behind strategic and technological change as a precipitant of intelligence reform. We have seen how few intelligence communities ever failed as often or as spectacularly as imperial Japan's, nowhere more consequentially than at Pearl Harbor, where one of history's most impressive tactical successes temporarily masked one of its most costly strategic failures.

Accommodation (1945–1991)

Physical devastation—the wartime loss of blood and lucre from which many states never recover—is indisputably the greatest cost a nation must bear. And by definition, the consequence of such defeat is a definitive shift in a nation's strategic environment. But Japan and its intelligence community did recover from their devastation. By the early 1970s, Japan was the second-richest nation in the world, a model of reconstruction and—for the second time since the Meiji Restoration—of industrial development. Alignment with Washington, the postwar hegemon, was essential to this reconstruction, but in rebuilding their nation from the ashes, Japanese strategists had to bear the collateral costs of accommodation to its conqueror's ambitions for global leadership. Access to U.S. markets and technology during the Pax Americana was extraordinarily salutary for Japanese reconstruction. But, like every other U.S. ally during the Cold War enjoying a cheap ride on national security, Japan found itself locked into an unequal relationship with Washington that distorted the shape and capacity of its intelligence community. The limited intelligence community that did operate after the war often found itself in uncomfortable service to U.S. power. It was directed to focus on U.S. concerns—most notably counterintelligence at first related to a possible nationalist resurgence and then aimed at communist agitation. To be sure, America's anticommunist zeal was shared by Japan's conservative elites. Unlike America's Canadian, British, Australian, or even New Zealander "Five Eyes" allies, however—each a victor in the Asia-Pacific War—the Japanese intelligence community also found itself handicapped by its own domestic illegitimacy. After all, the public no longer had a stomach for war, for the military, or even for discussion of national security affairs. This was a fine line to walk: the Japanese security community, and the intelligence units within it, were aligned with the United States but had to accommodate to both antimilitarist sentiment at home and often unwelcome U.S. demands from abroad.

This was apparent from the beginning of the Occupation, when the urgency of intelligence chief Major General Charles Willoughby's anticommunist crusade converged with the ambitions of unsavory former military intelligence officers like Arisue Seizō and Hattori Takushirō. They avoided being tried as war criminals by making themselves indispensable to credulous new masters they mistakenly imagined they could soon shunt aside. Fortunately for Japanese democracy and for the alliance, Washington proved less naïve than the "loveable fascist" (and inept intelligence officer) Willoughby; and unfortunately for the Japanese intelligence community in the short run, the Japanese public proved vigilant in defending its new rights. Contra Willoughby's ambitions, his handpicked and unpurged, but never fully rehabilitated, former intelligence officials did not take charge of a reborn and autonomous Japanese military and intelligence establishment. But neither could the more pragmatic Yoshida Shigeru and his allied bureaucrats create the comprehensive and effective intelligence apparatus they sought by putting an end to the endemic problem of silos that undermined the system. Instead, the Cold War—and U.S. preferences that each military service and each civilian unit (themselves stovepiped) connect separately with its Japanese counterpart—reinforced the predilection of Japan's intelligence units to splinter and compete with one another on shaky and increasingly narrow ground.

Chapter 3 documented how U.S. dominance and domestic antimilitarism complicated every element of Japan's Cold War intelligence community. The capacity to collect and analyze intelligence was surely the victim of these shifts. Japan was forced by public opinion to limit its overseas human intelligence (HUMINT) capabilities and to focus collection efforts on open source (OSINT) economic data. Politicians shied away from demanding national intelligence estimates from the intelligence community, and after chasing ultranationalists for a time, counterintelligence came to be narrowly and unsuccessfully focused on communists at home. Soviet agents operated unmolested in what they referred to as "spy heaven." With foreign espionage formally curtailed, as late as the 1980s the authors of the Self-Defense Force's annual white papers were compelled to represent monitoring activities as limited strictly to Japanese territory and the immediate vicinity. The editors took pains to refer repeatedly to how Japan's military intelligence activities conformed to international law and to the national policy of strictly defensive defense. The number of military attachés was limited, and intelligence sharing—even with Washington—was deficient. Each of Japan's intelligence units—civilian as well as military—was determined to protect its turf, and Tokyo was unable to establish a centralized intelligence agency.

Oversight was also imperfect and noninstitutionalized but surprisingly stout. Multiple efforts to promulgate anti-espionage legislation were undone by public fears that doing so would set Japan on a slippery slope to wartime surveillance and controls. To be sure, this indicated that the new democratic order was growing roots. But without Diet or judicial oversight, Japan was left with suboptimal intelligence capabilities. A bureaucratic scrum, characterized by competitive and mutually incompatible intelligence units, operated under what for many was the increasingly annoying direction of the United States. The door to moral hazard remained wide open, as resentment of U.S. control—often referred to as "anti-Americanism" (*kenbei*)—expanded within the Japanese intelligence community. As one retired U.S. intelligence official put it bluntly: "The Japanese believed they could never fully rely on us, and resented having to reinforce their own dependence. Their view was 'it sucks that we have to suck up to the United States.'"[1]

One manifestation of that resentment was the willingness of some Japanese "patriots" to support radical efforts to undermine the status quo.

Although it has not attracted much attention, some apparently did so with the support of individuals in the intelligence community. The most prominent—and troubling—example was the support that the novelist Mishima Yukio received for his private army from at least one military intelligence officer in the Ground Self-Defense Force, who lectured Mishima's "troops" on psychological warfare at GSDF facilities. Rather than being punished, this colonel (a former Imperial Army intelligence officer) was promoted to major general after Mishima's ill-conceived coup d'état failed. A different case, the (ultimately aborted) kidnapping of South Korean dissident Kim Dae-jung from his Tokyo hotel room, seems to have benefited from more formal involvement by a unit within military intelligence, the so-called Musashi Kikan, whose agents reportedly harbored significant resentment of Japan's subordination to the United States.

These extreme cases aside, even many of America's closest Japanese allies may not have been fully on board Washington's Cold War bandwagon. Most were openly motivated by the need to make the Japanese intelligence community more autonomous. We are reminded of the efforts of Gotōda Masaharu, the former Home Ministry official who worked his way through the NPA and CIRO to reach the highest levels of the LDP and who, as chief cabinet secretary to Nakasone Yasuhiro, advocated building the longest "rabbits' ears" Japan could sustain. As noted in chapter 3, Gotōda, who often spoke derisively of Japan as a "vassal" of the United States, may even have protected the Musashi Kikan official who fingered Kim Dae-jung.[2] Yet, like many LDP politicians, he was reported to be receiving covert financial support from the U.S. intelligence community and was a key political actor in the subsequent effort to stand up an integrated Defense Intelligence Headquarters for the first time. We have learned that resentment of dependence on U.S. intelligence did not drive Japanese intelligence reform, but that it abetted it at critical moments.

There were plenty of good reasons for the Japanese intelligence community and its political allies to seek to acquire longer ears of their own—and there were important Cold War successes and failures that made such reform easier. In 1983, for example, Japan's military intelligence earned global approbation when it captured Kremlin orders to shoot down a commercial jetliner that had strayed into Soviet airspace. But even that case illuminates how Japan's political leadership had lost control of its own intelligence to the United States. Once the frustrated Gotōda learned that the SDF was automatically sharing SIGINT with Washington before sharing it with Tokyo, he ended all automatic transmissions.

Indeed, the road to improved collection and analysis during the Cold War was blocked by the convergence of other technological and organizational

intelligence failures. One notable instance occurred when the defecting Soviet fighter pilot Viktor Belenko dared to fly his MiG-25—the newest in the
Soviet air fleet—unchallenged through Japanese airspace. As if performing in
a Keystone Kops comedy, Japan's ministries and agencies displayed unbridled
jurisdictional infighting even while the "Foxbat" jet was on the commercial
tarmac in Hakodate. Their competing demands to take charge overrode the
ability of any organization to do so, and no sum of their ambitions could
make up for the comprehensive reform of the Japanese intelligence community that was so clearly lacking. A second notable illustration was MITI's
disregard of international technology trade regulations that facilitated delivery of highly sophisticated milling machines to the Soviet Union in 1985 at
the height of U.S.-Japan trade frictions. Moscow's acquisition of this equipment enabled the Soviet navy to retrofit its submarines with silent propellers, a technological advance that had to be met at great expense by the U.S.
military.

In sum, the Cold War was an extended period of restraint on the more
determined proponents for thorough intelligence reform and, in particular,
for the creation of an autonomous Japanese intelligence capability. Remarkably, there emerged for the first time effective intelligence oversight when
the Communist Party unmasked the Musashi Kikan and when civic groups
mobilized to block Prime Minister Nakasone's draconian espionage law. Japan's leaders and intelligence practitioners were fully cognizant of—and constrained by—problems generated by Japan's subordinate position in the Pax
Americana. But there was little that could be done. This seemed to change
once relative U.S. power began to decline in the early years of the twenty-first
century. Prior to that, however, there was a period of apparent uncertainty
regarding how best to respond to America's unipolar moment in the first
decade after the Cold War.

Tinkering (1991–2001)

It is tempting to assume that the sudden end of the Cold War left the underdeveloped Japanese intelligence community clueless about what was in
store. But as a result in large measure of their discomfort with the power and
information asymmetries in the alliance with the United States, that was not
the case. Without waiting for external provocation, senior Japanese bureaucrats and politicians had already begun thinking about how to enhance the
capacity and autonomy of Japan's intelligence. Their first target was military
intelligence; they had already begun making plans to tinker with it before the
Soviet Union collapsed. Still, it was not an easy row for them to hoe. As one

indication of the political context constraining them, editors of "Defense of Japan," the Defense Agency's white paper, continued to emphasize the legal and normative limits of their intelligence reach. But Gotōda Masaharu, one of the "tinkerers in chief" during this and the previous period, recognized that even a half century after the Asia-Pacific War, intelligence remained toxic to some—even in his own LDP. As documented in chapter 4, he was determined to use the uncertainty engendered by the end of the Cold War to get some traction for such a project, and found an artifice acceptable to the Japanese public to clear the way forward.

With the support of Prime Minister Hashimoto and other LDP heavyweights—as well as with allies embedded in senior bureaucratic posts—Gotōda hitched plans for military intelligence reform to the effort to achieve more comprehensive and popular administrative reform. He was betting that the Japanese public had become almost as disenchanted with the policy dominance of bureaucrats as they were with the militarists who had by then receded farther in their rearview mirrors. He read the mood clearly: there was support for budgeting to be more transparent and for the administrative state to be more streamlined. Gotōda seized the opportunity. Moving intelligence reform forward in tandem with—and under the cover of—major administrative reform, he and Nishihiro Seiki (Japan's most senior defense bureaucrat) engineered consolidation of military intelligence, specifically signals and imaging, by shepherding through the January 1997 formation of the Defense Intelligence Headquarters.

As also reported in chapter 4, however, this new early warning unit failed its first major test. One of the justifications for its creation had been the JDA's inability in May 1993 to anticipate and warn Japan of the first test by North Korea of an indigenous ballistic missile, the Nodong-1 which landed short of, but uncomfortably near, the Noto Peninsula, which juts into the Sea of Japan from central Japan. The Japanese public took notice but did not rise up in indignation to demand better tools, much less a military response. In September 1998, however, the DIH failed to detect preparations for the launch of a longer-range North Korean Taepodong-1 that flew through Japanese airspace. This time, echoing the way that Washington stood up NASA in July 1958 after the Soviets had put Sputnik into orbit, Tokyo's politicians took the bit between their teeth. Within months the government retreated (informally for the time being) from its decades-long policy banning the military use of space and initiated an indigenous spy satellite program. But in an awkward arrangement entirely consistent with Japan's history of fractured intelligence, the program was placed under the nominal control of the National Police Agency. This was just more evidence that during this first post–Cold

War decade, Japan would content itself with tinkering with its underpowered and dependent intelligence community. Comprehensive intelligence reform would have to wait until greater threats manifested themselves and until new leaders emerged who were willing to expend the political capital necessary for comprehensive reform.

Reform would also have to overcome political and bureaucratic inertia. In the case of the former, it would also have to overcome the troubling ability of politicians—some much more powerful than others—to suppress inconvenient truths. As reported in chapter 4, this was particularly evident in the "conspiracy of silence" that shrouded the abductee issue in the early 2000s. Rather than another case in which the intelligence community failed the policy community, here we learned what could happen when policy makers fail the intelligence community and allow an already difficult problem to escalate into a convulsive national hysteria. We learned that the National Police Agency, and possibly other agencies, may have withheld early evidence that Japanese youngsters had been kidnapped decades ago by North Korean agents, and there is disturbing evidence that senior LDP and opposition party politicians who sought normalized relations with North Korea—as well as Communist Party leaders who were negotiating their own rapprochement with Pyongyang—stifled a public accounting. In the case of the JCP, we recall how politicians stood aside as bureaucratic obstacles blocked the Public Security Intelligence Agency, Japan's major counterintelligence organization, from disabling the murderous Aum Shinrikyō cult before it snuffed out thirteen lives on a Tokyo subway in March 1995.

Reimagining (2001–2013)

By the mid-2000s, as a "new world order" was finally taking shape, and as the threats associated with it were clarifying themselves, many of the same media that had locked arms to reflect and to shape antimilitarist public opinion during the Cold War turned critical of the government for its insufficient intelligence capability. Though some remained skeptical of government initiatives in this domain, others exhorted political leaders who had once shied away from engaging the intelligence community as a matter of electoral survival to focus on intelligence reform. It was time to stop tinkering and to start reimagining intelligence reform in a concrete and comprehensive way. Even the Japanese military was emboldened. In 2007, at long last, the SDF comfortably changed the section heading "Collection of Military Information" to "Military Intelligence Gathering" in its annual white paper.[3]

Japan's intelligence community became the object of mounting criticism. Taking stock of the state of the intelligence community in 2008, one influential analyst judged that considerably more work needed to be done "to conquer" three critical, persistent "bottlenecks"—each conforming to elements explored in this volume. Kaneko Masafumi called for improvement in circulation and sharing, presentation, and ending leaks—*mawatte, agate,* and *morenai* in Japanese.[4] Indeed, a small industry dedicated to intelligence reform emerged calling for institutional reform and strengthening, an argument another influential analyst dubbed the "jōhō kinō kyōkaron."[5] As reported in chapter 5, these and multiple other exhortations from media, think tanks, and scholars undergirded a cascade of government reports and recommendations from the political class that began to argue seriously, substantively, and compellingly for comprehensive intelligence reform. For its part, moreover, public opinion seemed to be becoming more accustomed to—and accepting of—formal discussion of threat.

As in the early years after the Cold War, attention was focused more on the military than on the civilian side. Apparently the SDF's experience in Iraq after 2003 stimulated calls to enhance the ground forces' tactical intelligence capabilities, and contracts were let for significant new ISR capabilities, including large numbers of a new indigenous maritime patrol aircraft. And the long-standing fiction regarding the non-military use of space was formally abolished. A new generation of political leaders, impatient with the slow pace of more pragmatic predecessors, emerged to advocate Japan's becoming a "normal nation" (see the epigraph at the beginning of this chapter) and displayed an open and unself-conscious eagerness to enhance Japanese defense capabilities and the intelligence community that would support them.

Although Japan's intelligence community was actively reimagined during this period, there was still no consensus on the best way forward, in part because this eagerly pro-reform generation of leaders had yet to fully consolidate power. Indeed, Japan's political leadership remained quite unsteady. In just the first six years after the retirement of Prime Minister Koizumi in 2006, Japan had seven prime ministers, eleven foreign ministers, and sixteen defense ministers from two different major parties. Some, like Abe Shinzō, were "normal nation-alists," while others, like Fukuda Yasuo, were more tentative.[6] Not surprisingly, then, intelligence reform initiatives undertaken by some were undone by others, as when Prime Minister Abe's 2006 effort to overhaul Japan's foreign policy decision-making apparatus was blocked the following year by Fukuda, his immediate successor. Several non-LDP governments favored intelligence reform but were not indulged by the LDP, which was eager to regain power. There were occasional efforts to burnish the image of Japan's once imperial intelligence community—as when a former commander of the once-secret Musashi Kikan wrote in his memoirs that "the DNA of Akashi Motojirō has been inherited by the Self-Defense Forces—indeed, by the Japanese people."[7] But until Abe returned to power in early 2013, the endemic failures of units within the intelligence community to communicate with one another and the incapacity of the intelligence community as a whole to communicate with the political class continued to define Japanese intelligence and undermine national policy.

The initiative for reform had to come from outside, as when a bilateral intelligence-sharing agreement was signed with the United States and was followed in short order by a half dozen more. But there were limits to how much Tokyo could achieve, even with U.S. support. Most glaring was the failure of Tokyo and Seoul to find a way to get past each other's politicians' use of their unpleasant history for domestic political gain and enable intelligence sharing regarding their common adversary, North Korea, support their common ally, the United States, and address other shared interests. Even though Japan's intelligence capabilities had been improved during and after the Cold War, there were still limits to intelligence reform.

Reengineering (2013–)

Thus, despite a widening recognition that the intelligence community was under-resourced and misaligned, elements of Japan's competitive and inadequately coordinated wartime intelligence system continued well beyond the Occupation and even decades beyond the Cold War. It seems that cheap riding on U.S. security guarantees had left the Japanese government insufficient incentive to establish a comprehensive central intelligence system. By the second decade of this century, however, a new world order—one characterized by the diffusion of global power—came into sharper focus for Japanese strategists. Post–Cold War threats, at first limited to non-state actors and to terrorism, gave way to an even more consequential shift in the strategic environment—the rise (and expansion) of China, the nuclearization of North Korea, and the concomitant relative decline of the United States. Japanese strategists have had to consider what one scholar has aptly called the "strategic insolvency" of the United States—the possibility that Washington would lose its capacity to effectively manage the gap between its strategic commitments and its national objectives.[8]

Even if they could not openly declare it, Japanese strategic planners, led by Prime Minister Abe and his closest allies in the LDP and the Foreign Ministry, seemed finally to appreciate that America's unipolar moment may be receding. In the absence of an obvious alternative to the alliance with Washington, they worked diligently to shore it up without boxing themselves in. Judging a security hedge to be the most prudent course in the face of declining U.S. capabilities relative to China, they eagerly accepted U.S. exhortations to improve their military and their intelligence system. Washington was pushing on an open door.

Effectively positioning the alliance to transcend the alliance should it become necessary to do so, the Japanese government moved in several directions simultaneously to expand its own intelligence capabilities.[9] The boldest move was the simultaneous creation in 2013 of the "twin pillars" of intelligence reform discussed in chapter 5—the Designated State Secrets Law and the National Security Council. The former created postwar Japan's first official document classification system, something long sought by Washington. The latter was an even more sweeping reform of foreign policy decision making—including a National Security Secretariat to streamline communication across intelligence units and between the intelligence community and the policy community. This was a direct frontal assault on long-standing, widely recognized impediments to effective intelligence in a system in which there was diminished, but still lingering, resistance to national security issues within the general public. But the political costs were contained, and these institutional reforms were accepted by the public without damaging the Abe administration.

So too were other, less controversial initiatives. Determined to extend defense to outer space and to bring indigenously developed and domestically produced space-based intelligence resources in line with Japan's new security infrastructure, the Abe government rewrote its predecessor's Basic Space Plan in late 2013 even before the ink had dried. It followed this a year later with a Cybersecurity Basic Law which created a Cybersecurity Headquarters to engage formally with the brave new dangerous world of cyber threats. The Abe administration proceeded thereupon to stand up a new Counterterrorism Unit ahead of the 2016 G7 summit in Iseshima and the 2020 Tokyo Olympics. Then, in late 2017, a year in which cyberattacks had increased by 20 percent—the MOD announced plans to create a joint cyber and space command under the direct control of the minister on the same reporting level as the ground, air, and fleet commands. It also announced an increase in the number of military attachés deployed to Southeast Asia to cooperate with the Philippines, Vietnam, and Malaysia to coordinate intelligence operations regarding China. The SDF revealed in April 2018 that it would deploy a new long-range radar system in the Ogasawara island chain one thousand kilometers south of Tokyo to monitor the South China Sea, and for its part, the Japan Coast Guard announced it would install radar sites on twenty-three remote southwestern islands explicitly to monitor Chinese and North Korean maritime activity. The JCG's 2018 budget also included money for new patrol aircraft and a significant increase in personnel—including sixty new pilots, radar technicians, and mechanics to improve aerial surveillance near the disputed Senkaku Islands in the East China Sea.[10] In December 2017 the government announced plans for research on space-based quantum cryptography communications. Suddenly intelligence reform and enhancement had a new spring in their step.[11] Clearly, these initiatives were driven by newly energized political leaders and accepted by a newly amenable public concerned about shifts in the strategic environment and technology.

This forward motion notwithstanding, the ambitions of Japan's intelligence reformers still were not fulfilled, making it difficult to be overly optimistic about the prospects for better coordination within the Japanese intelligence community. Even after periods of intense reimagination and substantive reengineering, the Japanese intelligence community remained riven by familiar, long-standing jurisdictional competition. Significantly, this condition was owed not only to the nature of bureaucratic politics in general or to secrecy in the specific case of intelligence everywhere. The problem has a Japanese character to it—the well-documented Japanese predilection for stovepiping in every bureaucratic endeavor, what the Japanese refer to as "the evils of bureaucratic sectionalism" (*tatewari gyōsei no heigai*). In the intelligence domain, there was no law requiring cooperation across constituent units until 2013, and LDP plans in 2015 to resurrect a serious HUMINT capacity and centralize intelligence by standing up a "Japanese-style CIA" (Nihonban CIA) were rejected by the Abe government as moving too far and too fast.[12] And even after intelligence cooperation was identified as critical to national policy, the law creating the National Security Council only required intelligence units to submit their data and analyses to the NSS. NSS officials could provide feedback, but could not share it across the intelligence community or generate their own analyses.

Meanwhile, the Cabinet Intelligence and Research Office continues to enjoy direct access to the prime minister in parallel to the National Security Secretariat. In what was described in chapter 6 as its "catchment" function, CIRO officials, all from the Police Agency, sit atop most of the recently established intelligence units—even those in the military. Indeed, not only did silos persist after the NSS was established in 2013, but also military intelligence reverted to its stovepiped norm in 2018, when the MOD stepped back from its 2007 commitment to joint intelligence by transferring supervision of its Military Intelligence Command (Chūō Jōhōtai) from the civilians in the ministry to the officers in the GSDF's Ground Component Command. So, despite the recognition of the problem, the demands of many, and the expectations of some, stovepipes never went away, and a robust HUMINT capability has yet to arrive.

Lessons Learned

Historical studies are often constructed to fit a narrative arc, but this history of the Japanese intelligence community seems more like a sine curve—one in which Japan's intelligence infrastructure expanded, receded, and now is poised to expand again. We can draw several lessons from the shape of this curve about how the Japanese intelligence community and its constitutive elements were shaped by two additional factors—leadership and public support—which, when present, operated in conjunction with the broader factors used to frame this volume. Both derive from the obvious fact that intelligence reform never occurs in a political vacuum. How could we be surprised to learn that intelligence reform was both possible and substantial when determined leaders who enjoyed public support were animated by shifts in the strategic environment, compelled to adjust to technological change, and/or had to respond to costly failure? But in our closer look at the Japanese case, we observe that this vacuum has been filled at different times and to different extents by differently motivated leaders, and we learn how these variations have combined irregularly with these factors to shape the contours of Japan's intelligence community.

As visions of an expanding empire seized the imagination of Japanese militarists before and during the Asia-Pacific War, they grew their intelligence community energetically. In the main, the public supported their efforts—especially after the experiment of Taishō democracy crashed and burned. But their shared energy proved to be entropic. In the absence of consistent, coordinated, strategic control by broad-minded leaders—and without even the pretense of oversight—the Japanese intelligence community expanded willy-nilly. At times, undisciplined and self-interested ruffians roamed the continent in the name of the empire but operated beyond the control of its leadership. At other times, better-disciplined intelligence professionals operated effectively, but too often in service to the parochial aims of their immediate organization. And as is often the case elsewhere, much of the intelligence generated by disparate units was ignored by a political class that was better at wishful thinking than at strategic thought.

Their failure had lasting trans-war consequences. Leaders seeking to reform and expand Japan's intelligence infrastructure during the Cold War found themselves far more constrained. They had to accommodate to citizens who were no longer imperial subjects, who no longer had a stomach for supporting foreign wars, and who understandably had become jealous guardians of their new right to live free of surveillance at home. Postwar efforts to consolidate the intelligence community by leaders who enjoyed the political support of the United States, like Yoshida Shigeru in the 1950s and Nakasone Yasuhiro in the 1980s, were blocked by an attentive public worried that any step in that direction would be the first on a slippery slope to wartime repression. Japanese citizens, much like American or British ones, never fully freed themselves from state surveillance, of course, but they did embrace and use the postwar Constitution and the courts to ensure that its use would become more transparent.

But now the strategic environment shifted. The unexpected end of the Cold War and prominent intelligence failures in its wake helped turn public opinion toward acceptance of the need for a professional intelligence service. But even as creative politicians continued to struggle mightily against entrenched bureaucrats—at times as much against one another as in regard to what was happening in the outside world—they now had more room to maneuver. This was first evident when Prime Minister Hashimoto Ryūtarō used public enthusiasm for administrative reform to stimulate intelligence reform in the late 1990s, and again when Prime Minister Abe overhauled the foreign policy–making process and intelligence infrastructure in 2013. But that room was not unbounded. Even the electorally secure Abe, facing direct military threats from North Korea and China, understood the popular limits to intelligence reform and faced an entrenched bureaucracy. His gimlet eye fixed on world affairs and domestic politics in equal measure, Abe modified some of the more draconian elements of his Designated State Secrets Law and rejected ambitious plans to enhance HUMINT.

We are therefore directed to examine how leadership and public opinion converged unexpectedly on the least examined element in our model: oversight. Formal intelligence oversight never existed in authoritarian Japan, and, while slowly emerging as a norm in the postwar system, it was not established legally for decades. In observing its emergence over time, I have documented support for oversight from even conservative legislators and intelligence practitioners. I also have observed a counterintuitive relationship between intelligence oversight and counterintelligence failure: several efforts to surveil Japanese citizens—on both the left and the right—and successive efforts to protect state secrets mobilized the public and led to court challenges which resulted in legal changes that limited state power. Intelligence oversight is not as robust in Japan as in some other industrial democracies which also, it must be noted, came to it rather late. But thanks to an engaged public, neither has it been moribund.

One final related, but more disturbing, lesson for intelligence in democratic politics emerges from (but surely is by no means limited to) the Japanese case. It derives from the several moments at which parts of the Japanese intelligence community skated onto the dangerously thin ice of subversion. As reported in chapter 3, and as reprised briefly in this chapter, a Japanese military intelligence officer who cooperated with Mishima Yukio's effort to challenge the postwar order was rewarded with a promotion. Then, several years later, the intelligence officer who apparently acted on behalf of military intelligence to abet the KCIA's kidnapping of dissident Kim Dae-jung from his Tokyo hotel room seems to have been protected by Chief Cabinet Secretary Gotōda. Asked about these cases, and about a failed 1961 coup d'état by an ultranationalist Imperial Army veteran and his associates, some of whom were in the SDF, one Japanese official grew defensive and insisted: "These cases are exaggerated. We cannot confirm what really happened and need to examine the credibility of the claims" that have been made in public.[13] It is certainly possible that these actors were isolated and that these incidents have been sensationalized—though not as much as the "abductee issue," which also involved political interference with the intelligence community— and we know that the nostalgic ultranationalist and his associates were apprehended by a vigilant state. However rare, these incidents call attention to a system in which Diet representatives have no formal oversight power and that relies on the media and courts to prevent intelligence excesses. If, as is indicated here, leadership and public support are central elements of effective intelligence reform, and if Japan's intelligence infrastructure now is poised to expand again, we should expect enhanced oversight to be targeted more explicitly than before.

Going Forward and Looking Ahead

Returning to Heraclitus's powerful metaphor, this discussion ends by asking about the future of the Japanese intelligence community. Where, at what depth, and how fast will the river of security environment, technological change, and failure carry it? There are at least three prospects for near-term shifts in Japan's strategic environment, some more plausible than others, but each of which will require Japan's leaders to make choices that would privilege different elements of the intelligence community in future reforms.

We can begin by assuming that the status quo—Japan's effective and low-cost military alliance with the United States—continues. This choice would reveal Tokyo's expectation that Washington will remain the dominant player in the system, and that Japan will be safest when aligned with it, even as the system becomes bi- or multipolar. During the 2016 U.S. presidential campaign, Donald Trump threatened to end Japan's cheap ride and to make defense more costly for Japan, but Japanese alliance managers and Prime Minister Abe talked him down from that ledge. He was, in any event, pushing on another open door. Abe and his allies long had chafed under limited defense budgets, and with the convergence of Trump's earlier pressure and the distractions of North Korean missile and nuclear tests in 2017, Abe indicated he would no longer be constrained by a long-standing normative limit of 1 percent of GDP. But he did not follow through when his government's 2018 record defense budget of 5.2 trillion yen ($46 billion) remained under that ceiling. This restraint continued when the Abe government announced it would allocate a total of 27 trillion yen ($240 billion) for the five year period from 2019 to 2023.[14]

A continued status quo—including President Trump's high-profile diplomatic maneuverings of mid-2018 involving North Korean denuclearization—would require the United States to continue to maintain bases on the archipelago and provide extended deterrence to Japan. We should also expect Sino-Japanese trade and economic relations to remain robust in the interest of both nations. Meanwhile China would continue its military expansion and provocations in the South and East China Seas, but would likely refrain from stepping out beyond "gray area" confrontations between its merchant fleet—its so-called "maritime militia"—and the Japan Coast Guard.[15]

Since change in the status quo is the scenario against which Japan has begun to hedge, the outline of its impact on the intelligence community is already clear. Intelligence reform would continue to focus on technological improvements and organizational enhancements. In the case of the former, this would entail acquiring better ISR for the military, both seaborne and airborne, as well as boosting space-based IMINT and SIGINT capabilities. We should expect more of this to be joint—across SDF service branches—and to see much more combined intelligence, that is, between the U.S. and Japanese militaries, which, by 2017, were exercising together with shared command and control of the airspace. In the case of Japan's military, we should expect renewed efforts to reduce the inefficiencies that remain embedded in the relationship between the NSS and CIRO. The Japanese government would also respond positively to the 2018 call by an influential Washington study group that it further enhance its intelligence capacity and "move promptly to adopt the security protections required to make its inclusion in Five Eyes a realistic possibility."[16] In this scenario, Japan could continue to use the alliance to transcend the alliance should that be necessary—and in the process would continue to derive benefits from intelligence sharing with the world's longest-eared rabbit.

Alternatively, whether by choice or (more likely) by default, Japan might opt to acquire and sustain an independent military capability. "Autonomous defense" (*jishu bōei*) has long been a part of the Japanese security discourse, and while it did not receive much public support during the Cold War, when politicians shied away from promoting it too vigorously, autonomous defense began to gain traction within the chattering classes as the relative decline of the United States came into sharper focus in the 2010s. The number of Japanese-language news items featuring the term *jishu bōei* soared fivefold in four years, from 708 in 2014 to 3,640 in 2017.[17]

Choosing this very expensive and politically divisive defense posture could be motivated by one or more of several developments: Japanese leaders could judge that the likely political and economic costs of U.S. assistance would exceed the certain costs of going it alone; they might determine that Chinese aggression and U.S. relative decline are threats of equal measure; they might feel threatened by a pacification of the Korean Peninsula; and/or they might be jarred by U.S. abandonment and/or the realization of a long dreaded "G2" agreement by which Washington and Beijing would collude to manage Asia jointly. In any of these contingencies, there would no longer be reason for Japan to hedge its bets on the rise of China or on the relative decline of the United States. Japan would do what it must: provide for itself in a "self-help" world. It would build metaphorical fences and dig metaphorical moats to preserve its sovereignty and independence, and in doing so not only would untether itself from the 1 percent limit on defense spending but also likely would at least double or even triple defense spending. Without the protection of the United States, and facing nuclear-armed neighbors in China and North (or even a unified) Korea, Japan would have to end its long-standing nuclear hedge and deploy its own nuclear deterrent.[18]

The implications of autonomous defense for the Japanese intelligence community are fairly evident. In order to deal on its own with contingencies on the Korean Peninsula, to deter Chinese aggression in neighboring seas, to deal with the possible rise of Islamist violence in Southeast Asia, and to protect against a reassertion of Russian power in Northeast Asia, Japan would have to enhance its intelligence capabilities in every respect. It would need to rebalance its technology-heavy collection apparatus by adding considerable human resources, including new training institutions and operations units designed to facilitate covert action, areas in which the Japanese intelligence community once excelled but that atrophied as dependence on the United

States increased during the Cold War. It would need to acquire real-time ISR capabilities to support strike missions, and it would have to invest far more heavily in space and cyber capabilities than heretofore. In the case of cyber capabilities, it would have to expand its defensive efforts (protection), and—to the extent that it is not already engaged in them—it would have to add exploitation (collection) and increase its efforts to develop offensive capabilities that were laid out prominently in the 2018 National Defense Program Guidelines.[19] And it would have to undertake all this without access to U.S. research on how to identify and counter new threats, including robots, germs, hackers, drones, and "deep fakes."[20] A fully re-reengineered Japanese intelligence community would be realized only at great political and economic cost, but would be indispensable in this circumstance.

Bandwagoning with China is a third strategic option for Japan. Rather than relying on a United States it judges to be in relative decline, and rather than distancing itself from both Washington and Beijing by adopting an autonomous defense posture, Tokyo would align with Beijing. It would discount China's economic domination and its military threat, as well as the costs of alienating Washington, emphasizing instead the benefits it could derive from a healthy economic relationship with the new global economic giant. This would contribute to the consolidation of a China-centered East Asian economic bloc, a process already under way after President Trump removed the United States from the Trans-Pacific Partnership in 2017. Indeed, within months of the U.S. withdrawal, Prime Minister Abe announced that the Japanese government would support participation by Japanese firms in China's "One Belt, One Road" and Asian Infrastructure Bank initiatives, and in October 2018 Abe and President Xi Jinping, both feeling pressure from President Trump on trade, agreed in Beijing to enhance economic cooperation more generally.[21] Japan would not "miss the China bus" after all. This was not the same as going "all in" with Beijing, but it did suggest the plausibility of this scenario, one that might leave room for a regional China-Japan condominium, the global impact of which would be the acceleration of a post-Washington economic consensus and the global multipolarity that was already under construction. In the event that such a position is achieved and sustained, Japan would likely have helped engineer a favorable power shift to East Asia and will have secured new possibilities for growth and innovation in the region.

In this scenario, there would be considerable pressure on Japan to reassure its new partner and avoid provoking China by fiddling too overtly with its intelligence community. The result might be a more well-rounded intelligence capacity that privileges civilian and military capabilities equally. But intelligence ties with "Five Eyes" states would be dialed back, as might deployment of powerful new radars and new satellites capable of enhanced imaging that Beijing opposes. And, of course, the Japanese intelligence community would certainly have to resist enhancing its HUMINT collection in China beyond beefing up JETRO-like economic collection and analysis. There also would likely be less pressure for Japan to take active measures to eliminate its remaining intelligence stovepipes, and indeed, such a radically altered Sino-Japanese relationship might even involve intelligence cooperation with China, something that began to stir in late 2018, as reported in chapter 6.

Each of these scenarios can be associated with likely Japanese intelligence failures. In the status quo case, we can anticipate Japanese intelligence failing an early test in the event of war on the Korean Peninsula or in Taiwan involving Japan-based U.S. forces. Although Japan's imaging and signals intelligence was exemplary during the 2017 North Korea missile and nuclear crises, it is not clear if Japan will have the more demanding intelligence required to anticipate and guide a safe evacuation of noncombatants. If the national reaction to the government's inability to protect teenagers from abduction by North Korea in the 1980s is a plausible prologue, avoidable deaths of Japanese civilians during a poorly coordinated and misapprehended evacuation would carry devastating domestic political consequences for Japan's leaders and their intelligence officials. Nor is it safe to assume that the intelligence community will advise the policy makers of the long-term consequences of the arrival of tens of thousands of refugees onto Japanese territory—or if they do, we cannot be sure that Japan's policy makers will hear and act upon such an unwelcome message.

There seem to be many more opportunities for intelligence failure under the autonomy strategy than either of the others. For starters, Japan would have returned to the world of covert action, one that was disorderly and disruptive during the Asia-Pacific War, the last time Tokyo dabbled in it. The political and diplomatic downsides of any massively embarrassing failed operation abroad would be enormous. The demands of autonomous defense may also invite a weakening of democratic oversight due to the associated rapid expansion of demands for secrecy, a situation that would stimulate enormous domestic protest. This in turn would limit the Japanese government's ability to mitigate the effects of bureaucratic stovepiping. We should also expect Japan's intelligence community to become more militarized in this scenario. As one national intelligence officer stated, "The SDF is always eager to accept expanded roles and missions, and already has legitimate and historically established intelligence capabilities."[22] It will be difficult for political leaders to resist increasing their reliance on the SDF for intelligence at a time when, as this volume has documented, they are expanding it in every direction all at once. And this, of course, would invite recalibration of civilian control of the military.

But, as noted earlier, the costs of autonomy—always high—are increasing, and Japanese leaders may continue to find the autonomy option untenable. As a former director of national intelligence, Admiral (ret.) Dennis Blair, points out, "Japan has continually striven for greater capability of its own [but] has found it much more expensive than relying on the United States."[23] Should Japan transition from its asymmetric alliance with the United States to one in which it relies entirely on itself, the most likely and most costly intelligence failure would derive from a reduction of access to advanced U.S. technology on the newest and most untested intelligence frontier—cyberspace. As reported in chapter 6, cyber and traditional intelligence are located administratively in different ministries and, even within the Cabinet Office, within different offices. As the technologies advance, and as their connections to intelligence multiply and blur, we can expect more of what we have already seen: each of the traditional players will lay claim to this space, and new entrants will be keen to raise their profile by formally entering the intelligence community. The likely result will be new levels of confusion and new vulnerabilities at just the moment when Japan would most need security.

This chapter began with the wisdom of the sixth-century BC philosopher Heraclitus, and it—and the book—end with the wisdom of the fifth-century BC historian Herodotus, who taught that "the worst pain one can suffer is to have insight into much and power over nothing." On the basis of the evidence presented in this volume, one could conclude that the reverse—having power over much but insight into nothing—can also have devastating consequences. The Japanese intelligence and security communities have experienced each kind of imbalance. During its imperial expansion Japan had great power but limited insight, and during the American century it had greater (often derivative) insight but much more limited power. The failure to strike an effective balance between power and insight has come at great cost to Japan and to its neighbors, no less than it has to its ally the United States, during its own imperial moment.

Notes

Preface

1. The White House vignette is from Andrew 1995, 164. "Licensed skullduggery" is from John le Carré's 2017 novel *Legacy of Spies*.
2. Turney-High 1971, 112. See Andrew 2019 for a global history of espionage.
3. Federation of American Scientists 1996, 1.
4. Andrew 1995, 16–17.
5. This perspective is often associated with former defense secretary Donald Rumsfeld, but it has long been part of intelligence lore. See Thomas 1988, 217.
6. Lathrop 2004, 325.
7. Laqueur 1985, 4.
8. Deacon 1983, 2; Elphick 1997, 36; Strategic Services Unit 1946, 29.
9. China Military Online, 6 June 2017, http://english.chinamil.com.cn/.
10. Kotani 2013, 189. Frustration with the lack of community was expressed more often in the interviews conducted for this book than any other single point.
11. Kuroi 2005a, 236.
12. See interview with Magosaki Ukeru in Kuroi, 2008, 261.
13. Kōno, Mabuchi, and Yamauchi 2013, 94–95.
14. Interview, former Ministry of Defense official, 29 November 2017, Tokyo.
15. The National Defense Program Guidelines issued in December 2018 emphasized both offensive and defense cyber capabilities.
16. Quoted in Warner 2014, 19.
17. "Glaring failure" is from Haynes 2009, iv.
18. Abe is cited in Maruya 2005, 135.
19. Grabo 2002, 26; Lefebvre 2004, 237; Johnson 2003a, 20.
20. Davis 2002, 5.
21. Kotani 2013, 191.
22. Hirajō 2010, 192.
23. See Samuels 2003a.

1. Driving Intelligence

1. Warner 2014, 74; Andrew 1995; and Codevilla 2002.
2. Handel 1992, 187.
3. For compelling evidence, see Zegart 2005, 80–82.
4. See Rovner and Long 2006 for a thoughtful critique of the idea that shifts in the international security environment require reorganization of intelligence agencies.

5. Some of these issues are explored in Hastedt 1991 and in Fry and Hochstein 1994. See also Handel 1981.

6. *Economic Times*, 6 April 2015; *The Diplomat*, 3 December 2013; Antara News, 28 August 2014.

7. For India, see Panneerselvam 2016, and for Australia, see Cook and Wilkins 2014. See also the special issue of *International Affairs*, "Japan Pivots in Asia," July 2018.

8. O'Connell 2004.

9. Chopin 2015.

10. See the comprehensive report by Chalk and Rosenau 2004.

11. Handel 1989.

12. McNeil 2014, 25; Andrew 1995, 24.

13. For the personal account of the cryptanalyst who broke the Japanese codes during the treaty negotiations, see Yardley 1931.

14. A 2008 study by the U.S. Directorate of National Intelligence concluded that the post–World War II demobilization of IMINT capability significantly handicapped U.S. forces in Korea in 1950. See *The Quint*, 22 September 2015.

15. *New York Times*, 5 January 1990. For the British program, see Royal United Services Institution ed. 1944, and for the Russian effort, see Cohen 2000.

16. Some of these grainy photographs have been declassified at https://www.cia.gov/library/center-for-the-study-of-intelligence/csi-publications/books-and-monographs/corona.pdf.

17. See Laqueur 1985, 27–28, for an accessible history of the evolution of intelligence technologies. See also Treverton 2001, Gaddis 1992, and Handel 1989.

18. Gaddis 1992, 102. Andrew 1995, 255, concurs that remote sensing "helped to stabilize the Cold War." Fry and Hochstein 1994, 21, is the more pessimistic assessment. See also Treverton 2001, 108.

19. To be sure, excellent SIGINT can come from a chain of steps in which a human agent plays a role, whether by suggesting who or what to bug, planting a microphone or a sensor, or inserting software on a phone, a single computer, or an entire network. The raw intelligence that results may not qualify as HUMINT because it did not come directly from an officer running an agent, but humans did things that sensors or hackers alone could not—at least before artificial intelligence matured.

20. On Israel, see *Haaretz*, 19 May 2011. On the UK, see http://www.techweekeurope.co.uk/workspace/mod-creates-command-unit-to-counter-cyber-threats-32802. For the French, Russian, Iranian, and other cases, see http://www.2501research.com/new-blog/2014/10/14/world-cyber-commands-in-their-own-words.

21. Fravel 2019, Cheng 2016.

22. See http://www.iips.org/en/research/2016/02/03180408.html. The proclaimed (and apparent) focus of the Japanese cybersecurity operation is on cyber defense.

23. *Nihon Keizai Shimbun*, 18 February 2018. For the 2018 budget, see https://www.nisc.go.jp/active/kihon/pdf/yosan2018.pdf.

24. *Bloomberg Business*, 20 July 2011.

25. Harris 2014, xxiv; Gartner, Inc., cited in *Forbes*, 9 March 2016. The estimate for 2018 is from Cybersecurity Ventures. See https://cybersecurityventures.com/cybersecurity-market-report/.

26. "Cyber military-industrial complex" is from *Toronto Globe and Mail*, 28 March 2011. The projection is from Gartner, Inc., as reported in *Forbes*, 9 March 2016. The $1 trillion estimate is from https://cybersecurity ventures.com/cybersecurity-market-report/.

27. These firms and others participate in the Cyber Security Working Group of the Federation of Economic Organizations, Nippon Keidanren. The record 2019 Japanese cyber budget was reported in *Nihon Keizai Shimbun*, 5 November 2018.

28. Lindsay 2017 is a sober reminder that cyberwarfare is subject to institutional constraints.

29. *Daily Mail*, 4 May 2012; *Times of India*, 3 July 2014; *Amsterdam Herald*, 14 October 2014.

30. *DOD News*, 19 March 2015.

31. *Jane's Intelligence Review*, 28 December 2014; *Financial Times*, 3 September 2007. In May 2014 the U.S. Justice Department charged five members of the PLA with cyber espionage and the FBI issued wanted posters for their capture and arrest. *DOD News*, 19 May 2014. See also *New York Times*, 18 February 2013, on the PLA's secret Unit 61398, suspected of targeting North American political, military, and economic entities for intelligence.

32. The coordinated U.S.-Israeli "Stuxnet" operation against Iran in 2010 has received the most attention (see Sanger 2012). *Jane's Intelligence Review*, 28 December 2014, also speaks of the cyber activities of the United States and its "Five Eyes" partners, discussed later in this chapter.

33. In 2013 the *Washington Post* published secret data on the annual U.S. National Intelligence Program, which constituted about 70 percent of total spending on intelligence. That year, it dedicated $4.3 billion to "conducting cyber operations," out of a total budget for the program of $52.6 billion. See http://www.washingtonpost.com/wp-srv/special/national/black-budget/.

34. See https://www.nisc.go.jp/active/kihon/pdf/yosan2018.pdf, *Nihon Keizai Shimbun*, 5 November 2018.

35. This rough approximation is based on data from Naikaku Saibā Sekyuritī Sentā ed. 2017, https://www.nisc.go.jp/active/kihon/pdf/yosan2017.pdf. The budget for this office rose from 1.6 billion yen in 2015 to 5 billion yen in 2018. See www.cas.go.jp/jp/yosan.

36. Jervis 2010, 2.

37. Bar-Joseph and McDermott 2017 identify a robust literature on intelligence failure. See also Laqueur 1985, Levite 1987, Betts 2007, Reisman and Baker 1992, Jervis 1986–87, and 2010.

38. Betts 1978, 62–63.

39. Unnamed senior State Department official quoted in Lathrop 2004, 326.

40. Hedley 2005, 438. Bar-Joseph and McDermott 2017, 240–41, make a similar point.

41. This astute evaluation is from Levite 1987, 18–19.

42. Posner 2006, 2. See also Garicano and Posner 2005 for an application of organizational economics to intelligence failure.

43. This is the observation of Jervis 2018.

44. Cordesman 2004, 5.

45. See Best 2004 for a review of some two dozen commissions and their recommendations for reorganizing the U.S. intelligence community from 1949 to 2004.

Jervis 2010 is a particularly intimate study of intelligence failure. See also Hedley 2005, 441; Federation of American Scientists ed. 1996, 7; and Zegart 2005, 79, on the inability to adapt to the rise of terrorism after the Cold War.

46. Journal of Palestine Studies ed. 1974. See chap. 3 of the report at https://israeled.org/wp-content/uploads/2015/06/1974.4-Agranat-Commission-of-Inquiry-Interim-Report.pdf. See also Bar-Joseph and McDermott 2017, 184–234, for a case study.

47. See paragraphs 311–20 in the so-called "Franks Report" of January 1983, "Falkland Islands Review: Report of a Committee of Privy Counsellors," http://fc95d419f4478b3b6e5f-3f71d0fe2b653c4f00f32175760e96e7.r87.cf1.rackcdn.com/E415E0802DAA482297D889B9B43B70DE.pdf.

48. See "Executive Summary of the Kargil Committee Report," 25 February 2000, http://fas.org/news/india/2000/25indi1.htm; and Kanwal 2012.

49. Federation of American Scientists 1996, 1–2.

50. Latell 2012.

51. See Jervis 2010 for a comprehensive analysis of the CIA's failure to anticipate the Iranian Revolution. Bar-Joseph and McDermott 2017, 14, provide a list of World War II surprise attacks, a tactical element used effectively by both sides in the conflict.

52. Laqueur 1985, 231, invokes President Dwight Eisenhower's explanation that "[intelligence] success cannot be advertised." Bar-Joseph and McDermott 2017 focus on failure and success.

53. Andrew 1995, 151.

54. Jervis 2010, 5.

55. Bar-Joseph and McDermott 2017 examine how individual decision makers process failure and learn how to succeed. See also Dahl 2013, who compares intelligence failure to intelligence success.

56. Interview, Gregory Treverton, 29 March 2016.

57. Richelson 2011. The case of Libyan disarmament, an intelligence success, is discussed in Nonproliferation Policy Education Center ed. 2014 and in Tobey 2017.

58. Davis 1991, 98; Kent 1949.

59. See Donovan 1946, 447, on the moles; Macintyre 2007 on the Double-Cross; and Boyd 1993 on Magic.

60. "Golden Age" aspirations were reported in the New York Times, 22 November 2013. See Wohlstetter 1962 for the classic analysis of Pearl Harbor.

61. Wark 1986, 198.

62. Knox quoted in Lathrop 2004, 157–58.

63. This is from Schelling's foreword to Wohlstetter 1962, vii.

64. Betts 2007, xi. For useful reviews of impediments to effective intelligence, see Levite 1987, chap. 1; Laqueur 1985; Betts 2007; Garicano and Posner 2005; Dahl 2013; and Bar-Joseph and McDermott 2017.

65. Hulnik 1986, 217, credits Kent. Phythian 2013, 7, says the origins of the "cycle" are difficult to pin down but that Kent's 1948 work Strategic Intelligence for American World Policy popularized the cycle in the United States. For use of the model, see Treverton 2001, 105; Johnson 2003a; O'Connell 2004; Commission on the Intelligence Capabilities of the United States Regarding Weapons of Mass Destruction ed. 2005, 584 (hereafter cited as Commission on Intelligence Capabilities).

66. O'Connell 2004, 190, uses the term "old-fashioned." Johnson 2003 includes "planning" in the model. Warner 2002, 231, argues that "only in textbooks" does it make sense to distinguish "separate 'information,' 'decision,' and 'implementation' phases."

67. Warner 2012, 226, calls them "constitutive elements."

68. Johnson 2003a.

69. Warner 2002, 227.

70. Levite 1987, 14. See also Davies and Gustafson 2013b, Kello 2013, Gartzke 2013, Lindsay and Kello 2013, and Lindsay 2017. Corn and Isikoff 2018 is a well-sourced journalists' account of the Russian meddling.

71. Johnson 2003a, 17; Andrew 1995, 260.

72. Richelson 2011, 17, lists these agencies. For the 2016 budget numbers, see the Federation of American Scientists' Intelligence Resource Program, http://fas.org/irp/budget/.

73. Thanks to Robert Jervis for pointing this out in private conversation. For more on MASINT, see Humphrey 2007.

74. Interview, General (ret.) Kunimi Masahiro, 5 October 2017, Tokyo. General Kunimi was also the first director of the Cabinet Satellite Intelligence Center. See chapters 4 and 5 of this volume.

75. Johnson 2003a, 24.

76. Mercado 2007.

77. Warner 2002, 229; George 1959.

78. Johnson 2003a, 18.

79. See Avey and Desch 2014. As Avey and Desch note, previous scholars have also pointed out the extent to which policy makers act on the basis of strictly open, unclassified sources.

80. Cole 2014, 8.

81. *Financial Times*, 10 July 2015; Schwartz 2015.

82. The German, French, and New Zealand programs are reported in an article in *Salon*, 26 October 2013, based on an undated story in the *Global Post*.

83. Betts 2007, 69.

84. Laqueur 1985, 32; Turner 1985, 271.

85. Jervis 1986–87, 161.

86. Kent is quoted in Betts 1978, 69.

87. The best compilations of these impediments are Jervis 1976, Betts 1978, Laqueur 1985, Levite 1987, Grabo 2002, Garicano and Posner 2005, and Bar-Joseph and McDermott 2017.

88. Handel 1989, 20.

89. Johnston 2005, 22; Laqueur 1985, 102.

90. Hilsman 1956, 46.

91. Cordesman 2004, 4. Or, as Gaddis 1992, 88, notes, "The price of 'listening in' is inundation."

92. Bar-Joseph and McDermott 2017.

93. Levite 1987, 9–10.

94. Handel 1987, 14. See also Hastings 2018, 51, who concludes that "if wars are too important to be left to the generals, intelligence is too important to be left to the spymasters."

95. Steury ed. 1994, ix.

96. Hedley 2005, 442. This pattern was repeated in 1998, when the American intelligence community failed to give advance warning of the Indian nuclear test because they could not imagine that the Indian government would be so irrational as to act in a way contrary to its best interests. See Riley 1998.

97. Betts 1978, 62–63, refers to them as "the pathologies of communication." For concurring analyses, see Levite 1987, Schoenfeld 2005, Andrew 1995, Johnson 2003b. Rovner 2011 focuses closely on the persistent and costly miscommunication between analysts and policy makers.

98. Treverton 2001, xiii. See also Stiefler 2004, chap. 1; and Bar-Joseph and McDermott 2017, 241.

99. Knudsen and Haridimos 2005.

100. Richelson and Ball 1985, 239; Herman 2003, 46.

101. Betts 1978, 77.

102. Statement of Lieutenant General Hoyt S. Vandenberg before the Armed Services Committee of the U.S. Senate on S758, the National Security Act of 1947, 29 April 1947, available at www.foia.cia.gov/collection/crest-25-year-collection-archive.

103. See the review by Davies 2012.

104. Chopin 2015, 1.

105. Grono 2007.

106. Fleischer 2013, 8.

107. Bar-Joseph and McDermott 2017, 241, could be describing Japan when they posit the "American tendency" toward bureaucratic rivalry.

108. Tab C, page 1, of the Report of the Joint Congressional Committee on the Investigation of the Pearl Harbor Attack, available at www.foia.cia.gov/collection/crest-25-year-program-archive.

109. Andrew 1995, 166; Federation of American Scientists 1996.

110. Laqueur 1985, 33. Handel 1989, 4, spoke of the "[perpetual] political tug of war between civil and military authorities" in the United States, and Russell 2002, 1, describes the "uneasy relationship" between the military and the CIA since the agency's inception.

111. Andrew 1995, 257.

112. Turner 1985, 236. Apparently the rivalry also has cut the other way. According to a declassified document, the CIA conducted a major SIGINT operation that overlapped with and excluded the NSA during—and after—the Cold War. See the 2015 report of the National Security Archive at http://www2.gwu.edu/~nsarchiv/NSAEBB/NSAEBB506/.

113. *New York Times*, 24 July 2003. See also Zegart 2005 for analysis of 9/11 failure and the difficulty of the intelligence community in adapting.

114. Commission on Intelligence Capabilities ed. 2005, 14. The Senate Committee on Intelligence came to the same conclusion; see Select Committee on Intelligence ed. 2004, 4.

115. Tama 2005, 10.

116. *Boston Globe*, 26 March 2014.

117. This "Unclassified Summary of Information Handling and Sharing Prior to the April 15, 2013 Boston Marathon Bombings" is at http://www.dni.

gov/files/documents/ICIG_Forum_Boston_Marathon_Bombings_Review_-_
Unclassified_Summary.pdf.

118. This particularly evocative internal assessment was published in 2007; see
http://www.ni-u.edu/ni_press/pdf/Improving_the_Law_Enforcement_Intelli
gence_Community.pdf.

119. Rovner 2011, 5. Hersh 2018 provides a career's worth of examples of "the
misuse of intelligence" in his memoir. See also Stiefler 2004.

120. Jervis 2010, 157.

121. Bar-Joseph and McDermott 2017.

122. Churchill is quoted in Lathrop 2004, 188.

123. Handel 1989, 5, 15.

124. Hulnik 1986, 215–16.

125. Treverton 2001, 15.

126. Jervis 2010, 159.

127. *Washington Post,* 17 August 2018.

128. The debate is reviewed in Davis 1991. For the original canon—what Davis
calls "a doctrinal shootout between champions of the detached and close-support
approaches" (91)—see Kent 1949 and Kendall 1949.

129. Donovan 1946, 448. See Treverton 1987 for background on the political
battles over the creation of the CIA.

130. Dulles quoted in Lathrop 2004, 322.

131. Steury ed. 1994, xx.

132. Rovner 2011, 177, argues that policy makers ignored the ambiguity in existing intelligence (and the debates within the intelligence community) and "wildly"
overstated the quality of their information regarding Iraqi WMD, thereby exaggerat-
ing the certainty of the threat.

133. Select Committee on Intelligence ed. 2004, 16. Betts 2007, 91, pulls no such
punches, calling this "the nadir" of politicized intelligence. Jervis 2006 reviews the
salience of politicization in three major reports on the U.S. government's 2003 intelligence failure in Iraq.

134. "Ideological blinders" is from Johnson 2003a, 4. The metaphor of the drunk
is from Hughes, cited in Handel 1987, 14.

135. Treverton 2001, 2; Handel 1989, 5.

136. Turner 2004, 54.

137. Kent is cited in Davis 1991, 93. Betts 2007, 3, articulates this view as well.

138. Johnson 2003a, 11.

139. Turner 1985, 250.

140. Johnson 2003a, 19.

141. Richelson and Ball 1985, 136–37.

142. Richelson and Ball 1985, 1–2. See also Johnson 2003a.

143. Andrew 1995, 152.

144. Richelson and Ball 1985, 171–72.

145. Johnson 2003a, 17. See also Davies 2002, 62.

146. Richelson and Ball 1985, 239.

147. Commission on Intelligence Capabilities ed. 2005, 381.

148. Morris-Suzuki 2014, 3.

149. Johnson 1988.

150. See http://www.businessinsider.com/obama-nsa-surveillance-reforms-edward-snowden-press-conference-2013-7#ixzz3ff2nrTRU. The American Civil Liberties Union does not believe this will suffice; see https://www.aclu.org/feature/end-mass-surveillance-under-patriot-act.

151. These terms are from Executive Order 12356 and relate to the unauthorized revelation of "secret," "classified," and "top secret" documents, respectively.

152. This list is from Gioe 2014, 51, and Gioe 2015, 3. See also Godson 1995, xii.

153. Cole 2014, 7.

154. See http://www.opensocietyfoundations.org/publications/global-principles-national-security-and-freedom-information-tshwane-principles.

155. Warner 2012, 225. The most comprehensive explorations of covert action are Treverton 1987, Johnson 1989, Warner 2002, Daugherty 2004, and Prados 2006.

156. Kibbe 2010, 570; Stempel 2007, 125.

157. There has been debate regarding whether or not covert action is a "constituent element" of intelligence. Warner 2012, 223–30, lays out both sides and ties covert action to the other elements through their common "economy of secrecy"; that is, secret action generates decision and action advantages which, in turn, are optimized when analysis and action are co-located in the same organization. See also Stiefler 2004, 632.

158. Johnson 1989, 84, lays out the full range of covert actions. In 1989 he judged propaganda to account for 40 percent of covert actions, political intervention 30 percent, economic manipulation 10 percent, and paramilitary action 20 percent. Treverton 1987, 13, offers similar estimates. See also Reisman and Baker 1992; Godson 1995; Hulnick 1996, 146–47; Stempel 2007; Rosenbach and Peritz 2009; and Lowenthal 2015.

159. Daugherty 2010, 621.

160. See the intelligence community assessment of Russian active measures in U.S. elections produced in declassified form by the director of national intelligence in 2017, https://www.dni.gov/files/documents/ICA_2017_01.pdf.

161. Sheldon 1997.

162. Stempel 2007, 122.

163. Daugherty 2010, 611.

164. Scott 2004 traces the lexical shifts. Levchenko 1988 speaks of "active measures" from his perspective as a former KGB agent. For the use of "active measures" by Russia to assist the Trump campaign, see http://www.atlanticcouncil.org/blogs/ukrainealert/russia-s-active-measures-are-back-with-a-vengeance.

165. Daugherty 2010, 609; Godson 1995, 19–20.

166. See Hulnick 1996, 148.

167. Rudgers 2000, 253–54; Hulnick 1996, 148.

168. Stiefler 2004, 635–37. Kennan's NSC 10/2 expanded covert action from propaganda to direct intervention in the politics and economies of foreign countries. See Treverton 1987, 36.

169. There is a rich literature on these activities. See Meyer 1980, Daugherty 2010, and Mistry 2011. Depending only upon the public record, Wettering 2003, 564, offers a remarkably long list of unsuccessful postwar covert actions.

170. Doolittle is quoted in Hulnick 1996, 149.

171. Stiefler 2004 reports that CIA enthusiasm for covert action peaked in 1965. Stempel 2007, 133, says that the U.S. postwar "romance with covert action" ended in the 1970s.

172. For legal analysis of how U.S. law applies to covert action, see Baker 2010. See also Hulnick 1996.

173. Krieger 2009, 217.

174. Baker 2010, 589.

175. Treverton 1987, 5.

176. See Johnson 1989 and Born and Jensen 2007.

177. The Twentieth Century Fund's report "The Need to Know: Covert Action and American Democracy" is discussed in Daugherty 2004, 18.

178. Sagar 2013, 3. For more on oversight, see also Bruneau and Boraz 2007 and Lester 2015.

179. For excellent reviews, see Born and Jensen 2007 and Krieger 2009. For a thorough review of oversight in the United States, see Daugherty 2004, chap. 6.

180. Krieger 2009, 218. For an explanation of consociationalism, see Lijphart 1968.

181. Krieger 2009, 226.

182. Daugherty 2004, 28–29.

183. Caparini 2007, 3.

184. See Johnson 1989 and Hamilton and Inouye 1987. Kibbe 2010, 570, discusses the 1991 Intelligence Authorization Act, which resulted from the Iran-contra fiasco.

185. Russell 2016, 155–56; Bauman et al. 2014; *The Guardian*, 5 June 2015.

186. Krieger 2009, 212.

187. See Caparini 2007, 12, on the independence of the media and Sagar 2013 on the limits to the media's role.

188. Interview, Tokyo, 22 December 2015.

189. Berkowitz 2001, 611.

190. Kent is cited by Davis 1991, 93.

191. Grabo 2002, 8.

192. Jervis 1986–87, 141. This status differential was acknowledged and derided by President Eisenhower, himself a retired military commander of distinction. See Andrew 1995, 200.

193. Johnston 2005, 23. See also Garicano and Posner 2005.

194. For background on the elocutionary somersaults that Japanese bureaucrats must complete in order to avoid the appearance of inconsistency in national security policy, see Samuels 2007.

195. Handel 1987, 9.

2. Expanding Special Duties (1895–1945)

1. For a scholarly look at that earlier period, see Nish 1984, 17. For the Dutch, see Clulow 2014. For the Koreans, see Toby 1991.

2. Hall 1988, 443, discusses the *oniwaban*. He also attributes Hideyoshi's failed invasions of Korea and China in the late sixteenth century in part to inaccurate intelligence (269–71).

3. Kotani 2009c, 6. Tachikawa 2015, 148, reports that the second Japanese military attaché was future prime minister Katsura Tarō, whom he credits with first

suggesting the model to Yamagata, and who was sent to Germany in 1875. The Imperial Navy followed suit five years later. Tachikawa 2015, 151. See also Allen 1987, 548–49. For the full context of the epigraph from Yamagata at the beginning of this chapter, see Ōyama 1966, 95.

4. Orbach 2018, 10. These business ties included sponsorship of many of Japan's most ambitious zaibatsu leaders, such as Iwasaki Hisaya of Mitsubishi and Baron Ōkura of the Ōkura Group.

5. "Agents of chaos" is from Orbach 2018, 34.

6. Nish 1984, 19–20; Inaba, Fält, and Kujala 1988.

7. Allen 1987, 549.

8. Orbach 2018 cites Sasaki 1994. Patalano 2015, 75, reports that many believe the Imperial Navy underestimated the importance of intelligence.

9. Nish 1984, 27.

10. Drea 1984, 66–73; Nakamuda 1985, 25–47, 82. The Imperial Navy also had the assistance of Captain Fred T. Jane, a British naval attaché in Tokyo whom the Japanese hired upon his retirement to provide assessments of foreign naval capabilities. His assessments became the basis for *Jane's Fighting Ships*, the world's most authoritative open source on the topic. See Jane 1904.

11. Hansen 1996, 26.

12. Kotani 2009c, 7.

13. Ishimitsu 1988, 208, 302.

14. Ishimitsu 1988, 571–74. Orbach 2018, 9, describes a similar case of a spy ring created much earlier, in 1884, by Arao Sei, a junior officer in the IJA, and an expatriate Japanese pharmacist, Kishida Ginkō. See Inaba, Fält, and Kujala 1988 for more on how military intelligence officers set up shop across Russia's Far East posing as barbers, priests, haberdashers, and photographers.

15. Zachmann 2011 reports that in 1898 Konoe disavowed the idea of a "same race alliance" after harsh criticism and that he later came to embrace the Anglo-Japanese alliance.

16. Reynolds 1989b, 19.

17. Maruya 2012.

18. The "Dark Ocean" refers to the narrow body of water separating Japan from Korea, pointing to the society's expansionist designs. Jourdonnais 1963, 6, suggests that many in these groups were young ultranationalists whom the army sent away in order to keep them from making mischief at home.

19. Crowdy 2006, 216.

20. Ishitaki 2010, 199.

21. Postwar U.S. intelligence mistakenly judged mapping "one of the major failures of Japanese intelligence." See GHQ Intelligence Summary no. 1475, 20 April 1946, 14. See also Jansen 1954.

22. Reynolds 1989b, 18. Orbach 2018, 28, refers to the ambivalent relationship of the adventurers to the Japanese state, and cites then opposition leader Hara Kei's diary, in which he noted that MOFA used the adventurers when they were useful but had no compunctions about tossing them aside when they were not.

23. Jacob 2014, chap. 5.

24. Mutsu 2015, 24.

25. Jacob 2014, 46–47, 52–53.

26. Tōyama et al. 2008, 226–28, 232.

27. Maesaka 2011, 100–101, 164–65. Documents related to Akashi's covert activities in central / eastern Europe are housed at the Japan Center for Asian Historical Records, https://www.jacar.go.jp/english/nichiro/cloud_akashi.htm. (Some links are broken.) There is little documented evidence of Akashi's connection to Lenin, but one detailed journalistic account describes their meeting during the Russo-Japanese War at Lenin's home in exile. Akashi reportedly offered cash to Lenin, which was accepted with the warning "Beware of spies." See the *Japan Times and Mail*, 24 August 1931. Another is Inaba 1995, who speculates that Akashi and Lenin met in Geneva, where Lenin was in exile from 1903 to 1905, when Akashi visited under the cover of a Japanese delegate to the International Red Cross. Inaba 1988a does not mention such meetings in his short profile of Akashi's career.

28. Deacon 1983, 47–50; Crowdy 2006, 217; www.alternativefinland.com/finland-grafton-affair/.

29. See Ishitaki 2010, 199 and 34–35, 44 in the appendix containing the Genyōsha member list. See also http://www5e.biglobe.ne.jp/~isitaki/page045.html.

30. See https://rnavi.ndl.go.jp/kensei/tmp/index_uchidaryohei.pdf and http://www.fl.reitaku-u.ac.jp/~rsakurai/siryo/aka2.html. For more on the overlapping memberships of the Kokuryūkai with the Genyōsha and the Tōa Dōbunkai, see Jacob 2014, 56–62.

31. Jacob 2014, 72.

32. Inaba, Fält, and Kujala 1988, 83.

33. Maesaka 2011, 193–96; Hirajō 2010, 6. Castravelli 2006, 44, insists that Akashi's destabilization budget was ten times greater: 1 million yen.

34. Pałaz-Rutkowska 2011.

35. Maesaka 2011, 180–81; Masunaga 2017, 4.

36. Maesaka 2011, 172, 175–78.

37. Maesaka 2011, 182.

38. Kurobane 1976, 74–75.

39. Deacon 1983, 56.

40. Maesaka 2011, 102. See Inaba, Fält, and Kujala 1988 for an English translation of parts of *Rakka Ryūsui*.

41. Masunaga 2017, 31–32. See the discussion later in this chapter for details on these special duty units (*tokumu kikan*).

42. Masunaga 2017, 21, 34.

43. Gunji Kenkyū ed. 2006, 155.

44. Doihara Kenji Kankōkai ed. 1972, 203–4, 267; Kuroi 2011, 48. The operative he used, Amagasu Masahiko, had been forced to retire from the army after murdering a Japanese civilian in 1923. Amagasu later became the head of Manchukuo's National Police Agency and Pu Yi's bodyguard. Kuroi 2011, 48, 56–59.

45. Gunji Kenkyū ed. 2006, 145–76.

46. Gunji Kenkyū ed. 2006, 156. Also see Kuroi 2011, 54–55.

47. Seki 2016, 108.

48. Nish 1984, 19.

49. Seki 2016, 108, 308, 240–41.

50. Nish 1984, 19.

51. Seki 2016, 62–67.

52. Orbach 2018.

53. This paragraph is based on Gaimushō Hyakunenshi Hensan Iinkai ed. 1969a, 740–42, 1032, and 1036. Also see *Asahi Shimbun*, 17 January 1920.

54. This paragraph and the next are based on Gaimushō Hyakunenshi Hensan Iinkai ed. 1969b, 180, 182,190–205.

55. *Asahi Shimbun*, 27 December 1933.

56. *Asahi Shimbun*, 7 December 1940.

57. Barnhart 1987.

58. U.S. Strategic Bombing Survey 1946, 2.

59. Sugita 1988, 22–23. For more on this disdain, even within Japan's elite covert operations training academy, see Mercado 2002, 23.

60. Kotani 2009c, 91.

61. Barnhart 1984, 447.

62. I am grateful to Stephen Mercado for this insight. For detailed career data on officers, including intelligence hands, see *Toyama 1981*.

63. Harries 1991, 376.

64. Much of the discussion that follows is based on Kotani 2009c, 94, 96, 103.

65. Mercado 2002, chap. 3.

66. See Kotani 2009c, 98–99. See also Bennett, Hobart, and Spitzer 1986, 3, on the relationship between operational commanders and their intelligence officers.

67. Barnhart 1984, 432.

68. The term *tokumu kikan* has been translated most literally as "special activities agency," and variously as "special services agency," "secret service organization," and "spy network," inter alia. I use the term "special duty unit," in part because the original Japanese term has been applied to more than just covert operations units and because doing so establishes a distinction in Japanese practice that is analogous to the one used in the U.S. military between standard combat units—replicable building blocks for larger brigades and divisions, such as tank or artillery units—and nonstandard units that are formed and funded for specific missions. These latter units may be assigned to any headquarters' functions—logistics, intelligence, and so on—and when the functions are complete, they are shut down. See https://history.army.mil/html/forcestruc/tda-ip.html for this distinction in the U.S. case. In the Japanese case, these nonstandard "special duty units" have been associated most closely with intelligence, but the term was applied to nearly everything: logistics, resource acquisition, HUMINT recruiting, influence operations—whatever their senior officers had in mind and had money to fund, including private businesses that generated cash flow and profits diverted to all sorts of public and private use. Thanks to Lance Gatling for working through this translation problem with the author.

69. The U.S. Strategic Bombing Survey 1946, 38, describes Japan's *tokumu kikan* in flattering terms. See also GHQ Intelligence Summary no. 1620, 8 October 1946, 9–10.

70. Ishimitsu 1988, 858–65, 886–90.

71. This account is based on Ishimitsu 1988, 858–906, 985–99, 1077.

72. This account is from GHQ Intelligence Summary no. 1619, 7 October 1946, 10.

73. Mercado 1994, 49; Tachikawa 2015, 179.

74. Sugita 1988, 25.

75. Sugita 1988, 62.

76. U.S. Strategic Bombing Survey 1946, 1; Kotani 2009b, 9.

77. Strategic Services Unit ed. 1946, 184.

78. Sugita 1988.

79. National Archives, Naval Attaché Reports, 1886–1939, RG38, box 729, subject E-8-a, register 6406c.

80. Sugita 1988, 11–12, 59. See also Bennett, Hobart, and Spitzer 1986, 3.

81. GHQ Intelligence Summary no. 1531, 25 June 1946, 11.

82. GHQ Intelligence Summary no. 1532, 26 June 1946, 10.

83. Nakamuda 1985.

84. Kotani 2009c, 91.

85. Kotani 2009c, 22. Pałaz-Rutkowska 2011, 26–27, reports that the Imperial Japanese Army developed particularly close ties with Poland in the 1920s and 1930s. It used Warsaw-based attachés to collect intelligence on the Soviet Union, nearly all of whom were elite officers focused on Russia in the Second Department of the Army General Staff or in special duty units in Manchuria. One, Ueda Masao, returned to Japan to become director of the Nakano School, the army's intelligence training academy, discussed later in this chapter.

86. Kotani 2009c, 15.

87. Much of this assistance was channeled through the efforts of Sugihara Chiune, a diplomat and intelligence officer who worked closely with Polish exiles to collect intelligence on the Soviet Union. Sugihara is better known for aiding the exit of Jewish émigrés from Lithuania. See Pałaz-Rutkowska 2011, 26, 32–35. Also see Military History Section ed. 1955 and Masunaga 2017.

88. National Archives, Naval Attaché Reports, 1886–1939, RG38, box 729, subject E-8-a, register 6406b, 13 July 1935; Sugita 1988, 27.

89. Cited in Bennett, Hobart, and Spitzer 1986, 14.

90. GHQ Intelligence Summary no. 1555, 23 July 1946, 12–13.

91. Nakamuda 1985, 83. Ironically, the United States had earlier broken Japan's codes and knew each of its negotiating positions at the 1921 Washington Naval Conference.

92. Drea 1991, 187–88.

93. Drea 1991, 189.

94. Drea 1991, 189. Drea's judgment is consistent with that of Nakamuda Kenichi, a naval officer responsible for decrypting naval SIGINT who suggested that Japan's capabilities "greatly excelled" at this sort of traffic analysis. Nakamuda claims that this capability was critical to the IJN's success in the Solomon Islands in 1942 (90–93). Bennett, Hobart, and Spitzer 1986, 22, point out that although large Allied fleet movements were always noted by Japanese intelligence, the target and timing of the attacks were not often correctly determined.

95. Elphick 1997, 43–45, describes this unit. This account of Rutland is based on Kotani 2009c, 79–83; Loureiro 1994; Everest-Phillips 2006, 264–66, 276.

96. Everest-Phillips 2006, 276.

97. GHQ Intelligence Summary no. 1491, 9 May 1946, 10.

98. Loureiro 1994, 198; Krebs 1996, 194. Lowman 2001 justifies the internment of Japanese Americans on the basis of Magic intercepts.

99. Loureiro 1994, 202.

100. See Loureiro 1994, 198, on Nomura and Everest-Phillips 2006, 260, on the House Un-American Activities Committee's hearings. For Mercado's concurrence with Lowman 2001, see Mercado 1994, 51.

101. Krebs 1996, 194.

102. For the Munson Report, see Munson 2000 and https://encyclopedia. densho.org/sources/en-denshopd-i67-00005-1/. The Ringle Report is available at https://www.history.navy.mil/research/library/online-reading-room/title-list-alphabetically/r/ringle-report-on-japanese-internment.html.

103. Loureiro 1994, 199. According to Kumamoto 1979, 48–50, the Office of Naval Intelligence and the Military Intelligence Division of the U.S. Army were receiving reports in 1934 that Japanese intelligence officers were active in Panama, near the Canal Zone, and throughout the rest of the decade there were episodic reports of Japanese espionage in the Pacific Northwest and elsewhere.

104. Kumamoto 1979, 45, 47. In personal correspondence, 3 April 2018, Professor Eiichi Azuma explained that "dangerous enemy aliens" were identified on the basis of their occupation, organizational membership, and community leadership, adding that "their arrests were not specifically tied to espionage charges." He noted too that "there were more German enemy aliens than their Japanese counterparts in the pool of arrested individuals."

105. Everest-Phillips 2007 insists this is because there were none. See also Burton et al. 2002.

106. Loureiro 1994, 203–4.

107. Loureiro 1994, 203–4; Hansen 1996, 27.

108. Jeans 2009; Krebs 1996; Zacharias 1946; Matthews 1993, 22.

109. Allen 1987, 549.

110. Mercado 1994, 50.

111. U.S. Strategic Bombing Survey 1946, 50.

112. Statement of Lieutenant General Hoyt S. Vandenberg, director of central intelligence, before the Armed Services Committee of the U.S. Senate, 29 April 1947, regarding S.758, "The National Security Act of 1947." Note that the report of the Joint Congressional Committee on the Investigation of the Pearl Harbor Attack, established in September 1945, came to a different conclusion—that it was "impossible to credit them with superior intelligence." The statement and the report are both available at www.foia.cia.gov/collection/crest-25-year-program-archive.

113. On the openness of Pearl Harbor, see Farago 1967, 144. Everest-Phillips 2007, 248, credits Japan with superior tactical intelligence that was undermined by "limited analytical skills."

114. This account is based on Brown 1960, 25–30.

115. Katō 1998, 28.

116. Harris 1994, 96.

117. Everest-Phillips 2006, 263, speaks of Japan's "conspicuous" intelligence failure at Nomonhan. Brown 1960, 31, says that Nomonhan "revealed serious defects in organization and technique" in the Kwantung Army intelligence. See Drea 1984, 66, for more on how the intelligence failure at Nomonhan was emblematic of the IJA's "endemic" intelligence weaknesses. Barnhart 1984, 435, called Japan's performance

at Nomonhan "a useful illustration of the poor coordination between operational planning and intelligence gathering in prewar Japan."

118. Drea 1984, 66.

119. Coox 1992, 264.

120. Handō 2007, 196–200.

121. Iwashima 1984, 193.

122. Handō 2007, 196–200.

123. Kotani 2009c, 122, makes the distinction between effective tactical and ineffective strategic intelligence during the battle. Drea 1984, 66, calls Japan's Nomonhan tactical intelligence "simply inadequate."

124. Brown 1960, 32–33.

125. GHQ Intelligence Summary no. 1539, 4 July 1946, 11–12.

126. Brown 1960, 33.

127. Barnhart 1984, 435; Handō 1998, 196–200.

128. Drea 1984, 66; Handō 1998, 273, 276, 290–91.

129. Military History Section ed. 1955; Brown 1960.

130. Kotani 2009c, 100.

131. Elphick 1997, 41, reports that foreign military attachés routinely visited most imperial military installations well into the 1930s, but never the Nakano School. The most comprehensive study in English of the Nakano School is Mercado 2002. See also Katō 1998; Mercado 2002–3; GHQ Intelligence Summary no. 1545, 11 July 1946, 10; Kotani 2009c, 30–31; and Allen 1985, 9–10. See also the literature on the affiliated Noborito Research Institute, formally the Army Ninth Technical Research Institute, and the only research unit under the supervision of the IJA's Intelligence Department. Counterfeit currencies, phony identification papers, and much of the rest of the operatives' paraphernalia were manufactured in Noborito's labs. According to Mercado 2002, 3, Noborito "shap[ed] the tools for the military's war in the shadows."

132. Mercado 2002, 7, 23.

133. Katō 1998, 34.

134. GHQ Intelligence Summary no. 1546, 12 July, 1946, 11.

135. GHQ Intelligence Summary no. 1545, 12 July, 1946, 10.

136. On 13 August 1945 the Imperial Headquarters directed the Nakano School to establish an underground resistance organization, to be activated in the event that the occupying forces failed to preserve the Japanese national polity. See Katō 1998, 34.

137. Few, though, were commanded by Nakano School graduates, because by war's end the most senior grads were still only mid-level officers. For a comprehensive list of the special duty units and their commanding officers, see Nihon Kindaishi Kenkyūkai ed. 1989, 208–16. Fuller biographical details of Nakano School graduates are in Hata 1991.

138. Allen 1987, 558–59.

139. Seekins 1999. Mercado 2002, 52, reports that the effort to arm Aung San was launched "with great expectations [but] soon sank under the weight of inter-service rivalry and suspicion."

140. Strategic Services Unit ed. 1946, 48; Katō 1998, 81–84; Hansen 1996, 25.

141. Bennett, Hobart, and Spitzer 1986, 74–75.

142. Bennett, Hobart, and Spitzer 1986, 31. Direction of the INA was only part of their remit, which also included counterintelligence, propaganda, and collection and analysis of intelligence reports.

143. Fujiwara 1983, 5.

144. Fujiwara 1983, xii–xiv.

145. Fujiwara 1983, xviii.

146. The definitive study of the relationship of Bose and Fujiwara is Lebra 2008. Ogura 2015, 88–93, reports that the Japanese government eventually betrayed Bose, but his ashes have been kept in a Nichiren temple in Tokyo, and during his first official visit to India in 2007, Prime Minister Abe Shinzō visited the Bose family in Calcutta.

147. The Fujiwara Kikan was an eleven-man team led by Fujiwara plus five junior officers and one NCO, all Nakano School graduates. One of the Nakano grads, a First Lieutenant Yamaguchi, had Foreign Ministry cover, and another had cover as an employee of the trading company Dainan Kōshi. See Kuwada 1996, 225.

148. GHQ Intelligence Summary no. 1620, 8 October 1946, 9–10; GHQ Intelligence Summary no. 1568, 7 August 1946, 11.

149. Maruya 2012 is a fascinating study of the South Manchurian Railway Company's intelligence organization. He estimates that the number of intelligence analysts in the company rose from 1.7 percent of total employees in 1917 to 3.7 percent in 1932. By 1940, he estimates that it had more than 2,300 intelligence staff. See Maruya 2012, 3.

150. The OSS report is summarized by Sugita 1988, 265. The effectiveness of Tōa Dōbun Shoin as a source of intelligence professionals is also mentioned in a U.S. intelligence report that reviewed the capabilities of Japan's naval attachés during the war. See GHQ Intelligence Summary no. 1474, 19 April 1946, 10. See Brooks 1989 for more on Tōa Dōbun Shoin.

151. Reynolds 1989b, 19. Note also that the nationalist and pan-Asianist Ōkawa Shūmei, who was tried as a Class A war criminal by Occupation authorities, founded Japan's first school for tradecraft focused on Islamic peoples for MOFA in the late 1930s. See Jacob 2014, 121, and Aydin 2007.

152. Imperial Ordinance no. 542, dated 7 May 1946, was published in the *Official Gazette*, no. 27.

153. This is from Arisue 1982, his memoir. In chapter 3 we see how the resourceful and ambitious Arisue was able to avoid the postwar purge and insinuate himself into a privileged role with Occupation intelligence.

154. Kotani 2008, 49. Dōmei was broken up into Kyodo News and Jiji Press after the war.

155. Iwashima 1984, 131–39.

156. GHQ Intelligence Summary no. 1475 20 April 1946, 14.

157. Allen 1987, 557.

158. Mercado 1994, 50; Bennett, Hobart, and Spitzer 1986, 7, 18.

159. Allen 1987, 556.

160. Bennett, Hobart, and Spitzer 1986, 6; Kotani 2009c, 135, 315–16.

161. Bennett, Hobart, and Spitzer 1986, 9–10.

162. Kotani 2009c, 9, reports that OSINT accounted for more than half, even in the last half year of the war.

163. At war's end a cache of 100,000 ersatz IBM punch cards was found in the Cabinet Printing Office. See Allen 1987, 556.

164. Mercado 1994, 51–52.

165. Strategic Services Unit 1946, 118.

166. Military History Section ed. 1955.

167. Strategic Services Unit 1946, 184; Bennett, Hobart, and Spitzer 1986, 4–5, 60. Bennett, Hobart, and Spitzer do suggest, however, that coordination was possible when the portfolios of the Ministry of Foreign Affairs and of the Greater East Asia Ministry were held by the same minister.

168. Lieutenant General Oikawa's testimony before the International Military Tribunal for the Far East on 25 July 1946, MacArthur Memorial Archives, Norfolk, VA, GHQ/SCAP Records, IPS-16 R07: 0659–0660.

169. Lieutenant General Oikawa's testimony on 25 July 1946, MacArthur Memorial Archives, GHQ/SCAP Records, IPS-16 R07: 0660–0661.

170. Kuroi 2011, 120–21. See also *Japan Times*, 30 August 2007.

171. Kuroi 2011, 120–23. Amakasu was a "deposed officer turned adventurer" who worked with other adventurers to bomb the Japanese consulate in Harbin in 1931 in order to give the army an excuse to "restore order" in northern Manchuria. See Orbach 2018.

172. Kotani 2009c, 26.

173. The prewar numbers are from U.S. Strategic Bombing Survey 1946, 1. The late war numbers are from Kotani 2009c, 16.

174. Sugita 1988, 27.

175. Kotani 2009c, 96.

176. Allen 1987, 560, provides data. This does not seem entirely out of line with U.S. spending, though a comparison is difficult. There is no consolidated figure available for the total spent on military intelligence by the United States government during World War II, when total U.S. defense spending is estimated to have been nearly 40 percent of GDP. If we consider only the Office for Strategic Services, records show that its original (1941) budget was $10 million and that this increased to $43 million in 1945, when OSS had almost thirteen thousand employees—roughly the size of one army infantry division. During its four years of existence, OSS spent about $135 million, a bit more than $1 billion in today's dollars. Authorizing documents also show that its director's salary was limited to $10,000. See https://www.cia.gov/library/publications/intelligence-history/oss/art03.htm and https://www.cia.gov/library/readingroom/document/cia-rdp80-01240a000400090001-9.

177. Arisue 1982, 259–62. Bennett, Hobart, and Spitzer 1986, 116, suggest that "an appreciable amount" of the intelligence collected by Japanese officers in Europe and passed on to Tokyo was actually planted for the purpose of deception by Allied counterintelligence.

178. Bennett, Hobart, and Spitzer 1986, 55. Hansen 1996, 23–24, also identifies the conflation of propaganda and intelligence as a serious flaw in the Japanese system.

179. Kotani 2009c, 107; Kotani 2009b, 26.

180. These quotes from Japanese intelligence dispatches are reported in Kotani 2009b, 10, 12.

181. Coox 1992, 272–73; Kotani 2009c, 145–49. Iwashima 1984, 91–101, describes how Ambassador Ōshima's cable from Berlin to Tokyo about Germany's intention to attack the USSR was caught by the U.S. intelligence community, which then reported it to the British and the Soviets. But there is also the irony that in 1938 Ōshima dismissed Ribbentrop's private signals for the impending German-Soviet rapprochement as a bluff. See Suzuki 1979, 200.

182. Coox 1992, 274.

183. Coox 1992, 281. See Kotkin 2017 for Stalin's view of the prospects for Hitler's attack.

184. Coox 1992, 285.

185. Hori Eizō, an IJA intelligence officer, said that this delay may have resulted in the deaths of hundreds of thousands of Japanese soldiers. He is cited in Mercado 1994, 51. See also See Hori 1989, 134; Harries 1991, 377; and Mercado 1994, 50.

186. Drea 1984, 68.

187. U.S. Strategic Bombing Survey 1946, 46.

188. Bennett, Hobart, and Spitzer 1986, 55–56.

189. Hori 1989, 132.

190. Hori 1989, 130.

191. See Kotani 2009c, 151.

192. Kotani 2009c, 104–5.

193. Kotani 2009b, 26.

194. Bennett, Hobart, and Spitzer 1986, 101.

195. Sugita 1988, 251.

196. Sugita 1988, 251. According to the U.S. Strategic Bombing Survey 1946, 52, Japanese intelligence reported that fewer than one thousand U.S. troops were operating in the Guadalcanal campaign. The actual number was almost twenty thousand—nearly two marine divisions and two army battalions.

197. See "Japan Reaction to Our Conduct of the War in the Pacific," paper dated October 1945, MacArthur Memorial Archives, SCAP, Occupation of Japan Section, subseries 2, box 104, folder 2.

198. GHQ Intelligence Summary no. 1475, 20 April 1946, 13.

199. Kotani 2009a, 7.

200. "Brief of Interrogation of General Yamashita," MacArthur Memorial Archives, SCAP, Occupation Staff Sections, subseries 2, box 104, folder 2, and box 106, RG5, folder 6.

201. Arisue 1982, 262.

202. Kotani 2013, 189; Kotani 2009c, 98.

203. Kotani 2009c, 150; Inose, 2017.

204. GHQ Intelligence Summary no. 1475, 20 April 1946, 13.

205. Kotani 2009c, 162. Kotani 2005, 305–6, explains that within the same Imperial General Headquarters, the army General Staff and the navy General Staff operated separate code-breaking sections.

206. Kotani 2009c, 9.

207. Takahashi 1982, vi, xiv.

208. Kōketsu 2008, 17–19.

209. Zenkoku Kenyūkai Rengōkai Hensan Iinkai ed., 1976, 128.

210. Kōketsu 2008, 22.

211. Takahashi 1982, xv–xvi.

212. Kōketsu 2008, 26–31, 40–45.

213. Ōtani 1966, 377–80.

214. Hata 1991, 732; Kōketsu 2008, 24.

215. Kōketsu 2008, 49–50.

216. Estimates vary from 34,000 to 70,000 in total. See Ōtani 1966, 578–79, and Allen 1987, 553–54.

217. Zenkoku Kenyūkai Rengōkai Hensan Iinkai ed. 1976, 34; Ōtani 1966, 11.

218. Ogino 2012.

219. *Mainichi Shimbun*, 6 June 2014.

220. Whymant 1996, 54, 78–79.

221. Whymant 1996, 75, 78.

222. See the accounts in Johnson 1964 and in Andrew and Mitrokhin 2005. After the war, General Charles A. Willoughby made rooting out the remnants of the Sorge spy ring a priority. See MacArthur Memorial Archives, Papers of Charles A. Willoughby, series 3, Sensitive Material; and chapter 3 of this volume.

223. Saitō 1977, 263.

224. Hayashi, Wada, and Ōyagi 2011, 103, 108.

225. Mercado 2002, 4; Kotani 2009c, 20.

226. Mercado 2002–3.

227. Kotani 2009c, 88.

228. See Boyd 1993, Matthews 1993, Farago 1967, http://www.paperlessarchives.com/wwii-pearl-harbor-magic-files.html, and Iwashima 1984.

229. Drea and Richard 1999, 68.

230. Boyd 1993, 76–77.

231. For these judgments, see the U.S. Strategic Bombing Survey ed. 1946, 3; Bennett, Hobart, and Spitzer 1986, 32; and Murray cited in Kotani 2009c, viii.

232. Barnhart 1984 offers an exceptionally clear analysis of Japan's prewar intelligence failures. Also see Bennett, Hobart, and Spitzer 1986, 55–58, for their analysis.

3. Accommodating Defeat (1945–1991)

1. See Hansen 1996, 35, for "transformation" and Kotani 2009a, 1, for "discontinuity."

2. See the unsigned report titled "The Japanese Intelligence Service: Groups and Japanese National Revival Present and Future," dated 11 May 1951, in the U.S. National Archives CIA Names File—Hattori Takushirō, 14 (hereafter referred to as 11 May 1951 CIA Report).

3. Honda et al. 2005, 363.

4. Gotōda 1998, 1:230. The best account of postwar Japanese antimilitarism is Berger 1998. See Kaneko 2011 and Williams 2013a for concurrence regarding the ways in which postwar pacifist norms stunted the development of Japan's intelligence community.

5. For more on the Yoshida doctrine, see Samuels 2003a and Samuels 2007.

6. Johnson 1982 is the canonical "trans-war" history of Japan. See also Gordon 1985 and Samuels 1987.

7. PHP Kenkyūkai ed. 2006 and Kaneko 2011 are useful short histories of the evolution of the postwar Japanese intelligence community. See also Williams 2010.

8. Saitō 2005, 118, 121. Mercado 2002, 201, reports that they disguised Ba Naw as a Manchurian monk in a Niigata temple.

9. Saitō 2005, 158, 165.

10. Saitō 2011, 165–66, 195.

11. Petersen 2006, 199; U.S. National Archives Names File—Arisue Seizō, CIC document, 22 April 1946. See also Kaneko 2011, 301.

12. "Very clever turncoat" and the reference to Arisue's buried cash are from U.S. National Archives Names File—Arisue Seizō, CIC document, 22 April 1946. Terasaki Hidenari, the "diplomat and master spy" who directed MOFA's Information Bureau early in the Occupation and who worked as a liaison between SCAP and the imperial household to develop lists of war criminals, wondered why Arisue was never indicted. See Takemae 2002, 259.

13. The best accounts of this period—and the ones this section relies on—are Petersen 2006, the declassified 11 May 1951 CIA Report, Takemae 2002, and Mercado 2002.

14. "Sort of FBI" is from an undated memo edited by Willoughby in MacArthur Memorial Archives Series K–L Box 18, 17. The prophylactic is from Willoughby and Chamberlain 1954, 322.

15. His connection to Spanish fascists was already well established before the war. Kluckhohn 1952, reports that in 1936 Willoughby was toasted by the secretary general of the Spanish Falangist Party, who declared, "I am happy to know a fellow Falangist and reactionary."

16. General Willoughby's papers are archived at Gettysburg College in Pennsylvania, and copies are held at the MacArthur Memorial Archives. In series K–L, box 18, see his 25 September 1946 memo to General MacArthur's chief of staff warning of "varying degrees of leftist infiltration into GHQ" and singling out Thomas Bisson, Eleanor Hadley, and Theodore Cohen, all of whom later became well-known Japan scholars.

17. Takemae 2002, 162; Willoughby 1973, 136–37.

18. Willoughby 1973, 140–42.

19. Takemae 2002, 161.

20. MacArthur's' characterization is reported by Kowalski 2013, 58. See Bar-Joseph and McDermott 2017, 177–83, and Haynes 2009 for analyses of Willoughby's shortcomings as an intelligence officer.

21. Mercado 2002, 197.

22. Kowalski 2013, 56.

23. On Willoughby's protection of Arisue, see Mercado 2002, 203, and Prados 2006, 49–52. See Van Hook 2006 and le Carré 2016 on Gehlen.

24. Takemae 2002, 52; Drea 2011, 40.

25. In 1939, then Colonel Arisue, the IJA's military attaché in Rome, proposed a joint Japanese-Italian Islamic policy to Mussolini's government by which Japan would dispatch agents to Egypt, the Arabian Peninsula, and Persia to counterbalance China's inroads. The Italian government was not interested. U.S. National Archives Names File—Arisue Seizō dated 11 June 1944.

26. Willoughby recounts the pre-surrender meeting but mentions only Kawabe, who also attended. See Willoughby and Chamberlain 1954, 293. Kawabe took over the Manaki Kikan in Estonia in 1939. See Masunaga 2017, 46.

27. According to a 15 September 1959 CIA report in U.S. National Archives CIA Names File—Arisue Seizō, Willoughby authorized the formation of a "Kawabe Kikan" in late 1948. See also Mori 2008 and Yuasa 2013.

28. Takemae 2002, 53; Mori 2008, 54–55. Mercado 2002, 190–91, reports that Arisue was also protected by an old acquaintance, Colonel Frederick P. Munson, who had been a Japanese language officer attached to an IJA field artillery unit in 1935–36. Munson, an aide to General Joseph Stillwell during the war, helped "run interference" for Arisue when he met resistance from General Whitney.

29. Takemae 2002, 165.

30. Petersen 2006, 208, 211; U.S. National Archives CIA Names File—Arisue Seizō, 29 February 1952 report; 11 May 1951 CIA Report, 26. For more on Watanabe's strong-arm philosophy of military occupation, see Akashi and Yoshimura 2008. For more on Kodama's background from the perspective of the Occupation, see the declassified CIA file at https://www.cia.gov/library/readingroom/docs/KODAMA%2C%20YOSHIO%20%20%20VOL.%201_0004.pdf.

31. Drea 2011, 40.

32. Mercado 2002, 212–14; Takemae 2002, 165.

33. Charles A. Willoughby, "Demobilization of Japanese Armed Forces," page 2 of the report found in MacArthur Memorial Archives, SCAP, Occupation Staff Sections, subseries 2, box 104, folder 6.

34. Petersen 2006, 199.

35. MacArthur Memorial Archives Index to Daily Intelligence Summaries, March 1946–June 1948 box 77, RG box 6, folder 1.

36. Interview, former Japanese government official, 4 April 2016, Tokyo.

37. A 20 May 1949 CIA report on the Takematsu operation is in the U.S. National Archives CIA Names File—Arisue Seizō. See also Petersen 2006, 203–4.

38. These maps were by then in the office of General H. J. Casey.

39. Arima 2010a, 80–85; Arima 2014, 61–65. Mercado 2002, 220, reports that by 1951, more than fifty Japanese veterans were in this group, and the unit continued to be active until 1964 with covert U.S. support. This plan involved a so-called "White Unit" (Paidan), a preparatory group that arrived in Taiwan before the Giyūgun. See Arima 2014, 107, 136–37, and the 20 May 1949 CIA report in U.S. National Archives CIA Names File—Arisue Seizō.

40. Arima 2014, 108–9; 11 May 1951 CIA Report, 22; Takemae 2002, 166, 489.

41. This account is from a 20 May 1949 CIA report in U.S. National Archives CIA Names File—Arisue Seizō. See also Petersen 2006, 205.

42. The "current activities" of U.S.-supported Japanese agents are reviewed in a 13 November 1950 CIA report in the U.S. National Archives CIA Names File—Arisue Seizō. The Taiwan operations had to be rolled up when their operator, the Kawaguchi Kikan, had its cover blown in August 1950.

43. See the 14 September 1950 CIA report "The Fourth Expedition to Formosa" in the U.S. National Archives CIA Names File—Arisue Seizō.

44. See Mercado 2002, 223–32, on the Inchon landing.

45. Petersen 2006, 203–5; Drea 2011, 42.

46. 11 May 1951 CIA Report, 26.

47. 11 May 1951 CIA Report, 44.

48. Quoted in Kuroi 2009b, 220.

49. U.S. National Archives CIA Names File—Arisue Seizō, documents dated 25 October 1949 and 3 August 1950.

50. U.S. National Archives CIA Names File—Arisue Seizō FBZ64, undated, unsigned.

51. Petersen 2006, 206, says that U.S. intelligence was "badly compromised between 1945–1952, though it is uncertain to what extent Willoughby realized this," despite an investigation by the Strategic Services Unit in 1946 designed to be "on guard for peacetime organizing" by demobilized Japanese military officers. See Strategic Services Unit ed. 1946, 2.

52. MacArthur Memorial Archives, Papers of Charles A. Willoughby, series 3, Sensitive Material, 62.

53. Araki, for her part, reportedly was providing information from Willoughby to the Japanese government. See Petersen 2006, 206, and Drea 2011, 41.

54. Petersen 2006, 205–7.

55. Petersen 2006, 201. Mercado 2002, 211, 232, and Williams 2013, 142, offer a more positive evaluation of the contributions to U.S. policy made by Japanese agents.

56. The report noted that the skills and motivations of these informants also served them well as smugglers and black marketers. 11 May 1951 CIA Report, 15–16.

57. The Maritime Safety Agency was stood up in May 1948 to intercept smuggling from the Korean Peninsula but was often unable to keep up with smugglers and pirates. See Wile 1981, 38. It was not mentioned in the CIA report.

58. All direct quotations in this paragraph are from 11 May 1951 CIA Report, 1–2.

59. Untitled CIA report dated 29 June 1951 in U.S. National Archives CIA Names File—Arisue Seizō. See also 11 May 1951 CIA Report, 56, inter alia.

60. Drea 2011, 44.

61. Untitled CIA report dated 14 September 1950 in U.S. National Archives CIA Names File—Arisue Seizō and Petersen 2006, 206. Note how the cultural differences between these service branches persisted across the war and Japan's defeat. See Heginbotham 2003.

62. This Fuji School in Shizuoka was where Mishima Yukio and his "troops" received military training long after Sugita retired. See the discussion later in this chapter.

63. Handō 2007, 126–27.

64. Mercado 2002, 210; Mori 2008, 52; Arima 2010b, 179–80.

65. Drea 2011, 42–43; Handō 2007, 126–27.

66. CIA report dated 7 March 1952 in U.S. National Archives CIA Names File—Hattori Takushirō; "Statements by Hattori Takushirō Regarding his Activities and Relationship," CIA report dated July 1951 in U.S. National Archives CIA Names File—,Hattori Takushirō.

67. CIA report dated 18 April 1952 in U.S. National Archives CIA Names File—Hattori Takushirō; Drea 2011, 42–43.

68. Kowalski 2013, 57–59.

69. CIA report dated 18 April 1952 in U.S. National Archives CIA Names File—Hattori Takushirō; Arima 2010b, 180.

70. "Statements by Hattori Takushirō Regarding His Activities and Relationship," CIA report dated July 1951 in U.S. National Archives CIA Names File—Hattori Takushirō, 1. Kowalski 2013 is a rare and excellent first-person account of the Willoughby-Hattori episode.

71. See the declassified April 1952 CIA report accessible as document no. 519c d81f993294098d5169a7 at www.foia.cia.gov. Also see Yuasa 2013, chap. 10, for more

on Tatsumi, a former Japanese military attaché in London and confidant of Yoshida who U.S. officials expected would become the leader of Japan's postwar intelligence community.

72. 17 July 1953 CIA report in U.S. National Archives CIA Names File—Hattori Takushirō. See also "Information Report" dated "prior to 17 September 1952," and accessible as document no. 519cd81f993294098d5169e2 at www.foia.cia.gov. Arima Tetsuo, a Japanese scholar who examined this report closely, believes it was based on disinformation planted by Hattori's aide Tsuji Masanobu to intimidate Yoshida. See Arima 2010d, 130–38.

73. Petersen 2006, 214–15. Tsuji, who had instigated the 1939 Nomonhan incident described in chapter 2 and was regarded as one of the IJA's most bellicose strategists, later became a Diet member. He disappeared in Southeast Asia in 1961 under mysterious circumstances on what he described as a mission for the prime minister. See Kyodo, 26 July 2000.

74. The account in this paragraph is based on the 11 May 1951 CIA Report, 36.

75. Petersen 2006, 215.

76. *Asahi Shimbun*, 19 May 1954.

77. Shinoda 2006, 94, puts the staff size at seven. Kaneko 2011, 304–5, puts it at thirty. Yanase 2013 provides a history of the organizational changes in the postwar Japanese intelligence community. See also Ōmori 2005, 36–38, and Arima 2010b, 184. If the name of this office seems a bit nondescript, it is worth recalling that the original name of the CIA's covert operations division was the Office of Policy Coordination. See Andrew 1995, 173.

78. Arima 2010a, 164.

79. See Yuasa 2013, 345–46.

80. Yoshida 2012, 153–54; Arima 2010b, 171; Kaneko 2011, 304–5. Morris-Suzuki 2014, 5, reports that Ogata, who had been purged by SCAP for his association with the Imperial Rule Assistance Association, was a key CIA informant, and that among other emoluments, he received funds from the agency to pay for his son's college education in the United States. See also Williams 2013a, 154, and Williams 2018.

81. Interview, senior government official, 15 January 2015, Tokyo.

82. Williams 2013a, 147; Arima 2010b, 185.

83. Yuasa 2013, 348–53.

84. Yuasa 2013, 358.

85. Williams 2013a, 153; Katō 1998; Saitō 2005.

86. See Williams 2013a, 150. Canon and Yeong each made this accusation. For more on Murai's difficulties with competing agencies, see the May 1953 declassified CIA document no. 519cd81b993294098d516178, accessible at http://www.foia.cia.gov. Yuasa 2013, chap. 10, describes the fuller range of Murai's political enemies.

87. Yuasa 2013, 360–61.

88. Jourdonnais 1963, 1. See also Shinoda 2006, 94.

89. For a short but powerful critique of CIRO, see *Sentaku*, December 2011, https://www.sentaku.co.jp/articles/view/11178. For more contemporary reports of CIRO's involvement in domestic political investigations unrelated to national security, see *Sankei Shimbun*, 9 May 2009; *Yomiuri Shimbun*, 3 September 2007; *Yomiuri Shimbun*, 2 May 2015; and *Asahi Shimbun*, 27 July 2018.

90. MOFA's unwillingness to share cables is from former CIRO director Ōmori Yoshio. See Ōmori 2005, 36–38, and Shinoda 2006, 105–6.

91. Hansen 1996, 68; Williams 2010, 163. "Laughingstock" and "world's worst" are from *Sentaku,* December 2011.

92. Weiner 1994 reports that Gotōda was on the CIA payroll.

93. Shinoda 2007, 36.

94. Shinoda 2000, 10 and 72; Shinoda 2007, 32.

95. Gotōda 1998, 1:237.

96. *Tokyo Shimbun,* 4 July 2006.

97. "Hollow" is from Martin 2016, 13. "Barely functional" is from Kotani 2013, 182.

98. Kotani 2009a, 9. Kotani's account was confirmed in a 15 January 2016 interview in Tokyo with a retired senior official who participated in this process. See also Farson 1997.

99. Fuke 2016.

100. Kaneko 2011, 303.

101. Uyehara 2010.

102. Jourdonnais 1963. Kaneko 2011, 302–3, lists the various Occupation-authorized units in the Home Ministry and Justice Agency that were forerunners of the PSIA. The estimate of the number of Nakano School graduates is from interview, PSIA official, 17 October 2017, Tokyo.

103. Oros 2002, 7–8.

104. Interview, PSIA official, 17 October 2017, Tokyo. See also Jourdonnais 1963, 4.

105. Williams, 2018, 22, reports the U.S. agents practiced "poor tradecraft," including use of unsecured equipment.

106. Interview, PSIA official, 17 October 2017, Tokyo.

107. Interview, PSIA official, 17 October 2017, Tokyo.

108. *Zaibatsu* were the financial/industrial combines that dominated the Japanese economy before and during the war, and that were dissolved during the Occupation.

109. 11 May 1951 CIA Report, 26.

110. 11 May 1951 CIA Report, 18.

111. Kaneko 2007, 127.

112. Ōmori 2005, 103–6.

113. Kaneko 2007, 29.

114. PHP Kenkyūkai ed. 2006, 32.

115. Kaneko 2007, 129.

116. *Asahi Shimbun,* 10 January 1980.

117. Okazaki became the first head of the new bureau. See Kuroi 2008, 247–48, 256.

118. Shinoda 2006, 97; Kaneko 2011, 303.

119. *Asahi Shimbun,* 30 July 2000.

120. Interview, former CEO and chair of JETRO Hayashi Yasuo, 12 October 2017, Tokyo. This "special relationship" was also identified by a former Japanese ambassador and deputy CIRO director. Interview, 20 September 2017.

121. Interview, former CEO and chair of JETRO Hayashi Yasuo, 12 October 2017, Tokyo. Examples of Western identification of JETRO as an intelligence unit are found at Johnson 1982, 230; Deacon 1983, 254; and Sheehan 1996, 60, inter alia. See Taoka 1994 for analysis in Japanese that places JETRO in the Japanese intelligence community.

122. Andrew and Mitrokhin 2005, 307–8; Levchenko 1988, 102.

123. These were the regulations of the Coordinating Committee for Multilateral Export Controls that governed technology transfer from the western to the eastern bloc during the Cold War. For more on this case, see Kelley 1989 and Andrew and Mitrokhin 2005, 311.

124. Kuroi 2009a, 204.

125. Ao 2009, 82. See also Katō 1998, 100–102. For reminiscences of early commandants of this academy, see Kuroi 2009a, 200, 202.

126. Kuroi 2009a, 200.

127. Matsumoto 2008, 150.

128. Ao 2009, 83.

129. See chapter 2 for more on Fujiwara, and see the discussion later in this chapter for more on Yamamoto. Also see Ao 2009, 83, and Kuroi 2009a, 195.

130. Saitō 2005, 172–73, 174, 177–79; Ao 2009, 85. Its elite graduates formed an alumni association called Aogirikai, or Aogiri Gurūpu, to maintain contact with one another in the event of future mobilization.

131. Akahata Tokusōhan ed. 1978, 228–29, 248–50, 277.

132. Jourdonnais 1963, 5.

133. Kuroi 2009b, 220.

134. Interview in Kuroi 2009a, 198.

135. Hirajō 2010, 142.

136. Satō 2012, 89–94.

137. Kuroi 2009a, 202. It was based on a U.S. model and formally called the Military Intelligence Service Organization. See the account by Satō 2012, 97.

138. Kuroi 2009a, 194.

139. This is according to Tsukamoto Shōichi, former GSDF G-2 commander, in Kuroi 2009a, 196.

140. This is the view of Tsukamoto Shōichi, former GSDF G-2 commander, in Kuroi 2009a, 196.

141. Daitoku 2014, 10.

142. Kuroi 2009a, 200; Kuroi 2009b, 221; Weiner 1994.

143. Matsumoto 2008, 103–4.

144. Interview in Kuroi 2009a, 198.

145. Kuroi 2009a, 199.

146. Levchenko 1988, 81, 116.

147. This complaint has been leveled by many, including Kōno, Mabuchi, and Yamauchi 2013, 100.

148. Uyehara 2010; *Christian Science Monitor*, 21 December 1982; Levchenko 1988.

149. Williams 2013b, 498, 500. He notes that bilateral agreements with the United States contained state secret law penalties far tougher than domestic legislation. The United States penalized both the seeking and leaking of state secrets, whereas Japanese law addressed only the latter.

150. For Rastvorov, see *Yomiuri Shimbun*, 5 February 1954, and the *Washington Post*, 15 January 2006. For the USSR-JCP connection, see Andrew and Mitrokhin, 2005, 297–98. They also report Soviet plans to generate crises in U.S.-Japanese relations by fomenting an attack on the American Cultural Center during an anti-Vietnam rally in 1965 and by scattering radioactive material in Tokyo Bay with the expectation that it would be blamed on the U.S. Navy.

151. Kotani 2013, 193; Williams, 2013b, 494–95. After defecting, he worked for the CIA and even married his handler. See his obituary at https://groups.google.com/forum/#!topic/alt.obituaries/7C7LXTykBRQ.

152. Keisatsuchō ed. 1981, chap. 8, sec. 1.

153. This account is based on Levchenko 1988; UPI.com, "Defector Details KGB Activity in Japan," 11 December 1982, http://www.upi.com/Archives/1982/12/11/Defector-details-KGB-activity-in-Japan/2938408430800/; *Kokkai Kaigiroku* [Diet Records], House of Representatives, Justice Committee, session 98, no. 10, 25 May 1983, 1–26; and Trahair 2004, 166–67. For General Willoughby's account of earlier postwar Soviet subversion in Japan, see Willoughby and Chamberlain 1954, 322–27.

154. Andrew and Mitrokhin 2005, 304.

155. Andrew and Mitrokhin 2005, 303–4.

156. Levchenko 1988, 89. He claims that twenty-five full-time Soviet intelligence officers worked on extracting scientific and technical information alone (89). He also claims to have had access to MOFA intelligence files (91).

157. This "declaration" is oft cited but likely apocryphal. But in his memoirs Levchenko did describe Japan as a "treasure trove" of useful information for the KGB, adding that the KGB "systematically drained what it needed from Japan." Levchenko 1988, 99. Also see remarks by Hideo Yamada, government delegate, in Kokkai Kaigiroku [Diet Records], House of Representatives, Justice Committee, session 98, no. 10, 25 May 1983, 5.

158. Andrew and Mitrokhin 2005, 302.

159. See Weiner 1994, Samuels 2003a, and Petersen 2006, 219–20.

160. The U.S. side only learned of the code name "Musashi Kikan" after it ceased to be used in 1965. Note too that there have been several names assigned to this secret unit: Ground Staff Office Second Department Special Unit (Rikubaku Dainibu Beppan), Ground Staff Office Intelligence Department First Intelligence Office Special Unit (Rikubaku Nibu Jōhō Ippan Tokkinhan), and Ground Staff Office Intelligence Department Special Unit (Rikujō Bakuryō Kanbu Dainibu Tokubetsu Kinmuhan). The official name in English was the Military Intelligence Specialist Training. See Hirajō 2010, 182, and Akahata Tokusōhan 1978.

161. Hirajō 2010, 3; *Asahi Shimbun*, 20 July 2009; Kuroi 2009c, 232–39.

162. *Asahi Shimbun*, 1 August 2010.

163. Tsukamoto 2008, 179.

164. Hirajō 2010, 191.

165. See his interview in Kuroi 2009b, 220. He also points out that it was Japanese intelligence that instructed the United States to look for bicycles along the Ho Chi Minh Trail rather than trucks—"something the U.S. military could not even imagine."

166. Kuroi 2009b, 226.

167. Hirajō 2010, 138.

168. *Asahi Shimbun*, 6 June 2009.

169. Unless otherwise indicated, Ao 2009 is the rich source for the next three paragraphs.

170. Sejima, a graduate of the elite Imperial War College, was rumored to have been a direct pipeline to the Soviets for years after the war. Interview, former MOFA

official, 21 September 2017, Tokyo. See chapter 4 for more on Sejima's role in rebuilding the Japanese intelligence community.

171. *Asahi Shimbun*, 1 August 2010; Hirajō 2010, 192–97. This was equivalent to $2,777 in current dollars.

172. *Asahi Shimbun*, 6 June 2009.

173. Hirajō 2010, 182–85.

174. Hirajō 2010, 209; Satō 2012, 101.

175. See Tsukamoto 2008, Matsumoto 2008, Ao 2009, and Hirajō 2010. Kuroi 2009a and 2009b are fascinating interviews with several of these men.

176. Kuroi 2009b, 222.

177. Akahata Tokusōhan ed. 1978, 104–8. Also see Kokkai Kaigiroku [Diet Records], House of Councillors, Budgetary Committee, session 77, no. 5, 27 April 1976, 32.

178. Kokkai Kaigiroku [Diet Records], House of Councillors, Budgetary Committee, session 77, no. 5, 27 April 1976, 32.

179. Kokkai Kaigiroku [Diet Records], House of Councillors, Budgetary Committee, session 77, no. 10, 8 May 1976, 24.

180. Kokkai Kaigiroku [Diet Records], House of Councillors, Budgetary Committee, session 80, no. 8, 29 March 1977, 23–25.

181. Kokkai Kaigiroku [Diet Records], House of Councillors, Budgetary Committee, session 80, no. 22, 16 April 1977, 8–13.

182. Hirajō 2010, 150–51.

183. Kuroi 2009b, 225.

184. Kuroi 2009b, 222.

185. Hirajō 2010, 192. Hirajō recalls that their distaste for reporting to the U.S. military was one of his agents' main complaints—alongside the sacrifices required of their families and the limited funds available to support their operations (198). He suspects that it was agents dissatisfied with having to report to U.S. counterparts who leaked information about Musashi Kikan to *Akahata* (212).

186. Interview, 5 October 2017, Tokyo.

187. Kaneko 2011, 304, reports that by 1953, the U.S. Ōi station was being supported secretly by multiple Japanese civilian intelligence units.

188. *Asahi Shimbun*, 21 September 2004.

189. The name of this unit was changed in 1978 to Rikujō Bakuryō Kanbu Chōsa Dainika, also called the Chōsa Besshitsu or Chōbetsu. One of these facilities was the one that intercepted the Soviet communications in the Korean Airliner case described later in this chapter.

190. Ball and Tanter 2015a.

191. *Asahi Shimbun*, 21 September 2004.

192. Hirajō 2010, 143.

193. Much of the information here is from *Asahi Shimbun*, 23 September 2004.

194. Interview, retired MSDF officer, 9 January 2016, Tokyo.

195. *Shokun*, 1 December 1998.

196. This account is based on an interview with Sassa Atsuyuki, former director of cabinet security affairs, published in *Shokun*, 1 December 1998.

197. *Smena*, 18 January 2007.

198. Martin 2016, 7.

199. Interview, 17 December 2015, Tokyo.

200. *Shokun*, 1 December 1998, 103.

201. This account is based on Ōkoda 2001; Kotani 2013; Defense White Paper 1977, chap. 4; Satō 2012, 21–35; and interview with a retired senior military officer, 16 December 2015, Tokyo.

202. Hersh 2018, 266, reports that in their eagerness to accuse the Soviets of a heinous crime, U.S. politicians knowingly misrepresented the intelligence they had received from Japan.

203. This account is based on Gallagher 2017, 1–3, and Satō 2012, 40–61. Reference to the "retiring group of cryptologists" is from the NSA document, dated 19 July 2006, "Back in Time: The KAL-007 Shootdown," attached to Gallagher 2017. See also *Asahi Shimbun*, 21 September 2004, and Shinoda 2006.

204. Kuroi 2007, 120.

205. Kuroi 2007, 122–25; Kuroi ed. 2009, 346–47.

206. Kokkai Kaigiroku [Diet Records], House of Councillors, Audit Committee, session 140, no. 2, 1 May 1997, 5–6. Also see Kuroi ed. 2009a, 352; and chapter 4 of this volume.

207. *Asahi Shimbun*, 21 September 2004.

208. *Asahi Shimbun*, 21 September 2004 and 19 July 2013.

209. *Gunji Kenkyū*, September 2006, 80.

210. Kaneko 2007, 130.

211. *Asahi Shimbun*, 8 May 1987.

212. Kuroi 2007, 187.

213. See Scott-Stokes 1974 for a biography of Mishima. See also Yamamoto 1980, Kuroi 2009b, and *Asahi Shimbun*, 20 July 2009.

214. This account is based on Yamamoto 1980. See also Hirajō 2010.

215. Ao 2009, 230–31. Hirajō 2010, 215–16, claims to have been shocked by the abduction but does acknowledge the involvement of Tsuboyama, one of his former subordinates. Akahata Tokusōhan ed. 1978, 41–60.

216. Ao 2009, 230–31; Oberdorfer 1997, 43; *Washington Post*, 23 February 2003.

217. *Asahi Shimbun*, 29 June 2013.

218. *Asahi Shimbun*, 29 June 2013.

219. *Asahi Shimbun*, 29 June 2013; Akahata Tokusōhan ed. 1978, 4, 53.

220. Ao 2009, 230–31.

221. Kuroi 2011, 362–64.

222. *Asahi Shimbun*, 29 June 2013.

223. Sassa 2103, 167–68.

224. Williams 2013b, 496–97; Kaneko 2011, 305.

225. *Asahi Shimbun*, 8 June 1985; *Mainichi Shimbun*, 3 August 2014; Kaneko 2011, 305–7.

226. Hoshi 2013 argues that the Designated State Secrets Law of 2013 was modeled on this failed initiative. See chapter 5 in this volume. Also see Williams 2013b.

227. *Asahi Shimbun*, 22 October 1985.

228. *Asahi Shimbun*, 22 October 1985.

229. *Asahi Shimbun*, 6 April 1987.

230. Interview, 15 December 2015.

231. Gotōda is interviewed in Honda et al. eds. 2005, 365.

232. Kuroi 2005b, 236.

233. 11 May 1951 CIA Report, 62.

234. "Fierce rivalries" is from Petersen 2006, 202.

235. Interview, 15 December 2015, Tokyo.

236. Nishihiro is quoted in Sanger 1992.

237. 11 May 1951 CIA Report, 66.

238. This term is variously attributed to Russian spies originating with Yuri Rast-vorov and Stanislav Levchenko, but was still being used in 2006 by Suganuma Mitsuhiro, a retired chief of the PSIA's second division. His speech at the Foreign Correspondents' Press Club is available at https://www.youtube.com/watch?v=WA1X2gCImbQ. Hastings 2018, 50, reminds us that Soviet agents enjoyed a similarly "free range" of access in the United States for at least a half decade after the end of World War II.

239. Kotani 2013, 181.

240. Kaneko 2011, 300.

241. Kaneko 2011, 308.

242. I am grateful to Mayumi Fukushima for reminding me of this point.

243. Supreme Commander of the Allied Powers, General Matthew B. Ridgway, to CIA Director, General Walter B. Smith, 14 April 1952, declassified Top Secret document CIA-RDP80B01676R004000130052–9.

4. Tinkering with Failure (1991–2001)

1. For the connection between the end of the Cold War and the fall of the LDP, see Samuels 2003a, chap. 10.

2. Gotōda was well ahead of his contemporaries in many critical policy areas. In addition to intelligence reform, he pioneered electoral reform and political control of the bureaucracy, major policy changes that were taken up by subsequent prime ministers over the next four decades, most notably by Hashimoto Ryūtarō, Koizumi Junichirō, and Abe Shinzō. For more on Gotōda, see the undated newsletter of the Kokusai Ryūgakusei Kyōkai, "Gotōda Masaharu," http://ifsa.jp/index.php?Ggotoda. Also see Shinoda 2000, Shinoda 2007, and Shinoda 2013.

3. The full list of its members is available on the website of the prime minister's office, http://www.kantei.go.jp/jp/gyokaku/report-final/3.html.

4. See http://paperroom.ipsa.org/papers/paper_5412.pdf. For more on the earlier administrative reform efforts, see Samuels 2003b.

5. Gotōda refers to Nishihiro as "Mr. JDA." See the interview in Honda et al. eds. 2005, 363–65.

6. See Kasai 1996.

7. Emphasis added. For the full text, see http://japan.kantei.go.jp/971228final report.html.

8. Kokka Anzen . . . Yūshikisha Kaigai ed. 2014.

9. These quotes and the rest of the text of the Administrative Reform Council Final Report of 3 December 1997 is available at http://www.kantei.go.jp/jp/gyokaku/report-final/II.html.

10. *Asahi Shimbun*, 16 January 1998. Maruya 2005 provides a chorus of criticisms of Japan's postwar intelligence efforts; see 134.

11. Kaneko 2007, 138. The Joint Intelligence Committee (Gōdō Jōhō Kaigi) origi-nated in July 1986, convening officials at the director general level from relevant intel-ligence ministries and agencies.

12. "Guideline for Promoting the Restructuring of Central Government Orga-nizations," 27 April 1999, chap. 4, available at https://www.kantei.go.jp/jp/cyuo-syocho/990427honbu/housin.html.

13. The "Guideline" did not specifically make this recommendation. Kaneko 2007, 138.

14. Interview, 1 October 2017, Tokyo.

15. Kaneko 2007, 138.

16. The MOFA official is cited in *Asahi Shimbun*, 21 September 2004, and the analyst in Sheehan 1996, 64–65.

17. *Asahi Shimbun*, 21 September 2004.

18. Nakanishi 2011, 22.

19. One former MOFA official who was head of the North Korea desk insists that Sejima was also instrumental in helping the Soviets prop up the nascent Democratic People's Republic of Korea as a buffer state. Interview, Harada Takeo, 21 Septem-ber 2017, Tokyo.

20. Sejima 1996.

21. "Mysterious" is from an interview with a PSIA official, 3 October 2017, Tokyo. "Actual" and "invisible" are from an interview with former diplomat Harada Takeo, 21 September 2017, Tokyo.

22. The direct quotes from Sejima in this paragraph are from an interview in *AERA*, 24 January 1994, 32.

23. *AERA*, 24 January 1994, 32.

24. Kaneko 2007, 135.

25. See chap. 4, section 1 in MOFA *Diplomatic Bluebook*, 1992, https://www.mofa.go.jp/policy/other/bluebook/1992/1992-contents.htm; and *Asahi Shimbun*, 17 January 1994.

26. Taoka, 1994, 27.

27. MOFA, *Diplomatic Bluebook*, 1991, http://www.mofa.go.jp/policy/other/bluebook/1991/1991-5.htm.

28. The 1998 edition is a useful example. See http://www.mofa.go.jp/policy/other/bluebook/1998/V.html.

29. This system persisted until May 2003. See Kuroi 2005b, 240. Taoka 1994, 8, reports that there were thirty-eight defense attachés in thirty embassies as of 1994. Note that the U.S. system works very differently. U.S. defense attachés report through Defense Intelligence Agency channels, subject to review by their ambassador, who normally sees their cables after they are sent. Private conversation, Ambassador Chas Freeman, 6 December 2017.

30. Kuroi 2008, 250.

31. There were rumors that the Hashimoto government gave official develop-ment assistance to China for a hospital to keep the scandal quiet. The woman's father was said to have been promoted to ambassador to India. See http://www.indepen dent.co.uk/news/sleaze-scandal-japanese-style-lets-forget-it-1294428.html.

32. Shigeta 2006, 294.

33. Ōmori 2005, 45–46.

34. This account is based on Shibata 1994 and Akimoto 2012.

35. Interview by Mayumi Fukushima, 9 January 2016, Tokyo.

36. Taoka 1994; Ishihara 1995, 47–60.

37. See Ōmori 2005, 145–47, and Ishihara 1995, 51. Taoka 1994 also documents the continued dependence of the Japanese intelligence community on U.S. intelligence.

38. Satō 2010, 101.

39. See Williams 2010, 163.

40. For more on the Tokyo and Kobe quakes, see Samuels 2013, chap. 3.

41. Asō 2003, 114, details the "ossification of Japan's administrative structure."

42. Tierney and Goltz 1997, 5.

43. Taoka 1994, 27; interview by Mayumi Fukushima, 15 January 2016, Tokyo.

44. Ōmori 2005, 50–52.

45. Ōmori 2005, 53–54.

46. Taoka 1994, 27, reviews these. The list includes the Sekai Chōsakai for information on North Korea, the Tōnan Ajia Chōsakai, and the Minshushugi Kenkyūkai.

47. Kaneko 2007, 120, 135.

48. Asō 2001, 203–4; *Asahi Shimbun*, 17 January 1994; Taoka 1994, 28.

49. Kotani 2013, 185.

50. Subversive Activities Prevention Act, or Act no. 240 of 21 July 1952, available at http://www.japaneselawtranslation.go.jp/law/detail/?id=1982&vm=04& re=01.

51. Interview, 17 October 2017, Tokyo. For more on the politics of Soka Gakkai, see Ehrhardt et al. eds. 2014.

52. Handa 1999, 14–20, 47–49.

53. Interview, 17 October 2017, Tokyo.

54. Handa 1999, 26–27. Matsumoto was executed in July 2018.

55. *Asahi Shimbun*, 1 February 1997.

56. *Asahi Shimbun*, 1 June 1999 and 3 December 1999.

57. *Asahi Shimbun*, 7 December 1999.

58. Mizuno had been head of the Management and Coordination Agency and chairman of the LDP's General Council.

59. Administrative Reform Council, "Final Report," published 3 December 1997, chap. 3, available at http://www.kantei.go.jp/jp/gyokaku/report-final/.

60. Tanaka and Okada 2000, 168–69; Asō 2001, 206.

61. Administrative Reform Council, "Final Report," published 3 December 1997, chap. 3, available at http://www.kantei.go.jp/jp/gyokaku/report-final/.

62. Interview, PSIA official, 3 October 2017, Tokyo.

63. There were 1,742 PSIA personnel in 1997. The planned reduction of government personnel was part of a "Cabinet Decision on the Restructuring of Central Government Organizations," 27 April 1999, available at http://www.kantei.go.jp/jp/kakugikettei/990524sosiki.html. The 11 percent reduction was required in addition to the planned reduction of total government personnel by 25 percent in ten years. Also see *Asahi Shimbun*, 14 April 1999.

64. Central Government Organizations Reform Promotion Headquarters, "Guideline for Promoting the Restructuring of Central Government Organizations on April 27, 1999," chap. I, available at http://www.kantei.go.jp/jp/cyuo-syocho/990427honbu/housin.html.

65. A PSIA official insists that the PSIA is "basically a domestic organization, but some agents travel abroad." He reminds us that the PSIA was involved abroad as soon as it was stood up in 1952 because the communist movement it was designed to monitor was a global activity directed from Moscow. Much but not all the information agents collected on the Soviet Union was harvested from repatriated Japanese soldiers. Interview, 3 October 2017, Tokyo.

66. *Asahi Shimbun*, 17 January 1994; Taoka 1994, 28.

67. Kotani 2009a, 4; Kotani 2013, 185; interview, PSIA official, 3 October 2017, Tokyo.

68. Williams 2010, 166.

69. For the 1988 version, see http://www.clearing.mod.go.jp/hakusho_data/1988/w1988_03.html.

70. As we shall see, this changed suddenly in 1998, when Japanese intelligence failed to anticipate a North Korean long-range Taepodong missile flight through Japanese airspace.

71. Interview by Mayumi Fukushima, 9 January 2016, Tokyo.

72. Insight into the preferences of Nishihiro and Gotōda was provided by General Kunimi Masahiro, the first chief of the DIH. Interview, 5 October 2017. For more on the creation of the DIH, see Kotani 2009a and Kuroi 2005b.

73. *Asahi Shimbun*, 21 September 2004.

74. This account is based on Taoka 1994, 27–28; *Asahi Shimbun*, 21 September 2004; Honda et al. eds. 2005; Shinoda 2006, 99–101; Ball and Tanter 2015a.

75. See the interview with Gotōda conducted by Honda Masaru in Honda et al. eds. 2005.

76. *Asahi Shimbun*, 21 September 2004.

77. Gotōda says he was "really furious" (*honto ni hara ga tatta*). *Asahi Shimbun*, 21 September 2004, and Honda et al. eds. 2005, 364.

78. Honda et al. eds. 2005.

79. *Asahi Shimbun*, 14 January 1997 and 24 December 1998.

80. For more on the relationship of technology and national security in Japan, see Samuels 1994.

81. *Asahi Shimbun*, 25 November 1989.

82. National Institute for Defense Studies ed. 2014, chap. 1.

83. *Asahi Shimbun*, 31 July 1992, 17 January 1994, 14 January 1997, 26 September 2004, 24 July 2003, and 14 December 2005.

84. Kuroi 2007, 28–29; Richelson 1988, 256; *Asahi Shimbun*, 17 January 1994.

85. Kaneko 2007, 117; *Asahi Shimbun*, 14 January 1997; *Gunji Kenkyū*, September 2006, 103.

86. *Asahi Shimbun*, 21 September 2004; interview, General Kunimi Masahiro, 5 October 2017, Tokyo.

87. Samuels 2007, 103. Apparently Gotōda was fond of the rabbit ears metaphor. See chapter 3 of this volume for a separate evocation.

88. The important distinction between "policy support" and "operational support" was made by General Kunimi Masahiro, the first chief of DIH. Interview, 5 October 2017, Tokyo.

89. Interview, General Kunimi Masahiro, 5 October 2017, Tokyo.

90. *The Strategist*, 22 September 2015. General Kunimi explained that most of his early reports to the prime minister were from U.S. military intelligence. Interview, 5 October 2017, Tokyo.

91. Kuroi 2005b, 233–35.

92. Interview by Mayumi Fukushima, 15 January 2016, Tokyo.

93. The U.S. early warning was confirmed by an active duty senior military officer who insisted that the incident was therefore "not a failure of intelligence cooperation." Interview, 14 December 2015, Tokyo. This was reconfirmed by a former White House official. Telephone interview, 10 July 2018.

94. Sassa interview in *Shokun*, 1 December 1998, 97, 103.

95. Kuroi 2007, 188.

96. Kaneko 2011, 310.

97. Sunohara 2005, 113–32; Radcliffe 2010, 9.

98. *Shokun*, 1 December 1998, 103.

99. Radcliffe 2010, 9, reports that the choice of the MELCO system was made easier because the alternative was from NEC, which was in the middle of a procurement scandal. This is confirmed by Pekkanen and Kallender-Umezu 2010, 88.

100. See Kuroi 2008, 260–61.

101. Pekkanen and Kallender-Umezu 2010, 137, cite a 5 May 1999 *Daily Yomiuri* article regarding U.S. pressure on Japan to buy a U.S. spysat system; see also 143.

102. Interview by Mayumi Fukushima with former high-level government official familiar with the Japanese intelligence community, 15 January 2016, Tokyo.

103. Pekkanen and Kallender-Umezu 2010, 136, describe the Taepodong incident aptly as a "trigger" rather than as a cause; "politically untouchable" is from 137. See also Kallender and Hughes 2018.

104. Telephone interview, 10 July 2018.

105. Radcliffe 2010, 9–10.

106. Radcliffe 2010, 11; Pekkanen and Kallender-Umezu 2010, 144–45.

107. Pekkanen and Kallender-Umezu 2010, 136.

108. Nakayama quoted in Radcliffe 2010, 11, emphasis added.

109. *The Strategist*, 22 September 2015. The Taepodong incident also stimulated Japanese interest in acquisition of a ballistic missile defense system. See Namatame 2012, 3.

110. Kuroi 2005a, 235–36; Kallender 2016; Radcliffe 2010, 18.

111. Interview, 15 December 2015, Tokyo.

112. The DIH Imagery Directorate was stood up in 1997 when the Central Geography Unit of the GSDF was combined with imagery analysts from elsewhere in the SDF. Radcliffe 2010, 17–18.

113. Radcliffe 2010, 17.

114. *Yomiuri Shimbun*, 25 February 2007; *Asahi Shimbun*, 30 August 2010.

115. *Asahi Shimbun*, 14 April 2009.

116. *Warudo Interijensu*, 4 December 2008. Those politics, it should be noted, were bipartisan. Democratic Party politicians were as enthusiastic about nurturing a homegrown space-based intelligence system as were their competitors in the LDP.

117. *Asahi Shimbun*, 14 April 2009.

118. Kuroi 2005a, 235–36.

119. Matsuura Shinya in *Warudo Interijensu*, 4 December 2008.

120. Much of this account is from Samuels 2010. See also Arrington 2016, Mason and Maslow 2015, Johnston 2004, Morris-Suzuki 2009, Kitachōsen ni Ratchi Sareta Kazoku ni yoru Renrakukai ed. 2003, Yamagiwa 2004, and Satō 2004.

121. Mason and Maslow 2015, 45.

122. Interview, 16 December 2015, Tokyo.

123. *Sankei Shimbun*, 7 January 1980.

124. See Hyōmoto 2002 for a first-person account and *Akahata*, 17 November 2002, for the party's rebuttal.

125. Budget Committee, House of Councilors, 26 March 1988. It was later revealed that Li Eun-hye was abductee Taguchi Yaeko.

126. Chimura Yasushi and Hamamoto Fukie were abducted in Fukui. Hasuike Kaoru, Ōkudo Yukiko, Soga Hitomi, and Soga Miyoshi were abducted in Niigata. Ichikawa Shūichi and Masumoto Rumiko were abducted in Kagoshima.

127. The bureau chief was Katō Ryōzō, the future Japanese ambassador to the United States.

128. An NPA official acknowledged that the agency had been investigating the connection to North Korea when the *Sankei* article was published. Interview, 22 December 2015, Tokyo.

129. Interview, 15 December 2015, Tokyo.

130. Mason and Maslow 2015, 45, credit Yamagiwa 2004 for this observation. The same claim was repeated by intelligence journalist Haruna Mikio in an interview on 21 December 2015 in Tokyo, and a variant of it was confirmed in an interview with Harada Takeo, a former MOFA chief North Korean desk officer, on 21 September 2017 in Tokyo. According to former government officials, Nakayama Tarō, a future foreign minister, and Nonaka Hiromu, a future chief cabinet secretary, also may have intervened. Interviews, 21 September 2017 and 1 October 2017, Tokyo. Wada 2004 offers a more benign account, arguing that these and other politicians interested in normalizing relations with North Korea had "devoted energy to opening roads to Japan–North Korean diplomatic engagement" and were unfairly slandered by the media and "harassed" by rightists.

131. Interview, NPA official, 22 December 2015. Ozawa Ichirō was still in the LDP when he traveled to Pyongyang with Kanemaru and Socialist Party leader Doi Takako in 1990.

132. Interview, Harada Takeo, 21 September 2017, Tokyo; interview, 22 December 2015, Tokyo.

133. Interview, 22 December 2015, Tokyo.

134. Interview, 17 October 2017, Tokyo.

135. Interview, 2 October 2017, Tokyo.

136. Interview, 18 December 2015, Tokyo.

137. Taoka 1994, 28.

138. See *Shokun,* 1 December 1998.

139. Armitage et al. 2000, 4–5.

140. Henderson 1997, 229.

141. This observation is from Kaneko 2011, 337.

5. Reimagining Possibilities (2001–2013)

1. Steinhoff 2016.
2. Shinoda 2006 explores Koizumi's enthusiasm for improved intelligence. Koizumi's frustration with Japan's limited HUMINT capabilities and his call for *"ninja"* is noted in Samuels 2007, 103.
3. *Yomiuri Shimbun*, 20 and 21 January 2013.
4. See the press reports in *Mainichi Shimbun*, 21 January 2013; *Asahi Shimbun*, 22 January 2013; *Tout sur l'Algérie*, 4 February 2013.
5. Abe is quoted in *Yomiuri Shimbun*, 27 January 2013. For reports during the crisis, see *Mainichi Shimbun*, 21 January 2013; *Yomiuri Shimbun*, 20 January 2013; Agence France-Presse, 19 January 2013; Kyodo, 8 February 2013; and *Al Akhbar Online*, 20 January 2013. For a report on the ransom effort, see Kyodo, 13 March 2013.
6. Abe's speech is available at http://www.mofa.go.jp/announce/pm/.
7. Suga 2014, 110–11.
8. Interview, 14, December 2015, Tokyo.
9. Kyodo, 27 January 2013. Under then extant law, the SDF could repatriate Japanese nationals only from ports and airports, and then only when there was no risk of being drawn into conflict. *Asahi Shimbun,* 22 January 2013. The number of military attachés in Africa is from *Nihon Keizai Shimbun*, 24 January 2013.
10. *Sankei Shimbun*, 3 June 2015.
11. *Komentoraina*, 28 December 2007.
12. Kotani Ken, cited in Mercado 2010, 53.
13. Ōmori 2008, 101.
14. Interview, CIRO official, 22 December 2015, Tokyo.
15. Maehara's testimony is in Kokkai Kaigiroku [Diet Records], House of Councillors Special Joint Committee on Basic National Policies, session 163, no. 1, 19 October 2005, 5. Haraguchi's is in Kokkai Kaigiroku [Diet Records], House of Representatives Committee on Measures against International Terrorism, session 165, no. 7, 20 December 2006, 26. Genba's testimony is in Kokkai Kaigiroku [Diet Records], House of Councillors Committee of Diplomacy and Defense, session 180, no. 4, 17 April 2012, 19. Maruya 2005 provides a collection of statements by leading Japanese politicians, bureaucrats, and analysts of the intelligence community who were concerned about Japan's excessive dependence on the United States for intelligence.
16. For China's defense budget, see http://www.globalsecurity.org/military/world/china/budget-table.htm. Japan's can be found at http://www.mod.go.jp/e/d_budget/pdf/300227.pdf.
17. PHP . . . Kenkyūkai ed. 2006, 2.
18. Magosaki 2009.
19. *Voice*, September 2015, 97 (Sugimoto) and 98 (Hokazono).
20. For the German case, see Mounk 2017.
21. Tanaka 2008, 2. Interview, senior official, National Security Secretariat, 19 December 2015, Tokyo.
22. See Kaneko 2008 and Kaneko 2011, 312–13. Also see Kotani 2013. Martin 2016, 17, aptly refers to a "barrage of official recommendations."
23. *Sankei Shimbun*, 6 March 2015. At the same time, he also took up a second, related problem: classifying state secrets, which will be explored in detail in chapter 6.

24. Kotani 2006 and Kotani 2013.

25. Shinoda 2006, 97.

26. Shinoda 2006, 97–99. Magosaki is interviewed in Kuroi 2008; see 248 and 252.

27. Interview by Mayumi Fukushima, 15 January 2016, Tokyo.

28. The British model was critical to the MOFA report because it placed government-wide intelligence authority within the Foreign Office. The report in Japanese is available at http://www.mofa.go.jp/mofaj/press/release/17/pdfs/rls_0913a.pdf. See also Kotani 2006; Kotani 2009a; Ōmori 2005, 160–65.

29. See the interview with Machimura in *Sankei Shimbun,* 6 March 2015. See also Ōmori 2005, 160–65.

30. Kotani 2006, 3.

31. Williams 2010, 177.

32. Kotani 2013, 187.

33. See Jōhō Kinō . . . Kaigi ed. 2008, 1–2.

34. Machimura 2005.

35. The first quote is from interview, senior intelligence officer, 6 September 2017, Tokyo. Morimoto interview, 31 October 2017.

36. A senior author of the PHP report insists that it was funded entirely by PHP and undertaken independently, at PHP's own initiative. Interview, Kaneko Masafumi, 11 October 2017.

37. The full report is PHP . . . Kenkyūkai ed. 2006. See also Kaneko 2008 and Kobayashi 2012, 68.

38. Kuroi 2005a, 237–38.

39. Machimura interview in *Sankei Shimbun,* 6 March 2015.

40. See interview in Kuroi 2008, 251.

41. Kotani 2013, 192.

42. Kaneko 2011 provides details.

43. Naikaku Kanbō ed. 2010, 3

44. Kotani 2013, 187, also makes this observation. For an official description, see Naikaku Kanbō ed. 2010, 8. Also see Kobayashi 2015, 723. There are echoes, too, of the recommendations of the U.S. 9/11 Commission Report.

45. Kotani 2009a, 13. See also Kōno, Mabuchi, and Yamauchi 2013, a detailed suprapartisan recommendation for a new 20 billion yen, five-hundred-person foreign intelligence unit proposed by three Diet members (one a future foreign minister).

46. See Kaneko 2011, 315, for details.

47. During the Cold War, Radiopress—like the Foreign Broadcast Information Service in the United States—collected and assessed signals from communist bloc countries. Today it monitors North Korea closely.

48. Kobayashi 2015, 719–20.

49. Annual report for 2014, Financial Services Agency of Japan, 3, 22, https://www.fsa.go.jp/en/about/Annual_Reports/2014.pdf.

50. Interview with former intelligence official by Mayumi Fukushima, 15 January 2016, Tokyo.

51. Jōhō Kinō Kaigi ed. 2008. An early plan for this new council appeared in *Gunji Kenkyū,* 1 September 2006. See also Kallender and Hughes 2016, 12.

52. Green calls Kanemoto "Japan's first real DCI [director of Central Intelligence]." Telephone interview, 10 July 2018.

53. Telephone interview, 16 July 2018.

54. One could come from the private sector. Their primary job was to prepare national intelligence estimates for the prime minister. See Kotani 2013, 191; Kokka Anzen . . . Yūshikisha Kaigi ed. 2013; and Naikaku Kanbō ed. 2010.

55. Testimony of Chief Cabinet Secretary Machimura to the House of Councillors Cabinet Committee. See Kokkai Kaigiroku (Diet Records), session 169, no. 2, 25 March 2008. Machimura discussed intelligence reform as well. See Kokkai Kaigiroku (Diet Records), House of Councillors Committee on Diplomacy and Security Affairs, session 162, no. 7, 14 April 2005.

56. *Sankei Shimbun*, 3 June 2015.

57. *Sankei Shimbun,* 6 March 2015.

58. Ōmori 2008, 100.

59. Ōmori 2006, 71–76.

60. Cables to the State Department from Assistant Secretary for Intelligence and Research Randall Fort based on his conversations with Japanese government counterparts in Tokyo are available at https://wikileaks.org/plusd/cables/08TOKYO2980_a.html.

61. MOFA *Diplomatic Bluebook* for various years, 1990–2010. Also see Martin 2016, 18.

62. Interview by Mayumi Fukushima with former high-level government official familiar with the Japanese intelligence community, 15 January 2016, Tokyo. This former official added that this crossed the line between the intelligence and policy-making communities.

63. Kotani 2013, 183.

64. Kōno, Mabuchi, and Yamauchi 2013; *Gunji Kenkyū*, September 2006, 80.

65. Ōmori 2005, 36.

66. For more on the government's fumbled response to the Kobe quake, see Samuels 2013, chap. 3. See Williams 2010, 164–65, for more on CIRO personnel and jurisdiction during this period.

67. Interview, 14 September 2017, Tokyo.

68. *Asahi Shimbun*, 19 July 2013.

69. Shinoda 2006, 96.

70. See https://wikileaks.org/plusd/cables/08TOKYO2980_a.html and Dorling 2011. According to historian Kotani Ken, CIRO asked the U.S. government to accept its officers for tradecraft training, but the latter declined. Japanese trainees were sent instead to Australia's Secret Intelligence Service facility near Melbourne. Interview, 15 December 2015, Tokyo.

71. CIRO had been this size for more than a decade, and its previous effort to increase to a staff of one thousand in 2004 was rejected. Shinoda 2006, 94–97; Kotani 2013, 183; Kōno, Mabuchi, and Yamauchi 2013. Williams 2010, 164–65, reports that in addition to the forty secondees from the NPA, there were twenty from the PSIA and ten from MOD, with a smattering from MOFA, METI, and elsewhere.

72. See Kuroi 2005a, 233, and Shinoda 2006, 95.

73. Interview, 14 September 2017, Tokyo.

74. Kuroi 2005a, 234, suggests that because, unlike the NPA, MOFA, and the Defense Agency, CIRO could have no officers stationed abroad, its HUMINT resources resided in this Trading House unit. *Gunji Kenkyū*, 1 September 2006, includes an organizational chart of CIRO.

75. Interview, 12 October 2017, Tokyo. In chapter 6 we will see how CIRO and JETRO began collaborating in Africa in 2016. Data provided by JETRO. See also Kōno, Mabuchi, and Yamauchi 2013, 99.

76. The CIRO budget data are based on internal Ministry of Finance data.

77. Data collected from assorted years of the *Keizai Sangyō Handobukku* (METI Handbook).

78. Interview by Mayumi Fukushima with retired senior JETRO official, 13 June 2015, Tokyo.

79. Based on data from *Keizai Sangyō Handobukku* (METI Handbook), various years.

80. Yama is reported to operate multiple fixed monitoring facilities as well as truck-mounted mobile equipment. See Kuroi 2005a, 237; Mercado 2004, 289; Williams 2010, 167–68.

81. See Daugherty 2004, 86–87; Kuroi 2005b, 237; *Asahi Shimbun*, 12 February 2000, 18 February 2000, and 16 November 2000. Note, however, that Gotōda Masaharu, the godfather of postwar intelligence reform, addressed the problem of cybersecurity in his 1998 memoirs. See Gotōda 1998, 1:237–38.

82. Kallender and Hughes 2016, 12.

83. National Information Security Center ed. 2014.

84. *Asahi Shimbun*, 27 November 2000.

85. See press release from the government of Japan, 26 March 2002, https://www.nisc.go.jp/conference/tyousakai/dai4/4siryou3.html.

86. Ministry of Internal Affairs (Sōmushō), *Jōhō Tsūshin Hakusho* (Information and Communication White Paper), 2011, pt. 3, chap. 5, http://www.soumu.go.jp/johotsusintokei/whitepaper/ja/h23/html/nc353210.html.

87. *Asahi Shimbun*, 11 December 2005.

88. *Asahi Shimbun*, 11 December 2005.

89. NSA document dated 8 January 2007, "Request for ADET SIGDEV Materials to Be Used for Training the Japanese Directorate for SIGINT Personnel," attached to Gallagher 2017.

90. Tsuchiya 2012, 172, 177. Kallender and Hughes 2016 speak of this period as the moment when Japan began to militarize cybersecurity in earnest and put itself on the path to becoming a "cyber power" with U.S. assistance.

91. *Asahi Shimbun*, 30 June 2012.

92. *Asahi Shimbun*, 8 September 2012, 5 February 2014, and 11 May 2017. See also Ministry of Defense, ed., *Defense White Paper, 2016* (2017), pt. 3, chap. 1, sec. 2. Information on NSA intelligence sharing in the cyber domain was revealed in the Edward Snowden leaks. It increased in 2013 after Abe Shinzō returned to power. See Gallagher 2017, 12.

93. Interview, 30 October 2017, Tokyo. Kallender and Hughes 2016, 9, report that throughout most of the 2000s the Japanese cybersecurity effort remained highly sectionalized.

94. Kotani 2009a, 2.

95. See Shinoda 2006, 95–96.

96. Interview, senior MOD intelligence official, 17 December 2015, Tokyo. See also Tsukamoto 2008, 208, and http://www.mod.go.jp/gsdf/kodaira/gakkouenkaku.html.

97. Interview, 17 December 2015, Tokyo.

98. Kyodo, 27 November 2013.

99. Kuroi 2005b, 241.

100. *Sankei Shimbun*, 23 August 2015. See also the editorial calling for beefed-up intelligence capacity in *Yomiuri Shimbun*, 23 May 2015.

101. Shinoda 2006, 101.

102. Interview, 17 December 2015, Tokyo.

103. Interview, 14 December 2015, Tokyo.

104. See chapter 4 of this volume. Kotani 2009a and Kōno, Mabuchi, and Yamauchi 2013 also provide useful background.

105. See Samuels 2007 for details on Japan's system of civilian control.

106. Kuroi 2005b, 236–37. For the memoirs of one such commander, see Ōta 2008.

107. Email interview, Admiral (ret.) Lowell E. Jacoby, former director, Defense Intelligence Agency, 20 July 2018.

108. *Asahi Shimbun*, 21 September 2004; Shinoda 2006, 101; Kōno, Mabuchi, and Yamauchi 2013.

109. Kaneko 2007, 118. "The Defense of Japan, 2006," available at http://www.clearing.mod.go.jp/hakusho_data/2006/2006/html/i31c2000.html. Also see Kuroi 2007, 26–28.

110. Kuroi 2007, 29.

111. Ball and Tanter 2015a. An NHK special report, broadcast in May 2018, reported that the DIH's Radio Wave Bureau (Denpabu), discussed in chapter 4, routinely supplied the U.S. government with intercepted foreign communications. NHK also claimed that these intercepts were particularly useful to the United States military during America's post-9/11 wars, an evaluation reconfirmed by former NSC senior director Michael Green in a telephone interview, 16 July 2018.

112. Kuroi 2007, 30–33. His organizational chart (32–33) is especially revealing.

113. Telephone interview, retired U.S. National Security Council official, 19 July 2018.

114. Kuroi 2007, 30–31.

115. Kuroi 2005b, 233; Shinoda 2006, 101.

116. *Asahi Shimbun*, 20 September 2013.

117. Kuroi 2007, 187–90; Perret 2015, 1, review of Ball and Tanter 2015.

118. See Samuels 2007 for more on these Cold War constraints and chapter 4 of this volume for more on the origins of Japan's spysat program. Kallender 2016, 15, identifies three phases in the path toward the open military use of space: 1969–1998, 1998–2007, and 2007–present. See also *Asahi Shimbun*, 20 September 2004.

119. *Yomiuri Shimbun*, 21 August 1993. See also Ikegami 2008.

120. "The Defense of Japan, 2003," chap. 3, available at http://www.clearing.mod.go.jp/hakusho_data/2003/2003/html/15311300.html. Also see *Asahi Shimbun*, 20 September 2004.

121. Radcliffe 2010, 10.

122. *Asahi Shimbun*, 27 March 2003. At the same time, the JDA announced it would develop and deploy unmanned aerial vehicles to backfill missing images from incomplete satellite coverage. See Martin 2016, 7, and *Mainichi Shimbun*, 8 November 2014.

123. *Asahi Shimbun*, 14 April 2009 and 19 July 2013.

124. *Asahi Shimbun*, 14 April 2009.

125. Pekkanen 2015, 3.

126. *Sankei Shimbun*, 29 November 2009; *Yomiuri Shimbun*, 11 September 2006.

127. *Yomiuri Shimbun*, 28 August 2010.

128. *Sankei News*, 12 December 2011; Kyodo, 26 April 2013; *Nihon Keizai Shimbun*, 13 October 2014.

129. *Asahi Shimbun*, 22 October 2014.

130. General Tachikawa interviewed in Kuroi 2008, 264.

131. Kuroi 2008, 264–65, emphasis added. Japanese troops in Samawah benefited considerably from DIH cooperation with the IMINT units of other friendly countries. See Shinoda 2006, 102.

132. *Yomiuri Shimbun*, 31 December 2006. Also see *Gunji Kenkyū*, September 2006, 108.

133. For more on the Chūō Shiryōtai's OSINT work, see *Gunji Kenkyū*, April 2009, 195–96; Satō 2012, 97; Hirajō 2010, 136; and chapter 3 of this volume.

134. "The Defense of Japan, 2001," available at http://www.clearing.mod.go.jp/hakusho_data/2001/column/frame/ak134003.htm.

135. See *Yomiuri Shimbun*, 10 June 2004, and "The Defense of Japan, 2001," available at http://www.clearing.mod.go.jp/hakusho_data/2001/column/frame/ak134003.htm.

136. *Yomiuri Shimbun*, 16 January 2005.

137. *Yomiuri Shimbun*, 16 January 2005. See Konishi 2017 for details on GSDF tactical intelligence gleaned from freedom of information requests, including intelligence activities aimed at what he labels "non-military" threats, that is, psyops, sabotage, and guerrilla forces.

138. *Asahi Shimbun*, 1 August 2010.

139. *Yomiuri Shimbun*, 31 December 2006.

140. Defense White Paper 2010, chap. 2; *Yomiuri Shimbun*, 31 December 2006.

141. *Sankei Shimbun*, 29 July 2007; *Asahi Shimbun,* 7 June 2007.

142. *Sankei Shimbun*, 29 July 2007 and 24 January 2011.

143. *Asahi Shimbun,* 7 June 2007; *Mainichi Shimbun,* 7 June 2007; Matsumoto 2008, 100–105.

144. Konishi 2017 raises questions about the intentions and potential for this sort of activity. Gallagher 2018 reports that the DIH Radio Wave Bureau began intercepting and surveilling domestic emails and Internet sessions in the 2000s.

145. Kokkai Kaigiroku [Diet Records], House of Representative Committee on National Security, session 154, no. 5, 4 April 2002, 27–18.

146. Kokkai Kaigiroku [Diet Records], House of Councillors Committee on Diplomacy and Defense, session 166, no. 17, 7 June 2007, 1–5; Kokkai Kaigiroku [Diet Records], House of Representative Committee on National Security, session 154, no. 5, 4 April 2002, 27–18; *Sankei Shimbun*, 7 June 2007; *Mainichi Shimbun*, 7 June 2007; *Asahi Shimbun*, 7 June 2007; *Asahi Shimbun*, 27 March 2012.

147. *Sankei Shimbun*, 24 January 2011.

148. Asagumo Shimbunsha Shuppan Gyōmubu ed. 2016, 384.

149. Bōeishō ed. 2014.

150. See the blog Japan Security Watch, 17 January 2011, http://jsw.newpacifi cinstitute.org/?p=3745.

151. Kuroi 2005b, 239.

152. Asagumo Shimbunsha Shuppan Gyōmubu ed. 2016, 384.

153. Asagumo Shimbunsha Shuppan Gyōmubu ed. 2016, 388; Bōeishō ed. 2014.

154. Ball and Tanter 2012, 19–20.

155. Ball and Tanter 2012, 22.

156. Ball and Tanter 2012, 23–26.

157. Bōeishō ed. 2014. See Samuels 1994 for analysis of Japanese technonationalism and the strategic connection between commercial and military applications.

158. *Defense News*, 11 May 2015, reported that the MOD was concerned about dependence on U.S. drones and was moving to develop proprietary Japanese aircraft.

159. DefenseNews.com, 21 November 2014; Inoue 2015, 72.

160. *Gunji Kenkyū*, September 2006, 111; Defense White Paper 2006, 193, http://www.mod.go.jp/e/publ/w_paper/2006.html.

161. *Gunji Kenkyū*, September 2006, 111; Asagumo Shimbunsha Shuppan Gyōmubu ed. 2016, 330.

162. Inoue 2015, 72. Also see Bōeishō ed. 2014. Note that ASDF fighter aircraft would acquire significantly enhanced ISR capabilities after 2013, including an integrated sensor package in the F-35 that provides pilots 360-degree access to real-time battlefield information that is securely shared with commanders at sea, in the air, or on the ground.

163. Perret 2015, 1, based on Ball and Tanter 2015.

164. Busujima 2017, 106–7; *Jane's Avionics*, 24 January 2007. The sonar, similar to the U.S. Navy's AQS-13F, could actively scan underwater targets through a transducer lowered into the water from a hovering helicopter.

165. Busujima 2017, 105.

166. Busujima 2017, 105.

167. Asagumo Shimbunsha Shuppan Gyōmubu ed. 2016, 194.

168. Asagumo Shimbunsha Shuppan Gyōmubu ed. 2016, 194.

169. Busujima 2017, 36–37.

170. Asagumo Shimbunsha Shuppan Gyōmubu ed. 2016, 200.

171. Asagumo Shimbunsha Shuppan Gyōmubu ed. 2016, 201; Busujima 2017, 62–63.

172. Asagumo Shimbunsha Shuppan Gyōmubu ed. 2016, 202–3. By June 2017 the MSDF had acquired eight Sōryū-class submarines, with two more under construction.

173. *Sekai no Kansen*, March 2008, 90–92. Note that the DDH designation is ambiguous.

174. *Sekai no Kansen*, March 2008, 91.

175. Jieitai no Nazo Kenshō Iinkai ed. 2014, 28. Note, however, that news reports vary about its maximum capacity.

176. Asagumo Shimbunsha Shuppan Gyōmubu ed. 2016, 254–55; Busujima 2007, 100–101.

177. The MSDF had nine P-1s in service in March 2016, with thirty-three more on order by the end of the 2017 and at least seventy targeted for acquisition by 2020, which seems to some a misallocation of resources for a military on a limited budget.

Flightglobal.com, 12 October 2016; *Asahi Shimbun*, 27 June 2017; Busujima 2017, 100–101.

178. Interview, Admiral Futakawa Tatsuya, Commander Fleet Air Wing 31, Iwakuni, 15 November 2017.

179. Ball and Tanter 2015, 55.

180. Ball and Tanter 2015, 15.

181. Samuels 2007–8 reviews the JCG contribution to Japan's defense during this period.

182. *Yomiuri Shimbun*, 8 September 2017.

183. Interview, 23 October 2017.

184. Geospatial Information Authority ed. 2012, 24.

185. Geospatial Information Authority ed. 2012, 2.

186. *Yomiuri Shimbun*, 8 September 2017.

187. *Yomiuri Shimbun*, 31 January 2016; Kuroi 2007.

188. Kotani 2009a, 4

189. See the NSA document dated 23 October 2007 released by Edward Snowden, "NSA Liaison in Tokyo Opens New Office," attached to Gallagher 2017.

190. See Richelson and Ball 1985, 171, and Richelson 1989, 282. Ball and Tanter 2016, 2, report that during the Cold War, the United States operated some one hundred listening posts in Japan. In 2016 they estimated there were one thousand U.S. personnel engaged in SIGINT, Internet surveillance, and network warfare activities in Japan. They are mainly uniformed personnel stationed in Yokosuka, Misawa, Yokota, and Kadena, as well as in the U.S. embassy in Tokyo.

191. NSA document dated 16 March 2007, "NSA SIGINT Site Relocated in Japan: The Story behind the Move," attached to Gallagher 2017.

192. NSA document dated 21 July 2004, "Charlie Meals Opens New Engineering Support Facility in Japan," attached to Gallagher 2017.

193. Interview, 9 November 2017, Tokyo. Admiral Otsuka became head of the DIH in early 2018.

194. Gallagher 2017, 11.

195. Armitage et al. 2000, 5.

196. Interview by Mayumi Fukushima, 9 January 2016, Tokyo.

197. Interview by Mayumi Fukushima, 4 July 2014, Tokyo.

198. Interview, retired senior White House official, 25 July 2018, Washington, DC.

199. Telephone interview, 16 July 2018.

200. Interview, retired senior White House official, 25 July 2018, Washington, DC.

201. Matsumura 2013, 6. See also Williams 2013b, 510.

202. Matsumura 2013, 5.

203. "Security Consultative Committee Document U.S.-Japan Alliance: Transformation and Realignment for the Future," 29 October 2005, available at http://www.mofa.go.jp/region/n-america/us/security/scc/doc0510.html. Also see Kallender and Hughes 2016, 16–17.

204. See the NSA document dated 14 March 2007, "U.S., Japan Now Exchanging Collection from Reconnaissance Missions," attached to Gallagher 2017.

205. http://wikileaks.org.cable/2006/09/06TOKYO5624.html.

206. https://wikileaks.org/plusd/cables/06TOKYO6896_a.html.

207. https://wikileaks.org/plusd/cables/06TOKYO6896_a.html.

208. https://wikileaks.org/plusd/cables/07TOKYO2895_a.html.

209. https://wikileaks.org/plusd/cables/06TOKYO5515_a.html, emphasis added.

210. https://wikileaks.org/plusd/cables/06TOKYO5515_a.html.

211. https://wikileaks.org/plusd/cables/07TOKYO2895_a.html.

212. https://wikileaks.org/plusd/cables/07TOKYO2895_a.html.

213. "Joint Statement of the Security Consultative Committee Alliance Transformation: Advancing United States–Japan Security and Defense Cooperation," 1 May 2007, available at http://www.mofa.go.jp/region/n-america/us/security/scc/joint0705.html.

214. Henderson 1997, 228; Richelson 1989, 282; Richelson 2011, 349.

215. NSA document dated 23 October 2007, "NSA Liaison in Tokyo Opens New Office," attached to Gallagher 2017.

216. Kaneko 2011, 315.

217. Rudner 2010, 197; Richelson 2011, 349; Ball and Tanter 2015b, 399. "Clubbiness" is from telephone interview, 27 March 2018.

218. Interviews, 27 February 2017, Cambridge, MA; 14 September 2017, Tokyo; 20 September 2017, Tokyo; and 5 October 2017, Tokyo.

219. Telephone interview, 27 March 2018.

220. Interview, 25 July 2018, Washington, DC. Japanese officials began trying to revise that image in early 2019. See the report in *Nikkei Asian Review*, 10 January 2019.

221. The oblique reference is in the NSA document dated 19 November 2008, "What's NSA's Reputation among Third Parties? What Are the Japanese Like as SIGINTers?," in Gallagher 2017. See also Honda et al. eds. 2005; and Electrospaces.net, 15 November 2013.

222. Ball and Tanter 2015b, 399.

223. Rudner 2010, 197–98; telephone interview, senior U.S. military officer, 27 March 2018.

224. Interview, former CIRO chief, 15 December 2015, Tokyo. This official anticipated a 2018 call by Richard Armitage and Joseph Nye for Japanese inclusion in the "Five Eyes" network. See Armitage and Nye eds. 2018.

225. Interview, 19 December 2015, Tokyo.

226. See Ball 2006, 4, for the case of Australia.

227. http://www.mofa.go.jp/announce/announce/2012/5/0517_01.html and http://www.mofa.go.jp/press/release/index.html.

228. *Korea Times*, 17 July 2015.

229. Interview, senior intelligence officer, 6 September 2017, Tokyo.

230. *Signal*, 1 November 2013; *Khmer Times Online*, 9 June 2015.

231. NSA document dated 19 November 2008, "What's NSA's Reputation among Third Parties? What Are the Japanese Like as SIGINTers?," attached to Gallagher 2017.

232. Gallagher 2017, 14.

233. See NSA document 2, January 2013, "NSA High Frequency (HF) Collection Efforts with Japan," attached to Gallagher 2017.

234. Participant quoted in Kaneko 2011, 312.

235. The observation that "Japan's intelligence community is not really a community" was repeated in multiple interviews in Tokyo with former heads of the DIH, a former head of MSDF intelligence, a former deputy director of CIRO, and sitting senior intelligence officials in December 2015 and September–November 2017.

236. See Kuroi 2008, 249. Magosaki also claimed that analysts within MOFA, CIRO, and PSIA "can match the CIA" for analysis of North Korea. Quoted in Kuroi 2008, 256.

237. *Japan News*, 2 December 2015.

238. Kōno, Mabuchi, and Yamauchi 2013, 96.

239. Kaneko 2011, 326.

240. Interview, 15 December 2015, Tokyo.

6. Reengineering the Intelligence Community (2013–)

1. Interview, General (ret.) Kunimi Masahiro, 5 October 2017, Tokyo.

2. See http://www.japaneselawtranslation.go.jp/law/detail/?id=2543&vm=04& re=01 for an outline of the law (Tokutei Himitsu no Hogo ni kansuru Hōritsu) in Japanese.

3. *Mainichi Shimbun*, 2 December 2015. Diet Representative Iwaya Takeshi, an ally of Machimura in the LDP and a vocal proponent of creating a "Japanese-style CIA" (Nihonban CIA) who became minister of defense in 2018, insisted that Diet oversight—including budgeting and performance evaluation—would not be enhanced until intelligence capabilities are enhanced. Interview, 10 November 2017, Tokyo. See also *Sankei Shimbun*, 28 December 2015.

4. *Asahi Shimbun*, 27 November 2013.

5. Suga 2014, 115.

6. Suga 2014, 114–15.

7. *Nikkei Telecom 21*, 10 December 2013. It is possible that this need for foreign intelligence became more urgent once the 2020 Olympics were awarded to Tokyo at this same time. Interview with journalist Hoshi Hiroshi by Mayumi Fukushima, 9 July 2014, Tokyo.

8. Unnamed senior U.S. official cited in *The Nelson Report*, 7 February 2014.

9. Interview by Mayumi Fukushima, 9 July 2014, Tokyo.

10. Suga 2014, 115.

11. https://www.wsws.org/en/articles/2015/03/12/japa-m.html. This section is based on Fukushima and Samuels 2018.

12. A fuller account is Chijiwa 2012.

13. Samuels 1994.

14. Cha 2016 argues this was by Washington's design.

15. *Sankei Shimbun*, 28 August 2006.

16. Kokkai Kaigiroku [Diet Records], House of Representatives, Budgetary Committee, session 185, no. 2, 21 October 2013. Also see Kyodo World Service, 4 December 2013.

17. *Sankei Shimbun*, 23 January 2007; Sunohara 2014, 47–57.

18. Sunohara 2014, 133; *Sankei Shimbun*, 21 December 2006; *Yomiuri Shimbun*, 23 November 2006.

19. Sunohara 2014, 112–13.

20. *Kokka Anzen Hoshō ni Kansuru Kantei Kinō Kyōka Kaigi*, 27 February 2007, 7. http://www.kantei.go.jp/jp/singi/anzen/.

21. Sunohara 2014, 115; *Sankei Shimbun*, 3 June 2008.

22. *Sankei Shimbun*, 27 December 2012.

23. *Yomiuri Shimbun*, 9 February 2013. For another account of the formation of the NSC, see Liff 2018.

24. Kokkai Kaigiroku [Diet Records], House of Councillors Budget Committee, session 189, no. 4, 5 February 2015.

25. Kokka Anzen . . . Yūshikisha Kaigi ed. 2013, 4.

26. This was emphasized by Prime Minister Abe during House of Councillors Budget Committee interpellations on 20 February 2013. See Kokka Anzen . . . Yūshikisha Kaigi ed. 2013, 5.

27. Chijiwa 2012, 18–19. The other five ministries represented in the nine-minister meetings are Internal Affairs; Finance; Economy, Trade, and Industry; Land Infrastructure, Transport, and Tourism; and the Public Safety Commission.

28. Nakanishi 2015, 406.

29. The first regional team covers North America, Europe, Australia, India, and ASEAN. The second team is responsible for Northeast Asia and Russia, and the third team focuses on the Middle East, Africa, and Central and South America. The NSS consists of some seventy staff members, with some thirty from MOD, some twenty from MOFA, and some from other agencies, including the Cabinet Office, National Police Agency, METI, MOF, and others. See PHP Kenkyūjo ed. 2015, 33.

30. Interview, senior NSS official, 1 October 2017, Tokyo.

31. "Nihon no Gaikō to Anzen Hoshō" [Japan's Diplomacy and National Security], speech by Kanehara Nobukatsu, deputy secretary general of the National Security Secretariat, to the Keizai Dōyūkai, 18 October 2016.

32. Article 6 of the Partial Amendment of the Act for the Establishment of the Security Council of Japan, revised 30 September 2015.

33. Interview, 14 September 2017, Tokyo.

34. Kokkai Kaigiroku [Diet Records], House of Councillors Budget Committee, session 189, no. 4, 5 February 2015, 37.

35. Interview, former deputy secretary-general of the National Security Secretariat Takamizawa Nobushige, 19 December 2015, Tokyo.

36. Interview, 1 October 2017.

37. Interviews, various NSS officials, 17 December 2015; 25 December 2015; 12 September 2017; and 1 October 2017, Tokyo.

38. See Kokka Anzen . . . Yūshikisha Kaigi ed. 2013, 2.

39. Kokkai Kaigiroku [Diet Records], House of Councillors, Special Committee on the National Security, session 185, no. 2, 13 November 2013.

40. Interview, senior government official, 3 July 2014, Tokyo. Also see *Kokka Anzen . . . Yūshikisha Kaigi* ed. 2013.

41. Interview, senior NSS official, 1 October 2017, Tokyo.

42. *Sankei Shimbun*, 8 January 2015.

43. *Asahi Shimbun*, 8 January 2015.

44. Interview, CIRO official, 6 September 2017, Tokyo.

45. Data from Naikaku Kanbō at www.cas.go.jp/jp/yosan.

46. Interview with senior government official by Mayumi Fukushima, 29 June 2015, Tokyo.

47. Interview with senior government official by Mayumi Fukushima, 29 June 2015, Tokyo.

48. The *Asahi Shimbun* was still referring to "peaceful use of space" as national policy in October 2014. See *Asahi Shimbun*, 22 October 2014.

49. See Prime Minister Abe's remarks at the Strategic Headquarters for Space Development meeting on 9 January 2015, http://japan.kantei.go.jp/97_abe/actions/201501/09article1.html.

50. *Mainichi Shimbun*, 31 October 2014.

51. Kallender 2016, 11–12.

52. Kallender 2016, 9. This is a comprehensive review of Japan's Basic Space Plan and how it linked to both the new national security strategy and the alliance guidelines that took effect in 2015. In February 2018, the Cabinet Satellite Intelligence Center launched its fourteenth "intelligence-gathering satellite," the IGS-Optical 6. See *Spaceflight Insider*, 24 February 2018.

53. Jiji Press, 13 June 2018.

54. *Mainichi Shimbun,* 8 November 2014.

55. *Asahi Shimbun*, 18 November 2014.

56. The overview of results and detailed opinions collected are available at the Cabinet Office's website, http://www8.cao.go.jp/space/plan/plan2/kekka.pdf.

57. See the report "Policy Proposal of the Mt. Fuji Dialogue Special Task Force: Toward a Greater Alliance," Tokyo, April 2017, 7.

58. See comments by Mukai Chiaki, a former astronaut and member of the MEXT Space Exploration Sub-Committee, on 12 November 2014 at http://www.mext.go.jp/b_menu/shingi/gijyutu/gijyutu2/071/gijiroku/1354477.htm.

59. Anan 2013.

60. Interview, 17 December 2015, Tokyo.

61. Interview by Mayumi Fukushima, July 4, 2014, Tokyo. Machimura died in June 2015.

62. Interview by Mayumi Fukushima, 29 June 2015, Tokyo.

63. Interview, 14 September 2017, Tokyo.

64. *Sentaku*, September 2016, 54–55.

65. Interviews, 16 December 2015 and 23 October 2017, Tokyo.

66. *Asahi Shimbun*, 27 December 2016.

67. Interview, 6 September 2017, Tokyo.

68. Interview, Harada Takeo, 21 September 2017, Tokyo.

69. Interview, PSIA official, 3 October 2017, Tokyo.

70. See www.moj.go.jp/content/000112383.pdf and www.moj.go.jp/ENGLISH/PSIA/psia02-05.html. According to Seikan Yōransha ed. 2012 and 2017, the number of senior PSIA officials remained the same—just eighteen—while the rest of the Japanese intelligence community was rapidly expanding between 2012 and 2017.

71. Interview, senior PSIA official, 17 October 2017.

72. *Ryūkyū Shinpō*, 18 January 2017. The involvement of Chinese agents in anti-base demonstrations in Okinawa was confirmed by U.S. military officers, 13 November 2017, Kadena Air Force Base.

73. Zhou 2016.

74. *South China Morning Post*, 15 October 2015.

75. Kyodo World Service, 2 October 2015; *Themis*, November 2015; *Asahi Shimbun*, 26 October 2015. A PSIA official would neither confirm nor deny the press reports, suggesting instead that "the Japanese media are not necessarily credible." Interview, 3 October 2017, Tokyo.

76. NPA interview, 22 December 2015, Tokyo; MOD interview 17 December 2015, Tokyo.

77. *China Military Online*, 6 June 2017.

78. *Nikkei Asian Review*, 14 June 2017.

79. Reuters, 27 July 2017.

80. Kyodo, 19 September 2017.

81. Associated Press, 11 July 2018.

82. Interview, 6 September 2017, Tokyo.

83. *Yomiuri Shimbun*, 23 December 2018.

84. *NHK World*, 1 October 2015.

85. *New York Times*, 24 January 2014.

86. *Jihadist News*, 31 January 2015.

87. *Yomiuri Shimbun*, 6 February 2015.

88. Kokkai Kaigiroku [Diet Records], House of Representatives Budget Committee, session 189, no. 4, 5 February 2015, 38.

89. "Hōjin Satsugai Tero Jiken no Taiō ni Kansuru Kenshō Iinkai Kenshō Hōkokusho" [Report from the Review Committee on the Japanese Government's Response to the Terrorist Incident Killing of Japanese Citizens], in Hōjin Satsugai Tero Jiken no Taiō ni Kansuru Kenshō Iinkai ed. 2015.

90. *Yomiuri Shimbun*, 23 May 2015.

91. *Mainichi Shimbun*, 23 May 2015. A mid-career MOFA official with responsibility for Middle East policy explained how the dearth of Arabic-speaking officers handicaps Japanese intelligence and diplomacy. Interview, 12 September 2017.

92. Interview by Mayumi Fukushima, 29 June 2015, Tokyo.

93. Interview, 23 October 2017, Tokyo.

94. Interview by Mayumi Fukushima, 22 June 2015, Tokyo.

95. Interview by Mayumi Fukushima, 29 June 2015, Tokyo.

96. Interview, 17 December 2015, Tokyo.

97. Interview, 17 December 2015, Tokyo.

98. *Japan News*, 2 December 2015.

99. *Sentaku*, June 2016, 99.

100. *Senkaku*, March 2016, 98.

101. Interview, 12 September 2017, Tokyo.

102. Interview, 15 December 2015, Tokyo.

103. Kobayashi 2015, 728.

104. Interview, 14 September 2017, Tokyo.

105. Interview, Kotani Ken, National Institute for Defense Studies, 15 December 2015, Tokyo.

106. Interview, cabinet intelligence officer, 6 September 2017, Tokyo. Deputy Secretary General Kanahara Nobukatsu has made the same point. See "Nihon no Gaikō to Anzen Hoshō" [Japan's Diplomacy and National Security], speech by Kanehara Nobukatsu, deputy secretary general of the National Security Secretariat, to the Keizai Dōyūkai, 18 October 2016. Kaneko 2011, 327–28, explains how NIEs were processed before the NSC/NSS system began. The classic account of *ringi* decision making in Japanese organizations is Vogel ed. 1975.

107. See National Institute for Defense Studies ed. 2014 and Ministry of Defense, ed., "Defense of Japan, 2015, http://www.mod.go.jp/e/publ/w_paper/pdf/2015/H27DOJ_Digest_EN_web.pdf. Also see *Nikkei Asian Review*, 27 April 2015;

Kyodo, 10 September 2015; *Asahi Shimbun*, 22 October 2014; Martin 2016, 26; and Seffers 2013.

108. Interview, squadron commanders, Kadena Air Base, 13 November 2017.

109. Interview, Admiral Futakawa Tatsuya, Iwakuni, 15 November 2017. This point was amply illustrated when, in February 2018, the Japanese government released a video taken by a P-3C of a Maldivian tanker transferring oil in the East China Sea in the dead of night to a North Korean tanker, an exchange banned under a September 2017 UN Security Council resolution. See *Popular Mechanics*, 1 March 2018.

110. Email interview, 19 July 2018.

111. *Yonhap*, 18 December 2014; *Nikkei Asian Review*, 18 December 2014.

112. *Joong Ang Daily Online*, 26 December 2014.

113. Interview, 14 November 2017, Okinawa.

114. This accord, like GSOMIA, would face furious opposition and engender multiple threats of abrogation by both sides. See the analysis by Prakash Panneerselvam and Sandhya Puthanveedu in *The Diplomat*, http://thediplomat.com/2016/05/6-months-later-the-comfort-women-agreement/. *Yonhap*, 27 October 2016, connects the comfort women agreement to the resumption of GSOMIA talks.

115. *Yonhap*, 22 January 2016.

116. *Joong Ang Daily*, 3 April 2016.

117. *Yonhap*, 8 February 2016, for example, immediately insisted that public support would have to be a prerequisite. The original Han statement was reported in *Nihon Keizai Shimbun*, 8 February 2016.

118. Kyodo, 1 April 2016; *Yonhap*, 1 April 2016.

119. *Tokyo Shimbun*, 7 April 2016.

120. *Yonhap*, 2 September 2016.

121. *Dong-A Ilbo*, 27 October 2016.

122. *Asahi Shimbun*, 28 October 2016; *Dong-A Ilbo*, 29 October 2016. Noncombatant evacuation operations involving the Japanese military were opposed by local government officials in Korea. See Heginbotham and Samuels 2018.

123. *Nihon Keizai Shimbun*, 26 August 2017. Employing its typically overheated rhetoric, the official North Korean news agency called the pact "an extremely dangerous and criminal sycophantic and treacherous agreement paving a broader road of reinvasion on the Korean peninsula for the Japanese reactionaries bent on the revival of militarism, dreaming of realizing the 'Greater East Asia Co-Prosperity Sphere' under the cloak of 'exchange of intelligence.'" Korean Central News Agency, 5 September 2017.

124. *Korea Herald*, 19 November 2017.

125. *Sankei Shimbun*, 23 August 2018.

126. Interview, retired commander of GSDF Signals School, 16 December 2015, Tokyo.

127. Tatsumi 2015; *Yomiuri Shimbun*, 24 August 2016.

128. Kyodo, 3 October 2015.

129. Kyodo, 2 September 2015.

130. *Facta*, February 2016, 31.

131. Interview, 22 December 2015, Tokyo. Morimoto added two years later, "Although the CTU is an MI6-like prototype that can grow, we would need legislation to protect agents abroad, and that would be difficult." Interview, 31 October 2017.

132. Interview, 17 December 2015, Tokyo.

133. Interview, 6 September 2017, Tokyo.

134. See Daugherty 2004, 86–87; Kuroi 2005b, 237; *Asahi Shimbun*, 12 February 2000, 18 February 2000, and 16 November 2000. Note, however, that Gotōda Masaharu, the godfather of postwar intelligence reform, addressed the problem of cybersecurity in his 1998 memoirs. See Gotōda 1998, 1:237–38.

135. National Information Security Center of the Government of Japan ed. 2014.

136. *Asahi Shimbun*, 27 November 2000.

137. See press release from the Government of Japan, 26 March 2002, https://www.nisc.go.jp/conference/tyousakai/dai4/4siryou3.html.

138. Ministry of Internal Affairs (Sōmushō), "Jōhō Tsūshin Hakusho" [Information and Communication White Paper], 2011, pt. 3, chap. 5, http://www.soumu.go.jp/johotsusintokei/whitepaper/ja/h23/html/nc353210.html.

139. *Asahi Shimbun*, 11 December 2005.

140. *Asahi Shimbun*, 11 December 2005.

141. NSA document dated 8 January 2007, "Request for ADET SIGDEV Materials to Be Used for Training the Japanese Directorate for SIGINT Personnel," attached to Gallagher 2017.

142. Tsuchiya 2012, 172, 177.

143. *Asahi Shimbun*, 30 June 2012.

144. *Asahi Shimbun*, 8 September 2012, 5 February 2014, and 11 May 2017. See also Ministry of Defense, ed., *Defense White Paper 2016* (Tokyo, 2017), pt. 3, chap. 1, sec. 2. See also Kallender and Hughes 2016, 14. Information on NSA intelligence sharing in the cyber domain was revealed in the Snowden leaks. It increased in 2013 after Abe Shinzō returned to power. See Gallagher 2017, 12.

145. *Nihon Keizai Shimbun*, 7 November 2014.

146. NSA document dated 21 January 2013, "NSA Assistance to Japanese Directorate for SIGINT in Developing Capabilities," attached to Gallagher 2017.

147. *Nihon Keizai Shimbun*, 8 November 2017. In 2017 the number of cyberattacks increased by another 20 percent. See *Nihon Keizai Shimbun*, 28 February 2018.

148. This information and the quotes that follow are from an interview with Keidanren's Cybersecurity Working Group Staff, 30 October 2017, Tokyo.

149. http://www.nisc.go.jp/about/.

150. The 2015 Cyber Security Strategy is at http://www.nisc.go.jp/eng/pdf/cs-strategy-en.pdf.

151. Interview, 22 December 2015, Tokyo.

152. This JC3 unit is described at https://www.jc3.or.jp/about/index.html.

153. *Nihon Keizai Shimbun*, 23 December 2015.

154. On the "Delta Wall," see http://www.fsa.go.jp/news/29/sonota/20171020/20171020-1.html. The new office is the Cybersecurity Measures Planning and Coordination Office (Saibā Sekyuritī Taisaku Kikaku Chōsei Shitsu) under the Policy and Legal Division of the Planning and Coordination Bureau in FSA. An organizational chart is available at http://www.fsa.go.jp/policy/cybersecurity/index.html. The new office in the cabinet was reported in *Sankei Shimbun*, 5 January 2018.

155. Deloitte's *Asia-Pacific Defense Outlook 2016* (24 February 2016) is available at https://www2.deloitte.com/sg/en/pages/public-sector/articles/deloitte-2016-asia-pacific-defense-outlook.html.

156. *Asahi Shimbun*, 1 August 2013.

157. NISC, "Jōhō Sekyuritī Kenkyū Kaihatsu Senryaku Kaiteiban Kosshian" [Information Security Research and Development Strategy, revised version, summary draft], April 2014, http://www.nisc.go.jp/conference/seisaku/strategy/dai23/pdf/23shiryou03.pdf.

158. *Asahi Shimbun*, 28 February 2014.

159. *Nihon Keizai Shimbun*, 5 November 2018.

160. Gallagher 2017, 4, 10.

161. According to the Snowden leaks, this included XKEYSCORE, which sweeps nearly everything a user does on the Internet. See Gallagher 2017, 4, 8, 12, 15.

162. Gallagher 2017, 8, 12, 15.

163. These evolving relationships are reported in Gallagher 2018. See its attached leaked NSA document marked "Secret//SI//NOFORN," titled "The Current State of and Proposed Future Cooperation with Japan on SIGINT-Enabled Cyber Defense and the Development of a Japanese National Cyber Workforce."

164. https://wikileaks.org/nsa-japan/. See also Gallagher 2017.

165. Kyodo, 15 May 2014. Snowden had been sent to Japan by the NSA under the cover of an employee of a U.S. computer firm from 2009 to 2011. See Greenwald 2014 and Gallagher 2017, 12.

166. Abe is quoted in *Mainichi Shimbun*, 5 August 2015; Suga is quoted in the *Ryūkyū Shimbun*, 4 August 2015; and "subordinate and unproductive" is from *Asahi Shimbun*, 4 August 2015.

167. Kokkai Kaigiroku [Diet Records], House of Councillors Budget Committee, session 189, no. 4, 5 February 2015, 37.

168. Interview, 21 September 2017, Tokyo.

169. Interview, 20 September 2017, Tokyo.

170. Kōno, Mabuchi, and Yamauchi 2013, 97.

171. Interview, senior intelligence officer, 6 September 2017, Tokyo.

172. Interview, 14 September 2017, Tokyo.

173. Email interview, 19 July 2018.

174. Email interview, 19 July 2018.

175. Telephone interview, 16 July 2018.

176. Interview, Tokyo, 20 September 2017.

177. Ōmori 2005, 160–65.

178. Ōmori 2008, 98–99.

179. Kōno, Mabuchi, and Yamauchi 2013, 100.

180. Kobayashi 2012, 66–67.

181. The *Japan Times*, 24 January 2014, editorialized that at best "this may serve as a minor check against arbitrary designation" of secrets.

182. That is the claim of Kōmeitō representative Ōguchi Yoshinori, who nominated Shimizu. Interview by Mayumi Fukushima, 10 July 2014, Tokyo. Nakatani Gen, the LDP leader on this issue, says that working with Shimizu helped ensure passage of the legislation. Interview by Mayumi Fukushima, 9 July 2014, Tokyo.

183. Interview with Shimizu Tsutomu by Mayumi Fukushima, 9 July 2014, Tokyo. The critique was also noted in an editorial in the *Mainichi Shimbun*, 6 May 2014.

184. Interview with Shimizu Tsutomu by Mayumi Fukushima, 9 July 2014, Tokyo.

185. *Asahi Shimbun*, 21 July 2014.

186. *Nihon Keizai Shimbun*, 26 March 2014. In the lower house, the committee comprised five LDP members and one each from the DPJ, CGP, and Japan Innovation Party. In the upper house, four LDP, one CGP, and two DPJ members sat on the committee. The JCP had no representation at all. See *Yomiuri Shimbun*, 31 March 2014.

187. *Mainichi Shimbun*, 11 December 2014.

188. For more on the changes that were made during the public comment period, see *Nihon Keizai Shimbun*, 15 October 2014, and *Yomiuri Shimbun*, 14 and 15 October 2014.

189. *Mainichi Shimbun*, 18 December 2015.

190. *Mainichi Shimbun*, 31 March 2016.

191. This is from Kaye's preliminary observations, announced in Tokyo on 19 April 2016, https://www.ohchr.org/EN/NewsEvents/Pages/DisplayNews.aspx?NewsID=19842&LangID=E.

192. The government's formal rebuttal is here: https://www.ohchr.org/EN/HRBodies/HRC/RegularSessions/Session35/_layouts/15/WopiFrame.aspx?sourcedoc=/EN/HRBodies/HRC/RegularSessions/Session35/Documents/A_HRC_35_22_Add.5_E.docx&action=default&DefaultItemOpen=1. It was also reported, but never confirmed, that CIRO may have surveilled Kaye during his one week visit to Japan. See Fackler 2016.

193. For the Supreme Court's ruling, see Kyodo, 19 January 2018. For the Nukaga announcement, see *Mainichi Shimbun*, 27 January 2018.

194. *Asahi Shimbun*, 16 March 2017. Interview, senior intelligence officer, 6 September 2017, Tokyo.

195. Data from Seikan Yōran ed. 2012 and 2017 (spring editions).

196. Interview, LDP Representative Iwaya Takeshi (project team leader), 10 November 2017, Tokyo. See also *Sankei Shimbun*, 28 December 2017.

197. Interview, LDP Representative Iwaya Takeshi, 10 November 2017, Tokyo. Iwaya became defense minister in 2018.

198. This was one of eight key problems identified in the pre-NSC/NSS system by Kaneko 2011, 335.

199. Interview, 31 October 2017, Tokyo.

200. Interview, 23 October 2017, Tokyo.

201. See "Kokka Anzen Hishō Kaigi de Nairan Bappatsu" [Discord within the NSC], *Sentaku*, September 2007, 46.

202. Interview, General Kunimi Masahiro, 5 October 2017, Tokyo, emphasis added.

203. Interview, 23 October 2017, Tokyo.

7. The Past and Future of Japanese Intelligence

1. Interview, 16 July 2018. One anonymous reviewer of the manuscript of this book reminded the author that this was also true of MI6 and other allied intelligence services.

2. See also his doleful description of Japan as a "dependent nation" in Maruya 2005, 135.

3. "The Defense of Japan, 2007," http://www.mod.go.jp/e/publ/w_paper/2007.html.

4. Kaneko 2008, 4. His first two bottlenecks are what this volume refers to as horizontal and vertical communication, and his third is related to protection.

5. Shigeta 2006, 296

6. For a century-long genealogy of this and competing Japanese grand strategies, see chap. 1 in Samuels 2007.

7. See Hirajō Hiromichi 2010, 6.

8. Mazarr 2012, 8. See also "Japan Pivots in Asia," the July 2018 special issue of *International Affairs*.

9. "Using the alliance to transcend the alliance" was Ambassador Chas Freeman's apt formulation in private communication.

10. *Mainichi Shimbun*, 13 April 2018.

11. See chapter 6 for more on the proliferation of these offices. The increase in attacks was reported in *Nihon Keizai Shimbun*, 28 February 2018, and the increase in attachés is from *Taiwan Times*, 7 March 2018. Also, note that there was less bounce in that step when the government's 2018 cybersecurity budget allocated less than $700 million for cybersecurity to support just 150 staff. See *Yomiuri Shimbun*, 27 December 2017, for the new unit and the quantum cryptography initiative, and 2 February 2018 for JCG's radar plans. The 2018 budget is at https://www.misc.go.jp/active/kihon/pdf/yosan2018.pdf. For the cabinet announcement of the new strategies document, see *Mainichi Shimbun*, 18 January 2018.

12. *Sankei Shimbun*, 28 December 2015; interview, Iwaya Takeshi, LDP Diet representative, 10 November 2017, Tokyo.

13. Interview, counterintelligence official, 17 October 2017, Tokyo.

14. *Nikkei Asian Review*, 8 December 2018.

15. The term "maritime militia" is from Andrew S. Erickson and Connor F. Kennedy in an undated working paper available at https://www.cna.org/cna_files/pdf/chinas-maritime-militia.pdf.

16. Armitage and Nye eds. 2018.

17. These results were generated by the customized data search function in Google News. See Samuels 1994 and Samuels 2007 for the history of this strategic preference. For more on the recent uptick in this perspective, see Magosaki 2009; Kusaka and Itō 2011; Yanagisawa 2015; and Nishio, Nakanishi, and Kashihara 2017. See also Busujima 2017.

18. See Samuels and Schoff 2013 for analysis of Japan's nuclear hedge and other options.

19. These guidelines were explicit about the need for the SDF to "enhance intelligence capabilities" across the board. See http://www.mod.go.jp/j/approach/agenda/guideline/2019/pdf/20181218_e.pdf.

20. Wittes and Blum 2015 outline these threats. For more on "deep fakes"—the digital manipulation of sound and images to counterfeit people—see Chesney and Citron 2018 and 2019; *New York Times*, 4 March 2018; *The Economist*, 1 July 2017.

21. *South China Morning Post*, 4 December 2017; *Nikkei Asian Review*, 27 October 2018.

22. Interview, 6 September 2017.

23. Email interview, 19 July 2018.

BIBLIOGRAPHY

Aid, Matthew M. 2000. "The Time of Troubles: The U.S. National Security Agency in the Twenty-First Century." *Intelligence and National Security* 15, no. 3 (Autumn): 1–32.

Akahata Tokusōhan, ed. 1978. *Kage no Guntai: Nihon no Kuromaku, Jieitai Himitsu Gurūpu no Maki* [Shadow Military: Japan's Backroom Mastermind, the Self-Defense Forces Secret Group]. Tokyo: Shin Nihon Shuppansha.

Akashi, Yōji, and Mako Yoshimura. 2008. *New Perspectives on the Japanese Occupation in Malaya and Singapore, 1941–1945*. Singapore: National University of Singapore.

Akimoto, Daisuke. 2012. "The Shift from Negative Pacifism to Positive Pacifism: Japan's Contribution to Peacekeeping in Cambodia." *Ritsumeikan Journal of Asia Pacific Studies* 31: 120–32.

Allen, Louis. 1985. "The Nakano School." *Proceedings of the British Association of Japanese Studies* 10: 9–18.

——. 1987. "Japanese Intelligence Systems." *Journal of Contemporary History* 22, no. 4 (October): 547–62.

Amnesty International. 2014. "Japan: Submission to the United Nations Human Rights Committee: 111th session of the Human Rights Committee (7–25th July 2014)," London. http://tbinternet.ohchr.org/Treaties/CCPR/Shared%20Documents/JPN/INT_CCPR_CSS_JPN_17507_E.pdf.

Anan, Keiichi. 2013. "Administrative Reform of Japanese Space Policy Structures in 2012." *Space Policy* 29, no. 3 (August): 210–18.

Andrew, Christopher M. 1995. *For the President's Eyes Only: Secret Intelligence and the American Presidency from Washington to Bush*. New York: Harper Perennial.

——. 2019. *The Secret World: A History of Intelligence*. New Haven: Yale University Press.

Andrew, Christopher M., and Vasili Mitrokhin. 2005. *The World Was Going Our Way: The KGB and the Battle for the Third World*. New York: Basic Books.

Ao Hiromasa. 2009. *Jieitai Himitsu Chōhō Kikan* [The Self-Defense Force's Secret Intelligence Unit]. Tokyo: Kodansha.

Arima Tetsuo. 2010a. *Daihonei Sanbō wa Sengo Nani to Tatakattanoka.* [What Was the Imperial Military Headquarters Staff Fighting after the War?]. Tokyo: Shinchōsha.

——. 2010b. *CIA to Sengo Nihon* [The CIA and Postwar Japan]. Tokyo: Heibonsha.

——. 2010c. "*Mō Hitotsu no Saigunbi*" [Another Rearmament]." *Waseda Shakai Kagaku Sōgō Kenkyū* 10, no. 3 (March).

——. 2010d. *Daihonei Sanbō wa Sengo Nani to Tattakata no Ka* [What Did the Imperial Headquarters Staff Officers Fight Against?] Tokyo: Shinchōsha.

———. 2014. *1949 Nen no Daitōa Kyōeiken* [The Greater East Asia Co-Prosperity Sphere in 1949]. Tokyo: Shinchō-sha.

Arisue Seizō. 1982. *Seiji to Gunji to Jinji* [Politics, Military, and Personnel]. Tokyo: Fuyō Shobō.

Armitage, Richard L., et al. 2000. "The United States and Japan: Advancing toward a Mature Partnership." Washington, DC: Institute for National Strategic Studies.

Armitage, Richard L., and Joseph S. Nye, eds. 2018. "More Important Than Ever: Renewing the U.S.-Japan Alliance for the 21st Century." Washington, DC: Center for Strategic and International Studies.

Arrington, Celeste. 2016. *Accidental Activists: Victim Movements and Government Accountability in Japan and South Korea*. Ithaca: Cornell University Press.

Asagumo Shimbunsha Shuppan Gyōmubu, ed. 2016. *Jieitai Sōbi Nenkan 2016–2017* [The Self-Defense Forces Equipment Yearbook, 2016–17]. Tokyo: Asagumo Shimbunsha.

Asō Iku. 2003. *Jōhō Kantei ni Tassezu* [Intelligence That Never Reached the Prime Minister's Office]. Tokyo: Shinchō Bunko.

Avey, Paul C., and Michael C. Desch. 2014. "What Do Policymakers Want from Us? Results of a Survey of Current and Former Senior National Security Decision Makers." *International Studies Quarterly* 58, no. 2: 227–46.

Aydin, Cemil. 2007. *The Politics of Anti-Westernism in Asia: Visions of World Order in Pan-Islamic and Pan-Asian Thought*. New York: Columbia University Press.

Baker, James E. 2010. "Covert Action: United States Law in Substance, Process, and Practice." Chapter 36 in *The Oxford Handbook of National Security Intelligence*, edited by Loch K. Johnson. Oxford: Oxford University Press.

Ball, Desmond. 2006. "Whither the Japan-Australia Security Relationship?" APSNet Policy Forum, September 21. http://nautilus.org/apsnet/0632a-ball-html/.

Ball, Desmond, and Richard Tanter. 2012. "The Transformation of the JASDF's Intelligence and Surveillance Capabilities for Air and Missile Defense." *Security Challenges* 8, no. 3 (Spring): 19–56.

———. 2015a. *The Tools of Owatatsumi: Japan's Ocean Surveillance and Coastal Defense Capabilities*. Canberra: ANU Press.

———. 2015b. "US Signals Intelligence (SIGINT) Activities in Japan, 1945–2015: A Visual Guide." Nautilus Institute for Security and Sustainability Special Report, 23 December.

———. 2016. "US Signals Intelligence (SIGINT) Activities in Japan, 1945–2015: A Visual Guide." *Asian-Pacific Journal* 14. 6, no. 8 (15 March): 1–11.

Bandō Hiroshi. 1995. *Pōrandojin to Nichiro Sensō* [The Polish and the Russo-Japanese War]. Tokyo: Aoki Shoten.

Barger, Deborah G. 2005. *Toward a Revolution in Intelligence Affairs*, Santa Monica: RAND Corporation.

Bar-Joseph, Uri. 2004. *The Watchman Fell Asleep: The Surprise of Yom Kippur and Its Sources*. Albany: State University of New York Press.

Bar-Joseph, Uri, and Jack Levy. 2009. "Conscious Action and Intelligence Failure." *Political Science Quarterly* 124 (3): 461–88.

Bar-Joseph, Uri, and Rose McDermott. 2017. *Intelligence Success and Failure: The Human Factor*. London: Oxford University Press.

Barnhart, Michael A. 1984. "Japanese Intelligence before the Second World War: 'Best Case' Analysis." Chapter 14 in *Knowing One's Enemies: Intelligence Assessment before the Two World Wars,* edited by Ernest R. May. Princeton: Princeton University Press.

———. 1987. *Japan Prepares for Total War: The Search for Economic Security, 1919–1941.* Ithaca: Cornell University Press.

Bauman, Zygmunt, Didier Bigo, Paulo Esteves, Elspeth Guild, Vivienne Jabri, David Lyon, and R. B. J. Walker. 2014. "After Snowden: Rethinking the Impact of Surveillance." *International Political Sociology* 8, no. 2 (June): 121–44.

Bennett, J. W., W. A. Hobart, and J. B. Spitzer, eds. 1986. *Intelligence and Cryptanalytic Activities of the Japanese during World War II.* Laguna Hills, CA: Aegean Park Press.

Berger, Thomas U. 1998. *Cultures of Antimilitarism: National Security in Germany and Japan.* Baltimore: Johns Hopkins University Press.

Berkowitz, Bruce D. 2001. "Better Ways to Fix U.S. Intelligence." *Orbis* 45, no. 4: 609–21.

Berkowitz, Bruce D., and Allan E. Goodman. 1998. "The Logic of Covert Action." *The National Interest* 51 (Spring): 38–46.

Best, Anthony. 2002. "Intelligence, Diplomacy and the Japanese Threat to British Interests, 1914–41." *Intelligence and National Security* 17, no. 1 (Spring): 85–100.

Best, Richard A. Jr. 2004. "Proposals for Intelligence Reorganization." *CRS Reports for Congress,* 24 September.

Betts, Richard K. 1978. "Analysis, War, and Decision: Why Intelligence Failures Are Inevitable." *World Politics* 31, no. 1 (October): 61–89.

———. 1982. *Surprise Attack: Lessons for Defense Planning.* Washington, DC: Brookings Institution.

———. 2007. *Enemies of Intelligence: Knowledge and Power in American National Security.* New York: Columbia University Press.

Bob, Clifford. 2015. "Secrecy, Diffusion, and Democracy." Memo prepared for Workshop on Secrecy, Surveillance, Privacy, and International Relations, MIT Center for International Studies, 16–17 April.

Bōeishō, ed. 2014. "Bōeishō Jieitai no Keikai Kanshi Taisei ni Tsuite [The Ministry of Defense and the JASDF's Patrol and Surveillance Capabilities]." November.

Bond, Trudy, Benjamin Davis, Curtis F. J. Doebbler et al., eds. 2014. *Shadow Report to the United Nations Committee against Torture on the Review of the Periodic Report of the United States of America.* Cambridge: International Human Rights Clinic, Harvard Law School.

Born, Hans, and Fairlie Jensen. 2007. "Intelligence Services: Strengthening Democratic Accountability." Chapter 15 in *Democratic Control of Intelligence Services: Containing Rogue Elephants,* edited by Hans Born and Marina Caparini. London: Ashgate.

Boyd, Carl. 1993. *Hitler's Japanese Confidant: General Ōshima Hiroshi and MAGIC Intelligence, 1941–1945.* Lawrence: University Press of Kansas.

Brooks, Barbara J. 1989. "China Experts in the Gaimushō, 1895–1937." Chapter 11 in *The Japanese Informal Empire in China, 1895–1937,* edited by Peter Duus et al. Princeton: Princeton University Press.

Brown, Arthur Judson. 1919. *The Mastery of the Far East*. New York: Charles Scribner's Sons.

Brown, Richard G. 1960. "Anti-Soviet Operations of Kwantung Army Intelligence." *Studies in Intelligence* 4, no. 2 (Spring): 25–34. (Declassified and approved for release 17 December 2004.)

Bruneau, Thomas C., and Steven C. Boraz, eds. 2007. *Reforming Intelligence: Obstacles to Democratic Control and Effectiveness*. Austin: University of Texas Press.

Burton, Jeffery F., M. Farrell, F. Lord, and R. Lord. 2002. *Confinement and Ethnicity: An Overview of World War II Japanese American Relocation Sites*. Seattle: University of Washington Press.

Busch, Noel F. 1969. *The Emperor's Sword: Japan vs. Russia in the Battle of Tsushima*. New York: Funk & Wagnall.

Busujima Tōya. 2016. *Kaijō Jieitai no Sōbi no Subete* [Everything about the JMSDF Equipment]. Tokyo: Esubī Kurieitibu.

——. 2017. *Jieitai Jishu Bōeika Keikaku* [A Plan for Making the Self-Defense Forces Autonomous]. Tokyo: Takarajimasha.

Caparini, Marina. 2007. "Controlling and Overseeing Intelligence Services in Democratic States." Chapter 1 in *Democratic Control of Intelligence Services: Containing Rogue Elephants*, edited by Hans Born and Marina Caparini. London: Ashgate.

Castravelli, Nunzia. 2006. "In margine al conflitto russo-giapponese 1904–1905: Akashi Motojirō e i rapporti dell'intelligence giapponese con i rivoluzionari russi" [On the Sidelines of the Russo-Japanese Conflict, 1904–1905: Akashi Motojirō and the Relationships of Japanese Intelligence with Russian Revolutionaries]. *Il Giappone* 46: 43–48.

Cha, Victor D. 2016. *Powerplay: The Origins of the American Alliance System in Asia*. Princeton: Princeton University Press.

Chalk, Peter, and William Rosenau. 2004. *Confronting the "Enemy Within": Security Intelligence, the Police, and Counterterrorism in Four Democracies*. Santa Monica: RAND Corporation.

Chan, Steve. 1979. "The Intelligence of Stupidity: Understanding Failures in Strategic Warning." *American Political Science Review* 73, no. 1 (March): 171–80.

Chapman, J. W. M. 1987. "Japanese Intelligence, 1918–1945: A Suitable Case for Treatment." In *Intelligence and International Relations, 1900–1945*, edited by Christopher Andrew and Jeremy Noakes, 145–90. Exeter: University of Exeter Press.

Cheng, Dean. 2016. *Cyber Dragon: Inside China's Information Warfare and Cyber Operations*. Santa Barbara: Praeger.

Chesney, Robert, and Danielle Citron. 2018. "Deep Fakes: A Looming Crisis for National Security, Democracy, and Privacy?" Blog post. *Lawfare*, 21 February.

——. 2019. "Deepfakes and the New Disinformation War: The Coming of Age of Post-Truth Geopolitics," *Foreign Affairs* 98, no.1: 147–55.

Chijiwa, Yasuaki. 2012. "Historical Transition of the Security Organs Subordinate to the Cabinet and the Japanese Version of the National Security Council." *National Institute for Defense Briefing Memo*, no. 170, n.p.

Chopin, Olivier. 2015. "Intelligence Reform and Transformation of the State: A French Perspective." Paper presented to the annual meeting of the International Studies Association, New Orleans, February 17–22.

Clulow, Adam. 2014. *The Company and the Shogun*. New York: Columbia University Press.

Codevilla, Angelo. 2002. *Informing Statecraft*. New York: Simon and Schuster.

Cohen, C. J. 2000. "Early History of Remote Sensing." *Applied Imagery Pattern Recognition Workshop*. http://www.computer.org/csdl/proceedings/aipr/2000/0978/00/09780003-abs.html.

Cole, David. 2014. "The Three Leakers and What to Do about Them." *New York Review of Books*, 6 February 2014, 7–9.

Colley, Linda. 2002. *Captives*. New York: Pantheon.

Commission on the Intelligence Capabilities of the United States Regarding Weapons of Mass Destruction, ed. 2005. "Report to the President of the United States." Washington, DC, 1 March.

Cook, Malcolm, and Thomas S. Wilkins. 2014. "Aligned Allies: The Australia-Japan Strategic Partnership," Tokyo Foundation, 24 December.

Coox, Alvin. 1992. "Japanese Net Assessment in the Era before Pearl Harbor." Chapter 8 in *Calculations: Net Assessment and the Coming of World War II*, edited by Allan R. Millett and Williamson Murray. New York: Free Press.

Cordesman, Anthony H. 2004. "The 9/11 Commission Report: Strengths and Weaknesses." Center for Strategic and International Studies, revised 2 August.

Corn, David, and Michael Isikoff. 2018. *Russian Roulette: The Inside Story of Putin's War on America and the Election of Donald Trump*. New York: Twelve.

Crowdy, Terry. 2006. *The Enemy Within: A History of Spies, Spymasters, and Espionage*. New York: Osprey.

Dahl, Erik J. 2013. *Intelligence and Surprise Attack: Failure and Success from Pearl Harbor to 9/11 and Beyond*. Washington, DC: Georgetown University Press.

Daitoku, Takaaki. 2014. "Resorting to Latency: Japan's Accommodation with Nuclear Realities." Unpublished manuscript presented to Workshop on Nuclear Latency, Woodrow Wilson International Center for Scholars. Washington, DC, 2 October.

Daugherty, William J. 2004. *Executive Secrets: Covert Action and the Presidency*. Lexington: University Press of Kentucky.

——. 2010. "Covert Action: Strengths and Weaknesses." Chapter 37 in *The Oxford Handbook of National Security Intelligence*, edited by Loch K. Johnson. Oxford: Oxford University Press.

Davies, Philip H. J. 2002. "Ideas of Intelligence: Divergent National Concepts and Institutions." *Harvard International Review* (Fall): 62–66.

——. 2012. "Defence Intelligence in the U.K. after the Mountbatten Reforms: Organisational and Inter-Organisational Dilemmas of Joint Military Intelligence." *Public Policy and Administration* 28, no. 2: 196–213.

Davies, Philip H. J., and Kristian C. Gustafson. 2013a. "An Agenda for the Comparative Study of Intelligence." Chapter 1 in *Intelligence Elsewhere: Spies and Espionage Outside the Anglosphere*, edited by Philip H. J. Davies and Kristian C. Gustafson. Washington, DC: Georgetown University Press.

——. 2013b. "Legacies, Identities, Improvisation, and Innovations of Intelligence." Chapter 15 in *Intelligence Elsewhere: Spies and Espionage outside the Anglosphere*, edited by Philip H. J. Davies and Kristian C. Gustafson. Washington, DC: Georgetown University Press.

Davis, Jack. 1991. "The Kent-Kendall Debate of 1949." *Center for the Study of Intelligence, Studies Archives Indexes* 35, no. 2 (March): 91–103.

——. 2002. "Improving CIA Analytic Performance: Strategic Warning." *The Sherman Kent Center for Intelligence Analysis Occasional Papers* 1, no. 1 (September): n.p.

——. 2003. "Strategic Warning: If Surprise Is Inevitable, What Role for Analysis?" *The Sherman Kent Center for Intelligence Analysis Occasional Papers* 2, no. 1 (January): 1–16.

Deacon, Richard. 1983. *Kempeitai: A History of the Japanese Secret Service*. New York: Beaufort Books.

Doihara Kenji Kankōkai, ed. 1972. *Hiroku Doihara Kenji* [Secret Record on Doihara Kenji]. Tokyo: Fuyō Shobō.

Donovan, William J. 1946. "A Central Intelligence Agency: Foreign Policy Must Be Based on Facts." Speech delivered at the *New York Herald Tribune* High School Forum, New York, 13 April 1946, and reprinted in *Vital Speeches of the Day* 12, no. 14 (May): 446–48.

Dorling, Philip. 2011. "WikiLeaks Unveils Japanese Spy Agency." *Sydney Morning Herald*, 21 February.

Drea, Edward J. 1984. "Missing Intentions: Japanese Intelligence and the Soviet Invasion of Manchuria, 1945." *Military Affairs* 48 (April): 66–73.

——. 1991. "Reading Each Other's Mail: Japanese Communications Intelligence, 1920–1941." *Journal of Military History* 55, no. 2 (April): 185–206.

——. 2011. "Tortured History: How a Massive Project to Write MacArthur's War Story Exploded into a Strange Battle of Egos and Agendas." *World War II* (May–June): 38–45.

Drea, Edward J., and Joseph E. Richard. 1999. "New Evidence on Breaking the Japanese Army Codes." *Intelligence and National Security* 14, no. 1: 62–83.

Dubovský, Peter. 2006. *Hezekiah and the Assyrian Spies: Reconstruction of the Neo-Assyrian Intelligence Services and Its Significance for 2 Kings 18–19*. Rome: Editrice Pontifico Istituto Biblico.

Dudden, Alexis. 2014. "Abe's NSA? The Japanese Government Embraces Secrecy." *Dissent*, January 28. http://www.dissentmagazine.org/online_articles/abes-nsa-the-japanese-government-embraces-secrecy.

Dundar, A. Merthan. 2008. "Three U.S. Reports Concerning Japanese Pan-Asianism and Pan-Islamism." *Annals of the Japanese Association of Middle East Studies*. Special issue, *Japan and the Middle East before WWII*. Tokyo: Japanese Association of Middle East Studies.

Duns, Jeremy. 2017. "This Is How Five Eyes Dies," *Foreign Policy*, 30 March.

Ehrhardt, George, Axel Klein, Levi McLaughlin, and Steven R. Reed, eds. 2014. *Kōmeitō*. Berkeley: Institute of East Asian Studies, University of California.

Elphick, Peter. 1997. *Far Eastern File: The Intelligence War in the Far East, 1930–1945*. London: Hodder & Stoughton.

Everest-Phillips, Max. 2006. "Reassessing Pre-War Japanese Espionage: The Rutland Naval Spy Case and the Japanese Intelligence Threat before Pearl Harbor." *Intelligence and National Security* 21, no. 2 (April): 258–85.

——. 2007. "The Pre-War Fear of Japanese Espionage: Its Impact and Legacy." *Journal of Contemporary History* 42, no. 2: 243–65.

Fackler, Martin. 2016. "The Silencing of Japan's Free Press." *Foreign Policy*, 27 May, n.p. https://foreignpolicy.com/2016/05/27/the-silencing-of-japans-free-press-shinzo-abe-media/.

Faludi, Susan. 2007. *The Terror Dream: Fear and Fantasy in Post-9/11 America*. New York: Metropolitan Books.

Farago, Ladislas. 1967. *The Broken Seal: The Story of "Operation Magic" and the Pearl Harbor Disaster*. New York: Random House.

Farson, Stuart. 1997. "Review Essay: Japan: Better Intelligence or Convenient Bogeyman?" *Journal of Conflict Studies* 17, no. 2 (Fall): n.p. https://journals.lib.unb.ca/index.php/JCS/article/view/11757/12534.

Federation of American Scientists, ed. 1996. "The Evolution of the U.S. Intelligence Community: An Historical Overview." http://fas.org/irp/offdocs/int022.html.

Finnegan, John P. 2011. The Evolution of US Army HUMINT: Intelligence Operations in the Korean War." *Studies in Intelligence* 55, no. 2: 57–70.

Fleischer, Julia. 2013. "The Coordination of Homeland Security Policy in Germany." Paper prepared for the European Commission Project on Coordinating for Cohesion in the Public Sector (COCOPS). Speyer: German Research Institute for Public Administration.

Fravel, M. Taylor. 2019. *Active Defense: The Evolution of China's Military Strategy since 1949*. Princeton: Princeton University Press.

Frühstück, Sabine. 2014. "A 'Dynamic Joint Defense Force'? An Introduction to Japanese Strategic Thinking." *Asia-Pacific Journal: Japan Focus*, 18 March. http://japanfocus.org/events/make_pdf/213.

Fry, Michael G., and Miles Hochstein. 1994. "Epistemic Communities: Intelligence Studies and International Relations." In *Espionage: Past, Present, and Future*, edited by Wesley K. Wark, 14–28. Portland, OR: Frank Cass.

Fujiwara, Iwaichi. 1983. *F. Kikan: Japanese Army Intelligence Operations in Southeast Asia during World War II*. Hong Kong: Heinemann Asia.

Fujiwara Kiichi. 2013. "Tokutei Himitsu Hogi Hōan: Shiranai Kenri mo Kiken [Special Designated Secrets Bill: The Right to Not Know Also in Danger]." Tokyo Daigaku Seisaku Bujiyon Sentaa, 22 November. http://pari.u-tokyo.ac.jp/column/column102.html.

Fuke Takahiro. 2016. "Sanmu Jiken Josetsu [Introduction to the Three Noes Incident]." *Shakai Kagaku* (Doshisha University) 46, no. 3 (November): 1–26.

Fukushima, Mayumi, and Richard J. Samuels. 2018. "Japan's National Security Council: Filling the Whole of Government." In *Japan Pivots in Asia*, edited by Richard J. Samuels and Corey L. Wallace. Special issue of *International Affairs* (Spring): 773–90.

Gaddis, John Lewis. 1992. *The United States and the End of the Cold War: Implications, Reconsiderations, Provocations*. New York: Oxford University Press.

Gaiji Jiken Kenkyūkai, ed. 2007. *Sengo no Gaiji Jiken: Supai, Rachi, to Fusei Yushutu* [Postwar Intelligence Incidents: Spies, Abductions, and Illicit Exports]. Tokyo: Tōkyō Hōrei Shuppan.

Gaimushō Hyakunenshi Hensan Iinkai, ed. 1969a. *Gaimushō no Hyakunen Jō* [One Hundred Years of the Ministry of Foreign Affairs, vol. 1]. Tokyo: Hara Shobō.

——. 1969b. *Gaimushō no Hyakunen Ge* [One Hundred Years of the Ministry of Foreign Affairs, vol. 2]. Tokyo: Hara Shobō.

Gallagher, Ryan. 2017. "Japan Made Secret Deals with the NSA That Expanded Global Surveillance." *The Intercept*, 24 April, n.p. https://theintercept.com/2017/04/24/japans-secret-deals-with-the-nsa-that-expand-global-surveillance/.

——. 2018. "The Untold Story of Japan's Secret Spy Agency." *The Intercept*, 19 May, n.p. https://theintercept.com/2018/05/19/japan-dfs-surveillance-agency/.

Garicano, Luis, and Richard A. Posner. 2005. "Intelligence Failures: An Organizational Economics Perspective." *Journal of Economic Perspectives* 19, no. 4 (Fall): 151–70.

Gartzke, Eric. 2013. "The Myth of Cyberwar: Bringing War in Cyberspace Back Down to Earth." *International Security* 38, no. 2 (Fall): 41–73.

Gazit, Shlomo. 1980. "Estimates and Fortune-Telling in Intelligence Work." *International Security* 4, no. 4: 36–56.

Gellman, Barton, and Greg Miller. 2013. "'Black Budget' Summary Details U.S. Spy Network's Successes, Failures and Objectives." *Washington Post*, 29 August.

George, Alexander L. 1959. *Propaganda Analysis*. Evanston, IL: Row, Peterson, and Co.

George, Roger Z. 2006. "Fixing the Problem of Analytical Mindsets: Alternative Analysis." Chapter 25 in *Intelligence and the National Security Strategist: Enduring Issues and Challenges,* edited by Roger Z. George and Robert D. Kline. Latham, MD: Roman and Littlefield.

Geospatial Information Authority of Japan, ed. 2012. "Geospatial Information Authority of Japan, 2012." Tsukuba, Japan.

GHQ U.S. Army Forces Pacific Military Intelligence Section, ed. Various dates. "General Staff Daily Intelligence Summary." Tokyo: G.H.Q. U.S. Army Forces Pacific Military Intelligence Section.

Gioe, David. 2014. "Tinker, Tailor, Leaker, Spy." *The National Interest* (January–February): 51–59.

——. 2015. "Treachery in Historical Perspective: Comparing Cyber-Spy Edward Snowden and the Cambridge Five." Paper presented to the annual meeting of the International Studies Association, New Orleans, 17–22 February.

Godson, Roy. 1995. *Dirty Tricks or Trump Cards: U.S. Covert Action and Counterintelligence*. Washington, DC: Brassey's.

Goldman, Adam. 2014. "U.S. Spy Freed by Cuba Was Longtime Asset." *Washington Post*, 18 December.

Goodman, Michael S., Frances Robles, and Mark Mazzetti. 2014. "Crucial Spy in Cuba Paid a Heavy Cold War Price." *New York Times*, 18 December.

Gordon, Andrew. 1985. *The Evolution of Labor Relations in Japan: Heavy Industry, 1853–1955*. Cambridge: Harvard University Press.

——. 2009. *A Modern History of Japan*. New York: Oxford University Press.

Gotōda Masaharu. 1998. *Jō to Ri: Gotōda Masaharu Kaikoroku* [Sentiment and Reason: Memoirs of Gotōda Masaharu]. 2 volumes. Tokyo: Kenkyūsha.

Grabo, Cynthia M. 2002. *Anticipating Surprise: Analysis for Strategic Warning*. Washington, DC: Joint Military Intelligence College Center for Strategic Intelligence Research.

Greene, Graham. 1955. *The Quiet American*. London: Heinemann.

Greenwald, Glenn. 2014. *No Place to Hide: Edward Snowden, the NSA, and the U.S. Surveillance State*. New York: Metropolitan Books / Henry Holt.

Grønning, Bjørn, and Elias Mikalsen. 2018. "Operational and Industrial Military Integration: Extending the Frontiers of the Japan–US Alliance." In *Japan Pivots in Asia*, edited by Richard J. Samuels and Corey L. Wallace. Special issue of *International Affairs* (Spring): 755–72.

Grono, Nicholas. 2007. "Australia's Response to Terrorism: Strengthening the Global Intelligence Network." Washington, DC: Center for the Study of Intelligence.

Gunji Kenkyū (journal), ed. 2006. "Kyūnihongun Tokumu Kikan no Zenbō [The Full Story of the Former Imperial Military's Special Agencies]." September, 145–76.

Hackett, Roger F. 1971. *Yamagata Aritomo in the Rise of Modern Japan*. Cambridge: Harvard University Press.

Hall, John Whitney. 1988. *The Cambridge History of Japan*. Volume 4. Cambridge: Cambridge University Press.

Hall, Simon. 2014. "Imperial Japanese Army Intelligence in North and Central China during the Second Sino-Japanese War." *Salus Journal* 2, no. 2: 16–30.

Halperin, Morton, and Molly Hofsommer. 2014. "Japan's Secrecy Law and International Standards." *Asia-Pacific Journal: Japan Focus* 12.37, no. 1 (4 August September): n.p. https://apjjf.org/-Molly-M--Hofsommer--Morton-H--Halperin/4183/article.pdf.

Hamilton, Lee H., and Daniel K. Inouye. 1987. *Report of the Congressional Committees Investigating the Iran-Contra Affair*. Washington, DC: U.S. Government Printing Office.

Han, Sang Il. 1974. "Uchida Ryōhei and Japanese Continental Expansion, 1874–1916." Ph.D. dissertation, Faculty of Asian Studies, Claremont Graduate School.

Handa Yūichirō. 1999. *Yōkai suru Kōan Chōsachō* [The Meltdown of the Public Security and Intelligence Agency]. Tokyo: Gendai Shokan.

Handel, Michael I. 1981. *The Diplomacy of Surprise: Hitler, Nixon, Sadat*. Cambridge: Harvard University Center for International Affairs.

——. 1987. "The Politics of Intelligence." *Intelligence and National Security* 2, no. 4: 5–46.

——. 1989. "Leaders and Intelligence." Chapter 1 in *Leaders and Intelligence*, edited by Michael I. Handel. London: Frank Cass.

——. 1992. "Intelligence in Historical Perspective." Chapter 9 in *Go Spy the Land: Military Intelligence in History*, edited by Keith Nielson and B. J. C. McKercher. Westport, CT: Praeger.

Handō Kazutoshi. 1998. *Nomonhan no Natsu* [That Summer in Nomonhan]. Tokyo: Bungei Shunjū.

——. 2007. "Hattori Takushirō to Tsuji Masanobu: Bōsō suru Sanbō Konbi no Musekinin [Hattori Takushirō and Tsuji Masanobu: Reckless and Irresponsible Staff Leaders in Tandem]." *Bungei Shunjū* (June): 126–31.

Hansen, James H. 1996. *Japanese Intelligence: The Competitive Edge*. Washington, DC: National Intelligence Book Center.

Harkabi, Yehoshafat. 1984. "The Intelligence-Policymaker Tangle." *Jerusalem Quarterly* 30 (Winter): 125–31.

Harries, Meirion, and Susie Harries. 1991. *Soldiers of the Sun: The Rise and Fall of the Imperial Japanese Army.* New York: Random House.

Harris, Shane. 2014. *@War: The Rise of the Military-Internet Complex.* 1st edition. Boston: Eamon Dolan/Houghton Mifflin Harcourt.

Harris, Sheldon. 1994. *Factories of Death: Japanese Biological Warfare, 1932–45, and the American Cover-Up.* London: Routledge.

Harrison, E. J. 1946. "Famous Judo Masters I Have Known." *Budokwai Quarterly Bulletin* (July): 16.

Hastedt, Glenn. 1991. "Towards the Comparative Study of Intelligence." *Conflict Quarterly* 11, no. 3 (Summer): 55–72.

Hastings, Max. 2018. "Smoke and Mirrors." *New York Review of Books,* 27 September, 49–51.

Hata Ikuhiko. 1991. *Nihon Rikukaigun Sōgō Jiten* [The Japanese Army and Navy Dictionary]. 2nd edition. Tokyo: Tokyo University Press.

Hayashi Takeshi, Wada Tomoyuki, and Ōyagi Atsuhiro. 2011. "Kenkyū Nōto Gunki Hogohō no Seitei Katei to Mondaiten" [The Military Secrecy Protection Law: Its Enactment Process and Problems]." *National Institute for Defense Studies Bulletin* 14, no. 1 (December): 87–109.

Haynes, Justin M. 2009. "Intelligence Failure in Korea: Major General Charles A. Willoughby's Role in the United Nations Command's Defeat in November 1950." M.A. thesis presented to the U.S. Army Command and General Staff College, Fort Leavenworth, KS.

Hedley, John Hollister. 2005. "Learning from Intelligence Failures." *International Journal of Intelligence and Counterintelligence* 18, no. 3: 435–50.

Heginbotham, Eric. 2003. "Military Organizations, Domestic Politics, and Grand Strategy: Explaining Military Doctrine in Developing States." Ph.D. dissertation, Department of Political Science, Massachusetts Institute of Technology.

Heginbotham, Eric, and Richard J. Samuels. 1999. "Mercantile Realism and Japanese Foreign Policy during and after the Cold War." Chapter 6 in *Unipolar Politics: Realism and State Strategies after the Cold War,* edited by Michael Mastanduno and Ethan Kapstein. New York: Columbia University Press.

——. 2018. "With Friends Like These: Japan-ROK Cooperation and U.S. Policy." *Asan Forum,* 1 March, n.p. http://www.theasanforum.org/with-friends-like-these-japan-rok-cooperation-and-us-policy/.

Henderson, Robert D'A. 1997. "Reviews and Commentary: Reforming Japanese Intelligence." *International Journal of Intelligence and CounterIntelligence* 10, no. 2: 227–38.

Henry, F. 1943. "Japanese Espionage and Our Psychology for Failure." *US Naval Institute Proceedings* 69: 639–41.

Herman, Michael. 2001. *Intelligence Services in the Information Age: Theory and Practice.* London: Frank Cass.

——. 2003. "Counter-Terrorism, Information Technology, and Intelligence Change." *Intelligence and National Security* 18, no. 4 (Winter): 40–58.

Hersh, Seymour M. 2018. *Reporter: A Memoir.* New York: Alfred A. Knopf.

Hilsman, Roger. 1956. *Strategic Intelligence and National Decisions.* Glencoe, IL: The Free Press.

Hirajō Hiromichi. 2010. *Nichibei Himitsu Jōhō Kikan: "Kage Guntai" Musashi Kikanchō no Kokuhaku* [The Secret U.S.-Japan Intelligence Organization: Confessions of the Commander of the Shadow Army Unit "Musashi"]. Tokyo: Kodansha.

Historic Wings, ed. 2012. "By Foxbat to Freedom," 6 September. http://fly.historic-wings.com/2012/09/by-foxbat-to-freedom/.

Hōjin Satsugai Tero Jiken no Taiō ni Kansuru Kenshō Iinkai, ed. 2015. "Hōjin Satsugai Tero Jiken no Taiō ni Kansuru Kenshō Iinkai Kenshō Hōkokusho [Report from the Review Committee on the Japanese Government's Response to the Terrorists' Killing of Japanese Citizens]." 21 May.

Honda Masaru et al., eds., 2005. *Jieitai: Shirarezaru Henyō* [Self-Defense Forces: The Unknown Changes]. Tokyo: Asahi Shimbunsha.

Hori Eizō. 1989. *Daihonei Sanbō no Jōhō Senki: Jōhō naki Kokka no Higeki.* [The Intelligence Strategy of the Imperial Military Headquarters' Staff: A National Tragedy without Intelligence]. Tokyo: Bungei Shunjū.

Hoshi Hiroshi. 2013. "Himitsu Hogi Hōan, Ano Goro no Jimin Nara [The Secrets Protection Bill: If We Were Citizens at That Time]." *Asahi Shimbun,* 17 November.

Hulnick, Arthur S. 1986. "The Intelligence Producer–Policy Consumer Linkage: A Theoretical Approach." *Intelligence and National Security* 1, no. 2: 212–33.

———. 1996. "U.S. Covert Action: Does It Have a Future?" *International Journal of Intelligence and Counterintelligence* 9, no. 2: 145–57.

———. 2006. "What's Wrong with the Intelligence Cycle." *Intelligence and National Security* 21, no. 6 (December): 959–79.

Humphrey, Peter. 2007. "MASINT Frontiers" *American Intelligence Journal* 25, no. 1: 21-8.

Hynd, Alan. 1943. *Betrayal from the East.* New York: R. M. McBride and Company.

Hyōmoto Tatsukichi. 2002. "Fuwa Kyōsanto Gichō wo Samon Seyo [Investigate Communist Party Leader Fuwa]." *Bungei Shunju,* no. 12:174–83.

Ikegami Toshihiko. 2008. "Wagakuni no Uchū Kaihatsu no Keii [The History of Japan's Space Development]." Presentation to the Ministry of Defense Space Development and Utilization Promotion Committee, 7 November.

Inaba, Chiharu. 1988a. "Akashi's Career." In *Rakka Ryūsui: Colonel Akashi's Report on His Secret Cooperation with the Russian Revolutionary Parties during the Russo-Japanese War,* by Chiharu Inaba, Olavi K. Fält, and Antti Kujala, 16–19. Helsinki: Societas Historica Finlandiae

———. 1988b. "The Politics of Subversion: Japanese Aid to Opposition Groups in Russia during the Russo-Japanese War." In *Rakka Ryūsui: Colonel Akashi's Report on His Secret Cooperation with the Russian Revolutionary Parties during the Russo-Japanese War,* by Chiharu Inaba, Olavi K. Fält and Antti Kujala, 67–83. Helsinki: Societas Historica Finlandiae.

———. 1995. *Akashi Kōsaku: Bōryaku no Nichirō Sensō* [Akashi's Maneuvers: Plots of the Russo-Japanese War]. Tokyo: Maruzen.

Inaba, Chiharu, Olavi K. Fält, and Antti Kujala. 1988. *Rakka Ryūsui: Colonel Akashi's Report on His Secret Cooperation with the Russian Revolutionary Parties during the Russo-Japanese War.* Helsinki: Societas Historica Finlandiae.

Inose Naoki. 2017. *Shōwa 16 Nen Natsu no Haisen* [Defeat in the Summer of 1941]. Tokyo: Chūō Kōronsha.

Inoue Kazuhiko. 2015. *Jieitai no Saikyō Sōbi* [The Self-Defense Forces' Finest Equipment]. Tokyo: Futabasha.

Ishihara Nobuo. 1995. *Kantei 2668 Hi: Seisaku Kettei no Butai Ura* [2,668 Days in the Prime Minister's Office: Behind the Scenes of Policy Decisions]. Tokyo: NHK.

Ishimitsu Makiyo. 1988. *Ishimitsu Makiyo no Shuki* [The Autobiography of Ishimitsu Makiyo]. Tokyo: Chūō Kōronsha.

Ishitaki Toyomi. 2010. *Genyōsha: Fūin Sareta Jitsuzō* [Genyōsha: Its Long-Sealed True Nature]. Fukuoka: Kaichōsha.

Iwashima Hisao. 1984. *Jōhōsen ni Kanpai shita Nihon* [Japan's Utter Defeat in the Intelligence Battle]. Tokyo: Hara Shobō.

Jacob, Frank. 2014. *Japanism, Pan-Asianism, and Terrorism: A Short History of the Amur Society (The Black Dragons), 1901–1945*. Bethesda, MD: Academia Press.

Jane, Fred T. 1904. *The Imperial Japanese Navy*. London: W. Thacker & Co.

Jansen, Marius B. 1954. *The Japanese and Sun Yat-sen*. Cambridge: Harvard University Press.

Jeans, Roger B. 2009. *Terasaki Hidenari, Pearl Harbor, and Occupied Japan*. Lanham, MD: Lexington Books.

Jervis, Robert. 1976. *Perception and Misperception in International Politics*. Princeton: Princeton University Press.

——. 1986–87. "Intelligence and Foreign Policy: A Review Essay." *International Security* 11, no. 3 (Winter): 141–61.

——. 2006. "Reports, Politics, and Intelligence Failures: The Case of Iraq." *Journal of Strategic Studies* 29, no. 1 (February): 3–52.

——. 2010. *Why Intelligence Fails: Lessons from the Iranian Revolution and the Iraq War*. Ithaca: Cornell University Press.

——. 2018. "Intelligence and International Affairs." Chapter 35 in *The Oxford Handbook of International Security*, edited by Alexandra Gheciu and William C. Wohlforth. Oxford: Oxford University Press.

Jieitai no Nazo Kenshō Iinkai, ed., 2014. *Jieitai no Saishin Saikyō Heiki 99 no Nazo* [99 Puzzles about the Self-Defense Forces' Newest and Most Powerful Weapons]. Tokyo: Saizusha.

Johnson, Chalmers A. 1964. *An Instance of Treason: Ozaki Hotsumi and the Sorge Spy Ring*. Stanford: Stanford University Press.

——. 1982. *MITI and the Japanese Miracle: The Growth of Industrial Policy, 1925–1975*. Stanford: Stanford University Press.

Johnson, Loch K. 1988. *A Season of Inquiry, Congress and Intelligence*. Chicago: Dorsey Press.

——. 1989. "Covert Action and Accountability: Decision-Making for America's Secret Foreign Policy." *International Studies Quarterly* 33: 81–109.

——. 1997. "The CIA and the Question of Accountability." *Intelligence and National Security* 12, no. 1: 178–200.

——. 2003a. "Bricks and Mortar for a Theory of Intelligence." *Comparative Strategy* 22, no. 1: 1–27.

——. 2003b. "Preface to a Theory of Strategic Intelligence." *International Journal of Intelligence and Counterintelligence* 16, no. 4: 638–63.

——. 2011. *National Security Intelligence*. Cambridge: Polity.

Johnston, Eric. 2004. "The North Korean Abduction Issue and Its Effect on Japanese Domestic Politics." Japan Policy Research Institute Working Paper 101, June.

Johnston, Rob. 2005. *Analytic Culture in the US Intelligence Community: An Ethnographic Study.* Washington, DC: Center for the Study of Intelligence, Central Intelligence Agency.

Jōhō Kinō Kyōka Kentō Kaigi, ed. 2008. "Kantei ni okeru Jōhō no Kyōka no Hōshin [A Plan for Strengthening Intelligence in the Cabinet Office]." Internal memorandum, 14 February.

Jourdonnais, Adam. 1963. "Intelligence in the New Japan." *Studies in Intelligence 7,* no. 3: n.p. https://www.cia.gov/library/center-for-the-study-of-intelligence/kent-csi/vol7no3/html/v07i3a01p_0001.htm.

Journal of Palestine Studies, ed. 1974. "Israel: What Went Wrong on October 6? The Partial Report of the Israeli Commission of Inquiry into the October War." *Journal of Palestine Studies* 3, no. 4: 189–207.

Joyal, Paul M. 1996. "Industrial Espionage Today and Information Wars of Tomorrow." Paper presented at the 19th National Information Systems Security Conference, Baltimore, 22–25 October.

Kahana, Ephraim. 2005. "Analyzing Israel's Intelligence Failures." *International Journal of Intelligence and CounterIntelligence* 18, no. 2: 262–79.

Kahn, David. 1980. "Codebreaking in World Wars I and II: The Major Successes and Failures, Their Causes and Their Effects." *Historical Journal* 23, no. 3: 617–39.

——. 2001. "An Historical Theory of Intelligence." *Intelligence and National Security* 16, no. 3: 79–92.

Kaido Yuichi. 2013. *Himitsu Hō de Sensō Junbi, Genpatsu Suishin* [The Secrecy Law Promotes War Preparation and Nuclear Energy]. Tokyo: Sōshi-sha.

——. 2014. *Han Genpatsu e no Iyagarase Zenkiroku* [A Full Record of Harassment Activities against Antinuclear Movements]. Tokyo: Akashi Shoten.

Kallender, Paul. 2016. "Japan's New Dual-Use Space Policy: The Long Road to the 21st Century." *Asie Visions,* Institut Français des Relations Internationales 88, November.

Kallender, Paul, and Christopher W. Hughes. 2016. "Japan's Trajectory as a 'Cyber Power': From Securitization to Militarization of Cyberspace." *Journal of Strategic Studies,* 26 September. https://www.tandfonline.com/doi/full/10.1080/01402390.2016.1233493.

——. 2018. "Hiding in Plain Sight? Japan's Militarization of Space and Challenges to the Yoshida Doctrine." *Asian Security,* 5 March. https://www.tandfonline.com/doi/full/10.1080/14799855.2018.1439017.

Kam, Ephraim. 1988. *Surprise Attack: The Victim's Perspective.* Cambridge: Harvard University Press.

Kaneko Masafumi. 2007. "Komyunitii Seijuku e no Nagai Michinori [A Long Way toward a Mature Intelligence Community]." In *Sekai no Interijensu: Nijū Isseki no Jōhō Sensō wo Yomu* [Global Intelligence: Understanding Intelligence Warfare in the 21st Century], edited by Kotani Ken. Tokyo: PHP Kenjyūjo.

——. 2008. "Kantei no Interijensu Kinō wa Kyōka Sareru Ka [Will the Cabinet's Intelligence Function Be Strengthened?]." *PHP Policy Review* 2, no. 6 (29 February).

——. 2011. "Japan: Sōō no Jitsuryoku wo Moteru no Ka [Japan: Do We Have Suitable Capabilities?]." Chapter in *Interijensu Naki Kokka wa Horobu* [States without Intelligence Will Be Ruined], edited by Ochiai, Kōtarō. Tokyo: Aki Shobō.

——. 2014. "Sekkyokuteki Heiwashugi no Keifu [The Pedigree of 'Proactive Pacifism']." *PHP Sōken Kenkyūin Koramu*, 19 February. http://research.php.co.jp/blog/kaneko/2014/02/19.php.

Kano Tadao. 2011. "Interijensu no Ima wo Yomitoku 58 [Understanding the Current Status of Intelligence, Issue 58]." *Keizaikai* 953 (18 October).

Kanwal, Gurmeet. 2012. "Defense Reforms in India: Slow but Steady Progress." *CSIS Issue Perspective* 2, no. 4: 1–3.

Kasai, Akio. 1996. "National Intelligence in Japan: Myth and Reality." Chapter 7 in *Post–Cold War, Democratization, and National Intelligence: A Comparative Perspective*, edited by Jin-Hyun Kim and Chung-in Moon. Seoul: Yonsei University Press.

Katō Masao. 1998. *Rikugun Nakano Gakkō no Zenbō* [The Whole Story of the Imperial Army's Nakano School]. Tokyo: Tendensha.

Keisatsuchō, ed. 1981. *Keisatsu Hakusho Shōwa 56 Nen* [Police White Paper, 1981]. Tokyo: Keisatsuchō.

Kelley, Stephen D. 1989. "Curbing Illegal Transfers of Foreign-Developed Critical High Technology for CoCom Nations to the Soviet Union: An Analysis of the Toshiba-Kongsberg Incident." *Boston College International and Comparative Law Review* 12, no. 1 (December): 181–223.

Kello, Lucas. 2013. "The Meaning of the Cyber Revolution: Perils to Theory and Statecraft." *International Security* 38, no. 2 (Fall): 7–40.

Kendall, Willmoore. 1949. "The Function of Intelligence." *World Politics* 1, no. 4: 542–52.

Kent, Sherman. 1949. *Strategic Intelligence for American World Policy*. Princeton: Princeton University Press.

Kibbe, Jennifer D. 2010. "Covert Action, Pentagon Style." Chapter 35 in *The Oxford Handbook of National Security Intelligence*, edited by Loch K. Johnson. Oxford: Oxford University Press.

Kindsvater, Larry C. 2003. "The Need to Reorganize the Intelligence Community." *Studies in Intelligence* 47, no. 1: 33–37.

Kissinger, Henry A. 1969. "The Vietnam Negotiations." *Foreign Affairs* 47, no. 2: 211–34.

Kitachōsen ni Ratchi Sareta Kazoku ni yoru Renrakukai, ed. 2003. *Kazoku* [The Families]. Tokyo: Kobunsha.

Kitaoka, Shinichi. 2015. "Insights into the World: Five Key Steps for Shaping National Strategy." *Japan News*, 28 December.

Klass, Gary M. 2008. *Just Plain Data Analysis*. Lantham, MD: Rowman and Littlefield.

Kluckhohn, Frank. 1952. "Heidelberg to Madrid: The Story of General Willoughby." *The Reporter*, 19 August. http://www.maebrussell.com/Articles%20and%20Notes/Charles%20Willoughby.html.

Knudsen, Christian, and Tsoukas Haridimos. 2005. *The Oxford Handbook of Organization Theory*. Oxford: Oxford University Press.

Kobayashi Yoshiki. 2012. "Interijensu Komyunitei ni taisuru Minshuteki Tōsei no Seido [Systems for Democratic Oversight of Intelligence Communities].: *Kokusai Seiji* 167 (January): 57–71.

——. 2015. "Assessing Reform of the Japanese Intelligence Community." *International Journal of Intelligence and Counterintelligence* 28, no. 4: 717–33.

Kōketsu Atsushi. 2008. *Kempei Seiji: Kanshi to Dōkatsu no Jidai* [The Politics of the Military Police: The Era of Surveillance and Intimidation]. Tokyo: Shin Nihon Shuppansha.

Kokka Anzen Hoshō Kaigi no Sōsetsu ni kansuru Yūshikisha Kaigi, ed. 2013. "Wagakuni no Jōhō Kinō ni Tsuite [Regarding Japan's Intelligence Functions]." Daisankai Kaigō Setsumei Shiryō [Handouts for the third meeting], 29 March.

Konishi Makoto. 2017. *Jieitai no Tōsho Sensō* [The Self-Defense Forces' Islands War]. Tokyo: Shakai Hihyōsha.

Kōno Tarō, Mabuchi Sumio, and Yamauchi Kōichi. 2013. "Nihongata 'Supai Soshiki' no Tsukurikata [How to Build a Japanese-Style Spy Organization]." *Chūō Kōron* (May): 94–101.

Kotani, Ken. 2005. "Could Japan Read Allied Signal Traffic? Japanese Codebreaking and the Advance into French Indo-China, September 1940." *Intelligence and National Security* 20, no. 2 (June) 304–20.

——. 2006. "Wagakuni ni Okeru Interijensu no Genjō to Kadai [The Current Situation and Problems of Intelligence in Japan]." *Bōei Kenkyūjo Nyūzu* 100 (May): n.p.

——. 2007. *Nihongun no Interijensu* [Japanese Military Intelligence]. Tokyo: Kōdansha.

——. 2008. "Nihongun to Interijensu—Seikō to Shippai no Jirei Kara [Japanese Military Intelligence: Examples of Success and Failure]." *National Institute for Defense Studies Journal* 11, no. 1 (November): 43–68.

——. 2009a. "Current Japanese Intelligence Reform." Paper presented to the Oxford Intelligence Group, Nuffield College, 13 March.

——. 2009b. "Japanese Intelligence in WWII: Successes and Failures." Tokyo: National Institute for Defense Studies Working Paper. http://www.nids.go.jp/english/publication/kiyo/pdf/2009/bulletin_e2009_2.pdf.

——. 2009c. *Japanese Intelligence in World War II*. Oxford: Osprey.

——. 2013. "A Reconstruction of Japanese Intelligence: Issues and Prospects." Chapter 10 in *Intelligence Elsewhere: Spies and Espionage outside the Anglosphere*, edited by Philip J. Davies and Kristian C. Gustafson. Washington, DC: Georgetown University Press.

Kotkin, Stephen. 2017. *Stalin: Waiting for Hitler, 1929–1941*. New York: Penguin Press.

Kowalski, Frank. 2013. *An Inoffensive Rearmament: The Making of the Postwar Japanese Army*. Annapolis, MD: Naval Institute Press.

Krebs, Gerhard. 1996. "The Spy Activities of Diplomat Terasaki Hidenari in the USA and His Role in Japanese-American Relations." Chapter 15 in *Leaders and Leadership in Japan,* edited by Ian Neary. London: Curzon Press Japan Library.

Krieger, Wolfgang. 2009. "Oversight of Intelligence: A Comparative Analysis." Chapter 9 in *National Intelligence Systems*, edited by Gregory Treverton and Wilhelm Agrell. New York: Cambridge University Press, 2009.

Kshetri, Nir. 2014. "Japan's Changing Cybersecurity Landscape." *Computer* 47, no. 1: 83–86.

Kumamoto, Bob. 1979. "The Search for Spies: American Counterintelligence and the Japanese American Community, 1931–1942," *Amerasia Journal* 6, no. 2: 45–75.

Kurobane Shigeru. 1976. *Nichiro Sensō to Akashi Kōsaku* [The Russo-Japanese War and Colonel Akashi's Operations]. Tokyo: Nansōsha.

Kuroi Buntarō. 2005a. "Wārudo Interijensu [Worldwide Intelligence]." *Gunji Kenkyū* (September): n.p.

———. 2005b. "Wārudo Interijensu [Worldwide Intelligence]." *Gunji Kenkyū* (November): n.p.

———. 2007. *Nihon no Jōhō Kikan* [Japan's Intelligence Organizations]. Tokyo: Kōdansha.

———. 2008. *Interijensu no Gokui!* [The Mysteries of Intelligence]. Tokyo: Takarajimasha.

———. 2009a. "Jieitai Jōhō Butai no Tanjō to Ayumi [The Birth and Development of the Self-Defense Force Intelligence Unit]." *Gunji Kenkyū* (April): 194–204.

———. 2009b. "Jieitai Jōhō Butai no Tanjō to Ayumi [The Birth and Development of the Self-Defense Force Intelligence Unit]." *Gunji Kenkyū* (May): 218–29.

———. 2009c. "Rikubaku Nibu Jōhō Ippan Tokkinhan Hitokumei 'Musashi' no Jitsuzō towa? [What Was the Ground Staff Office Intelligence Department First Intelligence Office Special Unit, Code-Named 'Musashi,' Really Doing?]" *Gunji Kenkyū* (September): 232–41.

———. 2009d. *Dainippon Teikoku Manshū Tokumu Kikan* [The Imperial Japan's Special Duty Units in Manchuria]. Tokyo: Fusōsha.

———. 2011. *Bōryaku no Shōwa Rimenshi* [The Dark Side of the Shōwa History]. Tokyo: Takarajimasha.

———, ed. 2009. *Sengo Hishi Interijensu* [The Secret History of Postwar Intelligence]. Tokyo: Daiwa Shobō.

Kusaka Kimindo and Itō Kan. 2011. *Jishu Bōei wo Isoge!* [Move Quickly to Autonomous Defense!]. Tokyo: Rihakusha.

Kuwada Etsu. 1996. "Hikari Kikan [The Hikari Special Duty Unit]." In *Shōwa Gunji Hiwa: Dōdai Kurabu Koenshu* [Secret Accounts of the Shōwa Military: Collected Speeches of the Dōdai Club], edited by Kanatomi Yoshiji, n.p. Tokyo: Dōdai Keizai Konwakai.

Laqueur, Walter. 1985. *A World of Secrets: The Uses and Limits of Intelligence*. New York: Basic Books.

Latell, Brian. 2012. *Castro's Secrets: The CIA and Cuba's Intelligence Machine*. New York: Palgrave Macmillan.

Lathrop, Charles E., ed. 2004. *The Literary Spy*. New Haven: Yale University Press.

Lebra, Joyce Chapman. 2008. *The Indian National Army and Japan*. Singapore: Institute of Southeast Asian Studies.

le Carré, John. 2016. *The Pigeon Tunnel: Stories from My Life*. New York: Viking.

———. 2017. *Legacy of Spies*. New York: Viking.

Lefebvre, Stéphane. 2004. "A Look at Intelligence Analysis." *International Journal of Intelligence and CounterIntelligence* 17, no. 2: 231–64.

Le Gallo, André. 2005. "Covert Action: A Vital Option in U.S. National Security Policy." *International Journal of Intelligence and CounterIntelligence* 18, no. 2: 354–59.

Lester, Genevieve. 2015. *When Should State Secrets Stay Secret?* New York: Cambridge University Press.

Levchenko, Stanislav. 1988. *On the Wrong Side: My Life in the KGB*. Washington, DC: Pergamon-Brassey's International Defense Publishers.

Levite, Ariel. 1987. *Intelligence and Strategic Surprises*. New York: Columbia University Press.

Liff, Adam P. 2018. "Japan's National Security Council: Policy Coordination and Political Power." *Japanese Studies*, 19 August. https://www.tandfonline.com/doi/abs/10.1080/10371397.2018.1503926?journalCode=cjst20.

Lijphart, Arend. 1968. *The Politics of Accommodation: Pluralism and Democracy in the Netherlands*. Berkeley: University of California Press.

Lindsay, Jon R. 2017. "Restrained by Design: The Political Economy of Cybersecurity." *Digital Policy, Regulation, and Governance* 19, no. 6: 493–514.

Lindsay, Jon R., Tai Ming Cheung, and Derek S. Reveron, eds. 2015. *China and Cybersecurity: Espionage, Strategy, and Politics in the Digital Domain*. New York: Oxford University Press.

Lindsay, Jon R., and Lucas Kello, 2013. "Correspondence." *International Security* 38, no. 2 (Fall): 181–92.

Loureiro, Pedro A. 1989. "The Imperial Japanese Navy and Espionage: The Itaru Tachibana Case." *Intelligence and Counterintelligence* 3, no. 1: 105–21.

——. 1994. "Japanese Espionage and American Countermeasures in Pre–Pearl Harbor California." *Journal of American–East Asian Relations* 3, no. 3: 197–210.

Lowenthal, Mark M. 2011. *Intelligence: From Secrets to Policy*. 5th edition. Beverly Hills: Sage.

——. 2015. *Intelligence: From Secrets to Policy*. 6th edition. Beverly Hills: Sage.

Lowman, David Daniel. 2001. *MAGIC: The Untold Story of U.S. Intelligence and the Evacuation of Japanese Residents from the West Coast during World War II*. Provo, UT: Athena Press.

MacCartney, John D. 2001. "John, How Should We Explain MASINT?" *Intelligencer: Journal of U.S. Intelligence Studies* 12, no. 1 (Summer): 28–34.

Machimura Nobutaka. 2005. *Hoshu no Ronri: Rin toshite Utsukushii Nihon wo Tsukuru* [The Logic of Conservatism: Creating a Dignified, Beautiful Japan]. Tokyo: PHP Kenkyūjo.

Macintyre, Ben. 2007. *Agent Zigzag: A True Story of Nazi Espionage, Love, and Betrayal*. New York: Crown.

Maesaka Toshiyuki. 2011. *Akashi Motojirō Taisa: Teisei Roshia Hakai Kōsaku Hōkokusho wo Yomitoku* [Colonel Akashi Motojirō: How to Understand Akashi's Report on his Subversive Activities against the Russian Empire]. Tokyo: Shinjinbutsu Ōraisha.

Magosaki Ukeru. 2009. *Nichibei Dōmei no Shōtai: Meisō Suru Anzen Hoshō* [The True Character of the U.S.-Japan Alliance: National Security Off Course]. Tokyo: Kōdansha.

Mahnken, Thomas G. 1996. "Gazing at the Sun: The Office of Naval Intelligence and Japanese Naval Innovation." *Intelligence and National Security* 11, no. 3 (July): 424–41.

Marrin, Stephen. 2002. "Homeland Security and the Analysis of Foreign Intelligence." Report of the Markle Foundation Task Force on National Security in the Information Age, 15 July.

Martin, Deirdre Q. 2016. "Trajectories of Intelligence-Building: Japan in the Post–Cold War." Paper prepared for the annual conference of the International Studies Association.

Maruya Akihiko. 2005. "Jōhō Kankei Kikan wo meguru Nihon no Genjō ni Tsuite [The Actual Situation of Intelligence-Related Organizations in Japan]." Chapter 8 in *Beikoku no Jōhō Kikan Kaikaku* [The Reform of U.S. Intelligence Organizations]. Washington, DC: CSIS Report.

——. 2012. "The South Manchuria Railway Company as an Intelligence Organization," Report of the CSIS Japan Chair, Center for Strategic and International Studies, Washington, DC, February.

Mason, Ra, and Sebastian Maslow. 2015. "North Korea and the Politics of Risk Framing." Chapter 3 in *Risk State: Japan's Foreign Policy in an Age of Uncertainty*, edited by Sebastian Maslow, Ra Mason, and Paul O'Shea. London: Routledge.

Masunaga, Shingo.2017. "The Inter-War Japanese Military Intelligence Activities in the Baltic States, 1919–1940." Ph.D. dissertation, University of Turku.

Matsumoto Shigeo. 2008. *Jieitai "Kage no Butai" Jōhōsen* [The Self-Defense Forces "Shadow Troops" Intelligence War]. Tokyo: Asupekuto.

Matsumura, Masahiro. 2013. "Deepening Japan's Information Security Regime: The Need of Domestic Legislation." Institute for National Strategic Studies, National Defense University, November.

Matthews, Tony. 1993. *Shadows Dancing: Japanese Espionage against the West, 1939–1945*. New York: St. Martin's Press.

May, Ernest R. 1992. "Intelligence: Backing into the Future." *Foreign Affairs* 1, no. 3: 63–72.

Michael J. Mazarr. 2012. "The Risks of Ignoring Strategic Insolvency." *Washington Quarterly* 35, no. 4: 7–22.

McNeil, Phyllis Provost. 2014. "The Evolution of the U.S. Intelligence Community: An Historical Overview." Appendix B in *Intelligence: The Secret World of Spies*, edited by Loch K. Johnson and James J. Wirtz. Oxford: Oxford University Press.

Mercado, Stephen C. 1994. "Japanese Army Intelligence Activities against the United States, 1921–45." *Studies in Intelligence*, 49–55.

——. 2002. *The Shadow Warriors of Nakano: A History of the Imperial Japanese Army's Elite Intelligence School*. Washington, DC: Brassey's.

——. 2002–3. "An Insight into Japanese CI." *International Journal of Intelligence and CounterIntelligence* 15, no. 4: 628–32.

——. 2004a. "The Japanese Army's Noborito Research Institute." *International Journal of Intelligence and CounterIntelligence* 17, no. 2: 286–99.

——. 2004b. "A Venerable Source in a New Era: Sailing the Sea of OSINT in the Information Age." *Studies in Intelligence* 48, no. 3: 45–55.

——. 2007. "Reexamining the Distinction between Open Information and Secrets." Center for the Study of Intelligence, *CSI Publications* 49, no. 2 (April): n.p. https://www.cia.gov/library/center-for-the-study-of-intelligence/csi-publications/csi-studies/studies/Vol49no2/reexamining_the_distinction_3.htm.

——. 2010. Review of Kotani Ken, *Nihongun no Interijensu: Naze Jōhō ga Ikasarenai no Ka* [Japanese Military Intelligence: Why Is Intelligence Not Used?] *Studies in Intelligence* 54, no. 1 (March): 51–53.

——. 2012. Review of "Intelligence in Public Literature—*KLO ui Hangukchon Pisa* [Secret History of the KLO in the Korean War]." https://www.cia.gov/library/center-for-the-study-of-intelligence/csi-publications/csi-studies / studies / vol.-56-no.-1 / klo-ui-hangukchon-pisa-secret-history-of-the-klo-in-the-korean-war.html.

Meyer, Cord. 1980. *Facing Reality: From World Federalism to the CIA*. New York: Harper and Row.

Military History Section of Headquarters, Army Forces Far East, ed. 1955. "Anti-Soviet Operations of Kwantung Army Intelligence, 1940–1941." Washington, DC: Office of Military History, Department of the Army. [Approved for release, CIA Historical Review Program, 22 September 1993.]

Mistry, Kaeten. 2011. "Approaches to Understanding the Inaugural CIA Covert Operation in Italy: Exploding the Useful Myths." *Intelligence and National Security* 26, no. 2–3 (April–June): 246–68.

Mori Ei. 2008. *Kuro no Kikan* [Black Special Duty Units]. Tokyo: Shōdensha.

Morris-Suzuki, Tessa. 2009. "Refugees, Abductees, 'Returnees': Human Rights in Japan–North Korea Relations." *Asia-Pacific Journal: Japan Focus* 7, no. 3 (24 March). https://apjjf.org/-Tessa-Morris-Suzuki/3110/article.html.

——. 2014. "Democracy's Porous Borders: Espionage, Smuggling, and the Making of Japan's Transwar Regime (Part 1)." *Asia Pacific Journal: Japan Focus* 12.40, no. 4 (6 October) https://apjjf.org/2014/12/40/Tessa-Morris-Suzuki/4198.html.

Mounk, Yascha. 2017. "Germany First." *The National Interest* (September–October): 33–39.

Munson, C. B. 2000. "Japanese on the West Coast." Chapter 6 in *Asian American Studies: A Reader*, edited by Jean Yu-wen Shen Wu and Min Song. New Brunswick: Rutgers University Press.

Murphy, David. 2005. *What Stalin Knew: The Enigma of Barbarossa*. New Haven: Yale University Press.

Murray, Williamson, and Kevin Woods. 2014. *The Iran-Iraq War: A Military and Strategic History*. New York: Cambridge University Press.

Mutsu Munemitsu. 2015. *Kenkenroku: Nisshin Sensō Gaikō Hiroku* [Secret Diplomatic Records Regarding the Sino-Japanese War]. 13th edition. Tokyo: Iwanami Shoten.

Naikaku Kanbō, ed. 2010. "Jōhō to Jōhō Hozen" [Intelligence and Intelligence Protection]." Internal memorandum, May.

Naikaku Kanbō Tokutei Himitsu Hogo Hō Shikō Junbi Shitsu, ed. 2014. *Tokutei Himitsu Hogo Hō Shikōrei Soan Setsumei Shiryō* [Explanatory Data for the Draft of the Special Secrets Protection Law Enforcement Order]. Tokyo: Naikaku Kanbō Tokutei Himitsu Hogo Hō Shikō Junbi Shitsu.

Nakamuda Kenichi. 1985. *Jōhō Shikan no Kaisō* [Reminiscences of an Intelligence Officer]. Tokyo: Asahi Sonorama.

Nakanishi Hiroshi. 2011. "Jōhō to Gaikō [Intelligence and Diplomacy]." *Kokusai Mondai* 600 (April): 18–25.

——. 2015. "Reorienting Japan? Security Transformation under the Second Abe Cabinet." *Asian Perspective* 39, 405–21.

Nakanishi Terumasa. 2007. "Nihon ni okeru Interijensu Kenkyū no tame Ni [Toward Intelligence Research in Japan]." In *Interijensu no 20 Seiki* [Intelligence in the 20th Century], edited by Terumasa Nakanishi and Ken Kotani, 1–13. Tokyo: Chikura Shobō.

Namatame, Norifumi. 2012. "Japan and Ballistic Missile Defense: Debates and Difficulties." *Security Challenges* 8, no. 3 (Spring): 1–17.

National Information Security Center of the Government of Japan, ed. 2014. "Jūyō Infura no Jōhō Sekyuritī Taisaku ni Kakaru Daisanji Kōdō Keikaku no Gaiyō [Summary of the Third Action Plan Regarding Information Security Measures to Protect Important Infrastructure]." 10 October.

National Institute for Defense Studies, ed. 2014. *East Asian Strategic Review 2014.* Tokyo: National Institute for Defense Studies.

Nihon Kindaishi Kenkyūkai, ed. 1989. *Nihon Rikukaigun no Seido, Soshiki, Jinji* [The System, Organization, and Personnel of Japan's Imperial Army and Navy]. Tokyo: Tokyo Daigaku Shuppankai.

Nish, Ian. 1984. "Japanese Intelligence and the Approach of the Russo-Japanese War." In *The Missing Dimension: Governments and Intelligence Communities in the Twentieth Century,* edited by Christopher Andrew and David Dilks, 17–32. Urbana: University of Illinois Press.

——. 1987. "Japanese Intelligence, 1894–1922." In *Intelligence and International Relations, 1900–1945,* edited by Christopher Andrew and Jeremy Noakes, 127–44. Exeter: University of Exeter Press.

Nishio, Kenji, Nakanishi Terumasa, and Kashihara Ryūichi. 2017. *Bringing Japan Back to Its Global Historical Position.* Tokyo: Shōdensha.

Nonproliferation Policy Education Center, ed. 2014. "Speaking Truth to Nonproliferation." Proposal cited with permission from principal investigator Henry Sokolski.

Oberdorfer, Don. 1997. *The Two Koreas.* Reading, MA: Addison-Wesley.

Obinata Sumio. 1992. *Nihon Kindai Kokka no Seiritsu to Keisatsu* [The Birth of the Japanese Modern State and the Police]. Tokyo: Azekura Shobō.

O'Connell, Kevin M. 2004. "Thinking about Intelligence Comparatively." *Brown Journal of World Affairs* 11, no. 1 (Summer–Fall): 189–99.

Office of the National Counterintelligence Executive, ed. 2005. "The National Counterintelligence Strategy of the United States." NCIX Publication no. 2005-10007, March.

Ogino Fujio. 2012. *Tokkō Keisatsu* [The Special Higher Police for Public Surveillance]. Tokyo: Iwanami Shoten.

Ogura, Kazuo. 2015. *Japan's Asian Diplomacy: A Legacy of Two Millennia.* Tokyo: LTCB International Library Trust.

Ōkoda Yahiro. 2001. *Migu Nijūgo Jiken no Shinsō* [The Truth of the MiG-25 Incident]. Tokyo: Gakushū Kenkyūsha.

Okudaira Yasuhiro. 2006. *Chian Ijihō Shōshi* [A Short History of Public Security Preservation Law]. Tokyo: Iwanami Shoten.

Ōmori Yoshio. 2005. *Nihon no Interijensu Kikan* [Japan's Intelligence Organizations]. Tokyo: Bungei Shunjū.

——. 2006. *Kokka to Jōhō* [The State and Intelligence]. Tokyo: WAC.

——. 2008. "Nihon wa Supai Kōsaku no Ejiki Da: Seifu wa Jōhō Kikan Saiken wo Isoge [Japan Is Prey to Spy Operations: The Government Should Promptly Rebuild Japan's Intelligence Organizations]." *Chūō Kōron* (June): 94–101.

Orbach, Danny. 2018. "The Military-Adventurous Complex: Officers, Adventurers and Japanese Expansion in East Asia, 1884–1937." *Modern Asian Studies*, 1–38. https://doi.org/10.1017/S0026749X17000543.

Oros, Andrew L. 2002. "Japan's Growing Intelligence Capability." *International Journal of Intelligence and Counterintelligence* 15, no. 1: 1–25.

Ōta Fumio. 2008. *Interijensu to Kokusai Jōsei Bunseki* [Intelligence and the Analysis of International Politics]. Tokyo: Fuyō Shobō Shuppan.

Ōtake Bushichi. 1941. *Kokubō Hoan Hō* [The National Defense Security Law]. Tokyo: Hata Shoten.

Ōtani Keijirō. 1966. *Shōwa Kempeishi* [The History of the Military Police in the Shōwa Period]. Tokyo: Misuzu Shobō.

Ōyama Azusa, ed. 1966. *Yamagata Aritomo Ikensho* [Yamagata Aritomo's Policy Proposals]. Tokyo: Hara Shobō.

Pałaz-Rutkowska, Ewa. 2011. "The Russo-Japanese War and Its Impact on Polish-Japanese Relations in the First Half of the Twentieth Century." *Analecta Nipponica* 1: 11–43.

Panneerselvam, Prakash. 2016. "Indo-Japan Maritime Security Cooperation in a Changing Environment." Speech delivered to the Young Scholars Forum of the East Asia Research Program, New Delhi, 19 August.

Patalano, Alessio. 2015. *Postwar Japan as a Sea Power: Imperial Legacy, Wartime Experience, and the Making of a Navy*. London: Bloomsbury Publishing.

Pavlov, D. B., and S. A. Petrov. 1994. *Nichiro Sensō no Himitsu* [The Secrets of the Russo-Japanese War]. Tokyo: Seibunsha.

Pekkanen, Saadia M. 2015. "U.S.-Japan Military Space Alliance Promises to Grow in 'New Ways.'" *Forbes*, 27 October.

Pekkanen, Saadia M., and Paul Kallender-Umezu. 2010. *In Defense of Japan: From the Market to the Military in Space Policy*. Stanford: Stanford University Press.

Perrett, Bradley. 2015. "Focused on China, Japan Expands Sigint Stations." *Aviation Week & Space Technology* 177, no. 33: 1.

Petersen, Michael. 2006. "The Intelligence That Wasn't: CIA Name Files, the U.S. Army, and Intelligence Gathering in Occupied Japan." Chapter 8 in *Researching Japanese War Crimes Records: Introductory Essays*, 197–232. Washington, DC: Nazi War Crimes and Japanese Imperial Government Records Interagency Working Group.

PHP Kenkyūjo, ed. 2015. *Kokka Anzen Hoshō Kaigi: Hyōka to Teigen* [National Security Council: Evaluation and Proposal]. Tokyo: PHP Kenkyūjo. 26 November.

PHP Nihon no Interijensu Taisei no Henkaku Kenkyūkai, ed. 2006. *Nihon no Interijensu Taisei: Henkaku e no Rōdomappu* [The Organization of Japan's Intelligence: A Roadmap for Reform]. Tokyo: PHP Sōgō Kenkyūjo. June.

Phythian, Mark. 2013. "Introduction: Beyond the Intelligence Cycle?" In *Understanding the Intelligence Cycle*, edited by Mark Phythian. London: Routledge.

Pillar, Paul R. 2012. "Think Again: Intelligence." *Foreign Policy*, 3 January.

Posner, Richard A. 2006. "Transcript of Speech." *Washington Post*, 30 March.

Prados. John. 2006. *Safe for Democracy: The Secret Wars of the CIA*. Chicago: Ivan R. Dee.

Radcliffe, William W. 2010. "Origins and Current State of Japan's Reconnaissance Satellite Program." *Studies in Intelligence* 54, no. 3, extracts (September): 9–21.

Ransom, Harry Howe. 1980. "Being Intelligent about Secret Intelligence Agencies." *American Political Science Review* 74, no. 1 (March): 141–48.

——. 1987. "The Politicization of Intelligence." Chapter 14 in *Intelligence and Intelligence Policy in a Democratic Society*, edited by Stephen J. Cimbala. Dobbs Ferry, NY: Transactional.

Reisman, W. Michael, and James E. Baker. 1992. *Regulating Covert Action: Practices, Contexts, and Policies of Covert Coercion Abroad in International and American Law.* New Haven: Yale University Press.

Repeta, Lawrence. 2013. "A New State Secrecy Law for Japan?" *Asia-Pacific Journal: Japan Focus* 11.42, no. 1 (October 21). http://japanfocus.org/-Lawrence-Repeta/4011.

——. 2014. "Japan's 2013 State Secrecy Act—The Abe Administration's Threat to News Reporting." *Asia-Pacific Journal: Japan Focus* 12.10, no. 1 (10 March). http://www.japanfocus.org/-Lawrence-Repeta/4086.

Reynolds, Douglas R. 1989a. "Training Young China Hands: *Tōa Dōbun Shōin* and Its Precursors, 1886–1945." Chapter 7 in *The Japanese Informal Empire in China, 1895–1937*, edited by Peter Duus, Ramon H. Myers, and Mark R. Peattie. Princeton: Princeton University Press.

——. 1989b. "Recent Source Books on *Tō-A Dōbunkai* and *Tō-A Dōbun Shōin*: A Review Article." *Sino-Japanese Newsletter* 1, no. 2 (March): 18–27.

Richelson, Jeffrey T. 1988. *Foreign Intelligence Organizations.* New York: Ballinger.

——. 1989. *The U.S. Intelligence Community.* New York: Ballinger.

——. 2011. *The U.S. Intelligence Community.* 6th edition. Boulder, CO: Westview Press.

Richelson, Jeffrey T., and Desmond Ball. 1985. *The Ties That Bind.* Boston: Allen & Unwin.

Riley, Patrick R. 1998. "CIA and Its Discontents." *International Journal of Intelligence and Counterintelligence* 11 (Fall): 255–69.

Rosenbach, Eric, and Aki Peritz. 2009. "Confrontation or Collaboration? Congress and the Intelligence Community: Covert Action." John F. Kennedy School of Government, Harvard University.

Rovner, Joshua. 2011. *Fixing the Facts: National Security and the Politics of Intelligence.* Ithaca: Cornell University Press.

Rovner, Joshua, and Austin Long. 2006. "Correspondence: How Intelligent Is Intelligence Reform?" *International Security* 30, no. 4 (Spring): 196–203.

Royal United Services Institution, ed. 1944. "R.A.F. Night Photography." *Royal United Services Institution Journal* 89, no. 544: 155–58.

Rudgers, David F. 2000. "The Origins of Covert Action." *Journal of Contemporary History* 35, no. 2: 249–62.

Rudner, Martin. 2010. "Hunters and Gatherers: The Intelligence Coalition against Islamic Terrorism." *International Journal of Intelligence and Counterintelligence* 17, no. 2: 193–230.

Russell, Adrienne. 2016. *Journalism as Activism: Recoding Media Power.* Cambridge: Polity Press.

Russell, Richard L. 2002. "Tug of War: CIA's Uneasy Relationship with the Military." *SAIS Review* 22, no. 2 (Fall): 1–18.

Sagar, Rahul. 2013. *Secrets and Leaks: The Dilemma of State Secrecy*. Princeton: Princeton University Press.

Saitō Dōichi. 1977. *Zoruge no Niniroku Jiken* [Sorge's 2/26 Incident]. Tokyo: Tabata Shoten.

Saitō Michinori. 2005. *Chōhōintachi no Sengo: Rikugun Nakano Gakkō no Shinjutsu* [Spies of the Postwar: Testimony of the Army's Nakano School]. Tokyo: Kadokawa Shoten.

———. 2011. *Rikugun Nakano Gakkō Gokuhi Keikaku* [Secret Missons of the Imperial Army's Nakano School]. Tokyo: Gakken Shinso.

Samuels, Richard J. 1987. *The Business of the Japanese State: Energy Markets in Comparative and Historical Perspective*. Ithaca: Cornell University Press.

———. 1994. *"Rich Nation, Strong Army": National Security and the Technological Transformation of Japan*. Ithaca: Cornell University Press

———. 2003a. *Machiavelli's Children: Leaders and Their Legacies in Italy and Japan*. Ithaca: Cornell University Press.

———. 2003b. "Leadership and Political Change in Japan: The Second Rinchō." *Journal of Japanese Studies* 29, no. 1 (Winter): 1–31.

———. 2004. "Politics, Security Policy, and Japan's Cabinet Legislation Bureau: Who Elected these Guys, Anyway?" Japan Policy Research Institute Working Paper no. 99, March.

———. 2007. *Securing Japan: Tokyo's Grand Strategy and the Future of East Asia*. Ithaca: Cornell University Press.

———. 2007–8. " 'New Fighting Power!' Japan's Growing Maritime Capabilities and East Asian Security." *International Security* 32, no. 3 (Winter): 84–112.

———. 2010. "Kidnapping Politics in East Asia." *Journal of East Asian Studies* 10, no. 3 (September–December): 363–96.

———. 2013. *3.11: Disaster and Change in Japan*. Ithaca: Cornell University Press.

Samuels, Richard J., and James Schoff. 2013. "Japan's Nuclear Hedge: Beyond 'Allergy' and 'Breakout.' " In *Strategic Asia, 2013–2014: Asia in the Second Nuclear Age,* edited by Ashley Tellis, 233–64. Seattle: National Bureau of Asian Research.

Sanger, David E. 1992. "Tired of Relying on U.S., Japan Seeks to Expand Its Own Intelligence Efforts." *New York Times*, 1 January.

———. 2012. *Confront and Conceal: Obama's Secret Wars and Surprising Use of American Power*. New York: Crown Publishing.

Sasaki Hirō. 1994. "Taga Muneyuki to Chūgoku Tairiku: Mōko e no Buki Yunyū Keikaku wo Chūshin to Shite, Tsu, Taga Muneyuki Kankei Monjo Mokuroku [Taga Muneyuki and the Chinese Continent: A Catalogue of Documents Relating to Taga Muneyuki and Tsu Related Primarily to Plans for the Import of Weapons into Mongolia]." *Kokushikan Shigaku* 2 (July).

Sassa Atsuyuki. 2013. *Interijensu no Nai Kokka wa Horobiru* [A Nation without Intelligence Goes to Ruin]. Tokyo: Kairyūsha.

Satō Katsumi. 2004. *Kitachōsen ni yoru Ratchi wo Kangaeru* [Thoughts on the Abductees in North Korea]. Tokyo: Meiseisha.

Satō Morio. 2012. *Jōhō Sensō no Kyōkun: Jieitai Jōhō Kanbu no Kaisō* [Lessons of the Intelligence Wars: Reminiscences of the Self-Defense Force Intelligence Bureau]. Tokyo: Fuyōshobō.

Schoenfeld, Gabriel. 2005. "What Became of the CIA?" *Commentary*, 1 May.

Schoppa, Leonard J. 1997, *Bargaining with Japan: What American Pressure Can and Cannot Do*. New York: Columbia University Press.

Schwartz, Mattathias. 2015. "Privacy and Surveillance Norms in Israel." Memo prepared for Workshop on Secrecy, Surveillance, Privacy, and International Relations, MIT Center for International Studies, 16–17 April.

Scott, Len. 2004. "Secret Intelligence, Covert Action and Clandestine Diplomacy," *Intelligence and National Security* 19, no. 2 (Summer): 322–41.

Scott-Stokes, Henry. 1974. *The Life and Death of Yukio Mishima*. New York: Farrar, Straus and Giroux.

Seekins, Donald M. 1999. "Japan's 'Burma Lovers' and the Military Regime." Japan Policy Research Institute Working Paper no. 60, September.

Seffers, George I. 2013. "Intelligence Leaders Seek Common Interests with China." *Signal*, November 1. http://www.afcea.org/content/?q=intelligence-leaders-seek-common-interests-china.

Seifu ni Okeru Jōhō Hozen ni Kansuru Kentō Iinkai, ed. 2011. *Himitsu Hozen ni Kansuru Hōsei no Seibi ni Tsuite: Seifu ni Okeru Jōhō Hozen ni Kansuru Kentō Iinkai Kettei* [Establishing a Legal Framework to Protect Secrets: Decision of the Government's Deliberation Committee on Information Security]. Tokyo: Seifu ni Okeru Jōhō Hozen ni Kansuru Kentō Iinkai. 7 October. http://www.kantei.go.jp/jp/singi/jouhouhozen/dai4/siryou1.pdf.

Seikan Yōransha, ed. Annual. *Seikan Yōran* [Government Handbook]. Tokyo: Seikan Yōransha.

Sejima Ryūzō. 1996. *Ikusangawa: Sejima Ryūzō Kaisōroku* [Ikusangawa: The Memoirs of Sejima Ryūzō]. Tokyo: Sankei Shimbunsha.

Seki Makoto. 2016. *Nisshin Kaisen Zenya ni okeru Nihon no Interijensu* [Japanese Intelligence Activities before the Sino-Japanese War]. Kyoto: Mineruba Shobō.

Select Committee on Intelligence. 2004. "Report of the Select Committee on Intelligence on the U.S. Intelligence Community's Prewar Intelligence Assessments on Iraq." United States Senate, 9 July.

Sheehan, Darrell C. 1996. "The Japanese Intelligence Community." *National Security Studies Quarterly* 2, no. 1: 59–67.

Sheldon, Rose Mary. 1997. "The Ancient Imperative: Clandestine Operations and Covert Action." *International Journal of Intelligence and Counterintelligence* 10, no. 3: 299–315.

Shibata, Akiho. 1994. "Japanese Peacekeeping Legislation and Recent Developments in UN Operations." *Yale Journal of International Law* 19, no. 2: 307–48.

Shigeta Hiroshi. 2006. "Nihon no Jōhō Kinō ni kansuru Genjō to Kadai [The Present Circumstances and Problems with Japan's Intelligence Functions]." *Seiron* (May): 294–98.

Shinoda, Tomohiro, 2000. *Leading Japan: The Role of the Prime Minister*. Westport, CT: Praeger.

——. 2006. "Nihon no Taigai Interijensu Komiyunitei [Japan's Foreign Intelligence Community]." *Nihon Seiji Kenkyū* 3, no. 2 (July): 92–111.

——. 2007. *Koizumi Diplomacy: Japan's Kantei Approach to Foreign and Domestic Affairs*. Seattle: University of Washington Press.

——. 2013. *Contemporary Japanese Politics: Institutional Changes and Power Shifts.* New York: Columbia University Press.

Shlaim, Avi. 1976. "Failures in National Intelligence Estimates: The Case of the Yom Kippur War." *World Politics* 28, no. 3 (April): 348–80.

Shulsky, Abram N. 1991. *Silent Warfare: Understanding the World of Intelligence.* Washington, DC: Brassey's.

Sims, Jennifer E. 2005. "Understanding Friends and Enemies: The Context for American Intelligence Reform." Chapter 2 in *Transforming U.S. Intelligence*, edited by Jennifer E. Sims and Burton Gerber. Washington, DC: Georgetown University Press.

Slotkin, Richard. 1973. *Regeneration through Violence: The Mythology of the American Frontier, 1600–1860.* Middletown, CT: Wesleyan University Press.

Steele, Robert David. 1995. "Private Enterprise Intelligence: Its Potential Contribution to National Security." *Intelligence and National Security* 10, no. 4 (October): 212–28.

Steinhoff, Patricia. 2016. "Transnational Ties of the Japanese Armed Left: Shared Revolutionary Ideas and Direct Personal Contacts." Chapter 7 in *Revolutionary Violence and the New Left: Transnational Perspectives*, edited by Alberto Martin Alvarez and Eduardo Rey Tristan. London: Routledge.

Stempel, John D. 2007. "Covert Action and Diplomacy." *International Journal of Intelligence and Counterintelligence* 20, no. 1: 122–35.

Stephan, John J. 1989. Review of Fält, Olavi K., and Antti Kujala. *Rakka Ryūsui: Colonel Akashi's Report on His Secret Cooperation with the Russian Revolutionary Parties during the Russo-Japanese War. Minumenta Nipponica* 44, no.3 (Autumn): 363–65.

Sternsdorff-Cisterna, Nicolas. 2015. "Food after Fukushima: Risk and Scientific Citizenship in Japan." *American Anthropologist.* doi:10.1111/aman.12294.

Steury, Donald P., ed. 1994. *Sherman Kent and the Board of National Estimates: Collected Essays.* Washington, DC: Central Intelligence Agency Center for the Study of Intelligence.

Stiefler, Todd. 2004. "CIA's Leadership and Major Covert Operations: Rogue Elephants or Risk-Averse Bureaucrats?" *Intelligence and National Security* 19, no. 4 (Winter): 632–54.

Strategic Services Unit, ed. 1946. "Japanese Intelligence Organizations in China." Declassified U.S. government document available at http://www.foia.cia.gov/sites/default/files/document_conversions/1705143/JAPANESE%20INTELLIGENCE%20ORGANIZATIONS%20IN%20CHINA%20%20%20%28WWII%29_0001.pdf.

Suga Yoshihide. 2014. "Abe Seiken wa 2014 Nen Nihon wo Kō Kaeru [How the Abe Administration Will Change Japan in 2014]." *Bungei Shunjū* (February): 110–18.

Sugita Ichiji. 1988. *Jōhō Naki Sensō Shidō* [Wartime Leadership without Intelligence]. Tokyo: Hara Shobō.

Sunohara Tsuyoshi. 2005. *Tanjō Kokusan Supai Eisei* [The Birth of Indigenous Spy Satellites]. Tokyo: Nihon Keizai Shimbun.

——. 2014. *Nihonban NSC to wa Nanika* [What Is the Japanese NSC?]. Tokyo: Shinchōsha.

Suzuki Kenji. 1979. *Chūdoku Taishi Ōshima Hiroshi* [Ambassador to Germany Ōshima Hiroshi]. Tokyo: Fuyō Shobō.

Svinth, Joseph R. 2003. "Professor Yamashita Goes to Washington." In *Martial Arts in the Modern World*, edited by Joseph R. Svinth and Thomas A. Green, 47–60. Santa Barbara, CA: Greenwood Publishing.

Tachikawa, Kyoichi. 2015. "Japan's Pre-War Military Attaché System." *NIDS Journal of Defense and Security* 16 (December): 147–85.

Takahashi Masae. 1982. *Gunji Keisatsu* [Military Police]. Tokyo: Misuzu Shobō.

Takahashi, Toshiya. 2014. "Japan's New Secrecy Law Revives Prewar Memories." *East Asia Forum* (24 December). http://www.eastasiaforum.org/2013/12/24/japans-new-secrecy-law-revives-prewar-memories/.

Takemae, Eiji. 2002. *Inside GHQ : The Allied Occupation of Japan and Its Legacy*. New York: Continuum.

Tama, Jordan. 2005. "Intelligence Reform: Progress, Remaining Deficiencies, and Next Steps." Princeton: Princeton Project on National Security.

Tanaka, Hitoshi. 2008. "The Crisis of Global Governance and the Rise of East Asia." *East Asia Insights* 3, no. 4 (September): 1–8.

Tanaka Kazukai and Okada Akira. 2000. *Chūō Shōchō Kaikaku* [Reform of the Central Government Ministries and Agencies]. Tokyo: Nihon Hyōronsha.

Tanin, O., and E. Yohan. 1934. *Militarism and Fascism in Japan*. New York: International Publishers.

Taoka Shunji. 1994. "Daremo Shiranakatta 'Kita' no Misairu Hassha [The 'Northern' Missile Launch That No One Knew About]." *Aera*, 17 January.

Tatsumi, Yuki. 2015. "To Fight Terror, Japan Must Fix Its Intelligence Apparatus." *The Diplomat*, 1 June.

Thomas, Stafford T. 1988. "Assessing Current Intelligence Studies." *International Journal of Intelligence and CounterIntelligence* 2, no. 2: 217–44.

Tierney, Kathleen, and James D. Goltz. 1997. "Emergency Response: Lessons Learned from the Kobe Earthquake." Preliminary paper no. 260, University of Delaware, Disaster Research Center.

Tobey, William. 2017. "Cooperation in the Libya WMD Disarmament Case." *Studies in Intelligence* 61, no. 4: 31–42.

Toby, Ronald P. 1991. *State and Diplomacy in Early Modern Japan: Asia in the Development of the Tokugawa Bakufu*. Stanford: Stanford University Press.

Toyama Misao, ed. 1981. *Riku-Kaigun Shōkan Jinji Sōran* [Personnel Guide to Officers of the Imprial Army and Navy]. Tokyo: Fuyō Shobō.

Tōyama Mitsuru, Inukai Tsuyoshi, Sugiyama Shigemaru, and Uchida Ryōhei. 2008. *Genyōsha to Kokuryūkai aruiwa Kōdōteki Ajiashugi no Genten* [The Genyōsha and Kokuryūkai or the Origin of the Aggressive Asianism]. Tokyo: Shoshishinsui.

Toyoda Minoru. 1987. *Jōhōshōgun Akashi Motojirō: Roshia wo Taoshita Supai Taishō no Shōgai* [Intelligence Shogun Akashi Motojirō: The Life of the Spy Who Overthrew the Russian Empire]. Tokyo: Kōjinsha.

Trahair, Richard C. S. 2004. *Encyclopedia of Cold War Espionage, Spies, and Secret Operations*. Westport, CT: Greenwood Press.

Treverton, Gregory F. 1987. *Covert Action: The Limits of Intervention in the Postwar World*. New York: Basic Books.

———. 1991. "Controlling Covert Action." Chapter 6 in *Controlling Intelligence*, edited by Glenn P. Hastedt. London: Frank Cass.

———. 2001. *Reshaping National Intelligence in an Age of Information*. Cambridge: Cambridge University Press.

Treverton, Gregory F., et al., eds. 2006. "Toward a Theory of Intelligence: Workshop Report." Santa Monica, CA: National Security Research Division, RAND Corporation.

Tsuchiya Motohiro. 2012. *Saibā Tero Nichibei vs. Chūgoku* [Cyberterrorism: Japan and the United States vs. China]. Tokyo: Bungei Shunjū.

Tsukamoto Katsuichi. 2008. *Jieitai no Jōhōsen* [The Self-Defense Forces' Intelligence War]. Tokyo: Sōshisha.

Turner, Michael A. 2004. "A Distinctive U.S. Intelligence Identity." *International Journal of Intelligence and CounterIntelligence* 17, no. 1: 42–61.

Turner, Stansfield. 1985. *Secrecy and Democracy: The CIA in Transition*. Boston: Houghton Mifflin.

Turney-High, Harry Holbert. 1971. *Primitive War: Its Practice and Concepts* 2nd edition. Columbia: University of South Carolina Press.

Ueki Chikako. 2015. *Heiwa no tame no Sensōron* [A Theory of War for Peace]. Tokyo: Chikuma Shinsho. UN News Centre. 2013. "Independent UN Experts Seriously Concerned about Japan's Special Secrets Bill." 22 November, http://www.un.org/apps/news/story.asp?NewsID=46560&Cr=japan&Cr1=#.U3Nx6HYvBGw.

United States Strategic Bombing Survey, Japanese Military and Naval Intelligence Division Japanese Intelligence Section, G-2, ed. 1946. "Japanese Military and Naval Intelligence." Washington, DC: United States Government Printing Office.

Uyehara, Cecil H. 2010. *The Subversive Activities Prevention Law of Japan: Its Creation, 1951–1952*. Leiden: Brill.

Uzaki, Masahiro. 2014. "What Japan's Designated State Secrets Law Targets." *Asia-Pacific Journal: Japan Focus* 12.21, no. 1 (May 25).

Van Hook, James C. 2006. "U.S. Intelligence and the Gehlen Organization." *Bulletin of the German Historical Institute* (Spring).

Van Wolferen, Karel. 1989. *The Enigma of Japanese Power*. New York: Alfred A. Knopf.

Vickers, Robert D. Jr. 1998. "The State of Warning Today." *Defense Intelligence Journal* 7, no. 2: 9–15.

Vogel, Ezra F., ed. 1975. *Modern Japanese Organizations and Decision-Making*. Berkeley: University of California Press.

Wada, Haruki. 2004. "Japan-North Korean Diplomatic Normalization and Northeast Asia Peace." *Asia-Pacific Journal: Japan Focus* 2, no. 3 (1 March).

Walsh, James Igoe. 2009. *The International Politics of Intelligence Sharing*. New York: Columbia University Press.

Walsh, Patrick F., and Seumas Miller. 2015. "Rethinking 'Five Eyes' Security Intelligence Collection Policies and Practice Post 9/11 Post Snowden." Paper presented to the annual meeting of the International Studies Association, New Orleans, 17–22 February.

Wark, Wesley K. 1986. "In Search of a Suitable Japan: British Naval Intelligence in the Pacific before the Second World War." *Intelligence and National Security* 1, no. 2: 189–211.

Warner, Michael. 2002. "Wanted: A Definition of 'Intelligence.'" *Studies in Intelligence* 46, no. 3.

———. 2012. "Fragile and Provocative: Notes on Secrecy and Intelligence." *Intelligence and National Security* 27, no. 2 (April): 223–40.

———. 2014. *The Rise and Fall of Intelligence: An International Security History.* Washington, DC: Georgetown University Press.

Weiner, Tim. 1994. "C.I.A. Spent Millions to Support Japanese Right in 50s and 60s." *New York Times,* 9 October.

Westerfield, H. Bradford. 1997. "American Exceptionalism and American Intelligence." *Freedom Review* 28, no. 2 (Summer): 27–37.

Wettering, Frederick L. 2003. "(C)overt Action: The Disappearing 'C.'" *International Journal of Intelligence and CounterIntelligence* 16, no. 4: 561–72.

Whaley, Barton. 1974. *Codeword Barbarossa.* Cambridge: MIT Press.

Whymant, Robert. 1996. *Stalin's Spy: Richard Sorge and the Tokyo Espionage Ring.* London: I. B. Tauris

Wile, Ted Shannon. 1981. "Sealane Defense: An Emerging Role for the JMSDF?" Master's thesis, U.S. Naval Postgraduate School.

Williams, Brad. 2010. "The Challenges of Intelligence Oversight in a Normalising Japan." Chapter 7 in *Democratic Oversight of Intelligence Services,* edited by Daniel Baldino. Sydney: The Federation Press.

———. 2013a. "Explaining the Absence of a Japanese Central Intelligence Agency: Alliance Politics, Sectionalism, and Antimilitarism." *Journal of East Asian Studies* 13: 137–64.

———. 2013b. "Japan's Evolving National Security Secrecy System: Catalysts and Obstacles." *Pacific Affairs* 86, no. 3 (September): 493–513.

———. 2018. "Explaining Conservative Hegemony in Japan: The Role of U.S. Intelligence." Paper presented at the annual meeting of the International Studies Association, April.

Willoughby, Charles A. 1973. *Shirarezaru Nihon Senryō* [The Unknown Story of the Occupation of Japan]. Tokyo: Banchō Shobō.

Willoughby, Charles A., and John Chamberlain. 1954. *MacArthur: 1941–1951.* New York: McGraw-Hill.

Wittes, Benjamin, and Gabriella Blum. 2015. *The Future of Violence: Robots and Germs, Hackers and Drones; Confronting a New Age of Threats.* New York: Basic Books.

Wohlstetter, Roberta. 1962. *Pearl Harbor: Warning and Decision.* Stanford: Stanford University Press.

Yamagiwa Sumio. 2004. *Ratchi no Kairyū: Kojin mo Kuni mo Utta Seiji to Medeia* [Currents of Abduction: The Politics and Media That Sold Out the Individuals and the Nation]. Tokyo: Kobunsha.

Yamamoto Kiyokatsu. 1980. *Mishima Yukio: Yūmon no Sokoku Bōeifu* [Mishima Yukio: A Lamentation on the Condition of His Beloved Nation's Defense]. Tokyo: Nihon Bungeisha.

——. 2001. *Jieitai Kage no Butai—Mishima Yukio wo Koroshita Shinjitsu no Kokuhaku* [Self-Defense Force Shadow Troops—Testimony for What Drove Mishima Yukio's Suicide]. Tokyo: Kōdansha.

Yanagisawa Kyōji. 2015. *Jieitai no Tenki: Seiji to Gunji no Mujun wo Tou* [Turning Point for the Self-Defense Forces: Questioning Political and Military Contradictions]. Tokyo: NHK.

Yanase Shō. 2013. "Wagakuni no Jōhō Kinō: Himitsu Hozen [Japan's Intelligence Functions: Preserving Secrets]." *Rippō to Chōsa* 347 (December): 15–33.

Yardley, Herbert O. 1931. *The American Black Chamber*. Indianapolis: Bobbs-Merrill.

Yokoyama Kendō. 1943. *Nippon Budōshi* [The History of Japanese Martial Arts]. Tokyo: Sanseidō.

Yoshida Noriaka. 2012. *Ogata Taketora to CIA* [Ogata Taketora and the CIA]. Tokyo: Heibonsha.

Yuasa Hiroshi. 2013. *Rekishi ni Kieta Sanbō: Yoshida Shigeru no Gunji Komon Tatsumi Eiichi* [Tatsumi Eiichi: Yoshida Shigeru's Forgotten Military Adviser]. Tokyo: Bungei Shunjū.

Zacharias, Ellis M. 1946. *Secret Missions: The Story of an Intelligence Officer*. New York: G. P. Putnam's Sons.

Zachmann, Urs Matthias. 2011. "Konoe Atsumaro and the Idea of Alliance of the Yellow Race." Chapter 6 in *Pan-Asianism: A Documentary History*. Volume 1. *1850–1920*. Edited by Sven Saaler and Christopher Szpilman. Lanham, MD: Rowan and Littlefield.

Zegart, Amy B. 2005. "September 11 and the Adaptation Failure of U.S. Intelligence Agencies." *International Security* 29, no. 4 (Spring): 78–111.

——. 2014. "Cloaks, Daggers, and Ivory Towers: Why Political Science Professors Don't Study U.S. Intelligence." Chapter 2 in *Essentials of Strategic Intelligence*, edited by Loch Johnson. Santa Barbara, CA: ABC-Clio.

Zenkoku Kenyūkai Rengōkai Hensan Iinkai, ed. 1976. *Nihon Kempei Seishi* [The True History of the Japanese Military Police]. Tokyo: Kenbun Shoin.

Zhou, Yongsheng. 2016. "Japanese Spies Are Deeply Hidden in China." *Global Times*, 3 August.

INDEX

Note: Page numbers in *italics* indicate illustrations; those with a *t* indicate tables.

Radiopress, Inc., 98, 144, *214*
Radio Wave Bureau (Denpabu), 150
Rastvorov, Yuri, 103, 124t, 291n238
Reagan, Ronald, 29
Reform Association (Kakushin Dōshikai), 43
Reilly, Sydney, 39
Research Data Leakage Incident (1978), 130t
Rice, Condoleezza, 196
Ridgway, Matthew B., 79, 123
Rikubaku Dainibu Beppan. *See* Musashi Kikan
Rogers, Michael, 7
Roosevelt, Franklin D., xii, 22
Roosevelt, Theodore, 26
Roundtable for Strengthening Diplomacy (Gaikō Kyōka Kondankai), 139
Roundtable on the Strengthening of External Intelligence Capabilities (Taigai Jōhō Kinō Kyōka ni kansuru Kondankai), 169, 172t
Rovner, Joshua, 19, 269n132
Rumsfeld, Donald, 196, 263n5
Rusk, Dean, 21
Russia, 38–39, 46–47, 243; Fascist Party of, *41*; U.S. election interference by, xvii, 6–7, 12, 26, 28
Russo-Japanese War (1904–5), xvii, 4, 33–35, 38–39, 43–44
Rutland, Frederick Joseph, 51–52

Sadat, Anwar, 16
Sagar, Rahul, 28
Saibā Bōeitai, 231
Sakata Incident (1963), 125t
Sakata Michita, 111–12
Sanwa Incident (1964), 126t
Sassa Atsuyuki, 112–13, 118, 152
satellites, spy, 5, 153, 217, 308n52
Satō Eisaku, 108
Satō Yukio, 112
Satsuma Rebellion (1877), xvi, 4
Schelling, Thomas, 11
Schieffer, Thomas, 197, 198
Science and Technology Agency, 154, 185
Security Council of Japan, 208
Sedov Incident (1969), 127t
Sejima Ryūzō, 107, 138–39, 288n170
Seki Sanjirō Incident (1953), 124t
Self-Defense Forces (SDF), 100–105, 108, 186–87; foreign military attachés of, 181–82, 182t; forerunner of, 90, 121; intelligence reforms of, 146–51, 184; in Iraq

War, 163; Mishima on, 114–15. *See also* Ground Self-Defense Force
Self-Defense Forces Law, 101, 104
Shigeta Hiroshi, 141
Shimizu Tsutomu, 236
Shin Gwang-soo Incident (1985), 132t
Shinjō Kenkichi, 54, 55
Shinkōgan Incident (1957), 124t
Shiozaki Yasuhisa, 209
Siberian Expedition (1918–22), 46–48
signals intelligence (SIGINT), xvi–xviii, 4, 10, 183–85, 190, 194; during Cold War, 113–14, 247; development of, 50–51, 242, 244, 258; measurement and, 5, 136; mission areas of, 196; during Russo-Japanese War, 35; Seniors Pacific group of, 200; U.S. budget for, 13
"siloism," 17–18, 69–71, 174; CIRO and, 138, 178; disaster management and, 143.. *See also* "stovepiping."
Singapore, 58, 61, 84, 201, 231
Singh, Mohan, 61
Sino-Japanese War, 34–36, 43–44
Snowden, Edward, 14, 22, 24, 29, 312n165
Soka Gakkai (Buddhist organization), 144
Sono Akira, 93
Sony Pictures Entertainment, 215
Sorge, Richard, 72–74, *75*, 244
South Korea, 200, 201, 224, 231; Korean War and, 9, 87–89, 264n14
South Korean Central Intelligence Agency (KCIA), 116, 118, 257
Spanish Civil War, 82, 282n15
special duty units (*tokumu kikan*), xxi, 25–26, 46, 47, 243, 274n68; "commercial cover," 86; in India, 61; of Kwantung Army, 55–57, 66; in popular culture, *63*
Special Higher Police for Public Surveillance (Tokkō Keisatsu), 72, 93, 94, 244
Spitzer, J. B., 69
Spy Prevention Act, 119
Stalin, Joseph, xvii, 19, 61, 67–68
Stalingrad, battle of, 61, 76
"stovepiping," 16–17, 137, 139, 187, 212; disadvantages of, 241; removal of, 174. *See also* "siloism."
Strategic Services Unit (U.S.), xiii
submarines, 5, 184, 191–92, 199, 223, 248; Chinese, 110–11; German, 45; Soviet, 100
Subversive Activities Prevention Act (SAPA), 95, 96, 103, 144–45, 218
Subversive Organizations Control Law, 145
Suga Yoshihide, 165, 207